Selected Writings of Maureen O'Hara on the Art, Science, and Hope of Humanism

This book presents the work of the eminent British-American psychologist, Maureen O'Hara. It explores the trajectory of humanistic psychology over the last few decades, providing a link between its original proponents, notably Carl Rogers, and its contemporary manifestations.

The text reproduces 18 of O'Hara's original papers arranged in six parts, each of which reflects a significant area in which she has contributed her rigorous analysis and creative thinking, i.e., the person-centred approach, humanistic psychology, third force science, client-centred therapy, psychology futures, and education. A unique feature of the book is a series of dialogues about O'Hara's contributions in each of these areas with the book's editor, Keith Tudor. The dialogues reveal not only O'Hara's reflections on and further thinking about each area of her contributions, but also how prescient her analysis was, and how contemporary and relevant her thinking still is.

Bringing together a collection of O'Hara's works to a broader audience, this book will be of interest to humanistic psychologists and psychotherapists, as well as those studying and/or training in this field.

Keith Tudor is Professor of Psychotherapy at Auckland University of Technology, Aotearoa New Zealand, where he is also currently a co-Lead of Moana Nui Research in the Psychological Therapies. He is the author and/or editor of over 100 publications on various aspects of person-centred psychology, including (with the late Bernie Neville) *Eco-centred Therapy: Revisioning Person-centred Psychology for a Living World* (Routledge, 2023).

Maureen O'Hara is Director of the International Futures Forum US, Professor Emerita of Psychology at National University, San Diego, CA, and President Emerita of Saybrook Graduate School, San Francisco, CA. Working closely with American psychologist Dr Carl R. Rogers for two decades, she helped develop the person-centred approach to psychotherapy and large group process.

What an incredible set of essays from one of the most influential visionaries we've had in the person-centred/humanistic psychology group of approaches. The first chapter, on O'Hara's encounter with R. D. Laing, is worth the price of admission alone. The rest of the essays include ones on psychotherapy; intelligent, incisive analyses of the relationship of humanistic psychology to science; as well as prescient essays on the relationship of feminism, politics, and cultural world views to our Western, male, ego-centric psychologies (O'Hara was ahead of her time in writing about these things that have now become centre stage in academic therapy training programs). There is also a section entitled 'Psychology Futures' with prescient essays which provide insight into the troubling times we currently live in. Finally, there is a section education. The whole is complemented by insightful dialogues between O'Hara and the editor of the volume, Keith Tudor. A stimulating and thought-provoking book.

Art Bohart, *Professor Emeritus, California State University Dominguez Hills, and Adjunct Faculty, Santa Clara University, California, United States*

This collection of Maureen O'Hara's writings is a magnificent guidepost and seedbed for those interested in the person-centred approach, humanistic psychology, third force science, client-centred therapy, psychology futures, and education. From its powerful opening chapter, which describes the impact of a meeting between R. D. Laing and Carl Rogers, the book represents the very best of person-centred processes and principles, lived with courage and vulnerability. This is a book for the here-and-now and the henceforth, and especially for the younger generations who are now the catalysts in the areas represented in these covers. This collection provides a cornucopia of brilliance and creativity in ideation and writing, not least by means of the extensive and rich dialogue after each chapter between Maureen O'Hara, the author of the original papers, and her colleague and editor, Keith Tudor.

Gay (Swenson) Barfield, PhD., *Lic. (retired) MFT, Co-Founder and Co-Director of the Carl Rogers Institute for Peace, Hilo, Hawaii, United States*

Scholars typically produce a body of work pertaining to a specifically bounded arena of inquiry and discourse. However, in this future-oriented retrospective, we are gifted with a body of work that in its coherence, authenticity, congruence, depth, and originality is emblematic of the actualising imperative suggested by Miguel de Unamuno's image: 'throw yourself like seed… from your work, you will be able one day to gather yourself'.

In walking through the dialogic mindscape of this mystic scientist's narrative, we can perceive fauna whose seeds can grow towards understanding and transforming the aridness of modernity and the nihilistic impoverishment of postmodernity. This book is a faithful artifact towards a cultural history of postmodern psychology that can serve towards reigniting a refreshing coherence within the turbulence of our times. How welcome these intimations of a possible centre that can hold!

Aftab Omer, *President, Meridian University, Petaluma, California, United States*

In recent years, a presentation by Maureen O'Hara at a conference featuring the work of person-centred theorists has been considered a major event. She has captured her audiences with her astute analyses of the prevailing conditions of the cultural climates in which we find ourselves. She supports us in our search for meaning and value in our work as person-centred practitioners. This book brings together some of her most important academic papers.

The collection evidences the high level of critical thinking and dedication that Maureen O'Hara has put into a career that stretches from her first meetings with Carl Rogers and colleagues in the 1970s to the present day. Her dialogue with Keith Tudor reviewing her work adds reflective spaces to the book which help bring the work alive for a new audience. Shining through all her work is the voice of a woman who is acutely aware of the times when difference and diversity have not been respected. A particular highlight is her first-person account of being an observer and participant in the somewhat explosive encounter between R. D. Laing's UK-based team and that of the California-based Carl Rogers and colleagues. It was O'Hara's level of personal engagement and her ability to express her sense of what was happening at a cultural level that made a difference. That sensitivity and analysis continues throughout the book in papers that reflect her deep dive into the epistemological foundations of the person-centred approach and client-centred therapy, as well as the broader field of humanistic psychology, to all of which she has been a major contributor.

Most of all, this is a very human and thoughtful read, which I hope will inform future debate.

Jo Hilton, *Person-centred Practitioner and Trainer, Ceredigion, Wales, United Kingdom*

Amidst worldwide existential challenges to our shared humanity, the book *Vitalising Persons for Turbulent Times* is a rare and indispensable read. Maureen O'Hara's theoretical writing is informed by the scientific rigor she developed early in her career, as well as significant encounters with R. D. Laing, Paulo Freire, and other thought leaders such as Walter T. Anderson. Her extensive experience working with Carl R. Rogers on the potential in large groups for nurturing social change animates her commitment to creating leaders capable of that cultural midwifery.

Maureen's seminal writing, together with Keith Tudor's own intellectually rich responses are philosophically current, authentically personal, and deeply layered. The organically developed relational format of their shared, reflective chapters illustrates how deeply they have embodied the theory and practice of the person-centred approach, and is a gift to the reader. Reading this book brought me back to the excitement, freshness of thought, and growth I experienced working with Rogers myself and interacting with his original partners in developing the person-centred approach. That itself renews my hope, and hopefully yours.

Carol Wolter-Gustafson, *Independent Scholar, Boston, Massachusetts, United States of America*

Selected Writings of Maureen O'Hara on the Art, Science, and Hope of Humanism

Vitalising Persons for Turbulent Times

Edited by Keith Tudor with
Maureen O'Hara

Routledge
Taylor & Francis Group
LONDON AND NEW YORK

Designed cover image: The cover image is a Huichol yarn painting created from a vision ceremony for Maureen O'Hara by a Huichol shaman (1995). © Maureen O'Hara

First published 2025
by Routledge
4 Park Square, Milton Park, Abingdon, Oxon OX14 4RN

and by Routledge
605 Third Avenue, New York, NY 10158

Routledge is an imprint of the Taylor & Francis Group, an informa business

British Library Cataloguing-in-Publication Data
A catalogue record for this book is available from the British Library

ISBN: 978-1-032-85698-8 (hbk)
ISBN: 978-1-032-85697-1 (pbk)
ISBN: 978-1-003-51945-4 (ebk)

DOI: 10.4324/9781003519454

Typeset in Times New Roman
by KnowledgeWorks Global Ltd.

Contents

Introduction

Keith Tudor and Maureen O'Hara

This book presents key works of the eminent British-American psychologist, Maureen O'Hara.

Maureen was born during the Second World War in a small wool town in West Yorkshire, England. Starting out first as a biologist, she switched countries and fields in 1969 when she moved to the United States. In 1970, a brush with death brought her in touch with deeper and more existential questions and seeking answers she found humanistic psychology and the work of Carl Rogers who became a lifelong source of both clarity and mystery. In her search to make sense of experiences in diverse settings, she has followed the mavericks who pushed the boundaries of received knowledge to find better ways of understanding the gloriously diverse manifestations of human being.

I (Keith) first came across Maureen's work on person-centred therapy when I was studying that in the early 1990s. I resonated with the more social—and political—emphasis in her work. I also appreciated the connection she made between gestalt therapy and person-centred psychology (PCP) (O'Hara, 1984a, 1984b) as I first trained in gestalt therapy and contribution training with Peter Fleming and Anna Farrow in London, UK, and Montecorice, Italy, in the early 1980s.

Later, as I began attending international person-centred conferences, I met Maureen in person and, in addition to appreciating her intellect, fine mind, and thought-provoking presentations, I also came to know her as a person, which included appreciating her beautiful Yorkshire accent (I lived in Sheffield, South Yorkshire, 1965–1969 and 1992–2009) and great sense of humour. I remember a particularly lovely and long evening spent with her and other organismic theorists within PCP, notably Bernie Neville, Alberto Segrera, and Carol Wolter-Gustafson, at the 8th Conference of the World Association for Person-Centered & Experiential Psychotherapy & Counseling (WAPCEPC) in Norwich in 2008, talking about PCP, Rogers, theoretical similarities and differences, and life, a conversation somewhat facilitated by some tasty tequila that Alberto had bought from Mexico!

I last saw Maureen live and in person in Vienna, at the 13th WAPCEPC in 2018, where she delivered a keynote speech on hope (O'Hara, 2018), following which we had some discussions about epistemology and culture, and I asked her to consider delivering a keynote speech at the next World Conference due to be held two years

DOI: 10.4324/9781003519454-1

later in Auckland, Aotearoa New Zealand (which Brian Rodgers and I were organising). Unfortunately, this conference was affected by the coronavirus pandemic, postponed one year to 2021, and then redesigned and held as a hybrid (live and online) conference (as PCE2021), at which point, due to travel restrictions and ill-health, Maureen was unable to attend or present.

Although I—and others—appreciate Maureen's work and voice with the person-centred and experiential (PCE) community, I have also had a sense of a certain lack of appreciation for the depth of her work, and even a certain marginalisation. For instance, when I was editing a book on person-centred brief therapies (Tudor, 2008) and writing about the question of time in PCP, I re-read a paper of hers on 'Moments of eternity' (O'Hara, 1999) which I don't think is at all well-known. In it, she describes her work with one client who had a transformative experience in four sessions but, as Maureen points out:

> it wouldn't matter whether it had taken ten sessions or even thirty, it was the quality of the change that marks it as significant. It would miss her achievement altogether to think of what occurred in terms of "numbers of sessions", "symptom reduction", [or] "problem-solving"... this change permeated her whole existence. She had not only changed what she thought about the situation she was facing, she had changed *how* she was thinking. She had made an epistemological leap.
>
> (O'Hara, 1999, p. 73, my emphasis)

There are not many colleagues in PCP who talk in terms of epistemology, let alone epistemological leaps, but Maureen does—and does so in an accessible way. So, in the two years since PCE2021, and, having been involved with three other books which, in different ways, present the work and legacies of other colleagues—namely, Evan Sherrard (Tudor, 2017/2020), Claude Steiner (Tudor, 2020), and Bernie Neville (Neville & Tudor, 2024)—it came to me that I would like to do this not only for and about but also with Maureen. The rest, as they say, is history.

For my part, I (Maureen) confess I was both uplifted and excited when Keith proposed working together. Uplifted because the proposal came at a time when I was working through the onset of a neurological condition which, though it has not affected my thinking and writing, has made speaking and walking difficult. At the time, I was deep in a sense of despair at the loss of my voice of all things. So, Keith's invitation reminded me of who I am despite the loss and restored my sense of agency. I was also excited because, though we have enjoyed some rich conversations at conferences, I had not had the chance to work closely with him. So I did not hesitate. For some years, I have had a keen interest in the scope of his work, ranging as it does from finely drawn presentations of person-centred practice in many settings in and beyond the therapist's office, theory-building, a critical post-positivist philosophical stance, a willingness to keep PCT honest when it slides into accommodation with instrumentalist thought, and, more recently, his immersion in indigenous psychologies and the psychological and cultural impact of colonisation. Through his writing, his practice, and the few far-reaching conversations over food and drinks, I have come to trust Keith and for me, that opens up the relational space where creativity lives. I was up for it.

Keith (anticipating the dialogic structure of our co-authored chapters):

Thanks for that Maureen. I'm very touched by your interest in my work. I agree that our contact over the years, and our appreciation of each other's politics and passion for the person-centred approach has opened up the relational space that has facilitated this project. Moreover, I'm glad that my invitation came at the right time. What synchrony!

So, to the book itself.

The structure—and process—of the book

So, once Maureen had agreed to doing this, she provided a list of her work; I read and re-read most of Maureen's publications and came up with the idea of reproducing work that represents Maureen's contributions within and beyond PCP and demonstrates both a depth of thinking and the breadth of her interests. This has resulted in a book comprising 18 papers organised, following two introductory chapters, into six parts, focussing on the person-centred approach, humanistic psychology, third force science, client-centred therapy, psychology futures, and education: an order, notwithstanding the fact that these threads may be found in Maureen's writings over many years, nevertheless reflects a broad historical view of the development of her interests (by the date of the first publication in each part). Two other parameters guided my choice (with which Maureen agreed): (i) that the publications would be sole-authored ones and (ii) include writing or publications that are not easily available to the professional or lay reader (i.e., those without access to academic journals). Finally, as I wanted to create a sense of dialogue, I suggested to Maureen that she and I discuss these various contributions, which we do in short chapters following Chapter 1 and at the end of each part, i.e., Chapters 2, 5, 10, 14, 18, 21, and 25. Finally, as we were finishing Chapter 25, we realised that we needed a final reflection on the whole book and project and so wrote a short epilogue.

In order to create the dialogue, we set up an online shared folder for each of our co-authored chapters, and wrote paragraphs in response to each other. This we did on a daily basis during August and September 2023 and again in January 2024, which, for me (Keith), meant that, as we live in different time zones (±19 hours apart), I would get up in the morning to something from Maureen, often accompanied by an email signed with 'Luv' (a greeting from the North of England), to which I would then respond, and so on. This rhythm created a closeness, which was sometimes enhanced by realising that we were both 'in' (working on) a particular document at the same time (in which case we would sometimes leave each other more personal notes), all of which I think has facilitated a depth of dialogue. The purpose of our dialogue was to enhance and draw out Maureen's ideas, especially with regard to their contemporary relevance, rather than to restrict or conclude anything for the reader. Finally, as I am particularly keen that edited books or books of collected papers have coherence, in addition to the chapters that discuss Maureen's contributions to these fields, we provide internal references to papers and dialogues in other parts of the book, and some explanatory endnotes, have updated some of the more dated language, and have collated all the references from the original publications into one list of References.

Finally, the title of the book reflects the dual focus of Maureen's work, that is, on people's inner world and their inner strength or vitality ('Vitalising persons') as well as on the impact of the external, social, cultural, and political world ('Turbulent times'). In the subtitle, the reference to both art and science acknowledges her embracing and mastery of these traditions in psychology, and to hope her 'buoyant humanistic utopianism' (O'Hara, 1989c, p. 12).

Acknowledgements

First, in terms of the formal acknowledgements, we are both grateful to the following for their permission to reproduce the following papers:

- Chapter 1—Based on O'Hara, M. (1996). An untitled chapter originally published in *R. D. Laing: Creative Destroyer* (pp. 314–322, edited by B. Mullan), published by Cassell/Sage, reproduced with permission.
- Chapter 3—Based on O'Hara, M. (1989b). Person-centered approach as conscientização: The works of Carl Rogers and Paulo Freire. *Journal of Humanistic Psychology*, *29*(1), 111–136, reproduced with permission.
- Chapter 4—Based on O'Hara, M. (1995a). Carl Rogers: Scientist or mystic? *Journal of Humanistic Psychology*, 35(4), 40–53, reproduced with permission.
- Chapter 6—Based on O'Hara, M. M. (1983). Our foremothers as gurus. *Perspective: Association for Humanistic Psychology*, November, reproduced with permission.
- Chapter 7—Based on O'Hara, M. (1992b). Relational humanism: A psychology for a pluralistic world. *The Humanistic Psychologist*, *20*(2-3), 439–446, reproduced with permission.
- Chapter 8—Based on O'Hara, M. (1995b). Constructing emancipatory realities: Towards a feministic voice in humanistic psychology, a chapter originally published in *The Truth About Truth: De-Constructing and Reconstructing the Postmodern World* (edited by W. T. Anderson), published by Jeremy Tarcher, reproduced with permission.
- Chapter 9—Based on O'Hara, M. (1997a). Emancipatory therapeutic practice in a turbulent transmodern era: A work of retrieval. *Journal of Humanistic Psychology*, *37*(3), 7–33, reproduced with permission.
- Chapter 11—Based on O'Hara, M. (1983). A hundredth monkey myth, an essay originally published in the *Association for Humanistic Psychology Newsletter* (November 1983), reproduced with permission.
- Chapter 12—Based on O'Hara, M. (1988). Science, pseudoscience and myth-mongering, a chapter originally published in *Not Necessarily the New Age* (edited by R. Basil), published by Prometheus, reproduced with permission.
- Chapter 13—Based on O'Hara, M. (1995c). Is it time for clinical psychology to deconstruct constructivism? *Journal of Constructivist Psychology*, *8*(4), 293–303, reproduced with permission.

- Chapter 15—Based on O'Hara, M. (1997b). Relational empathy: From ego-centric modernism to socio-centric postmodernism, a chapter in *Empathy Reconsidered: New Directions in Psychotherapy* (edited by A. C. Bohart & L. S. Greenberg), published by the American Psychological Association, reproduced with permission.
- Chapter 16—Based on O'Hara, M. (2002). Moments of eternity: What Carl Rogers has to offer brief therapists, a chapter originally published in *Brief Therapy: Lasting Impressions* (edited by J. K. Zeig), published by The Milton H. Erickson Foundation Press, reproduced with permission.
- Chapter 17—Based on O'Hara, M. (1996b). Rogers and Sylvia: A feminist analysis, a chapter originally published in *The Psychotherapy of Carl Rogers: Cases and Commentary* (edited by B. A. Farber, D. C. Brink, & P. M. Raskin), published by Guilford Press, reproduced with permission.
- Chapter 20—Based on O'Hara, M. (2010). Another inconvenient truth and the developmental role for psychology in a threatened world. *The Humanistic Psychologist*, *38*(2), 101–119, reproduced with permission.

I (Keith) would like to thank, first and foremost, Maureen for her agreement to and engagement in this project; Bob Lucas, her partner, for his research on Maureen's publications, and, specifically, in sourcing papers and applying for permissions; Angie Strachan for her fine editorial skills, especially in helping to present disparate papers into a cohesive whole, including checking references, and helping with the compilation of the index; colleagues at Routledge and KGL Copyeditors, and, last but by no means least, Louise Embleton Tudor for her continuing support for my writing and editing projects.[1]

I (Maureen) would first thank Keith for his invitation to collaborate on this project. One of the effects of taking a path that is more person-centred than discipline-centred is that you never quite believe anyone else is listening. Keith's listening brought me back to reflect more deeply on where I have travelled. That has been priceless. I want to acknowledge all the people with whom I have journeyed. There are too many to mention individually and they are spread over the world, but chief among them are Carl Rogers who was both friend and co-learner and my colleagues in the Meridian Institute for Leadership, Learning and the Future who have met together for 40 years to struggle with the human dimensions of the challenges we face as a planetary community of communities. I, too, thank Angie Strachan for her help with production of the manuscript. Finally, as Keith noted, I give thanks every day for my husband Bob, for his tracking down copyrights, rifling through boxes to find files and hard copies of articles and scrolling through digital copies of articles, and, most importantly, for just being himself, being there.

Note

1 I also want to acknowledge Louise's generosity in the context of Maureen's withdrawal from PCE2021, and her delivery of a great keynote speech (Embleton Tudor, 2022).

Chapter 1

Streams

On becoming a postmodern person (1995)

Maureen O'Hara

I first met Ronnie Laing in 1977, in Brazil. He was presenting at an International Transpersonal Psychology Conference in Belo Horizonte, and my good friend Lika Bandeira was his translator. A week after the conference, thanks to the silver tongue of Lika's husband Eduardo Bandeira and my own narcissism, I was talked into convincing my friend and colleague Carl Rogers and the rest of our person-centered approach (PCA) workshop team—which was made up of Carl Rogers, Maria Villas-Boas Bowen, Natalie Rogers, John K. Wood, Jared Kass, Joanne Justin, and myself—to collaborate with Laing and his group on a large one-day event in London. This meeting was to prove a psychological and professional turning point in my life.

The program was scheduled for the summer of 1978 at the Hilton Hotel in London. The day before, the whole Rogers' team arrived at Laing's home a little after seven. We were all nervous. Natalie had an uncomfortable encounter with Laing earlier in the day, when she had arrived earlier than planned. His chilly reception puzzled Natalie and by the time we all arrived at the house on Eton Place, we were beginning to suspect that our group's understanding about the meeting was rather different from that of Laing and his people. Our team believed, because that was what Eduardo Bandeira had told us, that Laing had initiated the contact because he and his team wanted a chance to work with Carl Rogers. As it turned out later, Laing's team thought we were there because Carl wanted to work with Laing. Both thought they were responding to an initiative by the other.

We were shown to an office to one side of the main house. It was small for the number of people assembled: eight Californians and maybe ten of Laing's people, including Francis Huxley and Hugh Crawford. There were others whose names I never heard, including a striking blonde woman who spent the evening taking photographs.

The room seemed to be already vibrating as we entered: breathing in and out with its occupants. The feel and smell were strongly masculine. Pipe smoke was heavy, and the strong odor of tobacco clung to the clothes of several whose hands I shook. Straight-lipped British smiles revealed the usual tobacco-stained teeth untouched by orthodontics. Colors were dark: blacks, grays, and browns. Our California clothes seemed brash next to the sombre tweeds and worsteds.

DOI: 10.4324/9781003519454-2

As we got started, time began to slow down and stretch out as my own excitement mounted. I could feel myself slipping into another state of consciousness. Sounds, smells, and sights took on added intensity. As we took our places in the circle, and I looked around, my heart rate quickened, and my palms were uncharacteristically moist. I refused the marijuana being passed from hand to hand. I already felt like my mind was in the process of being 'blown' and I certainly needed no psychoactive assistance. Instead, I accepted the wine circulating like a communion cup.

Laing expressed a few words of welcome to Carl and suggested we begin the process of getting to know each other. Carl began in his characteristic way: an opening rite we had performed at the start of every PCA event. He invited us to introduce ourselves. Knowing the ritual from many repetitions, we spoke, one after the other, until everyone in the brightly dressed half of the circle had spoken.

I have little clear recollection of what anybody said. I said something rather precious and predictable about hearing Laing in Brazil and how I had sensed deep correspondences between his thinking and ours. I was probably articulate and undoubtedly very serious. I revealed nothing about the mounting apprehension pounding away beneath my sternum. As we Californians talked, one after the other in our blandness, I could see eyebrows beginning to lift on the tweedy side of circle. Instead of mirroring smiles, nods, and other signs of acceptance we were accustomed to, we were met with cold impassiveness and, in a couple of cases, outright smirks.

After all of us had spoken, there followed a long, loud silence. As we sat, waiting for someone to speak, my focus shifted rapidly in and out like a sports photographer. Click—Laing's quizzical face. Click—Carl's, calm as ever. Click, click—Maria, Jared. Click—my own hands shaking. With a shutter speed of milliseconds, I scanned the room and tightened up like a spring. I dared not breathe.

Francis Huxley, nephew of Aldous and author of *The Way of the Sacred*, spoke first. He was puffing on a pipe, as I recall. He spoke in a voice that announced privilege and erudition. Public school, Oxbridge education, and a lifetime of consort with the intellectual elite of British culture oozed forth with every rich syllable. It was the voice of superiority, unshakable self-confidence, and absolute indifference to the impact it had on its listeners—beyond, that is, its intention to dominate.

'My God!' he began. His tone feigned naive innocence but dripped derision. 'I can only imagine what kind of reaction you would have obtained from our gang, Ronnie, if you had asked any of us to perform so politely'. Laing smiled.

The air hung heavy, Huxley's salvo reverberating around the room. I sat in stunned silence. Carl recovered first. As he began to speak, his voice wavered just a little but quickly took on its familiar fluency as he gracefully articulated our creed about human nature and the nature of relationships. Just as I began to relax, Laing interrupted again with another salvo, this time at Carl directly. 'If you and I are to have any kind of meaningful dialogue', he declared, 'you are going to have to cut out the California "nice-guy" act and get to something approaching an authentic encounter'. Laing's group seemed to be enjoying our discomfort.

Now my head was swimming. I was feeling very protective of Carl. My California 'family' was being ambushed! At the same time, though, unbidden came a much less noble reaction. I had the urge to denounce Californians and to line myself up with the Brits. I began to feel like a vile and spineless creature. Suddenly there was no end to my potential for treachery. I could imagine myself standing aside from Jewish friends as pogroms proceeded. I remembered St. Peter and wondered how I had failed to identify with his denial before. After a lifetime of identifying myself either with the hero or with the victim in stories of oppression and persecution, I was brought face to face with a slimy invertebrate cowardice. I said nothing.

When Maria spoke up, I began to feel better. Her eloquent elaboration of the basis of our approach and the self-assured confidence in our grasp of truth calmed my disquiet, and I was able to align myself with my comrades once more. But I was mortally shaken, and I knew it. As the uneasy conversation continued, my loyalties wavered back and forth as Laingian followed Rogerian and so on.

The conflict centered on whether human beings should be considered fundamentally trustworthy. Could we interpret behavior as manifestations of a universal telos—the self-actualizing tendency, as Rogers had called it, that propelled us toward self-realization and self-healing? We believed yes, and Laing's folk believed no. The unspoken corollary to our credo was the idea that those who denied the reality of the self-actualizing tendency were either wrong, misguided, or too afraid to have faith. So, they needed to be convinced to surrender themselves to the benevolence of the universe. Empathy, non-judgmental acceptance, warmth, and congruence—key concepts in Rogerian theory—created the conditions wherein people might be so persuaded.

Corollary to the Laingian position was the idea that those who unconditionally trusted human nature and denied that it had a destructive, dark side were wrong, and probably dangerously so. Such people needed to be convinced that despite their 'niceness', their own unacknowledged dark side had tremendous power and could be heinously destructive. In particular, middle-class bourgeois values were suspected of covering up unacknowledged repressive violence against the passionate authentic self. In Laing's theory, this was the origin of most mental illness and of social pathologies such as fascism and violence. The antidote was to denounce all attempts to stifle the raw self by brutally and frankly confronting all manner of inauthenticity and hypocrisy that were hidden in bourgeois sensibilities.

Adding greatly to my personal inner turmoil was the increasingly troublesome awareness that a good deal of the Laingian position had some ring of truth about it for me. After all, here I was in mortal combat with a very dark side to my own nature. I wanted to hear the Laingian position and then again, I didn't. If I found their arguments convincing, did that mean I must adopt their brutishness, so reminiscent of the bullying I had experienced as a girl growing up in the industrial north of England? And if I rebuffed their assaults, refused to be written off as a California wimp, and instead stood up for love, gentleness, civility, and gracefulness in human relationships, did that mean I must deny the realities of both my present experience and those of my early life at the hands of the 'civilized' middle class?

The encounter continued. I spoke some, listened some, but while the surface presentation of me was performing its well-behaved dance of participation, another deeper reality was unfolding. Another consciousness—almost another Maureen—was awakened. As the voices of Rogerians and Laingians dropped into the background, images from my own past began to float into view.

I remembered Miss Grange, the very proper spinster landlady of our cold-water back-to-back. She came every week to collect the rent and we lived in terror that someday she would arrive and we would not have the money. It's not that she would have evicted us. She would have just looked very disappointed, and we would have died of shame. I recalled quiet-spoken Mr. McDonald, the 'man from the Pru', who picked up our penny insurance premiums. He used to slip his fingers into my blouse and threatened to tell my parents I'd asked for it if I said a word. Loud, coarse Elsie, who would have fought off tigers to protect her kids from their drunken father, came to mind. She alone kept her kids from being put into what was euphemistically referred to as 'the care of the local authority' by the social worker with the Morris Minor. I remembered with vivid humiliation, the teacher at the elite girl's school who singled me out on the first day. In front of the whole school assembly, she prescribed remedial classes for my 'atrocious use of the English language and my slovenly posture'.

As the instances of shame and humiliation at the hands of the middle class flooded back, the educated, poised neo-Californian, who championed the ideas of her beloved friend and teacher Carl Rogers, became not much more than a patina on the gritty Yorkshire kid who had fought her way out of the slums by virtue of native intelligence, solid family support, welfare-state structures that helped bright poor youngsters attend elite schools, and who had developed more than the little pugnacity and impudence required to survive it all. My escape from a life in the 'satanic mills' had also entailed turning my back on much of my own roots, learning to play the middle-class game, developing the 'right' accent, and minimizing my working-class affiliations. I had survived and I had prospered but I had been hurt—deeply hurt—in the process. Sitting there in Laing's home, I was aware of the scars for the first time.

Then another series of memories made their appearance: an altogether different picture of my relationships with the middle class. I remembered John Bates MD, the pathologist who had taken me under his wing at my first job, and who had persuaded my sceptical parents that I should go back to school, finish my A-Levels, and enter university; Dr Irene Manton, FRS (Fellow of the Royal Society), the Professor of the Leeds University Botany Department, where I had begun working toward a PhD in plant science, who had explained to me why women scientists should publish alone if they wanted credit for their ideas; and of course Carl's accepting response to my request that he sit on my Doctoral committee for my clinical psychology degree. Then there was my first therapist, who taught me the meaning of unconditional acceptance and helped me go beneath the abrasive defensiveness of my childhood and identify a 'fragile, tender, female soul' who inhabited my consciousness. I remembered, too, numerous experiences in PCA workshops, counselling sessions, and classes, when I was opened up to a sweetness, a delicacy, a fineness of spirit that would have been as unsustainable in my early life as mangos in Michigan. Nothing in the bleak nastiness of my West Yorkshire childhood had encouraged me to aspire to anything remotely like the life I now had. I was 35, living in a communal household in a Southern California beach community, on very little income but enjoying tremendous riches. Spiritually and psychologically, life was gentle, full of love and joy—even ecstasy, and I was not so chronically angry. Images floated in and out of my reverie as, for the first time in my life, perhaps, I pondered the multihued complexity of all my varied experiences.

I was still in this other image-filled place of being when somebody decided we should all leave to go get something to eat. Laing had offered to buy us all dinner and had reserved tables at a Chinese restaurant half a block up the street.

There was considerable animosity by this time. Both groups were muttering and mumbling amongst themselves. I hoped that eating together might serve as some kind of tribal hospitality rite and that we might get closer to each other. On the way over to the restaurant, I struck up a conversation with Hugh Crawford. I seemed to have a greater affinity for his down-to-earth Scottish sensibility than for either my California colleagues or the more contentious of the Laingians.

At the restaurant, one long table was positioned near the wall, along the length of the room. It was set up to hold all of us. Carl sat with his back to the wall, Californians by his side including his daughter Natalie. Hugh and I sat along that side too. After an awkward, clumsy dance of 'who sits where?', Laing took himself off to a separate, unprepared table at the other end of the room. He was joined by a young colleague, Stuart I think his name was, and by John Wood and Jared Kass of the California team. The set-up could not have been more suggestive if it had been directed by Hal Prince. A long table with Carl in the center, flanked by people anxious to be in his presence, and over to one side a small, intimate group around Laing and his lieutenant. At first, no one else was in the restaurant.

As the dinner progressed, Laing's performance intensified. He joked and bantered in his melodic Glasgow style. His wit was sharp and entertaining. I talked with Hugh, who made some apologies for the roughness of our earlier meeting. I got the distinct impression that this was not the first time he had been embarrassed by Laing's behavior and that he personally found the abrasiveness very uncomfortable.

The restaurant door opened. In walked two young men looking for a Chinese meal. As they took in the scene, they began making sport. From their accents, it was obvious they also were Glaswegian, their wit every bit as well-honed as our host's. Suddenly, Laing was upstaged, and it was clear he didn't like it. Already pretty drunk, he began upping his ante, intensifying the barbs of his comments as if in a word-to-word combat.

We were all unprepared for what happened next. Up until now, Laing had aimed wide, sending his arrows indiscriminately at both his people and ours. Suddenly, he half stood and pointed his finger in Carl's direction. Carl was looking extremely uncomfortable, no longer sure how to react. Unfamiliar with British humor, he was unsure if these proceedings were funny or not, but like a well-mannered guest in an alien land, he remained polite and noncommittal. Laing yelled to the newcomers, 'You see that bald-headed man over there?' And then, with an unmistakably scornful reference to Carl's most popular book, 'Well, he's no' a man, he's a person!' His alcohol-loosened tongue rolled out the 'r' in 'person'.

Silence fell. Everybody looked stunned. Carl's face turned bright red. The rest of us had a variety of responses from squirmy embarrassment to white-knuckled fury. I was deeply ashamed. Reliving some primitive experience of inappropriateness, I felt entirely responsible for Carl being in this situation. It was like inviting a well-bred classmate to my home only to have a family member get drunk and be abusive. In my shame, I was paralyzed. As the shame turned to fury, I began to tremble. I made some feeble attempts to smooth things out (principally my own dishevelment). It didn't work. Laing had us going and he knew it.

He came over to the table, and sat before me, making slurred conversation. He was insulting and teasing, and he was enjoying himself. He poured scotch into my glass—a sign of friendship and goodwill, I thought—and asked if I liked the liquor. To humor him I said I did, although in truth it was not a favorite of mine. Whereupon he leaned over and spat in my glass. 'Well how do you like it now?' he leered. Now beside myself with shame and rage, I picked up the glass and hurled its contents at his face. I believe I missed.

The assembly was breaking up, with people milling about and scurrying toward the door. Laing paid the bill and we spilled out onto the damp London pavement. Tempers were close to explosion. As we walked back toward Eton Place, Laing announced that we were not welcome in his house. Alcohol, fatigue, and intense emotion threatened to propel us into a physical encounter right there on the street outside his house. At least one member of our team, dark side surging to the fore, had to be restrained from throwing a punch. Several other people arrived, friends and family members of the California team, including my own intentional family, who had been told they could attend the post-meal meeting. Voices were shrill and confused, but in the middle of it all, I heard Carl declare he would not go through with the event the next day. He'd had enough of Laing, and his politeness had given way to anger and indignation.

Carl's announcement seemed to come as a surprise to Laing's team. 'What? Back out?' Apparently that had not occurred to them. The next moment someone decided we had to enter the house after all and 'get this bloody mess sorted out'.

This time we were ushered into a room inside the house. Laing greeted the newcomers like the consummate host, welcoming them in and generously offering them scotch and wine. My husband remarked later that he felt his mind bend as he juxtaposed our group's obvious extreme distress with Laing's noblesse and grace. The room we entered was absolutely lovely. In the slowed-down vision of heightened arousal, my eyes took in the marvellous rich colors of the antique Persian carpet, the evocative presence of various masks, effigies, artworks, and symbols collected on global travels by an eye tuned to the luminosity of sacred consciousness. 'How could such a boorish bully have such exquisite sensibility?' I wondered. Laing's private study was like a temple.

He started the proceeding with what I took to be his familiar opening ritual. 'There are only two rules. Nobody gets hurt and nothing gets broken'. People began to talk, both sides trying to say things that might magically heal the gulf between us. Our group was angry. Their group was showing signs of alarm as the reality of the next day's meeting at the Hilton began to impinge upon that night's proceedings. Even the more belligerent Laingians were now expressing trepidation about facing a large group with soft plans and hard feelings.

Carl, who had said nothing since we entered, finally asked Laing to give him one good reason why he should go ahead with the next day's event. Laing, suddenly assuming the self-righteous position of guardian of social etiquette, said, 'I'll give you a thousand. Those are all the people who have bought a ticket expecting to see both of us tomorrow'. Somehow that convinced Carl and the rest of us to once more commit to the next day's event and do whatever it took that night to salvage the program.

I tried to speak. The conversation was somehow dancing over and around Laing's behavior in the restaurant. I began to speak to him, to express my pain and shame. My voice was shrill. I was cut off by someone—I don't recall whom—implying that my feelings were unimportant. The next day's meeting was the agenda now.

Somehow that pushed me over the edge. My ordinary mind left and what followed was like nothing I had experienced before. I lost my mind. I saw the inside space of my skull expand to engulf ever-widening worlds: the room, the present situation, the continent of Europe with its history and traditions, and the New World, both north and south. Inside this expanded universe, I could see and feel the eternal battles raging—between old and new, between north and south, between rich and poor, between light and dark, between oppressor and oppressed, between madness and sanity, between London and California, between men and women, between acceptance and rejection, between love and fear, between good and evil, and ultimately between being and nonbeing. My private inner battle raged in the same polarized duality as the conflicts of external realities. The madness of it was unbearable—and inescapable.

As the paroxysms took hold of my body, the dam wall that until then had separated the neatly ordered contradictions of my being began to crumble. I had no more resistance. The uneasy disquiet I had felt throughout the planning process to bring my California reality 'home' to England now burst through the retaining walls with maelstromic fury. I—whomever that pronoun now referred to—could only watch as the pieces of shattered reality pulled loose from their designated places in my psychic landscape and sloshed about like so much flotsam. Out of my solar plexus emerged a long harping wail. I yelled, 'You son of a bitch!' or some such, at Laing, now the embodiment of archetypal nemesis. He smiled patronizingly and encouraged me to 'get it all out'. As I slipped further into chaos, Laing seemed interested in me for the first time—the psychological final straw! The last blocks of the dam fell away and for a time—only minutes, but it seemed like an eternity—I was engulfed in pure madness. I raged, screamed, and sobbed as the tidal wave swept everything before it. As I surrendered to unspeakable terror, the demons of a thousand lifetimes laughed in my face. The gargoyles and incubi of countless humiliations and vanities swirled around me, casting their taunts. Some wore Laing's face, and some wore Carl's.

Swept onward, I was aware only of an anonymous male presence close by. He did not touch me at first but the smell of his tobacco-tainted breath, and the rise and fall of his chest, were reassuring in some way. I surrendered, further giving myself up to other, kindlier ghosts and apparitions: madonnas, knights, and delicate maidens. By now, sweetness began to permeate my experience. I leaned into the maleness of my companion as oceanic calmness took the place of the tempest. After a few moments of utterly perfect sobbing, I opened my eyes to find Laing's young lieutenant offering his support and urging me to 'go on through it'. Laing had moved closer too. Their earlier antagonism and derision were gone, and so was Laing's patronizing air (perhaps I had only imagined it before). In their place was a steadying but non-interfering accompaniment. I was contained by their presence, which seemed to have become almost luminous. Neither exploited my fragility—both seemed more comfortable with madness than with rationality. Little by little, the violence left my body and I slipped into a relaxed calm that was at once empty and pregnant. They helped me out of the circle and onto a couch, where a hazy half-sleep cradled me until the meeting ended a couple of hours later.

The next day's meeting at the Hilton went off without incident and without any great moment. Ronnie conducted a dialogue with Carl in which he was respectful—even admiring. The experiential part of the program was not what any of our team had in mind, but I think the people who came enjoyed it. I was still so dazed that I hardly remember anything about it. The night before was still too vivid, marking, I was to come to realize eventually, a psychic turning point for me—the beginning of my own authentic story.

In that short explosion of madness, the structures of my psyche—the roles and conceptual schemata with which I navigated life—came unglued. For years, since my earliest interactions with the repressive demands of middle-class culture, and continuing all the way through to the equally demanding yet infinitely nicer California human-potential-movement culture, I had been busily accumulating ways of being, thinking, and acting that would make the people I admired like me, accept me, and, above all, teach me. Gradually, what I had learned from my teachers became reintegrated in ways that were more uniquely mine, more an expression of what I believed and understood, and less a reiteration of other's theories. No longer the disciple, safely tucked in behind some mentor or another, I now found myself willing to stand out in front and speak about things the way I saw them. I realize as I look back, it was after the meeting at Laing's house, pressed by Laing's willingness to challenge the boundaries of accommodation, that I began to develop my own voice, my own sense of authority and authorship.

Chapter 2

Reflections on becoming and being a postmodern person

Maureen O'Hara and Keith Tudor

Keith: When I proposed this book and the structure of the book, organised in parts and including our reflections in dialogue, I knew I wanted us to open with this paper as it's so powerful and poignant in describing a transformative moment in your life, set or occurring in the context of a significant meeting in the history of psychology in the late 20th century.

For me, the crux of it is what you refer to as the 'mortal combat with a very dark side of my soul', and describe what appears to be a form of psychotic breakdown, in which, as you put it, 'I lost my mind'. Looking back at that evening, now some 45 years ago, how do you see it?

Maureen: Over the years, working as a person-centred and gestalt psychotherapist and supervising others—neophytes and experienced practitioners—I have revisited this event in my life, comparing it with descriptions by others of such states. I no longer think of it as psychotic, though at first, I did. Laing certainly wanted to make that link, but I now think there is a significant difference—at least at the level and duration of the pain I experienced—between what I went through and what people who live longer in states of severe disorganisation experience. Today I see the experience more in terms of complexity or chaos theory. I think of the thought experiment of watching a sand pile form. At first it forms a more or less ordered cone with grains that land first at the bottom and those that arrive later in the higher layers. What we know, though, is that as more piles up, it puts disruptive pressure into the system and avalanches occur. They may be small, unpredictable, and not disruptive at first but eventually as pressure builds the whole form may collapse bringing older material to the surface mixing old with new. My sense of what happened was that the disruptive pressure of the extremely intense encounter presented me with more cognitive and emotional dissonance that I could manage. The defences I had used over my life to keep my consciousness coherent as I encountered new worlds had been adequate to keep the 'avalanches' of novel awareness

DOI: 10.4324/9781003519454-3

manageable—even exhilarating. However, as the relentless assault on my ways of being continued that evening, I got to the point where the edifice of my previous identity was unsustainable and there was nothing I could do to hold it (my *self*) together, and keep older and denied aspects of consciousness from coming into current awareness. Pain, desire, fear, and rage; experiences that had been long buried were alive again and were available to become reintegrated into an expanded sense of reality. My old mind was deconstructed and a new one began to reconfigure itself. So, rather than 'psychotic', I now think of the moment as a transformative avalanche.

Keith: Thanks, Maureen. I was hesitant to refer to your experience as psychotic, but felt that I know you well enough to say and risk it. Interesting to learn that Laing wanted to make that link. Did he do that at the time?

Maureen: I'm OK with using the term 'psychotic' informally to represent disorganised states where our reality melts and normal boundaries disappear, but I think Laing used it to mean a more permanent state of being where nothing can be counted on, and to refer to those more transient episodes of disorganisation such as that we might have with LSD, chaotic meditation, even intense therapeutic experiences. At the time, Laing was into 'rebirthing' to provoke such states.

Keith: Moving on to the more theoretical layer of this evening and the following day's event, while you write about the difference between the Laingians and the Rogerians, for instance, with regard to the trustworthiness of human beings, you also mention your sense of 'the deep correspondences' between Laing's thinking and Rogers'. What do see as these correspondences?

Maureen: I see correspondence in their positions with respect to power, though Rogers was slow to recognise the politics in the interpersonal. I'll give an example. While we were negotiating plans for the event, Laing mentioned Rogers' political stance as a point of similarity. Rogers denied it: 'I don't see my therapy as political'. Laing's reply was to point to the moment in Rogers' career when he brought his chair out from behind his office desk and sat face-to-face with his client as an equal, on the same level and without the trappings of psychiatrist power, as a profoundly radical and 'political' move. In time, and with help from Natalie, Rogers' more politically minded daughter, and others, including me, he came to see the political dynamics in his approach.

Another area of correspondence was more ontological. They both held a faith in human potential, and they trusted the organismic tendency towards growth and self-fulfilment as an animating force in the universe. They believed—and believed in—what their clients said and, though Laing was willing to offer interpretations where Rogers was not, both respected their clients as creative agents of their own existence. Though their personalities were quite different—Laing the extrovert (at least when inebriated, which was quite often) contrasted with Rogers' more introverted style—they both sought contact, authenticity, empathy, and offered deep non-judgemental listening. They were both process-focused and sought to attune themselves to their clients' cognitive, emotional, and physical process, listening for emergent themes of being in their clients' accounts. Finally, they were both sceptical of the use of medical models when it came to explaining psychological processes and were willing to take the wrath of established psychology and psychiatry in their search for a psychology that sought to celebrate the fullness of Being rather than reduce it to mechanisms and engineering.

Keith: What a clear, concise, and useful response—thanks, Maureen. I also appreciate you referring to all *four* of Rogers' therapist conditions, i.e., contact, authenticity, acceptance, and empathy.[1]

Picking up your own experience of both the correspondence as well as the discordance between Rogers' and Laing's positions and personalities, especially that evening, you offer a beautiful and poignant description of what you describe as a 'transformative avalanche', and a great and, I think, useful distinction between this kind of transformation and that of a psychotic breakdown—thank you. As the landscape is different (transformed) after an avalanche, I wonder to what extent you understood—or understand—this experience as contributing to you becoming a postmodern person?

Maureen: It took quite some time to work through the event and make sense of it, though in a way I was prepared by my early life trying to make sense of the multiple contradictions I encountered. My experience has always been situated in multiple and culturally diverse settings. I was born into an unlettered home at the hard scrabble end of the economic scale. Our parents cobbled together a living that was governed by the values and logic of survival. At the same time, my mother insisted that I enter a competition for a place at a local girls' grammar school that saw the world in terms of privilege, aspiration, and achievement. I learned early to code switch between these two worlds. As I got older and immersed myself in the logic and perceptive frames of science, the gap grew wider, severely alienating my father who saw his world through the frames of a blue-collar Catholic patriarch. Ultimately, after the encounter at Laing's house I came to see that the boundaries I was navigating were permeable: human constructs that added to the range of understandings rather than imposing constraints and so postmodern in its acceptance of the multiplicity of possible configurations of understanding of what it means to be a person.

Keith: Yes. In your paper, you write—again, beautifully and poignantly—about your upbringing and especially the impact of class, which, notwithstanding the work of some colleagues,[2] is, I think, an undervalued factor in the field of therapy. I appreciate your references to Miss Grange, Mr. McDonald, and Elsie, and to John Bates, Irene Manton, and, of course, Carl Rogers. This passage is a great example of the autobiographical impact on theory and a person's choice of theory.

One of the threads of your narrative in the paper concerns gender. You describe the feel and smell of the room at Laing's house as 'strongly masculine', and later, Laing's interaction with you, including spitting into your glass of whiskey, what these days would be referred to as 'toxic masculinity'. You also describe yourself as having a 'fragile, tender, *female* soul' (my emphasis). Is this significant for how you view yourself as a person, or a gendered person?

Maureen: I have always had a keen sense of being a girl and then a woman, though I was more androgynous than my peers. Attending an all-girls' grammar school, with all female staff and teachers was profoundly formative. In my neighbourhood, no one else went to grammar school. After-school flirtation, make-up, and hair was what my neighbour friends did while I did homework. As I got older and chose science as a career, I had to buttress my sense of female self between more 'feminine' women friends who were far more gender performative than I was and my scientist colleagues who, in the pre-feminist mid '60s, were blatantly sexist and thought nothing of calling me a dyke. In a strange way, it was Irene Manton—the consummate bluestocking spinster who was my professor at Leeds University—who provided cover by encouraging me to work with her rather than the men in the department, though she never said that was what she was doing.

Keith: Does this relate to what you refer to as Laing's willingness—I'd suggest, even determination—'to challenge the boundaries of accommodation'?

Maureen: I'm not sure. I do know that I secretly relished my double life. I was discovering sexual power at the same time as I realised I was a gifted biologist. I could push back at the sexism in the lab because I was doing good science, and I could enjoy flirting and more because I discovered my own desire and that sexual conquests were readily accessible for me. So, I pushed conventional boundaries on both the science and gender fronts. It's no coincidence, then, that when I switched fields from biology to psychology when I moved to the United States, my area of study was sexuality and gender. The title of my 1976 PhD dissertation was *Different Paths: Journeys of Sexual Self-Discovery* and consisted of self-reflection about my own sexuality and gender identity development and in-depth semi-structured interviews with professionals who represented what today we would refer to as belonging to the LGBTQI+ community. It is important to add here that I also explored the tension between what at the time were seen as the benefits and drawbacks to the identity politics that were just emerging where people felt a new socialised pressure to identify with one of the emerging labels.

Keith: From your writing[3] and my experience of you, I've always had a strong sense of your feminism. Do you think that the Rogerian emphasis on the person discounts the impact of differential socialisation—and, worse, oppression—on the basis of gender, and how do you view this in the context of more recent deconstructions of gender that support increased gender fluidity?

Maureen: In 1976, based on my doctoral research and my experience teaching human sexuality with thousands of participants who spanned the political spectrum, from religious conservative to radical rational left, I had already seen that commonly accepted sex and gender identity categories were largely socially constructed, and people knew it. Though conforming to social expectations in overt behaviour, in the safe space of an experiential workshop or consciousness-raising group, persons who were actively claiming their right to self-describe and who were searching for their own unique ways of being, rarely fitted neatly into any of the socially available categories. Their sense of self was more fluid, often more pluralistic and their expression modified, dance-like, in tune with their social or interpersonal contexts. When given the space, freedom, and solidarity from others similarly reaching for a fuller sense of themselves, growth is inevitably a transgressive act. It involves contact with the status quo and engagement with the social forces that restrict options and possibilities. On individual levels, stories of abuse and cruelty were common as gay, transgendered, and folks who were questioning shared what they had experienced. At a more collective or social level, participants were encouraged to unpack power dynamics and recognise the contours of a socialisation process that was experienced to varying degrees by everyone within the shared cultural context.

Rogers' concept of 'person' always considered the social context of their existence and, though his analysis was somewhat superficial, he always believed that a person's ability to fulfil their inherent potential required that they contend with social forces that had impeded their actualisation.

Keith: Thanks, Maureen. I think your last response is a great example of people challenging the boundaries of accommodation, of over-adaptation to social norms, and exploring what Piaget wrote about in terms of assimilation (as distinct from accommodation), what perhaps nowadays we tend to view as and refer to as integration.

I also appreciate the point you make about actualisation requiring some contention with social forces that impede such growth. To paraphrase Jerold Bozarth, I'd suggest that *social* conditionality is the bedrock of a theory of internalised psychopathology.[4]

Maureen: I am not sure what I think about the concept of internalised psychopathology within a humanistic or person-centred framework. I don't want to deny psychological pain but I don't know what standpoint you have to take to deem a 'psyche' to be 'pathological'.

Keith: You make a good point about psychopathology, which I generally view as describing different forms of alienation,[5] but my use of the term 'internalised psychopathology' may be an example of my over-adaptation to a social norm, in this case, mainstream psychological language. Well caught!

What a great start. I'm appreciating both your reflections and our dialogue in this chapter which, I consider—and hope for the reader—have set the scene for the rest of the book in terms of your experience, background, politics, and transformative avalanche: all of which provide the base, bedrock even, for the range of theoretical interests represented by the works reproduced in this book.

Notes

1 For a discussion about these conditions, Rogers' (1957, 1959) necessary and sufficient conditions, and Truax and Carkhuff's (1967) 'core conditions', see Tudor (2000, 2011) and Tudor and Worrall (2006).

2 Jones (1974), Kearney (1996), Pérez Foster et al. (1996), and Ballinger and Wright (2007).

3 For example, O'Hara (1973, 1976, 1983a [Chapter 6 in this volume], 1983b, 1989b, 1995b, 1996b [Chapter 15]).

4 Bozarth's (1998) original assertion is that 'Conditionality is the bedrock of Rogers' theory of pathology' (p. 83).

5 See Tudor (1997, 2017, 2018a, 2018b, 2018c), and Tudor and Worrall (2006).

Part I

The person-centred approach

Chapter 3

Person-centered approach as conscientização[1]

The works of Carl Rogers and Paulo Freire (1989)

Maureen O'Hara[2]

Summary

In *Carl Rogers on Personal Power* (1977), Rogers devotes almost a whole chapter to what he sees as remarkable similarities between 'person-centred approaches' and the pedagogical strategies of Brazilian educator, Paulo Freire. During the last 13 years, I have heard such similarities debated in almost every context in which the social and political implications of person-centered approaches are considered. Many Rogerians and other North American humanistic psychologists believe there is a similarity. Freirians and many humanistic psychologists in technologically underdeveloped nations often disagree. This chapter introduces some new reflections on the work of both men that might be useful to those committed to a search for a more humane world. I hope to establish that the differences of opinion regarding the work of the two men are legitimate, that is, they are based in real differences. However, I also want to show that it is possible to reconcile these differences by considering the deeper underlying precepts of Freire and Rogers. Through examination of large group person-centered workshops, I suggest that a reconsideration of what may be at the base of the ideas of the two men could point the way to possible new discoveries about our human nature and our human future.

Radical humanism: the works of Carl Rogers and Paulo Freire

Ever since 1969, when I made the transition from natural science to behavioral science, the work of both Rogers and Freire has been a major source of inspiration. As I read *Pedagogy of the Oppressed* (Freire, 1970), I recognized instinctively (and probably naively) a correspondence between what I took to be both men's worldviews and my own. The unshakable faith in human beings and their potential, which illumined both men's work, resonates with my own buoyant humanistic utopianism. So, it came as a surprise to discover that Freire and many of those who follow his works reject this comparison.

The rejection is made primarily on ideological grounds. Freire and his followers point out that *Pedagogy of the Oppressed* is deeply rooted in a Marxist/

DOI: 10.4324/9781003519454-5

Christian worldview. They believe that attempts to draw comparisons between Rogers and Freire that fail to acknowledge these roots destroy the conceptual coherence and power of Freire's ideas. Even when well-intentioned, such comparisons are seen as resulting in a domestication of Freire's position (Fonseca, 1983). Another reason given for the rejection is that too little attention is given by those in technologically developed nations to the specific context from which Freire's ideas and methodologies emerged—the particularly miserable conditions of life in northeast Brazil, and elsewhere in technologically underdeveloped nations.

It is not my intention to destroy Freire's conceptual coherence, nor do I wish to overlook or underestimate the importance of the cultural and ideological roots of both Freire's ideas and Rogers'. The ideas presented here are, however, framed in the language of humanistic psychology from technologically developed nations. What I hope is that, despite the perils attendant on such cultural transposition, there is something to be gained by humanistic psychology in technologically developed nations in considering both men's work together.

Humanization and self-actualization: utopian ideals

Throughout the work of both Freire and Rogers runs a single thread. Both unabashedly celebrate human existence and our evolutionary potential. They write of their fascination with human capacity for self-regulation, self-understanding, and transcendence. Neither begs the intervention of a god, magic, manipulative technology, or supernatural forces. They are both radical humanists.

Rogers (1977) has placed his faith in what he describes as 'the formative tendency' or 'self-actualising tendency' for growth born in each person. He trusts that as long as life remains, this tendency remains. He even insists that the self-actualizing drive survives even in people so abusively dehumanized that it appears that nothing of their humanity remains:

> Belief in the worth of the free person is not something that can be extinguished even by all the modern technological devices—bugging of conversations, "mental hospitals" to recondition behavior, electric tortures and all the rest. Nothing can extinguish the human organism's drive to be itself—to actualize itself in individual and creative ways.
>
> (Rogers, 1977, p. 261)

Rogers never gives up on people, and nor does Freire.

Freire (1981) has profound Christian and Marxist convictions. He sees both these convictions (often said to be contradictory) as expressions of his belief that the destiny of humanity is humanization and to become subjects of free and authentic experience. He sees human beings as responsible participants in the continuous evolution of consciousness. This vision and his work to bring it about are the basis of what he terms his 'comradeship' with Christ and with Marx.

Freire's faith, like Rogers', in the inextinguishable push for transcendence, is unshakable. Whether speaking of downtrodden peasants, hot-headed terrorists, oppressed women, or even life-negating torturers or agents of oppression, he insists that all are born to live human lives, to be subjects of their own experience in a world of other conscious beings. Freire admits he is a utopian:

> Conscientização is clearly associated with utopia. It implies a utopia. The more conscious we are, the more capable we are of denouncing the inhuman or dehumanizing, and proclaiming the human. This is thanks to the commitment we make to transformation.
>
> (Freire, 1979, p. 28; translated from Portuguese)

Hammers and nails: technology is not neutral

There is a saying that the person who has only a hammer sees everything as a nail. The converse also seems to be true—when there are nails sticking up all over the place there is a tendency to see everything in terms of their potential use by a hammer. In a world full of suffering, oppression, dehumanization, fear, exploitation, and threat of annihilation by nuclear war, there is a similar tendency for those who are called to the cause of human emancipation to believe that everything they believe in or approve of will be a positive force for transformation.

Utopian ideals are shared by many in the humanistic community throughout the world. However, beyond this fundamental agreement is an overarching wish for human emancipation. Rogers and others have suggested technical or methodological similarities between the 'pedagogy of the oppressed', the Freirian method for adult education in peasant communities, and 'person-centred' or Rogerian approaches to therapy, education, and group facilitation. Rogers (1977) outlines them in *Carl Rogers on Personal Power*. I will summarize them here:

The role of the facilitator

- The facilitator is genuinely free of a desire to impose ready-made truths or to control the outcome.
- The facilitator has skills in helping people engage in genuine dialog.
- The facilitator respects the capacity of the group to discover the nature of their own problems and has skills in helping people express that capacity.
- A respectful hearing is given to all attitudes and feelings, no matter how 'extreme' or 'unrealistic'.
- The members of a group are permitted to choose, collectively and individually, their own process toward their own goals.

If these conditions apply, then a process is set in motion that has certain characteristics.

The process

- Long suppressed feelings will surface, many of them angry and bitter.
- Because these feelings are accepted and not judged, more people will express themselves and the range of feelings will widen.
- As people become vocal, visible, and known, trust and mutual respect will be strengthened.
- Irrational feelings lose their power both by being fully expressed and by feedback from others.
- Feelings based in common experience are clarified and strengthened, leading to a greater self and group confidence.
- Collective understandings become more realistic and less irrational.
- Power struggles between members are resolved and collaboration increases.
- Actions emerge that are aimed at changing the existing situation. In a good group, these actions will be innovative and transformational as well as realistic.
- Group solidarity is strong enough to support individuals to take even radical action.

Rogers based his thoughts on his own reading of Freire's book *Pedagogy of the Oppressed*, and although he notes that Freire 'is almost completely abstract', he tells us 'the principles he has come to build his work on are so completely similar to the principles of *Freedom to Learn* that I found myself open mouthed with astonishment' (Rogers, 1977, p. 106).

However, similar methods, techniques, or even principles do not necessarily guarantee similar outcomes—especially when they are rooted in different views about the nature of human reality.

I have suggested that there never has been a clear enough distinction in Rogers' writings between the purely technological aspects of the work, the more open-ended or investigative aspects of the work, and the frankly religious aspects (O'Hara, 1987). Coulson (1982) has explored the prevalence of what he calls 'psychosalvationism'—the tendency for humanistic psychologists to preach and persuade—which he believes comes from the abandonment of an open-ended investigative posture in favor of the application of person-centered techniques for specific predetermined moral ends. This lack of clarity leads to unresolvable discussions between practitioners as to what is or is not a 'person-centred' approach, with some pointing to techniques, others to end results, and still others to 'attitudes'.

Farson (1975) has discussed the contradictions for humanistic psychology that occur when too much emphasis is placed on technique. He points out, for instance, how emotional openness and dialog are enormously powerful techniques for the solution of some kinds of human problems. He cites, however, that between parties of unequal positions of institutionalized power, openness, and dialog favor the most powerful. There are situations in which silence may be the only power oppressed people have. Farson (1978) describes, as an example, encounter groups between Native Americans and Americans of European descent in which the groups actually favored the maintenance of illegitimate dominance by the Whites. Wooten (1981) makes the same (ghastly) point when he describes management techniques used by Albert Speer in Hitler's Ministry of Armaments as procedurally equivalent to present-day humanistic management approaches. Plum (1981) offers a brief review of writings that have raised similar concerns from a variety of contexts about the tendency to emphasize technique over purposes and intentions. It seems clear that the same technology can be used for vastly different (and sometimes completely opposite) ends.

If we wish, then, to understand the work of the two men, and of the people who identify themselves as followers or colleagues, we must examine not only methodologies or techniques but also the ideals to which their approaches are directed. When we ask about ends, we get a clearer picture as to what extent Freire's pedagogy and Rogers' person-centered approaches are based on similar ideals, comparable views of human life and analyses of social reality, and to what extent their practice is compatible.

Emancipation and humanization

One similarity that strikes most people immediately is the emancipatory thrust to all their efforts. Both men have consistently presented their work as strategies for use by those who wish to facilitate the rehumanization process of alienated people, the liberation of the oppressed, and achievement of full authentic human existence.

In his earlier work, Rogers was not yet promoting a particular model of *human*. He knew what a person was, more by its opposite—which he saw in the diminished and dehumanized people who sought his help as a counsellor—than by any formal standard of *health* or *personness*. Person-centered approaches have their origins in Rogers' search for strategies of liberation for people oppressed by dehumanizing ideologies, institutions, technologies, religious beliefs, personal myths, and orthodoxies. The end-goal of person-centered intervention was 'becoming a person'. Rogers was committed to helping people become who, in their deepest heart, they know themselves to be, however different from the crowd. His view of the fully functioning person was essentially Euro-American, which saw humans as individually autonomous and radically free to allow the authentic expression of an actualizing tendency that Rogers believed is present in all of Nature.

Freire, too, considers authenticity an essential aspect of full humanness. A Hegelian, he considers the oppressed as 'beingsfor-the-other', and the goal of his pedagogy is for people to become 'beings-for-themselves'—subjects of their own authentic experiencing, with their 'own authentic voice'. He suggests this is achieved through a process of critical education whereby the oppressed learn to read reality for themselves and to describe it in their own words.

Superficially, Freire's 'authenticity' may seem to be the same as Rogers' 'becoming a person'. However, Freire's concept of 'person' is quite different from Rogers'. For Rogers, a person is seen as distinct from society; separate, individual, and free to express themselves in unique ways. Rogers has an individualistic or egocentric concept of personhood. Freire's view, in contrast, is much more sociocentric. He considers a 'person' both as an individual center of consciousness and as a social reality. The 'own authentic voice' described by Freire is not an isolated voice uttering idiosyncratic opinions, but one that begins in a specific sociopolitical context.

In his lovely little book, *A Importância do ato de ler* [*The Importance of the act of Reading*] (1982), Freire describes his own early childhood experiences learning to read and write. He shows us a little boy surrounded by a world he did not create, populated by people who were there before him, who described the world to him as it made sense to them. He learned the meaning of words through a combination of his own subjective experience and the labelling by others, and with each meaning came a dense matrix of associations carrying in them many of the cultural elements of life in northeast Brazil. Out of this emerged his first sense of what is 'real'.

Later, as an old man, a return to the backyard of his childhood was to reveal much about the origins of his understandings and misunderstandings of reality. His sense of identity as an adult was partially given by the world in which he first developed language. When Freire speaks of 'self', he speaks of a self that can only be adequately comprehended as emerging from and coextensive with the concrete contexts of its history. This includes people known, words and meanings used, experiences lived, ideas accepted, lies believed, and knowledge acquired. Authenticity in this view is not so much a question of being 'different from the crowd' and free to construe the world uniquely, as it is for Rogers, but it is to be free from distortions in 'reading the world' created by myths, lies, and exploitation, perpetrated by one group for the purpose of maintaining oppression of another.

Traditional psychological and sociological thinking suggests that many forms of 'inauthenticity' or dehumanization occur because there exists an uneven balance of power between an individual and a group. The needs of the group (family, school, church, etc.) are seen as pitted against the needs of the individual, and generally the group wins out at the expense of the individual. The group's values and desires gradually become incorporated into the individual members in the form of 'introjections' that, especially in complex industrialized societies, are antagonistic to many of the felt needs and desires of the individual. On the macro scale, dominated groups will, in the interests of survival, be similarly obliged to introject the desires and values of dominant groups, even if this results in self-negation as it has been shown to do for women, for instance (Bernard, 1981).

When this happens, the individual or group lives under tension. Personal needs for self-assertion, individuality, integrity, and self-expression conflict with a sense of partness—the need to belong to a larger whole. Emphasis in humanistic psychology on autonomy, self-expression, self-fulfilment, self-assertion, uniqueness, and so on can be understood as a challenge to unfair, coercive advantages society (or a group) has over an individual. Oppressed groups, such as women, gay people, ethnic groups, and so on, have needed to express their truth, assert their identity, and achieve autonomy.

The work of both Freire and Rogers is aimed directly at this uneven balance of power: Rogers focuses on the disparity between the individual and various groups—family, community, culture, and so on, and Freire focuses on the disparity between dominant and dominated groups. As stressed earlier, both Rogers and Freire are committed to creating a society in which each human being is supported to become their full self. Although their stated or implied models of 'full personhood' may be quite different, both men share a conviction that what characterizes the fully human life is *consciousness,* and that the exclusively human activity is the *search for knowledge*. They share the belief that, to some extent, human evolution is in our own hands, and that history is made by human activity. More conscious beings create a more conscious world, and a more conscious world creates more conscious beings. In both cases, human beings are seen as architects of culture, and although both stress a secular, 'this-worldly' view of reality, both at the same time hold that a transcendent reality is at work in human nature.

The work of these two men involves re-examination of introjection and the ways by which the individual is diminished and limited in expressions of 'full humanness'. These introjections may be of individual psychological nature, as for example, 'I am not lovable when I get angry', or sociopolitical, as for example, 'The government knows better than a mere peasant'. In either case, these are views of human reality that have their origins outside the individual, and that are accepted acritically because of the individual's dependent and initially unconscious position vis-à-vis the group. Rogers and Freire have a common end-goal—the emancipation of persons from limiting 'false consciousness' through the development and exercise of critical consciousness or *conscientização*.

Rogers approaches the achievement of consciousness through exploration of the inner world of the individual and the intimate environment of the therapeutic relationship. He works to help individuals explore the myths they have of themselves and their relations in the world, to become conscious of inner resources and mobilize them for the fight to become more fully *self.* His writings are full of examples of expansion of individual consciousness. In his later work, which deals almost exclusively with group settings, Rogers recognizes the importance of groups as well as therapists in the facilitation of individual growth. Even in a group situation, however, what draws Rogers' attention is the (usually emotional) behavior of individuals. He frequently quotes examples in which individual outpouring of emotional expression has been the pivotal event in a group. In his evocative style, he tells us of such an event in Rust, Austria, of an encounter on the issue of Central America.

> Sunday morning the air was electric. The mood was different. The atmosphere in the general session was decidedly changed. There was recognition that there was hate, as well as pleasant feelings, involved. At different times several people expressed very bitter feelings against the United States; in one case, the person was surprised to discover how deep and strong his bitterness was. Two persons spoke of being torn between two cultures—Latin America and

the United States. Passionate speeches were made by the Nicaraguans and by others, but these were very different from presentations. Persons were talking to persons.

(Rogers, 1986b, p. 31)

In a group setting, Rogers did not talk about 'group issues' and usually responded on a personal level to anyone who did ask group-level questions. For example, in one group encounter in Europe, a woman wanted to discuss the male–female power dynamics in the group. Rogers responded to her by asking her to express how she was experiencing her own 'personal power' in the group at that moment. Gradually, the focus shifted from 'How come the men seem to be in charge here?' to 'How can I get closer to Carl?' and finally culminated in a cathartic release as the young woman acknowledged a deep frustration in her attempts to get close to her father. When an anonymous and massified member of a group is given the undivided attention of a figure like Rogers or of the group itself, the experience can be very powerful (Bowen et al., 1979). In the above case, everyone was deeply affected. Rogers gave her the gift of personal recognition, and in doing so facilitated the woman's 'rehumanisation' in her own, and in her society's, eyes. What was left hanging, however, was the whole question of male–female power issues in that group in particular and in society in general, not as issues between individuals but as issues of institutionalized prejudice. What had begun as an attempt to examine some of the structural aspects of dehumanization ended as a private individual experience. Even the comments by observers who had been deeply affected were limited to personal identifications with the woman's emotional longings.

Freire, however, focuses much of his attention on the group and on the relationships between groups in society, creating teaching strategies whereby people can explore the way groups function and how this has an impact on individual consciousness. Pedagogical approaches seek to create experiences whereby people may become aware of the ways in which groups can either enhance or damage the personness of their members and the ways in which the larger social forces sometimes promote, and sometimes conspire against, full humanness. Freirian educators hope this process will lead people to denounce systems of human organization, orthodoxies, and political ideologies that require the enslavement of souls for their functioning. They help the oppressed search for alternative ways to organize society, wherein the group does not parasitize the life force of individuals and one group does not unfairly exploit the labors of others.

Freire's facilitators are interested in individual personal experiences, but do not simply ask, 'What is your experience?' Rather, they inquire 'Your experience is of what?', thus turning the focus immediately back to the concrete conditions of daily life and the relationship between external reality and subjective experience. When an illiterate peasant claims to be powerless, Freire wants to know how this was learned and whether it is really true or merely an untested myth promoted by the dominant group, which the peasant has incorporated. In our Rogerian experience above, a Freirian would not have left the process here but would have facilitated the cognitive exploration of the relationship between the actual sexual power dynamics within the workshop, how they were isomorphic with those in the broader culture, how they were sustained by myths, ideologies, and practices to which the young woman and her father had been subjected throughout both their lives. The process would not end until all understood how the humanness of both was exploited by systems of economic and military power that need men to see themselves as breadwinner[s] and protector[s] and women to see themselves as angel[s] of the home and defenceless.

Perhaps more than any other humanistic thinker, Freire has taught us to blame neither the victims—whether it be their 'unconscious motives', their 'biological inferiority', their basic 'lack of motivation'—nor 'divine plan' or 'supernatural entities', for instance, for the injustices of society, but to search for understanding about how societies work—recognizing a historical dialectical interplay (or struggle) between the individual's yearning for full expression of their humanness and the group's tendency to dominate and consume. For Freire (1970), liberation involves becoming aware of oppression, and understanding how this oppression was accomplished. This is not abstract or theoretical knowledge, but knowledge achieved through a process of action upon the realities of existence. In attempting to improve the conditions of life, each new action brings the possibility of learning. Gradually, the dynamics of society that may either facilitate or impede achievement of humanization are confronted and comprehended.

For Freire, critical consciousness is an ongoing *achievement*, developing only through action in the world. By reflection upon the action, and its consequences in the world (and in their hearts), people become aware of aspirations to become fully human, and aware of the forces (internal and external) that conspire to enslave the human spirit. This open-ended process of action, and reflection upon the learnings from such action, Freire (1970) termed *praxis*.

What people become critically conscious *of* is of course vastly different in the different cultural and political contexts. The differences in perspective, worldview, and cultural contexts between the two men are most apparent when we consider what each of them sees as his field of interest and commitment. What Freire is conscious of, and believes other participants in the same reality as him will also become conscious of, is an established condition of institutionalized oppression that conspires to dehumanize the peasant and worker classes of technologically underdeveloped nations. What Rogers is conscious of, and similarly assumes his cultural companions will also become conscious of, is the condition of psychological oppression of individuals, which keeps them from achieving their full, unique personhood. Discussions between Freirians in technologically underdeveloped nations and Rogerians in technologically developed nations often become heated on this point. People who work with the *favelados*—slum dwellers of Rio or Recife—ask how it is possible to equate the psychological pain of urban middle-class North Americans or Europeans with the desperate situation of the poor in technologically underdeveloped nations. I think any honest answer has to be that it is not.

Patient impatience: trusting the process

Not disregarding the contextual differences, I think it is legitimate to say that the two approaches are comparable in the assertion by both men that becoming critically conscious *begins* with becoming fully awake to the local predicament in which one is situated—one's own actuality. Both Freire and Rogers believe this is the only valid place to begin a process of conscientização. Freire describes the essential attitude of a teacher as one of patient impatience—patience with those struggling to grasp their predicament and construct their solutions and impatient for the misery and oppression to be transformed. Rogers' approach is also characterized by this attitude. He faces those struggling to become with utter patience and yet remains impatient with a society that continues to dehumanize.

This patient stance in the face of pain is sustainable only because both of them have radical faith in the desire and capacity of human beings to become aware of their predicament. They both trust absolutely that inherent in human beings is a fundamental thirst for emancipation and consciousness that will, if nurtured, eventually bring people into contact with the concrete conditions of their existence. Their faith is grounded in love and respect, and both believe that people will eventually come to recognize the way they are oppressed *and* the way in which they may oppress others, and in the light of that awareness they will seek to create the conditions for a more humane world for themselves and others.

It is because of the conviction that critical consciousness can and must be achieved (it cannot be given) that both Rogers and Freire insist that the means of emancipation be congruent with the ends. Both thinkers insist that manipulation of people even 'for their own good' is always dehumanizing.

Because critical consciousness is an activity, and because a person becomes ever more conscious by the exercise of critical consciousness, methodologies of facilitation must be consistent with this at all stages. It is a profound contradiction for a liberational educator, community worker, humanistic therapist, or workshop convener to use techniques that, even momentarily, rely on the domination or objectification of another. In a world increasingly populated with manipulators—be they evangelists, gurus, Madison Avenue advertisers, party organizers, 'aquarian conspirators', or psychotherapists—this is a very radical stance: that all techniques must be subordinated to the achievement of critical consciousness. Freire (1980) decries revolutionary leaders or educators who 'massify' the oppressed, practising manipulation and indoctrination behind some rationalization:

> Propaganda, slogans, myths are instruments employed by the invader to achieve his objectives... In that manipulation encourages "massification" it categorically contradicts the affirmation by human beings as Subjects. Such affirmation can only come when those engaged in a transforming action upon reality also make their own choices and decisions. In fact, manipulation and conquest, as expressions of cultural invasion, are never means for liberation. They are always means of "domestication".

True humanism, which serves human beings, cannot accept manipulation under any name whatsoever.

(p. 114)

A Freirian educator relates to an illiterate farmer as a colearner, a co-explorer of reality. They enter a true dialogical relationship in the Buberian sense: together they can explore and act upon their shared actuality. According to Freire, it is a meeting of teacher–student and student–teacher in order to solve some real problem (Freire, 1970). Freire, describing his work with illiterate peasants, calls this his *pascoa* or 'Easter', wherein he dies as he was before and is reborn closer in his common humanness to his partner in the discovery. The revolutionary educator and the oppressed peasant become transformed by their *mutual* grasp of their shared reality, thereby approaching one another. Freire's teachers do not bring a ready-made truth to oppressed peasants: they bring themselves and surrender to a true relationship with them, acting and reflecting as authentic people, to build a society together ever more closely reflecting the highest human aspirations.

This radical position has caused Freire's work to be rejected by impatient ideologues of both the political 'left' and 'right' who search for technologies to create their image of a better society, quickly and predictably. They argue that the situation is too urgent and that they care too much about the plight of the poor to wait until the poor get around to reinventing the wheel. Freire believes such arguments indicate these leaders wish to objectify the poor, enlisting them in the leaders' unilaterally determined aims. He believes such strategies stem from contempt or pity, not love. Transformational educators or leaders participate wholeheartedly even in reinventing the wheel, because they have faith that what liberates is the achievement of critical consciousness. Furthermore, they believe that because consciousness implies creativity, human beings never quite reinvent so much as create something unique (Freire, 1970).

Rogers, too, has devoted a great deal of attention to describing what he sees as the essential attitude of the 'person-centred therapist', that of unconditional respect for the other. All tendencies to manipulate, control, interpret, persuade, or prescribe run counter to Rogers' radical faith in what he considers to be an 'actualising tendency' responsible for healing and growth. He has always maintained that the therapist does not position himself as an expert, imposing will or values on the proceedings, but enters into a relationship that is real and present for both. Because he believes the actualizing telos is positive, the direction and outcome of therapeutic encounter can be allowed to emerge from the encounter itself. Empathic contact implies participation in a shared actuality. As these parties (therapist and client, teacher and student, convener and workshop participant) bring themselves to bear on the same reality, they become united and they, too, undergo a pascoa in which previously held 'truths' or 'selves' yield, giving way to transcendent possibilities.

The work of a Freire educator or a Rogerian facilitator is theoretically very simple—surrender to the unfolding actuality, reflect upon the transformation, then be ready to act again, guided by the knowledge gained in reflection. In fact, it is very difficult to maintain. Vanities, greed, power, impatience, fear, laziness, naivete, magical thinking, politics, status, and so on, all act to prevent the formation of true transforming relationships. It may be just this paradox, theoretical simplicity, and the difficulty of achieving it (for more than just moments), that causes person-centered approaches to be written off as 'simplistic', even among humanistic psychologists. It is especially difficult for North Americans, accustomed as we are to responding to suffering by moving into action, simply to accompany a person in pain without feeling compelled to step in and solve the problem. As Farson (1975) puts it:

> But today's practitioners are impatient. They are not satisfied with such a pedestrian approach. They argue that if it is beneficial for people to talk about their feelings then perhaps it is good to make sure that they do so. To accomplish this all sorts of gimmicks have been invented to elicit expression of feelings… Authoritarian gimmickry seems irresistibly satisfying, even to humanistic psychologists. Rogers himself sometimes seems to be caught up in this trend. Performance seems to be winning over safety, aggressiveness over acceptance, emotionality over dignity.
>
> (p. xlii)

For people who pride themselves on ingenuity, knowhow, and technological excellence, it seems somehow 'uncaring' not to use one of our tried-and-true techniques or utter some wise counsel, if we believe we know what would help. Both Freire and Rogers knew that when we do this and resort to 'facilitative' expertise, we rob the other of the rich possibility for learning that exists in the actual difficulties we inevitably encounter any time we attempt to meet another in authentic dialog. Even techniques that actually facilitate achievement of open, noncoercive dialog, for example, may end up robbing participants of the opportunity to recognize for themselves the causes of coercion, and the reasons for silence.

Person-centered approaches and Freire's liberational pedagogy are thus not then best understood as technologies of persuasion or manipulation, but rather as methodologies for systematic exploration of human reality, methods for searching for knowledge and for creative power. Through painstaking, dialogic examination of actuality, the consciousness of all the parties to the dialog expands. Both men believe that such a process is emancipatory. It leads people to a greater consciousness of the inner subjective experience, of the interpersonal process of dialog, and of the broader social and (for Freire, if not for Rogers) political and historical realities of existence.

Psychology versus psychologism

As I have already discussed, a major difference between the work of Rogers and Freire is the level of human reality each addresses. Rogers' emphasis is personal: it is on the individual human being. Freire's focus, by contrast, is on the workings of human collectives or societies.

Freire is quite sceptical about psychology. In personal conversation, he expresses the view that there is a great danger of falling into empty and impotent 'psychologism' as long as the concern of psychotherapy remains too narrowly focused on the individual abstracted from their social context. He also points to a danger in simply extrapolating knowledge gained in the special conditions of psychotherapy to society at large. He believes this leads to a tendency to assume all human problems are psychological and have psychological solutions. Freire puts it to 'Rogerians'—in this conversation I was the 'Rogerian'—'You emphasize that your psychotherapeutic approach is one of dialogue. But I ask, "Dialogue about what?"' Freire accepts (and personally greatly values) the process of psychotherapeutic dialog insofar as it serves to identify illusions and distortions of perception—false consciousness—that interfere with a person's true 'vocation', that is, emancipation. Freire believes, however, that even the most intimate landscape of inner reality must always be seen as being *about* the world. If not, he believes, psychotherapy is bound to be an alienating process.

The current state of North American humanism seems to confirm Freire's fears. In recent years, we have seen a rising tide of social criticism that claims exactly that. Tom Wolfe (1976) referred to the phenomenon with the never-to-be-forgotten label 'the me generation'. Lasch (1979) identified what he considered to be a 'cult of narcissism'. Yankelovich (1981) pointed to a 'self-fulfilment contradiction'. Marien (1983) described the same process as the 'sandbox syndrome', and in their research, Bellah et al. (1985) discovered in North America a culture wherein individuals long for a sense of community yet feel isolated and alienated. All of these critics point at least one finger of blame at the human potential movement of the 1960s and 1970s and in particular decry the alienating consequences of a psychology such as Rogers' that is based in a version of self that is abstracted from the world of relationships, economics, social groups, politics, history, and biology.

These writers and others have argued that this retroflexive self-absorption leads people to a tendency to see all human suffering as originating in the intrapsychic realm of the individual, which in turn leads to 'blaming the victim' for their own suffering. It is not hard to come by glaring examples. In a recent radio broadcast, for instance, a humanistic psychologist was discussing California's newly instituted 'Task Force on Self-Esteem'. In her attempt to explain to the listeners how self-esteem influences all manner of social problems from the high divorce rate to high minority unemployment and the feminization of poverty, she was trying to make the case that studies have shown that Black teenagers who are addicted to drugs, drop out of school, or get pregnant have low self-esteem. She was maintaining that the Black family structure fosters low self-esteem in Black children and that it was, therefore, necessary or at least desirable to teach Black parents how to raise their children in ways that foster high self-esteem. Her proposed solution was to offer self-esteem and positive parenting workshops for inner-city parents. It sounded good to listeners (including several Black callers) and not even the usually astute show host drew any attention on the fact that the analysis and the remediation placed all the difficulties in the psychological realm—nothing was mentioned about long-standing racism, the actual conditions of life for many of these Black families, and how these influence not just self-esteem but every aspect of life. All the responsibility for both the problems and their solution was placed on other victims—Black parents trying to raise children under often dreadful circumstances. This is the psychologism Freire warns against.

It has been my experience as a humanistic educator, particularly in person-centered approaches, that Rogers' writings are often interpreted as providing theoretical support for the notion that changes in individual consciousness will be sufficient to bring about a humanization of society. The 'person-centred philosophy' has been credited—or rather discredited—as theoretical justification for many of the symptoms of the sandbox syndrome. The aforementioned California Task Force on Self-Esteem draws heavily on the ideas of Rogers.

Encounters in community: resolving the contradiction

For those who worked closely with him during the later years of his life, it is obvious that Rogers had become somewhat of a contradiction. While he never modified his individualistic core theory about the nature of consciousness, he nonetheless increasingly focused his attention on broader social questions and pushed his work ever further into frankly political arenas. In his last years, he worked in over 20 countries, including South Africa, where he facilitated encounters between Blacks and Whites; Latin America, where North encountered South; Europe, where Eastern Bloc Marxists met Western humanists; Ireland, where Protestants met Catholics; in Rust, Austria, where he brought together diplomats, politicians, and peace activists from Nicaragua, the United States, and other Central American and European countries to consider the problem of Central America; and the Soviet Union, where participants met each other in new and more open ways. Experiences in these experimental communities permit us, in fact I believe require us, to reconsider Rogers' theory in the light of the practice. And when we do, I think it becomes possible to reconcile some of the contradictions in Rogers' own work, and between Rogers and Freire.

Person-centered approach workshops were originally developed as a way to test the hypothesis, which originated in Rogers' experience in individual therapy, that under certain conditions not only will individuals move toward self-actualization and growth but so will communities and groups. Rogers and others have written several descriptions of these programmes (Bowen et al., 1979; O'Hara & Wood, 1983; Rogers, 1977). Findings from these experimental situations suggest the need to reconsider the meaning of such concepts as *person*, *self*, and *society*, and the relationship among them. The work has forced us to reject as illusory any egocentric conception of *person* as an entity that is abstractable from its social context. We have come to see that only a 'holistic' vision of *person* can provide an adequate base for a humanistic psychology. *Person* must imply a being who is at once autonomous, responsible, whole, *and* who is a constituent part of, heir to, and creator of larger social entities such as relationships, families, groups, classes, societies, and so on. Human beings can only be fully understood when we acknowledge that any time someone expresses 'self' fully, both individuality and belonging are perforce expressed at the same time.

An example will make this clearer. When I express myself authentically without reservations, my whole truth as I *experience* it, *understand* it, and *articulate* it, I also express my gender, nationality, class, ideology, cosmology, and what all these mean about my place in the world. The words I use, the meanings I make, the form and content of my expression are both uniquely mine and part of an intersubjective world to which I belong. Whether I am aware of it or not, these transindividual aspects of my identity can be recognized by others and will affect them.

That Rogers himself seems to have had some intimation of this without ever having articulated it fully is shown, perhaps, by his famous assertion that the 'most personal is the most universal'. Wood (1980) also has said, paradoxically, that when individuality is most exaggerated by members of a collective, unity is experienced in the group. Acts of martyrdom, heroism, and artistic or athletic mastery are the acts of single individuals, yet they are experienced by all as belonging to the collective in an essential and universal way. Throughout history, moments of supreme altruism have also been moments of intense self-expression.

In person-centered workshops, we have seen that in very special circumstances, it is possible for the conflicts between the individual and the group and between conflicting groups to become resolved in ways that take nothing (although much may be given) from either the individual or the group. It seems possible, for example, for a group and the individuals who are part of it to establish a relationship in which a high-order harmony is achieved. This is not a static harmony in which no discord is heard but is more like a conversation or a jazz group's improvisation, created by the contributions of individuals. Under these special circumstances, the group consciousness becomes isomorphic with the consciousness of the individuals (O'Hara & Wood, 1983).

A truly dialogical I–Thou relationship can occur not only between individuals in a group but between the individuals *and* the group, and between groups. There are moments when something can be created that is greater than the customary struggle between opposing elements or the separate voices of individual participants. This kind of group process can be wiser than even the wisest person. In these moments, it does not matter whether one speaks of someone's individual reality or of the group's reality, because at these moments they are identical. In other words, when the members of a group can understand how a particular 'voice' bears upon the collective predicament, the group as a whole takes a step toward knowledge and expansion of critical consciousness. The following example is from a multinational workshop in Europe:

> John, a Black North American, although wishing to participate in a group task was having difficulty accepting the views of a coparticipant, a White South African. John eventually exploded into spontaneous and whole-hearted (verbal) expression of his rage and anguish at apartheid. It was a moment of total self-assertion, experienced, however, by everyone present as a moment of integration.

> For the first time John experienced himself and was experienced by others as *part* of the group. Everyone participated in the act, passive but integrated as a group. When Nigel, the South African, responded in an equally autonomous and self-assertive manner, expressing the depths of his individual frustration at being a lawyer who had defended Blacks challenging pass laws (thereby incurring the suspicion of Blacks and Whites alike), a sudden shift occurred. Separateness melted as mutual comprehension took the place of antagonism. Both John and Nigel had found an ally where they had seen an enemy. They experienced a oneness of purpose, not through trying to understand or integrate themselves, but through vigorous assertion of their separateness (within the context of a mutual commitment to the same group task).
>
> (O'Hara, 1984a, p. 218)

The individual 'truths' about apartheid were expressed without inhibition, censorship, reservation, or judgment. Everyone present became more conscious of apartheid at every level of existence, from the uniquely personal to the broadly political. From that moment onward, each individual person and the group as a collective entity that is more than the sum of its parts had a greater grasp of the issues, a subtler feel for their consequences, and a greater ability to live and function in a world where such situations exist. Both the individuals and the collective had undergone a *pascoa*.

The context of Carl Rogers' working life differs markedly from that of Paulo Freire's. Rogers' work deals with middle-class members of a dominant culture, people very much like himself. Freire's work deals mostly with dominated people, illiterate peasants of technologically underdeveloped nations. These differences cannot be overlooked, especially when comparing the work of the two men on the level of ideology, techniques, or methodologies—approaches that may be emancipatory in one context may be oppressive in another. It is not, in my view, Freire's Marxist/Christian view or his passionate commitment to the struggles of peasants in technologically underdeveloped nations that makes it transformational—there are plenty of examples of people who share his ideology and speak equally passionately on behalf of the oppressed yet continue the tactics of domination. Freire's work is transformational because of its commitment to truth and the achievement of critical consciousness. Rogers' person-centered approach is also, at base, a process by which persons and groups can search for truth. It is not the 'necessary and sufficient conditions', nor 'nondirectiveness', nor the expression of emotions that makes person-centered approaches effective—it is knowledge or critical consciousness of oneself (in its individual and trans-individual aspects) and of one's place in the world, which heals.

People engaged in a search for knowledge, through dialog with each other and with their world, express their full human heritage. Although different contexts (Brazilian favela, North American counselling session, international community encounter, and so on) reveal different understandings of global reality, this essentially human activity is revolutionary, therapeutic, and transformational.

In searching for its own truth by listening to its members, a collective may heal itself, may learn, may evolve, and may achieve its own voice with respect to other groups. If we do not merely focus on the individual psychological gains made by John and Nigel but instead take note of the expansion of consciousness about the concrete conditions of each's life and of the lives of everyone else, we may be justified in speaking of this as a step in a process of conscientização.

What both Freire and Rogers offer us, separately and together, is the faith that truth both heals and emancipates, the uncompromisable position that we are all capable of becoming conscious, the conviction that we achieve that only through dialog with each other, and the hope that through such dialog, whenever, wherever, and however we have the opportunity, we can create a world where every one of us may live in dignity and may exercise our natural vocation to become ever more fully human. As humanistic psychology from technologically developed nations reaches out to bring its knowledge to the wider sphere of social and international relations, person-centered approaches, grounded in the work of Carl Rogers and sharpened by the thinking of Paulo Freire, have exciting possibilities. They offer a methodology and a theoretical paradigm that can embrace both the private unique world of the individual and the public intersubjective world of groups and societies. It is undoubtedly presumptuous to suggest, but Freire's process of conscientização, personalized by the psychological insights of Carl Rogers, may offer humanists in technologically underdeveloped nations a way to facilitate emancipation without either sacrificing the unique aspirations of the individual or falling into psychologism.

Notes

1 There is no exact English translation of 'conscientização' but the word means a process of becoming conscious or aware of inner and outer factors that affect our consciousness.

2 When this was published, Maureen was a long-time fellow of the Center for Studies of the Person, La Jolla, California; a teacher at San Diego State University, training gestalt therapists worldwide; in private practice in Encinitas, California; and serving as an associate editor for the *Journal of Humanistic Psychology* and also as a member-at-large of the Association of Humanistic Psychology's Executive Board.

Chapter 4

Carl Rogers: Scientist and mystic (1995)[1]

Maureen O'Hara[2]

Summary

Carl Ransom Rogers, one of the giants of 20th-century psychology, has been recognized for his immense contribution to the science of psychology. At the same time, millions have found his person-centered philosophy to be a deeply satisfying moral system and have been willing to place their faith in what can be seen as Rogers' metaphysics. This chapter examines Rogers' shift from positivist scientist to radical subjectivist and his continued ambivalence about both religion and objectivist science. It seeks to reconcile the seeming paradox in his work by suggesting that Rogers' work stands at the boundary between 19th-century positivism and 20th-century postpositive constructivism.

I always liked myself far better as a pure scientist.

(Carl Rogers)

The fine line between scientist and mystic

Carl Rogers said that of all the accolades and awards he had received in his career, it was the American Psychological Association's award for his distinguished scientific contributions that pleased him the most. He always felt most completely himself as a scientist and actually liked himself better as a pure scientist (O'Hara, 1995d).

Like most great scientists, researchers, or students of nature, Carl was already practicing his calling as a young boy. Whether it was night-flying moths or the arcane mysteries of the nutritional requirements of farm animals, by ten years old, Carl was already a serious student of mysteries of the universe. Throughout his life, Carl burned with that special luminosity of persons enthralled with the world, sure of their path, and unshakable in their vocation. He was first, last, and always a seeker, a questioner, a learner. Like most people who are consumed by a scientific passion, Rogers could also have been seen as a mystic—albeit an anti-religious one. It is not usually openly acknowledged by scientists, but at the heart of the scientific vocation is a basic metaphysical

DOI: 10.4324/9781003519454-6

belief that must be taken on faith if science is to continue: the fundamental faith that the universe is not random, capricious, or arbitrary but is in fact lawful, orderly, and understandable. As Polanyi (1958) said, scientists could not even begin their studies without some basic frame of belief in a harmonious and lawful universe within which new discoveries are understood. Like the mystic, the scientist is fired by a desire to come ever closer to a direct experience of this lawfulness or harmony.

Although for a few decades of the last century and the beginning of this one (during Carl's boyhood, not coincidentally), scientists have begun flirting with the idea of a meaningless universe, and for most of history, science, and mysticism have been intimately and synergistically involved with one another. Some of the greatest scientists who have ever lived readily acknowledged the sacred and mystical longings at the core of their work in science. Einstein was quite explicit:

> Still there are moments when one feels free from one's own identification with human limitations and inadequacies. At such moments, one imagines that one stands on some small spot of a small planet, gazing in amazement at the cold yet profoundly moving beauty of the eternal, the unfathomable: life and death flow into one, and there is neither evolution nor destiny; only being.
>
> (as cited in Nathan & Norden, 1960, p. 282)

Or, as Galileo is said to have responded to his inquisitors, 'If religion and science are properly understood there can be no conflict between them'.

Carl Rogers himself had once considered entering Christian ministry as his life's work. What is less well known is that he originally entered college to study natural science. His first choice of path was agriculture, stimulated by his boyhood experiences of farm life and his fascination with the natural world. It was only after a deeply moving experience in a student Christian group that he changed his focus to prepare to enter graduate seminary.

He quickly came to feel that this was a wrong choice for him. He has told us in *On Becoming a Person* (1961) how he came to feel that the search for truth through the study of religion was too confined by orthodoxy to permit a free search. So much the pure scientist, Carl was unwilling to bind himself to any pre-established beliefs and instead opted for a more open-ended search. He believed such a search might lead him into ever closer and deeper contact with the intrinsic order of things and—like the mystics—he acknowledged no greater authority than his own experience. If the universe were to speak to him, Carl wanted to hear it first hand and not in translation. He said of the experience:

> Experience is, for me, the highest authority. The touchstone of validity is my own experience. No other person's ideas, and none of my own ideas, are as authoritative as my experience. It is to experience that I must return again and again, to discover a closer approximation to truth as it is in the process of becoming in me.

> Neither the Bible nor the prophets—neither Freud nor research—neither the revelations of God nor man—can take precedence over my own direct experience…
>
> My experience is not authoritative because it is infallible. It is the basis of authority because it can always be checked in new primary ways. In this way its frequent error or fallibility is always open to correction.
>
> (Rogers, 1961/1967b, pp. 23–24)

These paragraphs provide us, I think, with a clue to why Carl, unlike Martin Buber or Thomas Merton, followed the path of scientific research, rather than a contemplative one, to truth. This last paragraph is a *scientist's* creed, forming the twin wings of the scientific endeavor in whatever discipline. It is clear that Carl was able to have faith in the authority of his experience and acknowledge human fallibility and proneness to error at one and the same time.

Carl's secure faith in the authority of his own understanding gives his work the power—the ring of truth—that so impresses his readers, students, and colleagues. This kind of authoritativeness takes Carl's ideas straight into the hearts of his audience, who recognize a quality of universality in the truth they are hearing. Such clarity can be very compelling. It can cause people to become ready converts to the new truth, taking on the glazed-eyed look of the true believer. Carl might easily have become some reluctant pope in a 'person-centred religion' if it were not for the other aspect of the scientist's creed. No sooner had he seen truth in a particular way then he began seriously to look for ways to check his truth against primary experience. Sometimes, particularly during his years in university settings, he and his colleagues invented elegant quantitative methods to test his ideas, but later he was content with qualitative methods (Gordon et al., 1954). His recognition and appreciation of human fallibility enabled him to hold truth lightly, put it to the test, and when it was time, let it go and move on, more often than not leaving at least some of his converts behind to go on practicing old orthodoxies.

I think that to understand what happened to Rogers' scientific career, one must keep in mind both the mystical nature of Carl's commitment to truth and the scientific nature of his chosen way of searching for it.

Positivism and psychological science

When Carl began his science, the dominant scholarly view—what Kuhn would call a paradigm—was positivist science. The physical sciences reigned supreme, and the scientists par excellence were the mathematicians. The closer a discipline was to mathematics, in terms of axioms and methodologies, the more valid or 'objective' it was thought to be. The hierarchy was topped by mathematics, followed by physics, chemistry, and biology in that order. Psychology was considered (and to a great extent still is) suspect unless it was sufficiently biological or physiological as to pass for natural science. Equating quantification, objectivity, and abstraction with 'hardness', and complexity, subjectivity, and ambiguity with 'softness', late 19th-century and early 20th-century psychologists proved their intellectual 'manhood' by producing hard data that were precise and quantifiable, and from which abstract and unambiguous laws could be deduced and predictions could putatively be made. Turn-of-the-century psychological scientists were interested in large samples, measurements, predictability, and control. This was especially true in America. Seen against this paradigm, Freud's methodology of detailed interpretive case histories of a very small number of cases upon which elaborate theoretical formulations were made, seemed unacceptably 'subjective', 'unscientific', and far too prone to 'observer' error.

It is no wonder, then, that when Rogers entered the field of psychological research, he would look for methodologies that were as 'hard' as possible. Rogers recognized that his subject matter—psychotherapy, the counselling relationship, and personality—was very complex and full of ambiguity. He nonetheless aspired to a highly precise, positivistic science that would be immune from the criticisms that it was 'unscientific'—criticisms that the more biological psychologists hurled at psychoanalysis.

Rogers believed that it was possible to design scientific investigations that would generate data upon which generalizations could be made, hypotheses generated and tested, and laws of nature discovered. In some of his early writings, it is almost possible to hear Carl's internal conversations with his potential critics. 'I'll show you', he seems to be saying, 'we are as much real scientists as the rat runners'.

The one orthodoxy Carl did embrace in those early days was that 'real' science was exact science, and that objectivity was possible and necessary and that even the most subtle of activities can be approached through the scientific experimental method. In his first book on the results of his research, Rogers (1954) writes:

> It is hard to imagine a field in which research is more difficult. It is also recognized that the essential elements of therapy are almost certainly subtle, are frequently intuitive, and often lie below the surface of the obvious situation. Yet this group is convinced that Thorndike's dictum is essentially correct—that "anything that exists, exists in some quantity that can be measured". It also has the belief, as it reviews the history of science, that important advances in science frequently follow when common observations are rigorously measured, under carefully controlled conditions, and when commonly held theories are put to objective test.
>
> (pp. 13–14)

Following these principles, Carl, his colleagues, and graduate students embarked on what remains today one of the most productive and successful programs of scientific research in psychotherapy ever conducted. His book *Psychotherapy and Personality Change* (1954) describes a program lasting almost a decade, conducted by over 30 scientists, postdoctoral students, and graduate students at the University of Chicago Counseling Center.

When the studies began, Carl had been a practicing clinician for a dozen or more years. Out of that clinical experience, he had generated some ideas, techniques, attitudes, and hypotheses regarding the elements of therapy that made it effective. It was these ideas he set out to put to the test, using research instruments that, although familiar now, were just then being developed. He made extensive use of Q sort to measure subtle changes in self-concept and used the Thematic Apperception Test and numerous personality and adjustment scales. Carl's team was also the first to use the new technology of sound recording to record actual therapy sessions.

What a phenomenal success this research turned out to be. *Psychotherapy and Personality Change* (1954) reported results on the evaluation of counselling, self-reference in counselling, the relationship between attitudes about self and attitudes toward others, language use and therapy, the interaction of client and counsellor, counsellor behavior and therapy outcomes, and several other studies on therapy outcome. In fact, much of what now we all take for granted regarding the process of psychotherapy and the nature of personality change was before this either unknown or known at the level of untested 'rules of thumb'. This is not the occasion to catalogue all of Carl's contributions to psychotherapeutic theory and practice, but perhaps it is worth mentioning a few. Carl's and his colleagues' research demonstrates, for example, that clients move toward health and integration; however, this is measured, when the relationship between client and clinician has certain characteristics:

- It is nonauthoritarian.
- The therapist is both authentic and warm.
- The therapist listens well.
- The client experiences basic acceptance by the therapist.
- The client is acknowledged as being essentially competent.

In 1950, when Fiedler (1950) compared expert therapists from different schools with novices from the same schools, he found the master therapists all resembled one another, whereas the novices were very different. And, although this was not acknowledged by Fiedler, the experts had all become 'Rogerians', that is to say, they were warm, transparent, empathic, accepting, and they saw the client as essentially competent. A study in 1989 came to similar conclusions and again revealed the essentially Rogerian feel to successful therapies—even psychodynamic ones. Luborsky (1989) reported that the two factors found to be important in the outcome of psychodynamic psychotherapy having to do with the psychotherapist and the therapeutic relationship are accurate empathy and the development of a positive therapeutic alliance. Wallerstein's (1989) extensive review of studies of psychotherapy also noted that the qualities associated with supportive therapies—warmth, empathy, acceptance—have infiltrated all successful therapies regardless of theoretical school. Lambert (1992) confirmed the findings.

I think it is fair to state that Carl's desire to discover some fundamental rules regarding the process of psychotherapy was fulfilled. I doubt that the future will do any more than modify or reframe these, as is the fate of even the greatest discoveries.

It is very important, especially given the current popularity of 'new paradigms', anti-positivist thinking in psychology, and ideas blurring the boundaries between science and mysticism, that we remember Rogers conducted his early research, posed his questions, and made his most important discoveries following—one might say religiously—the methods of *positivist science*. His intuitive, hands-on, personal experience in counselling, and so on undoubtedly were the sources of his glimpses of the universal, but his ability (and ours) to know that these glimpses were not mistaken or distorted but came through the vigorous discipline of painstaking and creative scientific research.

It is also important to know that from the beginning, Carl the therapist recognized that research in areas of human realities placed very special demands on the researcher. He encountered a contradiction that has plagued all human science: 'How can one be objective about people, without treating them like objects?' Or, as he puts it in an essay entitled *Persons or Science?*

> As I have acquired experience as a therapist, carrying on the exciting, rewarding experience of psychotherapy, and as I have worked as a scientific investigator to ferret out some of the truth about therapy, I have become increasingly conscious of the gap between these two roles. The better therapist I have become (as I believe I have) the more I have been vaguely aware of my complete subjectivity when I am at my best in this function. And as I have become a better investigator, more "hard-headed" and more scientific (as I believe I have) I have felt an increasing discomfort at the distance between the rigorous objectivity of myself as scientist and the almost mystical subjectivity of myself as therapist.
>
> (Rogers, 1961/1967b, p. 200)

Moreover, Carl was unable to set the problem aside precisely because he was so completely the mystic and scientist. Here was another puzzle, and he wanted to know what was at the bottom of it.

The unwitting postmodernist pioneer

By the 1950s, Rogers' experience of the contradictory nature of his 'double life' and his insatiable curiosity had forced him to grapple with some of the most puzzling philosophical questions of this century and plunged him into postmodern epistemological dilemmas within the social sciences that rage still.

- Is knowledge of the human world equivalent to knowledge of the natural world?
- In these post-Heisenberg times, is the idea of value-free objectivity realistic in even the physical sciences, let alone the human sciences?
- What is the relationship of the knower to the known?
- What is the relationship between an insider's knowledge and an outsider's?

- What is the purpose of human inquiry—understanding or prediction and control?
- Do the established scientific ways of asking questions determine the kinds of answers that may be generated?
- How can we do holistic contextual research and still make sense of our 'data'?

In the early 1950s when he was first encountering the puzzles, there were few philosophers of science out there ahead of him, at least not easily accessible in English. Michael Polanyi's book, *Personal Knowledge*, was not published until 1958, and Peter Berger and Thomas Luckmann did not write *The Social Construction of Reality* until 1969. Stephen Toulmen was probably still in graduate school. It seems to have been very difficult for psychologist Rogers to successfully move beyond positivist approaches to his science. Perhaps this was because Carl hung on so tightly to Thorndike's dictum, and to another great dictum of positivist science, that of Sir Karl Popper, that what separates scientific propositions from those from other discourses—such as religion, law, or the humanities—is that one can conceivably disprove scientific ones. It is to this that I wish to turn now.

In two camps: the training of a positivist, the experience of a postmodernist

By the early 1960s, it was clear even to lay people that a schism was opening up in the field of psychology. It was between the empiricists—the testers, experimenters, and measurers, that is, the 'hard' psychologists—and the new science of the mind that was developing out of the work of the European phenomenologists, the philosophy of Gilbert Ryle and Ludwig Wittgenstein, and the work of semanticists, semioticists, and others. The distinction between subjectivity and objectivity was fading and the question was reframed. During the 1960s and early 1970s, it was possible to read research reports produced in departments of psychology that ran the gamut from atomistic reductionism at one pole to pure solipsism at the other. Boundaries were blurring as we passed into the wildly experimental and conscientiously undisciplined times that are increasingly referred to as 'postmodern'.

Carl's dilemma, it seems to me, was that by history, competence, and training, he was on the side of the empiricists (he was proudest of his scientific award), but by temperament, by virtue of his calling as a therapist healer and a teacher, he was more drawn to the newly emerging approaches that suggested that much of positivist science in psychology was in fact 'scientism' and was based on an unrealizable ideal of objectivity. These new approaches attempted to examine issues such as consciousness, experiencing, meaning, and understanding and to redefine what we mean by reality.

Carl's years as a therapist had confirmed his long-standing—almost sacred—belief in the primacy of experience. He came to believe that personal experience was the ultimate standard of truth. He said many times that the most personal was the most universal. He embraced the 'third force' search for a new kind of science of persons, one that would not try to objectify, classify, or otherwise dehumanize its subjects but rather celebrate them, listen to them, and let them tell their own truths. The focus of humanistic science shifted from that of the outsider's view gained by objectivist experimental observation to an insider's view of persons as whole subjects investigated by researchers who were themselves whole subjects.

Carl was among the greatest of all adepts at gaining access to an insider's view. Not only was his own 'insider' view of his own reality—developed over a lifetime of practice—perceptive, subtle, and wise, but with others, either one-on-one or in the midst of groups of over a thousand, he could tune in and establish an empathic link, enabling him to sense the others' inner world with startling accuracy.

By the mid-1960s, we see no more positivist research from Carl. In *Carl Rogers on Encounter Groups* (1970), *Becoming Partners* (1972), *Carl Rogers on Personal Power* (1977), and *A Way of Being* (1980), what we see are exquisite, detailed, and inspired narratives of what he or his informants experienced, out of which Carl constructed theories about human nature and human cultures.

I think that we must recognize that at this point the nature of Carl's work changed quite fundamentally. We also have to think about his ideas in a different way. He had crossed over an invisible, but important, line between one kind of human inquiry and another. While the insider's view had always been his acknowledged starting point in his attempts to understand complex human events, previously he had followed this by subjecting any hypotheses generated to elaborate and vigorous tests for validity and error. From the 1960s onward, we see his writing based much more on his faith in certain principles, detailed personal accounts, and acquired knowledge of 'how to' do person-centered work. We see much more philosophical speculation and more promotion of the 'person-centred' point of view.

I do not mean to suggest by this that his later work is necessarily less valuable to us than his previous work. But I do mean that we need to look at it differently. It is a different kind of knowledge. It is personal. The personal knowledge of someone with Carl's experience and knowledge is very likely to have more truth to it than that of a newcomer to human studies. However, despite his authority, much of it gained as a consequence of his commitment to disciplined research, he can (as he himself insisted) be fallible. What he needed but had arrived at his understanding of the relationship between science and subjectivity too soon for, was a methodology that could elucidate and critically evaluate the link between his own inner reality and the external reality to which he was attending. Without a science such as that now being elaborated by researchers Karl Pribram, Larry Vandervert, and others on the cutting edge of brain–mind–consciousness studies, Rogers was left with raw subjectivity.

The specter of pseudoscience

In later years, I became increasingly distressed by the unwillingness of Carl and many who followed him to acknowledge this change. Most remained satisfied with his eloquent first-person accounts of his subjective experience. It is no secret—I have written about it extensively in the *Journal of Humanistic Psychology* and elsewhere—that I also became uncomfortable with the rising evangelism in not only Carl's work but much of what has become known as 'new-age science', as well as with a concomitant reluctance to put ideas to the test and vigorously search out errors, self-deception, and illusion (O'Hara, 1985a, 1985b, p. 1988, 1989a, 1995d). I believed, and I frequently told Carl so, that without critical evaluation of some kind, pure insider's knowledge, however deep, was bound to be an intellectual dead end. If we have no way to find the errors, to receive critical new input from others, or to set one's own personal knowledge up against others', we eventually bog down in superstition.

There are other serious objections to the insider view being considered sufficient on its own. What, for example, are we to do with different insider views. How are such differences to be resolved? Do we simply agree to disagree, do we fight it out in theoretical 'holy wars'? Or can there be agreed upon methods for using the differences between two perspectives to tease out new truths hidden to both?

There are also ethical questions to be addressed. When we consider actions and interventions based on this kind of unchallenged personal knowledge, what responsibility do we have to those involved? In a free society, we are each entitled to live our own life, basing it on whatever ideas about reality we want, but if we are to make or propose interventions in the lives of others, are we not ethically constrained to tell them on what basis we make our suggestions?

Over the last decade or so of his life, Carl and his colleagues, including many of us here today, generated from our personal experience, hypotheses, ideas, strategies, and techniques of working with groups, relationships, and individuals that I believe have great potential usefulness. Of particular interest to me is the person-centered approach work, some of which I participated in, aimed at larger social issues—including the projects in Russia, Northern Ireland, South Africa, and with the Sandinistas and Contras of Nicaragua and with North Americans in Rust, Austria (Rogers, 1986b). Over 20 years ago, many humanistic psychologists concluded that positivist science was no longer an acceptable paradigm with which to evaluate our hypotheses and techniques, but because no other reliable paradigm had yet been elaborated, Rogers (and many within humanistic psychology who followed him) settled for subjectivism and even pseudoscience.

What Carl needed were the narrative and other qualitative methodologies that have been developed recently in psychology, anthropology, and sociology. In particular, he needed methods based in the new postpositive, social constructivist epistemologies that would have provided him with a way to use both the insider's subjective views together with examination of aspects of a situation, like contexts, self-deception, misunderstanding, and bias, that may be visible only to an outsider (Douglass & Moustakas, 1985; Manicas & Secord, 1983; Mearns & McLead, 1984; Polkinghorne, 1983). Before he died, Carl himself had come to the same conclusion, but caught up as he was in spreading the news of person-centered approaches as far and as widely as he could, he looked to others to apply these methods to his work (Rogers, 1985).

Reclaiming the science agenda

The time is ripe for humanistic psychology to once more pick up the scientific trail and begin to submit some of Carl Rogers' later ideas to critical evaluation—especially those on large groups, the creation of creative and healthy communities, and working with politically, ethnically, and religiously diverse groups to achieve mutual understanding (Bowen et al., 1979; O'Hara, 1989a; Rogers, 1986b). In the course of such evaluation, we may find some areas of error, some aspects of person-centered theory that were more about Carl than about the situations he described or that were true only for one particular group or situation and not part of a generalizable larger truth about the human condition. However, because of my enormous respect for him as a scientist with 80 or more years of experience as an observer of complex realities, I have the feeling that if such research were to be conducted, we would find that many of Carl's personal knowings and hunches were pretty close to the mark.

Notes

1 A presentation given at UCLA Extension in memorial honor of Carl Rogers, November 7, 1987, and later published in the Fall 1995 issue of the *Journal of Humanistic Psychology*, *35*(4), 40–53.

2 At the time this was published, Maureen was the former president of the Association for Humanistic Psychology and had written extensively on issues in psychological theory and practice, postmodernism, feminism, pseudoscience, and philosophy of science. She was both a student and colleague of Carl Rogers and traveled internationally with him and a group of colleagues facilitating person-centered approach workshops and residential learning communities.

Chapter 5

Reflections on Maureen O'Hara's writings on the person-centred approach

Maureen O'Hara and Keith Tudor

Keith: I really enjoyed re-reading these papers on the person-centred approach *as an approach* as I think they each and both together deepen an appreciation of the philosophy that underpins the approach as an application of person-centred psychology to a range of human activities and endeavours. As you know, this was reflected in the term and the title of Rogers' last book, *A Way of Being* (Rogers, 1980/1995b), following which the phrase 'the person-centred approach' became more widely used. John K. Wood (1996), a close associate of Rogers, and with whom I know you worked, elaborated this when he argued that the person-centred approach:

> is not a school... itself, it is not a movement... it is not a philosophy. Nor is it any number of other things frequently imagined. It is merely, as its name implies, an approach, nothing more, nothing less. It is a psychological posture, if you like, from which thought or action may arise and experience be organized. It is a "way of being". (pp. 168–169)

Before we get into some of the substance of these two papers—and they are, indeed, substantial—I would love to hear your thinking about the significance of this last iteration (at least in Rogers' lifetime) from what was originally a 'newer psychotherapy' (Rogers, 1942) in the clinic to its wider application to and in life.

Maureen: This is an interesting (and deeply layered) issue. The genesis of the shift from client-centred therapy (CCT) to a person-centred approach (PCA) was a design meeting in preparation for the 1975 workshop to be held at Mills College in Oakland, California that Carl and Natalie Rogers, John K. Wood, Jared Kass, Maria Bowen, Joanne Justin, and myself were offering. Based on our experience of previous events, we felt the term Client-Centred Therapy and its Social Implications no longer described what actually happened. Given the reality that the staff sought to minimise power hierarchy, were present as co-creators of the process but

DOI: 10.4324/9781003519454-7

not directors of it, and like everyone else lived their reality as subjects, to consider participants as 'clients' and the process 'therapy' vastly underestimated the transformative potential of these gatherings. I believe, like John Wood, that the change to the terms 'person' and 'approach' rather than 'client' and 'therapy' marks a deep conceptual and practice shift—the importance of which is only now becoming clear. Of course, there are countless situations in which a person who is seeking help—a client—consults a person who offers expertise to help—therapy. However, at least in Rogers' later life, and for many radical person-centred practitioners, a distinction is made between creating a relational context in which an inherent impulse towards growth and self-organisation can be trusted (letting it be) and one in which a specific predetermined end goal is desired, a process designed to make it happen, and so-called 'objective' outcomes measured. When you trust the universe as Rogers' and other process philosophers do, you can act as midwife to the emergent creative flow of becoming.

In these days of hyper-manipulation by dead algorithms of individuals and whole societies, we may be losing the race for machines over persons and even life itself. A person-centred approach as a way of being may be an antidote to what to me is an existential struggle. Unless the centrality of living beings is reasserted by all of us, artificial intelligence (AI) may take game and match.

Keith: I agree about this being an interesting and layered issue. Your comment about AI (which I'd like to pick up in our reflections on psychology futures in Chapter 21) makes me think that the concept of person is not only interesting but also perhaps somewhat urgent to clarify and communicate.

Personally, I've always loved Rogers' emphasis on the person (and thus his use of the plural 'persons' rather than people), and I particularly love *On Becoming a Person* (Rogers, 1961/1967b), which I have always found both accessible and profound.[1] However, I have also been curious that, given the centrality of the concept to his thinking and approach, he didn't define it, a curiosity I share with Peter Schmid, who reports asking Rogers about his definitions of the terms 'organism', 'self', and 'person', a question to which Rogers replied:

> I use the term organism for the biological entity. The actualising tendency exists in the biological human organism. I use the term self when I am referring to the concept a person has of himself, the way he views himself, his perceptions of his qualities and so on… I use the term person in a more general sense to indicate each individual.
>
> (Schmid, 1998, p. 47)

Commenting on this, Schmid suggests that this makes 'person' a concept that is superordinate to those of the self and even that of the organism. However, in our work on the subject, I and Mike Worrall countered this by arguing that Rogers' use of the word person as synonymous with individual 'move[s] away from an interconnected, organismic perspective on the person as a whole individual and as an individual-in-relation, in a whole, holistic context' (Tudor & Worrall, 2006, p. 136). What do you think?

Maureen: I agree with Schmid. As you say, Rogers does use the word 'individual' sometimes synonymously with person. You are pointing out a real contradiction in his way of talking about persons and this probably does reflect on a linguistic level his embeddedness in an individualistic profession before the relational turn in thinking that was to blossom in the 1990s after his death. But, as Schmid and I observed, over his entire career Rogers saw groups as the generative context for becoming whole. Pointing to 'the definition of the "fully functioning person", not simply as an individualistic self, but as a self within society… and, by extension the political dimension of the person-centred approach… originating largely in experiences from small and large groups' (Schmid & O'Hara, 2013, p. 96). Rogers sees persons and their personhood as inseparable from their existing in the world as a conscious agent who participates in the creation of worlds. Rogers et al. (Bowen et al., 1979) describe the PCA group as creating a climate which 'responds to the human tendency to "reach out". The separate person "reaches" to become all they can become. As a consequence, an emotional energy is generated in the group and the "separateness" of consciousness is raised to a "oneness" of consciousness' (p. 116).

Keith: That's great, Maureen, not least as it gets us to the second aspect of this part of the book, which is the aspect of *approach*. As you know (but not all readers will necessarily know), Rogers' own thinking and emphasis changed—from relationship therapy (Rogers, 1939), through non-directive therapy (Rogers, 1942), client-centred therapy (1951), and person-centred therapy (Rogers, 1961/1967b), to the person-centred approach (Rogers, 1980/1995b).[2] You were around Rogers and other colleagues at the time of this last iteration, and the two papers that form the preceding chapters represent this. Before we discuss those papers in more depth, what, for you, was—and still is—the significance of the application of person-centred psychology beyond the clinic?

Maureen: My background as a child of deprived circumstances into a society where women were regarded as 'less than'—morally, intellectually, and politically—whose primary worth was in terms of our usefulness to a patriarchal order understandably pointed me in the direction to psychological applications that might offer a practice with which to address looming social challenges. I was drawn to the work of humanistic psychologists because they understood that a change in the collective consciousness was needed. I have observed that Rogers' interest in psychotherapy in particular,

> took place against a deeper and ultimately more ambitious mission, that of social reformer and cultural leader. Rogers' aim was to transform the world. Many, including Rogers himself, have referred to him as a "quiet revolutionary" (Rogers & Russell, 2002) but I think a more accurate designation is that Rogers was a 20th century prophet. Prophets are *cultural* leaders. They emerge at times of social turmoil and their genius is to makes sense of what is happening, and articulate the collective aspirations for a better future, to sense the emergent tide of history and offer vision and practices to shift the entire culture in the direction of the desired change.
>
> (O'Hara, 2024, pp. 463–464)

In the turbulence of the mid-20th century, recovering from a second world war, under the shadow of nuclear weapons, uprisings by oppressed and colonised peoples demanding that their rights be respected, and a dawning awareness of impending ecological catastrophe, socially engaged humanistic thinkers such as Rogers offered me a way to be a new kind of agent for change. His work is a rare example of a depth psychology which honours the inner experience of each person at the same time as it seeks new ways of being on a social scale.

Keith: I'm really appreciating both your passion and the sense of politics in your espousal of the person-centred *approach*. While some emphasise this iteration as a way of being and, as John K. Wood (1996) put it, 'a psychological posture' (p. 169), what you're clarifying is that for you (and others) it's more a way of being and acting in and on the world—which brings us, appropriately enough, to the two papers in this part of the book.

In the first, in comparing the work of Rogers and Freire, you also examine both the underlying methodologies of their respective work and techniques, and, as you put it, 'the ideals to which their approaches are directed' (p. 27). In this sense, the paper is both analytic and aspirational, which, it seems to me, mirrors not only your own perspective and journey, from natural to behavioural science, but also that of the person-centred approach—from the clinical treatment of the problem child (Rogers, 1939) to a psychology that, as you put it, 'celebrate[s] human existence and our evolutionary potential' (p. 24). Would you agree?

Maureen: This paper is based on a presentation to the first Forum for the Person-Centred Approach convened by Alberto Segrera in 1982 in Oaxtepec, Mexico. Alberto was eager to raise awareness to the substantial (and substantive) work going on beyond the United States. He particularly wanted to showcase the different concerns and diverse voices of the PCA in non-Eurocentric cultures such as Latin America and other non-English speaking societies. At that time, I was working in Brazil facilitating PCA workshops with Americans John K. Wood and Carl Rogers and Brazilians Rachel Rosenberg, Maria Bowen, Eduardo Bandeira, and a cohort of Brazilian professionals committed to the abordagem centrada na pessoa (ACP) (the person-centred approach). From 1976 to 1984, at the invitation of humanistic psychologists interested in a more integrative humanistic approach to growth and social transformation, I was spending about six months each year in Brazil offering training workshops in person-centred gestalt therapy, my own synthesis based on my theoretical background (O'Hara, 1984a). Working in Brazil at that time it was inevitable that conversations about human potential would encompass the political sphere. The years 1974 to 1988 were the period of *abertura* or opening—a process of demilitarisation and liberalisation—during which Brazil was emerging from a period of brutal dictatorship and aspiring towards a democratic constitution. Participants in our programmes saw in ACP (PCA) a framework for an emancipatory practice. They saw a process which could heal the trauma of the decades of brutal oppression by the oligarchs and violence by the military regime against any form of dissidence, at the same time as it offered a pedagogy that could prepare a silenced generation for effective life in a democracy. During the dictatorship, advocates for social justice such as liberation theologians, emancipatory educators like Paulo Freire, and artists who distilled collective pain into songs that stirred the soul, were exiled, and even murdered. With abertura, the political landscape began to open, albeit gradually and unevenly. Professionals sought ways to create safe spaces where persons, newly free to speak their truth, could express their pain, find their authentic voices, and create ways of being that (as I put it) 'celebrate[s] human existence and our evolutionary potential'. They had to be careful, though. Activists who were too overt in their social critique might still disappear. This is where person-centred approaches came in. As one colleague explained, Rogers' ideas in general and ACP encounter groups in particular could be seen as a Trojan Horse, introducing an emancipatory praxis to the oppressed and traumatised under the cover of psychotherapy (O'Hara, 2024).

Keith: Thanks for giving us the background to that paper. I have the volume of papers Alberto collated from that conference (Segrera, 1984); it's an astonishing collection and a great resource of 80 papers to which I still return when researching the PCA.

One of the similarities you draw between Rogers and Freire in your paper, and one which might surprise some readers, is their faith: Rogers, a Christian humanist, and Freire with, as you put it, 'profound Christian and Marxist convictions' (p. 24). However, their Christianity (or Christianities) seems to have focussed less on the redeeming role of Christ as the saviour of 'man' (kind or otherwise) but more on the capacity of humans for self-understanding and transcending—which I think you summarise very well (on pp. 27–34 above).[3] Given the antagonism of some humanists to any religion, how important do you think Rogers' beliefs and faith were—and still are—for the PCA?

Maureen: Great question. I agree that neither Freire nor Rogers focus on Christ the redeemer who exists in a realm outside of human life only through whom humans are saved from suffering and achieve spiritual fulfilment. When Freire and Rogers identify as humanists, they are deliberately placing redemptive and transcendent potential within human beings, making alleviation of suffering and transcendence our personal and collective responsibility. Whilst both were raised in religious homes—Rogers' a fundamentalist Protestant one and Freire's a Catholic and spiritualist one—by adulthood they had both left behind religious doctrine which each in separate ways regarded as disempowering and oppressive. Instead, they spoke in terms of core values that are integral to Christianity. They focused their service on expanding critical consciousness and action to facilitate empowerment of the oppressed. They wished to serve humanity, not any deity. Instead, they wanted to create a world in which every person is free to become actualised while alive and have their diverse cultures and ways of being respected. Their secular version of Christian love, then, when stripped of its dogma, became unconditional acceptance, empathy, and non-manipulative solidarity with persons as subjects, while their version of humanistic service was to build communities in which all persons regardless of their birth are free to attain fulfilment on their own terms. In my view this overlap of essential values with some Christian traditions explains the early uptake by pastoral counsellors of Rogers' work and liberation theologists of Freire's.

Since the early days of humanistic psychology, including the PCA, there has been tension between secular humanism and a more spiritually informed humanism. The worldview of secular humanists is based in Eurocentric modern science, rationality, and materialism, and rejects (and frequently derides) truth claims that rely on faith, religion, and call upon supernatural entities or non-material forces. Rogers took pride in being recognised by academic psychologists for his scientific contributions. Early in his research career, Rogers subscribed enthusiastically to a secular view but, as he immersed himself in the experiences of his clients in psychotherapy and experiences of 'oneness' that sometimes occur in encounter groups, and as he began to experience expanded states of consciousness himself, he began to accept that something beyond secular rationality was at play. Something as he says, 'clear[ly] involves the transcendent, the indescribable, the mystical' (Rogers, 1980/1995b, p. 130). Such experiences while not religious in any doctrinal sense were certainly what for eons human societies have considered 'sacred'. By the late 1970s, along with his more politically focused work in the former Soviet republics and Central America, in his own life, Rogers was experimenting with altered states of consciousness, seances, experiences with mediums and psychics, was interested in telepathy, spirit possession, and other claims of paranormal, and was open to participating in frankly spiritual events. He became more open to the ideas and practices of spiritually informed colleagues to an extent that I confess at the time I found inconsistent with the essential faith in human empowerment and expressed my fear that openness to everything left him and his followers vulnerable to manipulation and exploitation. I now think my fears of the PCA becoming a new religion that once again distrusted subjectivity in favour of gurus, priests, hypnotists, spiritual teachers, and new quasi-religious political ideology were overblown. The interest in experiences of the sacred never coalesced into any new PC religion or spiritual doctrine and most people espousing the PCA can handle the postmodern hybridisation of spiritual and scientific knowledge claims. They can, as my Brazilian colleagues put it, 'ride two horses with one behind'.

Keith: Thanks, Maureen. What you say about Rogers' later interest in experience and phenomena beyond secular rationality adds more background to your 'Scientist and mystic' paper which addresses Rogers' ambivalence about science and religion and, I think, offers a brilliant analysis of his work—and approach—as representing both 19th century positivism and 20th century post-positivism.

I'm amazed at the directions our reflections and dialogue take, and think we could discuss a lot more about the PCA as an approach but, in the interests of keeping an eye on the word count, will leave some of that for later—for instance, regarding the importance of critical thinking (see Chapter 12 and **check**)—and perhaps other discussions for another time. For now, in closing this particular reflection, I'd like to pick up a point about the language of faith. I notice a certain tendency in the field generally but, for our present interest, amongst person-centred practitioners to write about theory and practice using words such as believe and belief, and faith. In both papers, you catch something of this when you refer to Rogers' belief in the actualising tendency, and that it's positive; that a methodology or process is emancipatory (and/or effective); and in personal experience as the ultimate standard of truth; his faith in human beings and their potential; in the formative tendency; in the (positive) desire and capacity of human beings; and in others' faith in Rogers' metaphysics. I have always worried about the overuse of this language applied to psychological theories, most notably when advocates of the PCA talk about 'believing' in the core conditions. In this context, I was quite struck by your point that:

> at the heart of the scientific vocation is a basic metaphysical belief that must be taken on faith if science is to continue: the fundamental faith that the universe is not random, capricious, or arbitrary but is in fact lawful, orderly, and understandable.
>
> (pp. 40–41)

I would have thought that, at the heart of scientific vocation—and, indeed, the person-centred approach—is metaphysical *knowledge*, that a thing or, in this case, an approach works.

Maureen: I am talking here about what comes *before* knowledge—an intuition or grounding assumption that the universe is not random but rather is ordered even if we cannot yet see the order. Such an assumption makes the collective search for truth that we call science reasonable rather than capricious and our discoveries plausible (or implausible) even prior to knowledge acquisition. It allows us to indwell in the ineffable and to wait until some form emerges in the short term of a single inquiry or the longer term of the evolution of consciousness. Whether this view survives a world of AI is still an open question.

I do share your concern that in many writings about the PCA, there is a certain philosophical muddiness. This is a problem for psychology in general which has never become a unified philosophical paradigm with multiple epistemologies, ontologies, and practices contributing to the postmodern psychosphere.

Keith: Thanks, Maureen, this last point provides a good bridge to the next part of the book and some of your papers on humanistic psychology, so let's leave this particular dialogue there (for now!) and leave the reader to enjoy Part II.

Notes

1 I recently re-read this book and, specifically, the first three chapters, for an article exploring Rogers' ideas about helping (Tudor & Rodgers, 2023).
2 For reviews of which, see Tudor (2022a, 2022b).
3 A few colleagues have discussed the importance of Rogers' Christian beliefs (Leonardi, 2006; Steele, 2014; Thorne, 1991, 1998, 2002; Tudor & Worrall, 2006; Van Belle, 1980).

Part II

Humanistic psychology

Chapter 6

Our foremothers as gurus (1983)[1]

Maureen O'Hara

In a recent survey of attitudes about work, Yankelovich (1978) reports a sharp difference between those of women and men. Men were more egocentric; they valued autonomy, independence, initiative, and competition; and were more likely than women to equate job satisfaction with material rewards and status recognition as a leader. Their concern for recognition made them more likely to favor their own ideas over those of others, even when the others' were more suitable. Women were more loyal to their company, valued team effort, were more often satisfied with 'psychic rewards' rather than material ones, were more likely to help out a colleague, often without being asked, and took satisfaction from the fact that a problem was resolved well than from their own role in solving it. Other research shows that while men use so-called 'power language' which emphasizes individual achievement or failure, women more frequently use inclusive language.

We women use expressions like 'Let's all…' and 'Why don't we…?', a language form often called weak because it is not assertive. Carol Gilligan's (1982) research on women's development of moral reasoning clarifies further the differences between the (characteristically) male 'voice' which is egocentric, abstract, and categorical, and the (characteristically) female 'voice' which is inclusive, contextual, concrete, and is informed by a holistic view of reality. Men make choices informed by an ethic of fairness, equality, and justice; the choices of women are informed by an ethic of care and avoidance of inflicting hurt.

Probably because of its overwhelming success, egocentricism has become so dominant a worldview that in our society it has become equated with 'reality'. Judged with respect to norms derived from male experience, a reasoning based in an ethic of care appears naive, muddle-headed, and endlessly compromising. Women are considered, even by widely accepted 'psychological' theories, to be intellectually and morally 'immature'.

Gilligan's (1982) work confirms that women's reasoning is informed by different principles. Ours is a reason of connection and interrelatedness. A basic condition which must be met in the resolution of a conflict is that everyone involved must be considered concretely; another is that no one should be hurt.

A serious dilemma for women at present is that the female 'voice' is not taken seriously, especially in the public world. Personal success depends greatly on

DOI: 10.4324/9781003519454-9

mastery of the 'male mode'. Holistic awareness of connection, a sense of the 'whole', may make a woman an essential part of any effective group but it is unlikely to get her promoted. Most likely, it will be relied upon but taken for granted. Yankelovitch's (1978) study suggests that the best 'company-man' may be a woman, but he wonders if that just means that women are 'patsies', willing to work harder, for less money, and without the recognition afforded their male colleagues.

The temptation is great for women to adopt the individualistic, assertive, egocentric attitudes that have paid off so well for men. The strengths of the egocentric view are obvious and largely derive from its capacity to abstract principles from their context. Without it, for example, we would find such abstract concepts as 'equality', 'justice', 'individual human rights', 'fairness', etc. Impossibly vague—even absurd.

But it must also be obvious to anyone in a position to be aware of the existential challenges now faced by humanity, as the Club of Rome dubs it in *Limits to Growth* (Meadows et al., 1974), 'The global problematique', that abstract reasoning alone is insufficient by which to approach the vastly complex, interpenetrated web of problems faced by the global community. The challenge today is to begin to take care of the 'whole' in which exist, simultaneously, legitimate and often competing needs: often action which solves a problem for one isolated group will create a problem for some other group elsewhere.

It is common these days for progressives to condemn 'Western thought' and to look eastward or southward for philosophies and practices which may help 'us' develop a more holistic, inclusive consciousness. But, as we look more carefully at research on the differences between men and women in our culture, it becomes clear that it is not 'Western thought' which is exaggeratedly egocentric, but Western male thought.

Some may, as I do, find it ironic that, as evidenced by the current fascination with Eastern masters, it seems that many men are now willing to hear from their gurus what men have refused for centuries to hear from their women partners. Perhaps the holistic voice is more audible if it issues from the mouth of an admired male. But despite enormous potential gains from this emerging fascination with Eastern ideas and practices by members of American educated populations at this point in the history of consciousness in the longer run, I suspect that in the shorter run, there may be much more gained from a recognition of Western culture's largely hidden resource—the holistic, inclusive consciousness of women.

Women are socialized from birth to master the art and science of belonging, in relationships which are complex, concrete, and exist over time. Because we live in our relationships, we become expert at sensing the subtle intricacies of groups which place multiple demands on limited resources. Tuning into the flow of complex human systems is not a new skill for women, not something we have learned in encounter groups or new-age festivals. We have acquired our viewpoint as a legacy from our foremothers who learned it through the daily business of being female and doing female things.

I hope we women today resist the temptation to eliminate the present inequality between the sexes and the suffering this entails by becoming like men. Concrete thinking, awareness of 'part/whole' relationships, the balance between personal freedom and community well-being, and an ethic of avoidance of inflicting hurt have never been more urgently needed by our troubled world. I want us instead to continue to clarify and articulate the grounds upon which we make our claim that the female voice is indispensable to the global conversation, both locally and globally.

And I hope we insist that global as well as personal survival will depend upon acknowledgement of the value of a worldview attuned to the 'whole' and informed by an ethic of care and responsibility. We must insist that the women's voice be heard, and I passionately believe the sooner the better for everyone's world.

Note

1 A final version of this chapter was published in *Perspective: Association for Humanistic Psychology* (November, 1983).

Chapter 7

Relational humanism

A psychology for a pluralistic world (1992)[1]

Maureen O'Hara[2]

Introduction

At last count there were over 400 different therapies competing for the therapist's training dollars and the client's health insurance benefits. Whether major established schools or 'treatments of the month', all claim their approaches are valid and are 'true' in some objective way. On the basis of such claims, whole professions of helpers have evolved with elaborate legitimizing structures and procedures. Increasingly, patients/clients are taking their therapist to task (and to court) for failure to provide some abstract and absolute standard of care, basing their claims on scientistic assumptions about the nature of psychological knowledge.

At the same time, though, members of marginal groups, like women and people of different racial and ethnic groups, are busily deconstructing the whole edifice, advancing postmodernist arguments that the most firmly established theories and practices—whether medical model or humanistic—are based on modernist worldviews reflecting the habits of mind, realities, and values of the people who are inventing them. These post-structural critics believe all totalizing discourses—in ordinary words, grand theories of everything—are suspect, that even in the physical and biological sciences, knower and known are fundamentally inseparable, and that an advanced technological society has created a psychology in its own image. If that isn't confusing enough, a lively conversation exists within humanistic psychology, feminism, transpersonal psychology, critical theory, and some areas of analytical psychology that suggest that the image of psychological 'health' enshrined within the mental health community is actually deeply sick, and the treatments based upon it make people worse, not better.

Whether we are aware of it or not, we have all become postmodernists. When we include studies from social learning theory, cognitive science, neurological studies, perception, depth psychology, sociology, anthropology, and any number of critical studies, we come to the conclusion that the inner psychological world of human beings, our consciousness or Subjectivity, is a creative product. The 'I' each of us knows is produced through dialogical engagements with the world into which one is born and lives. Inner physical sensations and perceptions of external events are interpreted, symbols, narratives, and conceptual schemas generated,

DOI: 10.4324/9781003519454-10

against which new experiences are referred. This produces, with varying degrees of permanence or fluidity, our subjective inner symbolic map for the self-in-the-world. If this constructivist view is correct, then we should expect different socio-cultural landscapes to produce different kinds of inner selves—and they do.

Selves in cultural contexts

In Western cultures, especially in the United States, people seem to experience themselves with a clear, lived sense of the 'I', which they refer to as 'myself', and which is the same 'I' throughout life: a self that is clearly distinguishable from other selves. Radical transformations or discontinuities are expected to be accompanied by anxiety, often intense. Not to know clearly who one 'is' or to lose one's sense of coherence and continuity is felt as a loss of self. In Western culture, this kind of disintegration and disorder has become equated with mental illness or even madness. Freedom and respect for the integrity of that self by others is also highly prized. This ideal of an autonomous, clearly bounded, self-assertive, self-responsible individual, who acts consistently and coherently, is the definition—the sine qua non—of psychological health for both males and females. Recently, this view of self, which is the self firmly ensconced at the center of humanistic psychology, has been shown to be culturally and contextually exclusive. In other cultures overseas, among individuals from non-dominant and immigrant groups within our own culture, and under varying relational circumstances even within the same group, ideals of 'personhood' might not necessarily imply such a strong sense of a distinct, individuated, and stable self. We now know that far from representing some absolute 'ideal human nature', many cultures go to considerable lengths to discourage such psychological patterns for adults. The ideal person is not one with a strong sense of personal identity, expressiveness, and creativity, but is someone who participates within their own social contexts. This 'sociocentric' self is almost identical to the 'relational' self of feminist psychology, and the 'process' self I have described elsewhere.

The 'I' at the center of our worldview, our system of laws and social conventions, and the educational system of our psychology is based on a Western, egocentric view of the person. Within the humanistic psychological community, the egocentric version of self has been so central to self-actualization theory that the frequent observation that females and non-dominant males or ethnic groups often fall outside this description did not, until recently, result in any real modification of this picture. Rather, it resulted in discrepancies being attributed to failures within the 'deviants' themselves, who were deemed less developed and less psychologically healthy. In the time-honored tradition of blaming the victim, this conclusion was then used to justify traditional patterns of economic and political discrimination, and ultimately abuse. It also led to psychologists interested in the psychology of women and other marginal groups departing the humanistic psychology community in droves, greatly diminishing our intellectual vitality.

Postcards from the edge

In recent years, the egocentric bias in psychology has been subjected to increasing criticism—especially from those seen as 'other' to this cultural norm and as marginal to the definitional centers of society. Realizing how much of the research upon which maps of the human psyche were drawn reflected the theoretical schemas of the minds of privileged elites, or if empirical, were based upon studies of White male college students, feminists, people of color, and people from other non-dominant groups have begun to accumulate other views of the psyche drawn by phenomenological investigation of and by diverse peoples.

The feminist work is well developed and seems to show that women live their lives in their connections and relationships, evaluate their well-being in contextual, concrete terms, and appear to develop their sense of self in concrete, relational terms. Studies of women seem to suggest that psychological well-being is not an individualistic affair, as women concern themselves not only with how they themselves are doing, but also how their relationships are doing and how those they belong to, love, and care for are doing too. Self-concept—whom a woman believes herself to be—is multi-determined, moment by moment, and over time, by the different relational contexts in which she operates.

The postmodern discussion now underway—whether by feminists, non-European ethnic groups, or other 'others'—marks a return to the center of discussions in psychology of the experiencing Subject. Gaining ground throughout human studies is the recognition that human beings do not all live in the same perceptual universe, do not all have the same kinds of selves, do not all care about, value, or believe the same things. At the level of individual psychology, respect for individual Subjectivity, although long championed within humanistic psychology by people like Carl Rogers, Abraham Maslow, Clark Moustakas, Eugene Gendlin, and Rollo May, has nevertheless assumed a largely homogeneous (European, masculine, elite, modernist) cultural context. Now it is time to extend our theory to embrace the multi-hued, multi-voiced, multi-contexted worlds we actually inhabit and to recognize that any decontextualized abstraction that attempts to separate persons from their life-worlds is bound to seriously distort and misunderstand human experience.

We must now take responsibility for the ways in which our theories and observations are themselves formative acts serving to construct realities as much as to describe or define them. When abstractions are based in and reflect the particular interests and worldviews of the dominating elites, such discourses have the power to, and historically have led to, patterns of social and interpersonal abuse. It may also be the case that the desire for and popularity of abstract theory are themselves both effect and cause of a great deal of the psychological pain we see around us.

I would like to propose that if humanistic psychology is to seize the opportunity for intellectual leadership now offered it by virtue of the epistemological fragmentation occurring within mainstream psychology, it is time to develop nothing short of a new, postmodern psychology. In particular, we must take up the task left unfinished by our founding giants and advance a psychology reflective of, and which can contribute to, the pluralistic worlds we all now inhabit. Such a new humanistic psychology will need a contextual, relational, flexible vision that combines features of both the abstract-egocentric views of individual Subjectivity with which we are all familiar and the less familiar contextual-sociocentric views which try to understand psychological life within specific concrete relational contexts. We must also bring to our work what we have learned from social theory, anthropology, religious and cultural studies, political theory, feminism, and ethnic studies, toward a greater understanding of the interplay between individual Subjectivity and broader cultural forces.

In these postmodern times, it is no longer feasible for psychologists of any stripe—but particularly humanistic psychologists who have always granted epistemic validity to individual experience—to consider questions of psychological development, functioning, and psychotherapeutic treatment of anyone, without considering the specific, concrete situations, and contexts in which they participate, the basic worldview at the center of both the client's and therapist's psychological landscapes, and how these all interact within the therapeutic context. Once we accept that where the question of what constitutes the fully human life concerned there are no absolute answers, we—clients and therapists—become existentially free, and actually obliged, to make our own choices about who we shall be and how we shall live and what we will let matter to us.

Beware the backlash

This much freedom is a job for grown-ups. Life with no externally given moral compass or ready-made sources of meaning can be terrifying, overwhelming, and bewildering. Responses to such freedom are varied and often troubling. In the next decades, humanists who affirm the primacy of human experience must expect to become the targets of intensified attacks. Attempts to discredit our work will come from within mainstream psychology, from those who have made investments in the scientistic modernist traditions in psychology, as well as from 'true believers'—left and right—who see in the postmodern discourse nothing but anarchy, superficiality, and narcissistic inflation.

Humanistic emphasis on the pursuit of one's own authenticity and self-fulfilment has become a popular target for criticism in recent years. It has been condemned from conservatives as leading to selfishness, moral relativism, and the breakdown of traditional values, condemned from the radical left as hopelessly individualistic, and politically naive, and condemned by orthodox psychiatry as romantic, shallow, and irresponsible. Common to all these criticisms is an underlying misanthropy and suspicion that too much freedom and self-development is a dangerous thing. Such criticisms mis-frame the problem and take the symptom for the illness. The critics are correct when they say that Americans feel disconnected and alienated. They are also correct that the search for self-fulfilment can easily become an excuse for endless pursuit of self-gratification. Demands for freedom have increasingly come to mean freedom from commitments and responsibility rather than freedom to be one's own self. They are right to point to disintegration of our environment and communities, and responsibility rather than freedom to be one's own self. They are right to condemn the victimization of the vulnerable, as a social ill on a catastrophic scale. But they are wrong when they identify the humanistic search for self-fulfilment as the culprit, they are wrong when they suggest that the health of a community must always be pitted against the freedom of the individual, and they are dangerously wrong when they suggest that we have gone too far down the road to freedom, and it is time to roll back our freedoms 'for our own good'.

An increasingly significant voice within and without psychology points in another direction. People from the margins, those historically silenced by the dominating worldviews that have deemed them 'object', are discovering the vastly expanded sense of empowerment, creativity, and joy that comes when one first begins to recognize the truth within one's own experience. Humanistic psychologies have been the route for many to reclaim their subjective voice. In humanistic therapy, workshops, classrooms, and organizations, people have learned to base their actions and life choices on their own particular authentic experience. They have discovered that it is only by making such choices for oneself that one becomes a fully emancipated member of society.

Humanistic psychology has a long-standing love affair with individual human beings, seeing us not as children to be taught, patients to be cured, or as victims to be protected but as unique center s of consciousness, responsibility, intentionally, and choice.

The problem, as I see it, is not that humanism has gone awry because of too much emphasis on the search for fulfilment of the individual self, but rather that we have misunderstood the nature of that search and in some ways have made it impossible to succeed. So that instead of our searches for self-actualization leading to more meaningful lives as intended, they actually end up making us feel less connected, less whole, and more alienated. Because the self at the center of humanistic psychology has been framed in a modernist egocentric worldview, it misconstrues the nature of the selves to be realized, and in doing so fails to recognize that genuine individuality can only flower within those social contexts in which such individuality is protected, nurtured, and developed. Through a fabric of cultural forces, from religion to psychiatry, from Marxism to marketing, we in the West have lost touch with, and so have betrayed, the very sources of our humanness and have been persuaded to accept a shrunken version of ourselves. We have also been persuaded, and been very ready to be persuaded, to bolster this shrunken self-concept with externally derived compensations and fortifications. Bigotry, sexism, racism, turning people, including ourselves into categories—such as 'Adult Children of Alcoholics', the homeless, AIDS victims, senior citizens, White males, liberals and conservatives, and so on—are all ways of bolstering our puny stripped-down modern selves.

The personal and the political

When we started out, humanistic psychology was largely populated by compassionate idealists who had embraced the notion that the personal was political. Many of us took that to mean that if I perfect myself in some mysterious way, it would perfect the society, making the egocentric error of drawing the boundaries of self too close to our own skin. If we did enough inner work, if we found a good enough therapist, if we withdrew to our mountain top and into our private choices, and cut ourselves off from oppressive forces 'out there', many believed we could radically transcend the human condition. However, while we were turned inward, our communities were falling into the hands of the greedy, the glib, the slick, the cynical, and the fanatical. And because we are all woven from the fabric of our shared world, bit by bit, the poverty, fear, despair, violence, bigotry, and pollution that is the daily experience of millions of people—who are, after all, our co-creators—creeps into our consciousness and into our selves.

It is obviously important for all of us to develop greater awareness of our inner landscapes and to undertake the kinds of practices that for millennia have opened our consciousness, but relational selves cannot withdraw permanently into a private search for self and hope to keep on growing. It doesn't work. Eventually, we must reconnect. We must make a commitment to each other, to our communities, and to the earth we share. Relational selves sink or swim together.

A commitment to the emancipation of a human self, understood as a relational self, far from leading to hopeless relativism, nihilism, political correctness, self-indulgence, inevitable isolation, and atomistic disconnection—as our critics maintain—will lead to the development of one's own unique particular self. However, such development can only succeed if we make a shift towards responsibility, caring, accountability, and community. Once we come to view ourselves as creatively woven from experiences within the world around us, then that world takes on a whole new significance. No longer seen as a hostile impediment to true self-fulfilment or even as 'a worldly distraction' but as the very source of who we are and of who we might possibly become, it is no longer feasible to separate the work of self-realization from the work of the realization of the potential of the communities we inhabit. A fully humanistic psychology must see environment interests, community interests, and personal interests as the same thing.

I am convinced that our pluralistic world is waiting for a fully humanistic psychology: that is, one based in a new relational humanism that understands selves as contextual and relational, that will acknowledge individual Subjectivity in all its glorious diversity, and that will establish and value relational norms of mutuality, civility, responsibility, and accountability.

Notes

1 Originally published as a chapter in *The Humanistic Movement: Recovering the Person in Psychology* (edited by F. J. Wertz, 1994, Gardener Press).

2 At the time this was published, Maureen was the former president of the Association for Humanistic Psychology, was an associate editor of the *Journal of Humanistic Psychology*, was a long-time colleague of Carl Rogers at the Center for Studies of the Person in La Jolla California, had taught women's studies, and was a fellow of the Meridian International Institute, a San Francisco Bay-area think tank on governance and the future. She was in private practice as a marriage, family, and child counsellor in Encinitas, California.

Chapter 8

Constructing emancipatory realities

Toward a feministic voice in humanistic psychology (1995)

Maureen O'Hara

As Walt Anderson (1996) describes it, the field of psychology is buzzing with new ways of thinking about concepts such as 'self' and 'reality'.

Feminist theory and practice has, from the beginning, been in the thick of such arguments, and for good reason. When every 'truth' system we've ever known, from the oldest myth to modern medical science, has concluded that women are biologically, intellectually, and morally inferior, that we are, on the one hand, dangerous and, on the other hand, natural nurturers and homemakers, that we are unsuitable for public office, should be at once protected and subjugated, you bet feminists have a stake in conversations about 'reality'!

Contemporary feminist ideas about the nature of female reality fall into at least three different streams. One, more common among American feminists, takes the view that there is an essential female nature which is determined by and manifest through the female body, with its possibility for multiple orgasms, its internal sex organs, and its capacity for pregnancy, birth, and milk-nursing. This line of argument sees female nature violently repressed and compromised by patriarchal and misogynistic societies which have prevented women from fully knowing themselves, each other, and their nature. Through practices, customs, taboos, and restrictions that circumscribe every aspect of her life, she is pruned and doctored like a Bonsai tree so that by the time she is an adult she sees this as the natural state of affairs. She willingly contributes to the perpetuation of the process by cooperating with the pruning of the next generation—her daughters. The radical version of this line of thinking, exemplified by Mary Daly (1978) in *Gyn/Ecology*, leads to a separatist position, where women would remove themselves from all institutions currently created in man's image, and, in order to rediscover their lost 'sacred femininity', withdraw from all contact with men. They would create their own institutions, symbols, religions, mores, and forms of government that more faithfully reflect 'essential feminine consciousness'. Although not herself proposing separatism, Riane Eisler (1987), in *The Chalice and the Blade*, also argues for an essential female nature which results in matriarchal cultures being somehow more 'nurturant' when compared to male 'sword' nature.

Another major stream of theory comes from the French feminists such as Julia Kristeva, Luce Irigaray, and Hélène Cixous, who draw on both Lacanian

DOI: 10.4324/9781003519454-11

psychoanalysis and Marxism to argue that even the deepest layers of our psyche, the symbols, the desires, the fundamental structure of our sense of self, what Daly argues is 'Nature', are constructed by our minds as ways to account for what happens to women (because they have no phallus) in a misogynistic society. The third important stream is made up of post-structuralists like Chris Weedon, who argue that there is no such thing as 'feminine nature', that our biology is not our destiny but our consciousness, mediated through symbolic language, and is derived from the culture we live in. If our culture feels that women are inferior, then we will experience that as our nature. If our culture sees us as brood mares, then we ourselves will highly prize our reproductive natures rather than our minds or our athleticism. This line of thinking, drawing on the deconstructionist thought of Derrida, as well as Lacan, Foucault, Althusser, and others, focuses on the way language creates experience rather than merely reporting upon it. For post-structuralists, if we prize our mothering, it is not due to some biological imperative but because patriarchal societies require that we voluntarily accept roles such as child-rearing and domestic work and don't ask for payment for it.

Ideologies of 'femininity' arise, what Betty Friedan (1963) termed 'feminine mystique', which help solidify these work roles into aspects of identity. These codes of conduct feel so basic to us that we experience real anxiety if we try to go against them, thus reinforcing the belief that it is against our 'nature' to not want to mother or have sexual relations with men. When patriarchal interests shift, as in a war, for example, and women are required to work in the armaments factories, we are subjected to new propaganda urging us to downplay motherhood and promoting a new ideology of 'womanhood' that makes heroines out of Rosie riveters and aviatrixes. When the thinned ranks of men come home from the battlefield, the 'cult of motherhood' is reintroduced to get women out of the jobs the men need and to replace the population decimated by the war. This line of discussion sees our nature as 'man-made' and points to how it shifts from discourse to discourse, from community to community, and from era to era as evidence for the plasticity of 'female nature'.

There are, of course, enormous implications for the therapist in these two different positions. If you believe that a woman's meaninglessness and emptiness—her depression—stems from her alienation from some primordial femininity, then your therapy will be geared toward separatism, casting off the artifices of 'masculine consciousness' and reaffirming the 'essential feminine'. You will eschew activities associated with the 'masculine' and cleave to those that are womanist. You will see intuition, feeling, magic, sensuality, dance, poetry, and mysticism as facilitating your client's recovery of her 'divine female nature'; rationality, politics, education in established institutions, participation in established religions, law, heterosexual marriage, competition, business, etc., will be seen as taking her away from sense of self and, therefore, as a contributing factor in the depression.

Therapy informed by post-structuralist or constructivist positions (not quite the same but close enough for the purpose of this discussion) necessitates a heightened commitment to rationality, and it requires critical analysis of both the outer world of signs and language and inner subjectivity. It will involve consciousness-raising activities to challenge even deeply felt identifications and pulling apart cherished psychic structures with the view to realigning them with female emancipatory interests. Such a therapy has to be essentially activist, requiring women to get involved in the social, economic, and political structures of society in order to transform them from exploitative forms to emancipatory forms, and, in the crucible of our community conversations about reality, each of us becomes both a culture interpreter and a culture-maker.

Within the Association for Humanistic Psychology community, there has been a clear preference for the 'essential feminine' version of feminist psychology. I would like to argue that this is a mistake, albeit one that is very easy to understand. The idea of ourselves as 'goddesses' or 'priestesses' is a deeply comforting antidote to the usual sense of insignificance experienced by most women in their daily lives. Nonetheless, I think going in the direction of a 'goddess'-type language and affirmations of some inborn, biologically based 'femininity' in fact only serves to perpetuate ways of thinking about human realities which themselves form the justification for many attitudes and social practices which have disenfranchised women for millennia. When we look dispassionately at the newly emergent 'goddess'-type stories, one can hardly fail to recognize how derivative they are of myths about female nature which have been part of patriarchal societies since ancient times.

The constructivist position is a harder pill to swallow. Its arguments leave the question of biological contribution to consciousness veiled in mystery. It is not that our biology is irrelevant but that it serves as a lower boundary condition through which and upon which symbolic reality, both internal and social, must perforce be constructed. The content of consciousness, of the unconscious, of experience, even of 'self', is constructed from semantic and semiotic symbols we encounter in our interactive dialogue with the world. When, for example, in a moment of intense psychological disorganization, I saw hideous gargoyles and diaphanous sprites taunting me from the depths of the abyss, the constructionists would argue (and they would be right) that I had seen every one of those beings before on the pages of children's fairytale books, on the sides of Gothic churches, and in art museums I had been taken to before I could talk. It is not to say the drama these demons were engaged in within my psyche had ever been seen before, but, in the way 26 characters, half a dozen or so punctuation marks, and a space-bar can be organized into either *King Lear* or Dear Abby,[1] I had drawn upon my learned symbols and their socially agreed upon meanings to understand an event that needed more expressive language than I ordinarily used.

Some people feel the post-structural position leads to despair. Derrida himself is often quoted as saying he is in despair. I don't agree with them. Interestingly, it is not the feminist post-structuralists who cry out in angst, but the White, European males! I feel, and read in the work of feminist post-structuralists, an enormous sense of relief, hope, and responsibility. Far from despair, the idea that each of us recreates reality with each encounter fills me with a wondrous sense of hope, empowerment, and community connection. If there is no absolute truth 'out there' by which to create pristine 'expert systems' which can somehow solve our problems mathematically; if I am who I am because you are who you are; both of us who we are because they are who they are; if we accept that when we enter into dialogue, we both change; and if it's true, we *co-create* reality, which, in turn, creates us, then we are called to a new kind of community. If I can make culture, I must act responsibly, and if I can only ever be part of the creation, I must act humbly. I'd take that over a goddess any day!

Note

1 This refers to an American advice column, originally written by Abigail Van Buren, and carried on today by her daughter, Jeanne Phillips.

Chapter 9

Emancipatory therapeutic practice in a turbulent transmodern era

A work of retrieval (1997)

Maureen O'Hara[1]

Summary

Within the community of psychotherapists, there has always existed philosophical and methodological tension between objectivists who follow a medical model, romantics who favor humanistic approaches, and social constructivists who take a more sociopolitical path. The current health care crisis is forcing practitioners to take sides, is threatening to unravel this always uneasy coherence among psychotherapists, and is forcing practitioners to revisit questions of epistemology, ethics, and practice. I argue that as medical insurance funds dwindle and the assessment of 'medical necessity' comes increasingly to be defined according to strict patterns of specific 'symptoms', and as insurance-allowable treatment becomes restricted to short-term, emergency care, or medication-based treatment, humanistic psychologists should restate their commitment to a psychology that approaches the struggles and promises of human life in human terms and should refocus their efforts on quality of life, and spiritual and emancipatory concerns.

What is a good life?

How should we understand the nature of reality? What is happiness?

What is the nature and meaning of consciousness?

How do relationships, families, and communities thrive?

How should goods and privileges be distributed among people? What should guide ethical human conduct?

What is our relationship to and responsibility for the natural world?

How can we face pain, loss, and death without losing hope or the will to transcend suffering?

Any durable society must have shared myths or stories that successfully answer these and other essential questions for most of its members, most of the time (Shweder & Bourne, 1982). It must also have effective institutions and psychologically compelling socializing processes through which successive generations are

DOI: 10.4324/9781003519454-12

initiated into the stories of their forebears in ways that permit their society to be reproduced. Societies that accomplish this with the minimum expenditure of effort are more successful than those that must exert much of their precious community resources to function in an orderly way. In the more stable and harmonious communities, the master narratives, or *cosmology*—that complex, interwoven set of symbols, traditions, norms, patterns of expectation, and explanations for things from which societies derive their metaphysics, morality, and epistemology—become internalized into automatic psychic structures—the social constructions—of inhabitants. In coherent societies, members participate in coherent patterns of life and develop a coherent sense of self.

People who like to think about the big picture, including religion, politics, psychology, education, science, history, and popular culture, concur that in these last years of the 20th century, as we face (by the Christian calendar, anyway) not only the beginning of a new century, but of a new millennium, the entire world is well into another period of radical change. The 400-year-old Western mythos, which has formed the cultural consensus holding Europe and European-derived American communities together, is unravelling. Whatever benefits ultimately issue from these changes—and some futurists believe they could be very great—no one doubts that we are in for a rocky ride. The rising tide of political apathy, accelerating rates of senseless violence, the AIDS epidemic, continuing claims for enhanced human rights and intensifying reactions against such claims, the popularity of simple-minded talk-show hosts peddling comforting nostrums, human-made ecological disasters occurring more and more often, the alienation of the young, rising xenophobia, rising infant mortality rates in developed countries, an alarming reversal in health standards in the nations of the former Soviet Union, massive dislocation of peoples because of war and famine, and other worrisome indicators all echo the kinds of social ills experienced during other earlier periods of turbulence (Toulmin, 1990; Tuchman, 1978). As in any and all such transitional times, people in America are confused, anxious, and deeply divided. Searching for some kind of coherence, some kind of social glue that can prevent their world from flying apart—from disintegrating—they worry and argue about what is or should be the social mythos of our times.

Crisis of coherence in psychotherapy

The mental health professions together comprise a community or society, a cultural entity peopled by its own particular set of inhabitants—practitioners, consumers, administrators, teachers, students, opinion makers—with its own patterns of life, and its own symbols, master narratives, and language and social forms. It has been one of the more influential myth-making institutions in late 20th-century North America and Europe, coming behind the news media, popular culture, and education, but coming ahead of law, religion, and the fine arts (Bellah et al., 1985; Rieff, 1966). Its inhabitants include psychotherapists, counsellors, pastoral counsellors, psychiatric nurses, psychologists, psychiatrists, social workers, case-workers, holistic health practitioners, metaphysical counsellors, life-style educators, and school counsellors. Its rituals and traditions include psychotherapy, education, self-help groups, workshops, seminars, and a whole spectrum of books, tapes, and seminars that provide answers to the essential questions of life that are psychology based. Nowhere are the concrete consequences of the rising levels of cultural incoherence more visible than within the community of psychotherapists. Therapeutic psychology and its spin-offs, clinical social work, marriage and family therapy, psychiatric nursing, and organizational behavior are disintegrating as academic disciplines and as fields of professional practice. The field of psychology and the individuals who inhabit it are in the midst of theoretical, epistemological, methodological, and ethical meltdown. Pluralism in graduate school training, discussions about licencing and credentialing, variations in clinical theory and practice, debates about the status of psychological knowledge as science and as evidence in courts of law, shifting definitions of ethical and unethical behavior, and proliferation of antitherapist consumer protection laws are just some of the ways the postmodern crisis is already affecting the field. *And it will get worse.*

Daily, psychotherapists are confronted with situations that require them to make moral, methodological, and humanitarian decisions not accounted for either in their graduate training or in their professional codes of ethics. Actions chosen and how these are received by the general public will depend on the various philosophical assumptions on which any particular therapist's practice is based. These may be quite different. There exist unresolved fundamental philosophical disagreements among psychologists about the core questions of the field, its metaphysics—what practitioners believe about the nature of reality—its morality—what they believe to be the nature of the good life and the good society—and its epistemology—what they believe to be the status of clinical knowledge. These disagreements have existed at the center of clinical psychology for over a century. Because of this, legitimate clinical choices in diagnosis and intervention can be radically different from one practitioner to another, even among skilful and ethical practitioners (Miller, 1992).

There are at least three different kinds of responses to the fundamental questions currently coexisting within the mental health community. Gergen divided psychological discourse into modern objectivist, the modern romantic, and the postmodern constructivist responses (Gergen, 1994). Another designation might be biomedical modernists, the psycho-poetic depth psychologists who straddle the boundary between modern and postmodern, and the postmodern social constructivists and integrationists.

They frequently coexist, it should be added, within the same individual psychotherapist.

The biomedical majority

The dominant position among members of the American Psychological Association (APA), the American Psychological Society (APS), and the American Psychiatric

Association is firmly modernist. Even in psychology, the biomedical paradigm dominates, enshrined in the Boulder model of clinical psychologist as natural scientist and behavioral practitioner. The metaphysic of mainstream psychology is causal and materialist. Reality, including mind itself, is made up of measurable quantities of matter that behave in a predictable, law-like fashion. Its dominant epistemology is Cartesian or empiricist-objectivist. This position holds that valid knowledge is impersonal, gained only through strictly controlled experimental methods from which all sources of contextual contamination and observer subjective biases have been eliminated. As a logical consequence of these first two tenets, adherents to the modernist-objectivist position claim its truth to be precise, value-free, and generalizable.

The psycho-poetic romantics

The next most widely held position among American psychologists is the romantic-subjectivist or psycho-poetic, which places the unique, experiencing individual at the center of its metaphysics, epistemology, and moral theory. Stretching back to the earliest days of psychotherapy, the romantic view was part of the thinking of early psychoanalytic thinkers like Adler, Rank, Homey, and Jung. Its most widespread and popular manifestations, however, have been in the humanistic and transpersonal traditions, represented by members of the Association for Humanistic Psychology, the Association for Transpersonal Psychology, the American Academy of Psychotherapy, and members of the Division of Humanistic Psychology of APA, Division 32. Arising as a direct challenge to regarding psychological problems as diseases and to limiting the focus of psychological attention to questions of treatment and repair, the humanistic tradition refused the medical designation and instead, defined itself in growth, education, and wellness terms. This tradition reached back to the gentler, more tolerant, and inclusively humanistic visions of reality of pre-Cartesian Renaissance humanism. For the psycho-poetic therapist, the highest reality is transcendental reality—the whole that is greater than the sum of its material parts. Knowledge is personal knowledge, the most important and enduring answers to the eternal questions found deep within the individual subjective human being. Despite self-characterization as alternative or 'Third' and 'Fourth Force' movements within psychology, the modernist origins of a great deal of humanistic psychology are still clearly visible. Although arrived at through more personal or subjective processes of inquiry, continued emphasis on such Enlightenment universals as truth, freedom, and self reveal their (in my view, proud) modernist lineage.

The constructivists

The newest family in the psychological discourse neighborhood—one that is clearly offspring and kin of both modernist-objectivists and subjectivist-romantics—is a heterogeneous assortment of practitioners and theoreticians who approach questions of reality, knowledge, and morality from pluralist, contextualist, or social-constructivist perspectives. These newer voices—often referred to as postmodern—speak in the frankly politicized accents of previously marginalized groups such as women and ethnic, sexual, and religious minorities. They interpret psychological pain contextually, as the result of cultural and political forces that have forced people on the margins of society to internalize self-injurious conceptual maps and narratives, which lead to restricted patterns of life.

The postmodern discourse represents a conjunction of some recent extensions of both objectivist and subjectivist traditions. On the one hand, by casting an analytical and critical eye onto the processes of normal science itself, objectivist researchers have been able to show that when formerly tacit or invisible variables such as the values, investments, and interests of the investigators are put under scrutiny, claims about impersonal objectivity and moral neutrality prove unsustainable. On the other hand, by taking phenomenological, narrative, and interpretative research methods favored by romantic-subjectivists to their furthest extensions, they reveal psychological reality to be uniquely personal, as the romantics have long asserted, but at the same time coextensive with the cultural contexts—historical, class, gender, racial, ethnic, and linguistic—in which any individual develops consciousness. The postmodern discourse offers contemporary psychology the potential for reconciling and surpassing the limits of both objectivism and subjectivism. There are still important methodological, ethical, and developmental problems to be solved before a new postmodern psychotherapy can be satisfactorily described that is more than either of the psychologies it attempts to replace, but the postmodern discourse appears very promising (Neimeyer, 1996; Stricker, 1996).

A house divided

Despite its enormous social influence in creating the 20th-century worldview, psychology is a house divided. The deep philosophical differences and ever-present threat of schism among the modernist-objectivist, subjectivist-romanticist, and postmodernist-contextual discourses within psychology have gone unresolved for over three decades. After a brief period of openness in the late 1960s and early 1970s, the modernist Boulder model has come to dominate mainstream academic and government psychology. With a few remarkable exceptions (e.g., Duquesne University, Sonoma State University, and the State University of West Georgia), by the 1980s, in mainstream schools, humanistic and transpersonal approaches had been either banished to programs in counselling, marginalized within departments of psychology—which over the 1970s came to look and sound ever more like departments of zoology, biochemistry, or computer science—or had struck out on their own into free-standing alternative graduate schools like the Union Institute, Fielding Institute, Saybrook Institute, California Institute for Integral Studies, and the Center for Humanistic Studies.

Outside the academy, and outside scholarly journals, however, the vast majority of private mental health practices across the country, service professionals, and the general public had until recently accommodated to the schism.

Subjectivist-romanticist practitioners resolved their cognitive dissonance by convincing themselves they were 'playing the insurance game'—giving medical diagnoses to insurance companies while avoiding them within their actual practices. Conversely, modernist-objectivists supplemented their scientist-practitioner graduate training with workshops, clinical training programs, and growth experiences of all sorts, which offered a rich diet of both romanticist and postmodern growth opportunities and therapeutic training. During the 1970s and 1980s, people favored gestalt therapy, self-psychology, client- centered therapy, Eriksonian hypnosis, Jungian psychology, and transpersonal psychology. The postmodernists, who go by such names as narrative, deconstructionist, constructivist, relational, and contextual therapists, have gained ground in the last decade. In many ways ideally suited to the need to play more than one game, the postmodernists have been particularly visible among marital and family, feminist, and ethnic therapists.

Despite deep and seemingly irreconcilable theoretical contradictions, professional therapists have so far been remarkably adept at juggling the multiple discourses or paradigms that coexist within their field, speaking one language and idiom with their university professors, another with their clinical supervisors, another with the insurance companies, and yet another with their clients.

However, the ground is shifting once again, and the cracks are beginning to show. The paradigm wars are heating up—not only on an academic or theoretical level but in the more concrete arena of the business of practice. The always-incoherent center of professional psychology threatens to finally fracture into separate discourses.

The widening chasm

As the cultural divisions within the psychotherapy community widen, some practitioners try to resist the disintegration of their world with a flurry of activity within their various professional organizations, apparently aimed at consolidation of the modernist position before it slips away.

There are initiatives among practitioners within the APA to develop standardized treatment protocols for psychotherapists based on empirically validated treatments and to define standards of care in objective, operational terms. A Division 12 (clinical psychology) task force, for instance, recently proposed that APA create an authorized treatment manual that would endorse only those therapeutic approaches that had been subjected to randomly assigned, double-blind, symptom-specific outcome studies. Although the proposal was rejected by the majority within APA as overly restrictive, other attempts to establish therapeutic effectiveness on the basis of strict experimentalist and objectivist criteria are likely to follow in North America and worldwide. According to Auckenthaler, *Psychotherapie im Wandel: Von der Konfession zur Profession* [*Psychotherapy in Transition: From Speculation to Science*] by Grawe et al. (1997) has been very influential in the movement within European psychotherapy toward the objectivist position and away from either the romantic or postmodern positions (A. Auckenthaler, personal communication,

July 4, 1996). Recently, the APA voted to seek drug prescription-writing power for clinical psychologists, thereby moving even further along a biomedical path. As the managed care revolution in health care proceeds, demands for accountability in health care spending intensify. Shareholders and executives of the large for-profit health care entities begin to clamor for good returns on their money, and pressure is on psychotherapists to demonstrate therapeutic efficacy in terms that are acceptable to managed care executives and their corporate customers. Nonphysician psychotherapists, wary of losing their piece of the health care pie, are scrambling to play catch-up with the psychiatrists. Clearly, they have decided to put their money on the modernist-objectivist horse. There are serious challenges to APA's attempts to fortify its modernist-objectivist grounding for its claims about the effectiveness of psychotherapy, some of them coming from within the modernist-objectivist camp itself. It has been long recognized that training and credentialing processes employed by APA-accredited graduate schools of psychology and state licencing boards cannot be shown to result in more positive treatment outcomes for clients (Dawes, 1994). Others point out that from within the objectivist story favored by dominant voices within APA, no strong, validated evidence exists that verifies that specific therapeutic techniques, beyond such nonspecific factors as warmth and a sympathetic ear, actually correlate significantly and favorably with treatment outcomes (Dawes, 1994; Eysenck, 1952, 1983; Jacobson, 1995; Miller et al., 1995). Some researchers, although granting that people who consult psychotherapists do report benefits, nevertheless argue against considering such benefits therapeutic. Dawes, for instance, suggests that outpatient psychotherapy plays an educational or spiritual rather than therapeutic function in peoples' lives. He calls for the complete deregulation of outpatient psychotherapy and suggests that because it is not medicine, it be marketed on a caveat emptor basis like any other personal service or product. He argues that professional licenses should be required only by those therapists who work in institutional settings such as hospitals, prisons, and residential treatment programs, where inmates are relatively powerless and so need some kind of organized protection from abuse of psychiatric power. These debates over fundamentals within the modernist community are likely to become increasingly politicized.

Meanwhile, from without there rages a vigorous postmodernist antitherapy critique (Wakefield, 1996). By revealing the embarrassing history of racism and misogyny that has informed psychology's views of women, people of colour, strangers, nonconformists, and lesbians and gays, the postmodern critique argues that all theories of psychological life, systems of psychotherapy, strategies for change, values, and ethics are nothing more (or less) than shared traditions—myths or stories generated to protect the interests of particular dominant groups (Caplan, 1995). (Postmodernists have been slower to extend this analysis of interests to their own position.)

Virtually ignored by both modernist-objectivists and deconstructivist postmodernists are the very large numbers of practitioners and the dwindling numbers of academics who make up the ranks of the humanistic and transpersonal counsellors, psychotherapists, psychologists, and organizational consultants. Unacknowledged, or when acknowledged, devalued, or even disapproved of by APA-accredited clinical psychology programs, much of the actual clinical psychotherapy practice of the nearly 300,000 mental health practitioners across the United States, the majority of organizational-behavior practitioners, and virtually all of the practice within the self-help movement, is grounded in a romanticist-subjectivist language of humanistic psychology, often combined with the spiritual focus of transpersonal psychology. 'Becoming your own person', 'awareness', 'trusting what is deepest within you', 'listening to your unique inner self', seeking 'authentic experience', building 'empathic' and 'accepting' 'I–Thou' relationships with others, 'realising your true potential', embracing the 'freedom to be', experiential exercises, guided imagery that help people 'get in touch with their deeper selves', and stress reduction meditation techniques are familiar touchstones of actual practice for the vast majority of American practitioners and their clients. Although frequently sliding back and forth across the fuzzy boundary between modernism and postmodernism, this broad folk-psychology clearly derives much of its language, meanings, and behavioral conventions from the romanticist tradition.

The radical turmoil within the psychotherapy culture leaves a pervasive sense of pessimism and uncertainty among psychotherapists about their own futures in a profession that is in the process of being turned upside down. Bewildered and anxious, they buy books and newsletters and flock to conferences and seminars that offer to teach them managed-care-friendly, 'magic bullet', short-term techniques and programs on how to make their livelihoods outside the health care 'industry'. However, at the same time, a burgeoning therapeutic counter-culture of licensed and nonlicensed healers thrives in the widening cracks in the authorized mental health landscape—yet more evidence of centrifugal forces tearing the psychotherapeutic community apart (O'Hara, 1996a).

Culture wars

The therapeutic community can no longer deny that not only does it house multiple theoretical positions about psychological development and the practice of psychotherapy, but it embraces multiple ways of investigating the existential questions—everything from positive science to myth. It also has multiple views on the multiplicity! There is no coherent and universally accepted meta-story that can make sense of the pluralism of the mental health field and help clients make sense of it. Like the rest of society, mental health professionals find themselves caught up in contradictory and deeply divisive movements that become increasingly difficult to reconcile. In October 1996, the *American Psychologist* published a special issue on outcome assessment in psychotherapy that included 11 very different points of view about research about psychotherapy, ranging from vigorous defence of experimental treatment-focused methods to arguments favoring more contextual patient-focused approaches (VandenBos, 1996). In reviewing Hoshmand and Martin's book, *Research as Praxis: Lessons From Programmatic Research in*

Therapeutic Psychology (1995), Claiborn expresses his astonishment at how much of discussions of therapeutic outcome end up being discussions about 'methodology as distinct from findings' (Claiborn, 1996). Practitioners attempting to straddle more than one discourse community must come to terms with the dawning realization that the grounds for justification of *any* particular clinical approach, ethical consensus, or choice of action are in large part socially constructed. More confusingly, some are logically and ethically incommensurate one with another. When parallel but incommensurate logical, moral, and ethical systems collide, as they increasingly do within the mental health community, ensuing disagreements frequently become divisive, interminable—and shrill (MacIntyre, 1981). The strain this puts on any community is enormous. In the absence of any universally respected final authority—science, God, Truth—if disagreements are to be resolved at all, it is frequently through the exercise of force—coercive or brute—by the stronger over the weaker.

There is a real danger of strong-arm methods being used within psychology, by modernist-objectivists—who represent the powerful majority—denying legitimacy to both subjectivists and postmodernists and forcing them beyond the margins of acceptability. Of the 20 or so clinical treatments initially endorsed by the APA Division 12 Task Force on Practice Guidelines, all but one were cognitive behaviorist approaches.

To be included by the Division 12 Task Force as a proven effective treatment (in contrast to a treatment that is considered experimental or ineffective), a therapeutic process must pass muster when held to standards of evaluation derived from biological medicine and drug trials conducted under conditions that bear little or no relationship to the actual practice of psychotherapy. Only those therapies that have already been 'manualised'—broken down into clearly delineated, replicable, and quantitatively measurable operational steps—are considered. These selection criteria are based on the proposition that only by comparing psychotherapy outcomes with different therapists, specific client populations who are randomly assigned to either no treatment control groups or test groups, and the therapy conducted under specified clinical conditions can outcome results be confidently evaluated, and effectiveness claims justified (Barlow, 1996). Context, the experience or other personal dimensions of the therapist, or the unique life circumstances of the client have no place in this form of outcome assessment. They are 'out of paradigm' (Bohart et al., 1998). Such strict adherence to abstract standards of formal objectivity, long abandoned by biological and physical sciences, has been referred to by some critics as 'the cult of empiricism' (Toulmin & Leary, 1994). Regardless of its validity in assessing the effectiveness of some kinds of behavioral interventions, this type of research protocol effectively eliminates a priori the work of researchers interested in the subjective particularities of individual cases and in specific client–therapist relationships. Humanistic, transpersonal, or constructivist approaches did not survive the Division 12 cut. Nor for that matter did any feminist, depth psychoanalytic, family process, or sociocultural approaches. Within the modernist-objectivist logic of this Task Force, such an exclusion is logically and ethically coherent.

Within the real world of psychotherapy—as the enterprise is actually experienced by clients—a far wider range of therapeutic approaches can be shown to have successful outcomes for participants than the Division 12 validity criteria would have recognized, thus placing practitioners in a serious professional bind (Seligman, 1995). Because the stated goal of such manualization projects is to identify those treatments that pass empirical muster from those that do not, and by doing so endorse one set of methods over others, it is quite clear that methods not on the list—regardless of the questionable validity of such exclusion—are likely to be seen as substandard. This would leave any practitioner who uses nonendorsed methods open to charges of ethical violations for providing substandard care and vulnerable to malpractice lawsuits.

The new heresy hunters

The threat to psychotherapists is real—not just to those at the flaky fringe, but to all creative and innovative psychotherapists. Consider a recent case in California brought by the family of a client. The family accused a licensed marriage and family therapist of malpractice for performing what she referred to as shamanic healing. The case was settled in favor of the family. The therapist lost her license—and her livelihood. Her professional organization did not support her use of shamanic techniques. In another case, Thomas Szasz, a long-time antipsychiatry voice, was sued successfully by the family of a deceased physician. He had consulted Szasz for depression after having given up treatment with a previous psychiatrist who had prescribed lithium. The physician was fully aware that Szasz was well known for his antimedication stance. Several months after he had stopped seeing Szasz, the physician killed himself. The family won more than $600,000 in a malpractice settlement against Szasz for not insisting that the patient take medication.

So far, nonphysician psychotherapists have not had to fear this particular kind of lawsuit, but if efforts to secure prescription-writing power are successful, psychologists too will be expected to insist on medication. This is likely to create even more divisive pressures within the psychology community as prescription writers become differentiated from nonprescription-writing therapists in both training and worldview. At the 1995 annual convention of the APA, when *Journal of Humanistic Psychology* editor Torn Greening expressed his opposition to prescription authority for psychologists, a colleague active in promoting such authority told him he should resign from APA because 'his type of opposition could undermine and split the organisation, which should be united on this issue' (T. Greening, personal communication, October 1996). Similarly, in the August 1996 issue of the *APA Monitor*, Smason wrote:

> We've got PhDs, PsyDs, EdDs, clinical, counseling and school psychologists… some sociopaths and God knows what out there as licensed clinicians. Let's establish one method of training, and one degree first. Then let's begin requiring

> adequate predoctoral training in psychopharmacological prescription for doctoral students in clinically oriented psychology.
>
> (1996, p. 4)

Clearly, this urgency to obtain prescription privileges threatens to narrow the field of clinical psychology and to close off dialogue and support for diversity and creative alternatives, especially those who do not follow medical models of treatment.

Yet another battle is raging around the recovered memory question, and positivistic psychological researchers with bona fide credentials can be found on both sides of the debate. The debate has been very productive and has resulted in so-called false memory syndrome advocates coming to accept that there is good evidence for amnesia for traumatic events (FMS Foundation, 1993). At the same time, psychotherapists have become much more circumspect about the epistemic status of what their clients talk to them about. The fact that the debate has become so fiercely politicized, however, taking place in the popular press, in highly publicized court proceedings, and on TV talk-shows, is part and parcel of the psychological culture wars and has resulted in erosion of public confidence in both psychological research and psychotherapy.

In criminal cases, the role of mental health practitioners as expert witnesses is also hotly contested. Advocates for psychology as an exact and predictive science are frequently challenged by others who deny any such exactitude or objective reliability to psychological testimony.

Nor can therapists turn to the seductive illusion that as the field progresses and we have more 'real data', it will be finally possible to sort out truth from politics in such cases. Arguments on either side of such complex issues as these will always be able to be convincingly bolstered by experimental research, narrative science, or phenomenological or hermeneutic science, and in some cases, all three. Unless and until different ways of knowing and different ways of addressing important existential questions can be accepted for what they are and are not capable of contributing to understandings about human welfare, any attempts to arrive at a 'truth' that can be generally applied to all human affairs are bound to lead to acrimonious and interminable debates.

Faust's therapists

As if all these internal doctrinal pressures were not enough to tear apart the fabric of the psychotherapy community, another far greater external threat is barrelling down that will alter the practice of psychotherapy beyond recognition—the managed care industry.

In many ways, the threat is the latest extension into the field of human affairs of the Faustian bargain modern societies have made between stability and progress. Positivist science and the instrumentalist worldview brought improvements in the material lives of ordinary people. The average worker in the United States today lives a longer, more comfortable, and freer life, afflicted with less illness, pain, and tragedy than any medieval king. Social progress, too, has been brought about by such important, if still imperfectly implemented, cultural innovations as democracy, abolition of slavery, equal rights, and access to education—all inventions of the modern era. These mean that ordinary people have the opportunity to become emancipated and to make life, liberty, and the pursuit of happiness a feasible project for most everyone.

However, these gains came with a price, as Alexis de Tocqueville could already perceive by the mid-1800s. The psychic losses have been enormous. Alienated from traditional ways of life, displaced from Old World communities, and brutalized by life in disease-ridden cities and 'dark satanic mills', industrialized men and women lost faith in their religions, in each other, in their relationships, and in themselves. Then, as now, large numbers lost hope, and many were driven mad. The mid-1800s saw an epidemic of drug use, violence, sexual abuse, and insanity as people lost touch with the psychic core of their existence.

Psychiatry, or 'alienism' as it was then called, was invented as a response to this alienation and for its first several decades, whole-heartedly embraced the fix-it paradigm of the industrial age. There was heavy emphasis on mechanical devices such as restraints of one sort or another, psychic surgery, and electric shocks and the administration of a range of miracle drugs like opium, chloral hydrate, and lots of cocaine, putting modernist science to the service of deranged minds. The aim of early psychiatry was to engineer satisfactory adjustment to the demands of an ordered and mechanistic modern world (Showalter, 1985). This continued to be a major purpose until the early 1940s, when philosophical movements from war-weary Europe such as existentialism met up with thinkers like Adler, Rank, Horney, and Sullivan and the earlier American psychospiritual tradition of William James, and a new humanism began to permeate American psychological thought. Out of this potent alchemy, the humanistic revolution in American psychology was born.

Humanistic psychology, uninterested in and antipathic to behavioral engineering, focused its attention on the expansion of consciousness. Although many early pioneers might have been embarrassed by the word, their interests were in soul-craft (O'Hara, 1995a). Humanistic psychologists were not satisfied with a clinical practice whose ends were adjustment to what they felt were the dehumanizing effects of modernism but strove instead to heal that which was damaged and to restore what had been lost from human experience. Practitioners set out to rehumanize psychology. Existential, humanistic, and transpersonal psychologists in particular rejected the reductionist positions of both Freudian and behaviorist psychologies—which they saw as part of the problem, not the solution. Instead, they reached back to classical humanism—both Greek and Christian Renaissance—and to the romantic transcendentalism of Rousseau, Emerson, and Thoreau and sought to create a psychology aimed at releasing the very highest aspirations from within each human soul and facilitating the achievement or evolution of higher levels of consciousness—what Maslow called a 'psychology of being'.

The therapeutic relationship was to be a place where people—not patients—were free to reconnect with their exuberant, if unruly, passions and with what was best, highest, and most sacred within and between them and to explore human life as it is experienced. Clients who were drawn to these new psychotherapies screamed their primal screams, participated in emotional psychodramas and powerful gestalt exercises; they reached into their depths, confronted their demons and their angels; they encountered each other in deep and authentic ways; they touched; they meditated, experienced rituals, rediscovered the healing power of prayer, felt joy, sometimes even ecstasy. Anything but morally neutral, as Christian fundamentalists charged, humanistic psychology was from the outset a values-based psychology, designed to be an antidote to the alienation, ethical corruption, and emptiness of modern secular, commercial, and industrialized life. Anything but nonempiricist, as positivist scientists charged; radically empiricist in the Jamesian or Deweyian sense, humanistic science attempted to return psychological research to the study of actual experience and to place at its center the meaning-making, autonomous subject.

The industrial revolution arrives in the psychotherapy neighborhood

By all measures, the arrival of managed care to the field of psychotherapy threatens to produce a paradigmatic shift as great as that brought by the humanistic movement, only in quite another direction (Kuhl, 1994). For the first time, researchers on therapy effectiveness suggest that the corporate health care budgets should be included as a significant variable in outcome assessment (Newman & Tejada, 1996). Rapid changes in health care economics such as the rising marketplace power of health maintenance organizations (HMOs), preferred provider organizations (PPOs), and other forms of managed care and the clamor for reduced government spending on entitlement programs such as Medicare and veterans benefits are forcing changes in all mental health practice that unwittingly or wittingly, depending on how paranoid you want to be, is pushing all schools of therapy—modernist, romantic, and constructivist—into a mechanistic, medical model and is attempting to push psychotherapists into work environments that have more in common with the industrial production line than with a learned profession.

The humanistic revolution in psychotherapy was led by philosophers, psychological thinkers, social critics, and psychotherapists whose cause was human emancipation. They heard in the voices of their patients and clients individual iterations of the age-old struggle to become fully human. They shared a belief that psychotherapy should be a context in which individuals could heal soulwounds inflicted by an excessively materialist culture and could realize their potential as conscious beings.

Managed care revolutionaries have different visions of their brave new world. Most do not come into contact with patients and have no commitment to any emancipatory goals, but are business executives, financiers, bureaucrats, and shareholders, looking to make money—lots of it. A recent table appeared as part of a political advertisement in *The New York Times* (on September 6, 1996), which quoted statistics on the stock wealth of some of the CEOs of the top three managed care organizations in 1995—U.S. Healthcare, Columbia/HCA, and Humana Inc. They were $795.3 million, $248.6 million, and $232.6 million, respectively.

The money motive is not the only difference. Like all revolutions, this one too has an ideological base; it encompasses its own worldview or belief system. Managed care spokespeople openly describe their revolution as the industrialization of health care and, with unconcealed enthusiasm and frequently contempt, declare that the days of 'therapy as a cottage industry' are over. What is happening to therapists in the 1990s is equated with what happened to butchers, bakers, and candlestick makers in the 1800s. Therapists are told to get on board or get out of business (Kuhl, 1994; Wiley, 1992).

To the managed care industry, psychotherapy is a commodity, indistinguishable from wheelchairs, nurses' uniforms, and open-heart surgery, delivered by interchangeable 'service delivery systems'. In old-style production line industrial processes, it is not feasible to have the line workers or consumers make design decisions, and in industrialized mental health care, therapeutic decision making becomes centralized and removed, far from the actual therapeutic context. Company policy rather than independent professional judgment determines to whom, for what, how much, what kind, and by whom treatment will be offered. An irony worth mentioning here is that as the health care industry tries to imitate the production line, other large-scale industries are giving up on centralized control. With the help of business gurus, many greatly influenced by humanistic psychology, corporate America is discovering that creativity and performance is enhanced when the people closest to the point of any transaction and those most likely to be influenced by its outcome are the ones who make the best decisions about them (see, for example, Covey, 1989; Senge, 1990).

Autonomous professionals—people with the necessary advanced education to practice independently, who have demonstrated their competence before their peers, and who agree to be bound by ethics and practices of fellow professionals—do not fit well into the managed care framework. Increasingly, the entire practice of psychotherapy is becoming dumbed-down as higher order knowledge is replaced with short-term standardized treatments that can be applied by minimally trained workers.

Even more serious is that many of the gains in the direction of autonomy and empowerment of clients, made largely as a consequence of the humanistic revolution, are being lost as clients are told which therapist they must see, what the focus of treatment will be, and that they must accept whatever treatment protocol the assessment worker recommends. They might even find themselves coerced into seeing their problem in the company's terms. A July 1995 memo to providers in a San Diego-based HMO Vista Hill (now merged with a large nationwide HMO) made this explicit when it recommended that therapists 'set the expectation from the very beginning that therapy is temporary support... Be compassionate and gently steer them toward the short term model' (Vista Hill, 1995). Last year, a utilization reviewer for a national managed care company informed me that my suggestion that a woman I was working with needed to set the pace of her own therapy was 'hand holding' and had 'no place in the new era of health care accountability'. My client had been repeatedly sexually abused by both her father and her brother, sometimes while her mother watched. When I explained to the utilization reviewer that in my professional judgment, such cases needed time to establish a strong therapeutic alliance, he recommended that I attend a seminar on brief symptom-focused treatment.

Return to the fundamental questions

Whatever else it does, the managed care revolution is forcing psychotherapists, regardless of their theoretical orientation, to revisit struggles over their core values. Some clinical orientations—particularly those in the biomedical camp—will fit well with the managed care industrialized worldview. Humanistic approaches do not fit nearly so well (see Bugental & Bracke, 1992, for a discussion on this).

Many mainstream psychotherapists are betting their future on some version of the industrialized model. As noted above, recent actions from APA's Division 12 appear to coincide with the needs of the managed care industry, as does the APA College of Professional Psychology's move toward certification of specialists in the treatment of specific symptom-defined disorders such as substance abuse. However, there is evidence that opinion may not be all that homogenous even within APA. Dorothy Cantor, the APA president in 1996, advocated fighting for psychotherapist's freedom to treat their patients in the ways their best professional judgment and the client's own sense of what is effective for them (Cantor, 1990). APA's 1997 president, Martin Seligman, although a firm advocate for empirical outcome studies, is open to consumer feedback that values longer term, more client-centered therapeutic processes (Seligman, 1995), and the *APA Monitor* prominently featured a research study that showed that the active ingredient in the treatment of 225 depressed people was the clients' active participation and the strength and duration of the therapeutic bond between therapist and client (Newsline, 1996).

Nevertheless, graduate schools are rearranging their curricula to produce the line workers for the managed care industry. Professional schools of psychology, believing that part of their mission in the future will be to produce clinicians attractive to HMOs, are dedicating more courses to mastering the medical diagnostic systems and emphasizing brief therapy approaches and deemphasizing depth approaches (O'Hara, 1996a). In 1995, the APA presented its award for educational innovation to a graduate program that had included business courses in its doctoral program. Humanistic psychotherapy—and for that matter psychodynamic, Jungian, family systems, transpersonal, or relational psychotherapies—have a very limited place in the managed care world.

A large segment of the American public is not entirely happy with the state of affairs in the medical world. We know this because of the staggering amounts of money and effort they are willing to put into alternative medical treatments not covered by their health insurance. Also, students keep on pouring into graduate psychology programs that permit studies of philosophy, humanities, political theory, religion, and the arts. New findings in the neurosciences reaffirm the holistic, nonreductionist paradigms long favored by humanistic psychologists as they undermine the more mechanistic cause and effect paradigms of behavioral psychology. Additionally, clients continue to seek out therapists who will meet them in authentic relation, even if it means making financial sacrifices. Consumers of mental health care who may not know the difference between a Rolfing and a Rorschach do know the difference between being related to as a human being or as treated as a cost to be contained. They know the difference between being confirmed as an empowered agent of their own change, and as a passive patient to be acted on (Bohart & Tallman, 1996). The American public has come to expect freedom of choice in such intimate arenas of self-care. People have already discovered the important connection between their mind, body, and spirit.

Objections to some of the more egregious problems with managed care—lack of privacy, patient and therapist disempowerment, and lack of freedom of choice—are just now getting rolling, fuelled by both professional organizations and public sentiments. Two California ballot initiatives in the 1996 election—Propositions 214 and 216—were aimed at restoring balance and accountability to an out-of-control health system that's risking patient lives and sacrifices quality of care (Ballotpedia, n.d.). Both were defeated (58%–43% and 61%–39%), but when the massive amounts of money spent by insurance companies and business interests to defeat these measures are considered, it is clear that anti-managed-care voices did fairly well. The organizers of the initiative vow to be back in two years with another try. There are also several national coalitions and local consumer groups across the nation organizing to ensure the survival of traditional psychotherapy, and many individual practitioners are refusing to practice under HMO conditions (O'Hara, 1996a).

Mental health community as a microcosm

The field of psychology represents, in microcosmic form, the crisis of values affecting the society at large. If we read the signs of the times screaming at us everywhere from Oprah, the Republican National Committee, the White House, magazines and newspapers of every political persuasion, self-help groups, and metaphysical bookshelves, we can be left in no doubt that a new generation cries out for a return to the perennial questions with which I opened this chapter.

Contemporary culture desperately needs a coherent shared vision. Part of that need is for a new psychology of wellness, of the sacred, and of empowerment; a psychology that gives meaning and significance to individual human lives, that understands the central importance of stable families and communities, and that can make room for diversity, commonality, and the possibilities for significant connections among us.

From the private lives of individuals to the workings of institutions, governance, and business, the whole culture grapples with the question of what will be its fundamental values in the coming global era. If a new story is to emerge that can provide a coherent paradigm or mythos for a 21st-century mental health culture, it is most likely to come from some reconfiguration of the humanistic tradition, together with a holistic neuroscience of mind, consciousness disciplines from non-Western cultures, and various mind–body practices, all framed in the constructivist terms of postpositivist contextualist epistemology.

From their beginnings, humanistic, feminist, and ethnic psychologists, as well as radicals like R. D. Laing and Thomas Szasz, were unapologetic—even militant—about their rejection of medicalized psychology of adjustment in favor of a growth-focused psychology of individual and group liberation and self-realization. As the world turns itself inside out, the need for practitioners committed to this emancipatory vision is more important than ever.

Economic considerations—Making a living

Noble as such goals are, can psychotherapists make a living by taking such a position and rejecting the rewards of the industrialized health care system? The answer seems to be yes. Times may actually be very promising for mental health professionals with the courage to declare their independence and offer their psychotherapy practice not as a branch of industrialized medicine but as something closer to soul-doctoring or personal development service. Unlike the 1960s, when psychotherapy was something only for the very sick or the very rich, now well over one-third of Americans of all classes, ethnicities, and creeds have experienced some form of counselling or therapy—and most would do so again. More than 30 million people every year engage in some form of psychotherapy or counselling and buy almost a billion dollars' worth of self-help books, tapes, and seminars—this latter without the benefit of third party payments. Some of this massive expenditure is for severe and debilitating forms of mental distress and people afflicted by these conditions will require financial assistance from either government or insurance. However, when strict criteria of medical necessity are applied, a great many equally important, but less catastrophic quality of life concerns will have to be provided for outside the health care system.

Demand for demedicalized psychological services is likely to be high (O'Hara, 1996a). Most Americans are now aware that there is a deep and important inner life, which can seriously hamper or profoundly enrich their daily experience. People today set higher standards for the quality of their intimate relationships, psychological, and spiritual satisfactions than any previous population. They have learned that there is help for their pain and wish to grow, that there are ways to address past traumas, anxieties, despairs, and hopes. They understand more about the relationship between the psyche, the soul, and the body than any Westerners have before them, with much of this knowledge learned from consciousness disciplines with origins beyond Western culture and imported into American popular cultures since the 1960s. In human relations training at work, in their churches, in their women's and men's groups, with therapists, in abuse recovery programs, in relationship enhancement programs, on spiritual retreats, in self-help groups, and on TV talk-shows, Americans of all kinds have enthusiastically embraced the self, relationship, and social evolution agenda of the human potential movement.

There is also an important role to be played by mental health practitioners in prevention, a role that was set aside in the 1970s, once lucrative insurance reimbursements became available for individual treatment (Sarason, 1981). The new workplace, with its emphasis on emotional intelligence, teamwork, multi-tasking, diversity, and worker empowerment and responsibility, make new and higher order mental demands on workers from the executive suite to the shop floor. After a brief period of experimentation in the early 1970s, when humanistic, affective, or confluent education could be found at all levels, American education does not see its role as one of deliberately facilitating the achievement of higher orders of relational and self-mastery. This leaves a serious and frequently stress-inducing gap between workplace demands and worker mental capacities (Kegan, 1994). A growth-oriented psychotherapy geared to workplace competence has much to offer on the level of prevention and remediation of workplace pressure.

The potential demand for higher order ways of growth is expanding rapidly as Western society prepares itself for life in the 21st century. In a recent survey of Americans, social scientist Paul Ray believes he has identified the emergence of a new demographic group within American society: the 'Culture Creatives' who are 'seriously involved with psychology, spiritual life, and self-actualisation' (Ray & Anderson, 2001). Although the study appears to have some methodological flaws, Ray's conclusions echo findings of the study of Bellah et al. (1985) a decade before, that an increasing proportion of the American people were actively engaged in a self-development agenda. For many, the values embodied by the human potential movement forms the framing conceptual scaffolding of their pursuit of happiness and fulfilment (Bellah et al., 1985). The quintessential American insistence on individual freedom as a core psychological good render them characteristically resistant to systems they find dehumanizing. We can safely predict that these 'self-formers' are the people most likely to reject industrialized mental health care and to want emancipatory, transformational, or integral forms of psychotherapy.

A theoretically reinvigorated humanistic psychology that draws on the best of its past, on constructivist developments in theory, and on the newer neurosciences and advances in mind–body studies is well placed to provide the basis of a postmodern emancipatory psychology. Once it embraces its own polycentrism and unavoidable incoherence, its core values of privileging the unique experience of individual human subjects; placing human suffering, wellbeing, and the universal need to search for meaningful answers to existential questions at its center; embracing the need to contain and comfort the high anxiety now endemic on both individual and cultural levels; and committing itself to both abatement and prevention of suffering and to the further evolution of human consciousness suggests that the humanistic tradition has much of abiding value to offer individuals and groups in a postmodern world that is in the process of being born. Outside the highly bureaucratized and increasingly centralized health care industry, where the marketplace can act like a real marketplace, people are free to buy what they are looking for from those who wish to provide it, and there will be plenty of room for dedicated and enterprising professionals to make a decent living without selling their souls to the psychoindustrial complex.

Note

1 When this was originally published, Maureen had joined Saybrook Institute as the vice president for academic affairs in February 1997 and was the executive vice president and dean of faculty. She was a former president of the Association for Humanistic Psychology and had served on the executive committee of Division 32 of the American Psychological Association and as an associate editor of *JHP*. Although her first career was as a biological scientist, she began to escape the gravitational pull of modernism after a close encounter with death, falling in love with gestalt therapy, and finally traveling the world with Carl Rogers and colleagues convening large cross-cultural encounter groups. Her recent writings at the time included articles that appeared in the *Journal of Constructivist Psychology*, the *Journal of Humanistic Psychology*, and *Family Therapy Networker*, and book chapters on relational empathy, a feminist critique of a therapy session of Carl Rogers, and a memoir.

Chapter 10

Reflections on Maureen O'Hara's writings on humanistic psychology

Maureen O'Hara and Keith Tudor

Keith: In his introduction to the original chapter (an excerpt of which forms Chapter 1 of this book), Suhd (1995) describes you as 'a brilliant writer whose works will continue to expand our understanding of social, political, and humanistic thought' (p. 104), an assessment with which I heartily agree. While the four chapters that precede this one in this part of the book represent but a small element of this contribution, they nevertheless give us readers a good sense of your humanism.

The first aspect of this that strikes me is your consistent critical perspective and edge. In one paper, you acknowledge your 'buoyant humanistic utopianism' (O'Hara, 1989c, p. 12), but this is no soft, fluffy utopianism; it is, I suggest, a socialist utopianism, forged on the streets of Shipley, against the backdrop of those 'dark Satanic Mills', and honed (to continue to quote from Blake's [1804] *Jerusalem*), by 'Mental Fight' informed by your experience of class and gender oppression (to which we referred in Chapter 2).

Maureen: I like that you note a critical fierceness in my utopian perspective. I don't remember a time when I did not have such a double edge. I always had a kind of double vision. I did experience the unfairness (oppression as we now call it) of the way life was organised to favour the powerful (especially men) and abuse the poor (both men and women) and that made me angry. But at the same time, I was a confident and happy kid who saw the resilience and grit of her community and who saw no reason that the world could not be better for me and everyone else. So, I called out the injustice I saw around me and at the same time sought paths to cultural change that would level the playing field and create nourishing spaces where everyone had the chance to reach their full potential.

Keith: You're welcome. How could I not notice it!

The other strong thread to your critique and in your work derives from feminism, an early example of which is represented in your paper 'Our foremothers as gurus' (Chapter 8).[1] Two things about this strike me. The first is that you seem to find a way of acknowledging

DOI: 10.4324/9781003519454-13

differences between woman and men without collapsing into essentialism; and the second is your astute observation of the irony of—and, I imagine, deep frustration with—men turning to an idealised other, such as an Eastern guru, somewhere over there, rather than to the wise woman who may be standing next to them.

Maureen: I think you're right; I was sometimes frustrated, and never more than those occasions where I would hear my words or those of other wise women coming out of the mouth—without attributions I might add—of some esteemed man. Looking back, I see that my approach to such ironies has been to look for ways around them. I saw early that the one dimension of life I was deficient in was the effective and non-exploitative use of power, be that personal, interpersonal, or institutional. I set out quite deliberately to acquire such capacity and find ways to make a difference despite all that stands in the way of making a difference. I handled frustration by avoiding direct confrontation with it and instead seeking out spaces in which I could be heard, and I worked collaboratively with other women to create such spaces for others, and once in those spaces I learned how to avoid frustration by acting to change things. Bit by bit I found myself in settings where I was asked to take leadership roles and, whereas earlier I would have avoided what I feared would be frustration and failure, I gradually claimed my authority and capacity to have an impact. When, after several years as a board member, I was elected first as president of the Association for Humanistic Psychology and then the Society for Humanistic Psychology, a division of the American Psychological Association and ultimately as president of Saybrook Graduate School,[2] I felt ready to test what I had learned about how to handle power and frustration in a (still) patriarchal world.

Keith: What you're representing here—and elsewhere, notably in this collection in Chapter 1—is the autobiographical nature of theory or of our engagement with theory. In your paper on 'Relational humanism' (Chapter 9), you acknowledge that: 'firmly established theories and practices—whether medical model or humanistic—are based on modernist worldviews reflecting the habits of mind, realities, and values of the people who are inventing them' (p. 64). I suggest that, equally, the theories to which we're drawn are influenced by our worldviews, as well as changing worldviews, and, of course, in saying that, I'm aware that your reference to 'medical… or humanistic' applies to you. Before we get on to the aspects of your humanism represented in these papers, will you say a bit about how your background in natural science influenced and, indeed, may still influence your humanistic psychology?

Maureen: Of course, you are right. The relationship between the theories with which we resonate, and which illuminate what we already accept as 'real' or 'true' is reciprocal. We read and understand the world through the languages and cultural practices we already know, and as thinkers and practitioners we are drawn to theories to which we are primed by our history to see as a good fit with our experience. As the humourist Ashleigh Brilliant put it (Figure 10.1), 'I wouldn't have seen it if I hadn't believed it'.[3]

My life as a mid-20th-century European research cell biologist provided conceptual frameworks from within a modernist, objectivist paradigm with all the social norms that that encompasses. At the same time, though, my doctoral supervisor Professor Manton and her colleague philosopher Michael Polanyi whom she quoted repeatedly in our graduate seminars stressed that even scientific knowledge is fundamentally—and inescapably—personal. This reinsertion of the human subject into science primed me for humanistic theories like Rogers' and gestalt which by the 1970s had all but abandoned objectivism and were celebrating the epistemic legitimacy of persons with multiple ways of knowing situated within diverse cultural communities. Beyond the influence of my admittedly unorthodox scientific socialisation, the fact that my field was cell biology rather than, say, physics was also influential in my attraction to humanistic psychology. The language of 'growth', 'organismic process', 'organism', 'actualisation tendency', 'experience', 'sensing', 'becoming', and 'evolution', for instance, are concepts that are shared with biology. The idea that growth takes place driven by an inherent tendency to fully realise its inherent possibilities is a biological proposition as is the later ecological idea that such organismic growth occurs through synergistic webs of influence. These ideas form the basis of humanistic approaches. When I encountered the work of Rogers and other humanistic psychologists, I was instantly at home and, despite having taken not even one class in psychology, was

Figure 10.1 Seeing is believing (Brilliant, 1979)

able to find resonance with my own keen desire carried over from my life as a biologist to get closer to what it means to be fully alive.

Keith: Thanks. That makes a lot of sense and gives me—and others—more background as to why you not only represent the organismic basis and tradition of person-centred psychology and the PCA,[4] but also see this also and more broadly in humanistic psychology.

A central feature of your critical view of humanistic psychology is your emphasis on context, what you refer to (in Chapter 7) as 'socio-cultural landscapes' (p. 65). In that one paper alone, you deconstruct—or at least point to the necessity of deconstructing—concepts, including: 'I', 'self' (and 'myself'), 'is', 'autonomy', 'individual', 'self-concept', 'personhood' (and, thus, 'person'), 'subjectivity', 'experience', 'freedom', 'authenticity', and, by implication, much more!

Given that this was written in 1992, I think you were ahead of your time, not least, as both these chapters and that on 'Emancipatory therapeutic practice' (Chapter 9) strike me as very contemporary. I guess my question is, how come this perspective hasn't become more mainstream within humanistic psychology which still has some of the essentialism you discuss in your paper on 'Constructing emancipatory realities' (Chapter 8)?

Maureen: This a question I have asked myself many times without really arriving at a satisfactory answer. We need a little context here.

What makes generalising about humanistic psychology such a challenge is that from the very beginning, the field was theoretically and philosophically incoherent and still is. In the 1960s, psychologists who had mounted individual critiques of the shrunken views of human beings offered by both Freudians and behaviourists came together at the invitation of Abraham Maslow with the aim of establishing a new movement within psychology that would embrace humanity's full potential and would use research methods that were qualitative, phenomenological, and holistic. The group was decidedly male, White, and European and included Carl Rogers, Rollo May, Houston Smith, Victor Frankl, Eric Fromm, James Bugental, Clark Moustakas, Gregory Bateson, George Kelly, and Alan Watts, among others (Aanstoos et al., 2000). Though they shared a common antipathy towards dominant psychological theories, as a group they were heterogeneous and embraced diverse and sometimes incompatible viewpoints. This has resulted in theoretical fragmentation—even tribalism—where factions have gone on to create their own professional organisations, licences, separate journals, schools for training, forms of practice, and distinct worldviews.

After the identification of humanistic psychology as a 'third force', almost immediately there was a call for a fourth force 'transpersonal psychology' that would make room for realms of consciousness beyond the personal. Debate among the adherents of the different theories has been especially intense about such core concepts such as 'self', 'autonomy', 'individual', 'self-concept', 'personhood' (and, thus, 'person'), 'subjectivity', 'experience', 'freedom', 'authenticity', and 'consciousness'. Today psychological work is conducted that still reflects the various participants in Maslow's efforts which ranges from essentialist depth psychology to contextual emancipatory views. Most exciting for me is represented in the work of the Society for Humanistic Psychology's (APA Division 32) Task Force on Indigenous Psychology. One of its aims is to cultivate alternative cultural paradigms (ACPs) that address both the personal and cultural experiences of indigenous populations who have been victims of White brutality and seeks to facilitate emancipatory progress (Gone, 2022). This work reframes many of the old debates by deconstructing hegemonic constructs such as the ones listed here and, instead, exploring psychological concepts from within their particular cultural and historical contexts.

There are some conceptual transformations—avalanches as I describe them (see Chapter 1)—that are irreversible, when concepts that had once seemed 'baked in' suddenly appear malleable and their meaning dependent on their context. For me, such a transformation occurred around 1984 when I first encountered the emerging conversations about 'reality' that came under the umbrella 'postmodern'. At the time, I was still working in Brazil six months a year and spent a lot of time with young people who were in the throes of political change from dictatorship to democracy. Psychologists and educators were fired up about the revolutionary potential of the idea of radical plasticity in social and personal realities and sought practices by which to create change on personal and collective levels. Freire's work was a touchstone for those who looked forward to an open and free society which would be the crucible for a new creativity. The notion that one's 'self'—one's ways of being—was not predetermined, but, rather, was an emergent result of life in particular worlds, moved the focus of Brazilian humanistic psychotherapy and my own from the inner world to the social context. From then onwards, my interest moved to the person–community–person dynamic interface. The idea of a 'real self' abstracted from their context (which Rogers and others had described) gave way to a search for practices that could result in cultural transformations that would support growth and well-being in persons and their communities. What I found, however, was that among many of my American colleagues, the focus on change at a cultural level was less urgent. Americans—at least White, male Americans and the affluent women who attended humanistic events—were more essentialist—that is, interested in personal growth, individual freedom, and the search for transcendence. The contextual critique moved to the marginalised groups—women, African Americans, Latinx, LGBTQ, and people with disabilities—who put the critiques to use in their own emancipatory projects on their own terms.

Keith: Wow! Thanks, Maureen, for such a comprehensive and useful answer. As you acknowledge in the email you sent about this exchange, the question and answer could—and perhaps should—prompt a(nother) book!

There's a lot in what you write to which I relate, connect, and associate[5]—and, I am sure, readers of this book also will do. I think that what you say links well to the other two papers in this Part in which (in Chapter 8) you elaborate some alternatives to humanistic individualism, including the concept of relational selves, and values of mutuality, and diversity; and (in Chapter 9) go further and elaborate an emancipatory therapeutic practice which acknowledges 'a more sociopolitical path' (p. 74).

For myself, I am particularly appreciative of you introducing me to the APA's Task Force on Indigenous Psychology of which I have now been a member—I would say an ally member—for some years. This relates to one aspect of this discussion I'd like to pick up from another paper—on 'Values for a pluralistic world'—which is the idea that, as you put it 'our "truths" are a whole lot more local than we realised' (O'Hara, 1992a, p. 42). I relate this to the idea of local knowledge (van der Ploeg, 1993), as applied to therapy by Totton (1999), especially as it relates to indigenous knowledge, epistemology, and, therefore, practice.

Maureen: Yes, van der Ploeg's observation of how knowledge is local and often related to the crafts and labour routines in which they participate is relevant here, as is Nick Totton's notion of 'wild psychotherapy'. My Mexican colleague, Erica Camarena, who trained in expressive arts therapy with Natalie Rogers,[6] does workshops with Oaxacan villagers which aim to help indigenous people keep their local knowledge alive as they participate in the production of their art (O'Hara, 2024). A significant consequence to seeing perception and sense of reality as local and personal is that we can no longer rely on our treasured abstractions as a basis for psychotherapeutic practice. We have to get concrete and phenomenological and drop the labels and categorisation. 'Diagnosis' of 'psychopathology' for instance, only makes sense within a locality of medicine and mental illness. A Oaxacan artist has no need of them unless forced to interface with the health care system. I use the term 'psychosphere' to refer to those aspects of particular contexts—symbols, language, rituals, life patterns, economic systems, and explanatory narratives—that organise mental life.

Keith: Yes, and, of course, this is consistent with the critical perspective and deconstruction you offer in Chapter 8 with regard to 'reality' and 'nature'.

As we end this particular reflection, how would you summarise the role that humanistic psychology still has to play in our world?

Maureen: I would say that the general lack of critical consciousness and the rise of autocracy and fascism, even in industrialised democratic cultures that have taken democracy and human rights as a stable state of affairs, suggests a need for humanistic psychology to return to the work of facilitating empowerment of persons, increasing awareness of diverse voices and ways of life, and accepting human responsibility to co-create a sustainable and just future. In the 21st century, 60 years on from Rogers' and Freire's seminal contributions (discussed in Chapter 5), we can embrace a wider spectrum of human knowledge that includes science-based knowledge and respects the need for sacred and transcendent experiences at the same time as we remain critically alert to the manipulative potential of both.

Keith: Rawe! (Excellent) I'd like to finish this dialogue by quoting from one of my favourite English musicians and activists, Billy Bragg, which I think echoes some of the language(s) you use with regard to humanism, as well as your political perspective:

> I kept the faith and I kept voting
> Not for the iron fist but for the helping hand
> For theirs is a land with a wall around it
> And mine is a faith in my fellow man
> Theirs is a land of hope and glory
> Mine is the green field and the factory floor
> Theirs are the skies all dark with bombers
> And mine is the peace we knew
> Between the wars.
>
> (Bragg, 1984)[7]

Notes

1 See also O'Hara (1989b, 1996b [Chapter 17]).
2 From 1996 to 2006.
3 Brilliant (1979), reproduced with permission.
4 I note this as I don't take it for granted—see Tudor and Worrall (2006), Tudor (2010b, 2013, 2022b), and Neville and Tudor (2024).
5 Some of which may be found in Tudor (2010a, 2015, 2018a, 2018b, 2018c, 2021).
6 See N. Rogers (1993/2000, 2011), and N. Rogers et al. (2012).
7 BETWEEN THE WARS
Words and Music by STEPHEN WILLIAM BRAGG
© 1985 WARNER CHAPPELL MUSIC LTD (PRS)
All rights administered by WC Music Corp.
All Rights Reserved
Used by Permission of ALFRED MUSIC.

Part III

Third force science

Chapter 11

A hundredth monkey myth (1983)

Maureen O'Hara[1]

Bob Flasher's (1983) essay seems an example of the very problem I see facing the humanistic 'collective'. Bob has apparently accepted Watson's (1979) assertion that instantaneous transmission of knowledge across natural barriers does in fact occur. Flasher never says on what evidence or basis he admits this belief. My point is that this claim has yet to be substantiated. I still stand by that. If Bob Flasher or Lyall Watson or anyone else can come up with evidence more solid than hearsay regarding *speculations* which Japanese scientists (over 20 years ago) were reluctant to discuss publicly, no one would be more excited than I. Watson and Flasher clearly have the right and responsibility to hold their own beliefs and to base them upon whatever they wish. But, if they wish me to share their belief, the burden of substantiation is on them.

The burden of substantiation was also upon all the luminaries Flasher credits with effecting most of the positive changes in society. What makes luminaries is not, it seems to me, that people swim against the current until their ideas bring about a general consensus, as Bob suggests, but rather it is because they accept the burden of substantiation *impeccably*. In their different spheres of knowledge, they hold out their discoveries and their passions about the nature of things. *And they back it up.*

I believe they expect me to bring my whole being, my past, my knowledge, my experience, my heart, and my mind to the task of deciding for myself if what they are showing me—their truth and the basis for it—is more truthful than what I had previously believed. When Martin Luther King, Jr. says, 'I have a dream…', he doesn't stop there. He lays out concrete examples of what he means by injustice for me to come to grips with. I don't believe King because he is a consummate orator; I believe him because *I* now see the world differently. The great teachers, poets, mystics, social reformers, scientists, or sages ask me to reflect. They trust me to be fully human, to bring all my capacities of selectivity, creativity, and evaluation to independently and consciously come to my own understanding. This trust is precisely what is missing in those who resort to demagoguery, using techniques of propaganda, manipulation, coercion, and indoctrination.

Flasher seems to have bridled at my insistence on the need for rational thought. If by saying that rational thought is not sufficient he means abstract analysis and

DOI: 10.4324/9781003519454-15

critique is not sufficient on its own, then I could not agree with him more. It is clearly insufficient, but it is necessary.

There are times when we are called upon to abstract, to identify, differentiate, separate, and *even* judge. I believe now is one of those times for humanistic psychology. Jesus certainly did this when he separated from the Pharisees; as did Gandhi when he resisted the British, as is Helen Caldicott now doing as she exposes and debates (with demonstrable facts) the 'survivable nuclear war' fallacy; and as the people of Poland are now doing. But, for these people, the purpose of analysis and judgement is not to establish divisions between people, but the opposite. Their critique of the status quo is informed by a strong urge for the creation of a more harmonious unity—it is informed by strong feelings, by spiritual beliefs, and by love; aspects of our lives eminently rational.

Most of the highly complex problems and challenges of our collective predicament require of us both critical analysis and creative synthesis.

Another point which Bob's essay prompts me to touch upon comes from his emphasis on the role of leadership in social events. It brings to mind a line from the movie *Convoy*. Burt Reynolds is driving a truck at the head of the convoy. He is asked at one point if he is the leader. If my memory serves me, his reply was to the effect, 'Hell no! I'm not the leader I'm just in front'. An abiding assumption in our culture is that it is the influence of powerful leaders (monarchs, politicians, scientists, artists, prophets, generals, and the like) that brings about social transformation. This is an assumption worth examining. When Carl Rogers attributes the extent of the influence of his work to having offered the 'right idea *at the right time*', I believe he is expressing a profound and largely overlooked dimension of social reality.

Another reasonable way to view the process of history is possible. Rather than seeing the acknowledged leaders as bringing about these changes, it is reasonable to see the leaders themselves as products of changes already occurring in the collective consciousness. Rather than making the common consensus, perhaps the more sensitive are pushed by it.

This is not to minimize the importance of individual acts of imagination (or perfidy) but to do the opposite. I wish only to re-emphasize the importance of a collective composed of people willing to think critically and clearly. Whichever way we look at human history, we are still called upon by our human condition—our covenant with ourselves, each other, the global community and with the future—to act responsibly.

I know I have come a long way from monkeys so now I wish to return to them. One of the findings of the study (Koshima Island) was that no monkey ever did anything to actively teach another monkey—even its own child. I carefully did not say (as Bob indicates one did) that monkey mothers taught 100% of their offspring. I said that 100% of the offspring learned (sweet potato washing) from their mothers. The survival and inventiveness of monkeys depend not on their capacity to *teach* but on their eagerness to *learn*.

In conclusion, I want to make clear that my thesis is not that ideas do not spread rapidly through the collective 'mind' from time to time, nor is it that such events cannot bring about rapid changes in human society. I know that such events occur. General Motors knows it, James Watt knows it, Bagwan Rajneesh knows it, my mother knows it. My concern is how we can ensure that this collective 'mind' is *wise*, capable of responding to complex interpenetrated webs of common and often competing demands upon the global community's resources.

I am proposing that the hope for the evolution of a *wise* human collective lies in the exercise of the most human of all our capacities—the search for knowledge through thoughtful engagement with life and its mysteries (instead of unscrutinized speculation proffered as knowledge). We must try to understand how human society works, how we make mistakes, how we influence our reality. We must go into action informed by both our aspirations and our knowledge. And above all, we must be eager to learn from what we have done to be even more knowledgeable the next time we act.

Is this a job for monkeys?

Note

1 When this was published, Maureen was a board member and resident fellow at the Center for Studies of the Person and had worked with Carl Rogers investigating large group phenomena. She was formerly a biochemist, and was working with John K. Wood on a book on 'consciousness and group mind'.

Chapter 12

Science, pseudoscience, and mythmongering (1988)

Maureen O'Hara[1]

It's a fine thing to have an open mind—but not so open so as your brains fall out.
(attributed to an Episcopalian bishop)[2]

I first became involved with the whole question of the relationship between science and pseudoscience and New Age[3] thinking when I was researching an article for the *Journal of Humanistic Psychology* (*JHP*), debunking the thenpopular 'Hundredth Monkey' story—the widely promoted New Age myth that if enough monkeys could be persuaded to wash their sweet potatoes, something called a 'critical mass' would be formed, which would result in mind-to-mind knowledge transfer wherein all monkeys in and around Koshima Island would instantaneously take up potato washing. In that article, I tried to show how the so-called 'Hundredth Monkey Phenomenon' was a myth and a cryptofascist myth at that (O'Hara, 1985b). In another article for *JHP* (O'Hara, 1984b), I argued that another New Age notion, Rupert Sheldrake's hypothesis of 'morphic resonance',[4] was not a fine example of 'real new age science' (whatever that is), as had been suggested by New Age writer Ken Wilbur.

I had argued that it was, in fact, reductionist pseudoscientific clap-trap, which had nothing at all to offer real students of human nature (O'Hara, 1984b). In both these articles, and in subsequent writings and presentations for similar audiences, I have tried to explore what for me are the more interesting, and I believe ultimately more important, psychological, political, and philosophical questions that emerge when we look at stories like the 'Hundredth Monkey', theories like 'morphic resonance', and the whole cultural phenomenon of so-called New Age thinking. In particular, I have tried to understand what it is that makes members of professional organizations like the Association for Humanistic Psychology so vulnerable to pseudoscientific scams, paranormal claims, quantum flim-flam, and all manner of psychological ideas and ideologies that are often based on nothing more than popular acclaim and successful marketing. How do we account for the enormous fascination and gullibility of a broad spectrum of well-educated, well-meaning, largely middle-class Americans when presented with claims of the miraculous, magical, or paranormal? What are we to make of the obvious fact that rational people can be so

DOI: 10.4324/9781003519454-16

easily conned by Shirley MacLaine's 'trance-channelers' or be so willing to hand over a thousand or so dollars to walk over 'hot' embers?

I ask these questions as an insider, sympathetic—even enthusiastic—to the broader aims of those involved with humanistic approaches in psychology and with the consciousness movements. I have experienced many of the spiritual longings—and satisfactions—spoken of by such denizens of the New Age as Jean Houston and Ken Wilbur. For the last 17 years, I have worked all over the world with psychologist Carl Rogers, trying to put many of the principles highly prized by New Age writers to the test of concrete action. We have done this in villages in technologically underdeveloped nations and in elite universities in Europe, and Rogers himself has taken the work to Moscow and South Africa. I make my living as a humanistic psychologist, and I teach feminist studies at a university. I also serve on the board of the Association for Humanistic Psychology and as an associate editor of its journal.

It is precisely because I have such a stake in humanistic psychology, in what truly is a worldwide network of committed folks working in widely ranging settings to further humanistic values, that I think it is worthwhile—indeed urgent—to try to tease out some of the nonsense that has crept (flooded?) into humanistic psychology in recent years.

What began 25 years ago as a serious and successful challenge to Freudian and behaviorist orthodoxy in psychology quickly blossomed into a broader social movement calling for a greater democratization of American life. Humanistic psychology and its applied wing, the 'human potential' movement, invented techniques, theories, and attitudes that transformed the way we think of counselling, education, and even business management. It is doubtful whether these ideas could have been so phenomenally successful if its early leaders had not been superb scholars and thinkers dedicated to research excellence.

The Rogerian idea, for example, that a therapist's warmth, acceptance, genuineness, and willingness to listen were all that were necessary for effective psychotherapy was considered radical when first proposed. Now these ideas are taught to every mental-health professional as the *sine qua non* of good therapeutic practice. Rogers' work had credibility with practicing professionals and established academic psychologists because he was a brilliant thinker who based his claims on concrete, practical knowledge, and subjected his hypotheses to the most rigorous scientific evaluation.

The best of humanistic psychology is very good and offers, in my view, one of the only visions of human possibilities with the potential to guide us toward the next century and beyond. However, if we are to realize this potential and not become bogged down in ultimately empty—though perhaps deeply comforting—superstition, if we are not to be lured into a metaphysical dead-end by New Age Pied Pipers, we will need to take a hard look at our gullibility.

My intention here is to speak to people who are sympathetic to the humanistic vision, even in its New Age persona, and yet are willing to consider the movement with a critical eye.

Professional authority—Professional responsibility

Although I have aimed my arguments toward readers who would approve of the aims and methods of humanistic psychology, I must acknowledge that much of what I want to say is applicable not only to them. Obviously, it takes more than the 5,000 members of an organization like the Association for Humanistic Psychology, for example, to make best-sellers out of books like Marilyn Ferguson's *Aquarian Conspiracy*, Fritjof Capra's *The Tao of Physics*, Lyall Watson's *Lifetide*, and Rupert Sheldrake's *A New Science of Life*. Nor are we the only people who have been fooled by scams like the hundredth-monkey story; firewalking; 'Senoi Dreamwork'; spoonbending psychics; Carlos Casteneda's fantastic fabrications; mediums who claim to communicate with animals, visitors from far-off galaxies, dead relatives, and spirits of all manner of departed sages; and quackery both physiological and psychological. In many respects, humanistic psychologists are no different from perhaps the majority of people in American society. We all have, as William James (1896) once observed, a strong 'will to believe', but we seem to have neither the will nor the intellectual discipline to critique our beliefs.

Despite its small size, the Association for Humanistic Psychology and its publications have had a disproportionately large impact on the cultural picture of late 20th-century America. Its members have included Abraham Maslow, Carl Rogers, Rollo May, Gregory Bateson—all founders—as well as Fritjof Capra, Marilyn Ferguson, Charles Hamden-Turner, Jean Houston, Walter Truitt Anderson, Frances Vaughan, Michael Marien, Jim Bugental, and Virginia Satir, who are all active members today.

Our association is composed of bright, committed seekers dedicated to the advancement of human life through knowledge. In all our publications and public statements, it is clear that members wish to be taken seriously as professional scholars with the authority to advance human knowledge. We ask that our utterances be given credence, be considered valid, and duly established as 'real' by the public in the way that the reports of scientists are. A large proportion of our association's membership also offers services for a fee. A recent National Research Council report (Eisenberg et al., 1998) estimates that American corporations spend at least $30 billion on these kinds of services.

In claiming professional authority for their statements and propositions, members of a scholarly community tacitly agree to hold themselves and each other to higher standards of thinking and scholarly research, critical judgment, and professional integrity than is incumbent on the general public. In other words, when an organization or profession claims its truths are 'established' and offers them to the public so it can disseminate the 'new reality', they have an obligation to offer the public more than they can get in the *National Enquirer*.

How then are we to account for such a willingness on the part of serious people who are genuinely dedicated to search for truth to accept all manner of extraordinary and bogus claims with such eager enthusiasm?

The simple answer is that people are people. There is a great deal of research that shows that all people, but especially highly intelligent people, are easily taken in by all kinds of illusions, hallucinations, self-deceptions, and outright bamboozles—all the more so when they have a high investment in the illusion being true.

Many writers and speakers popular with New Age audiences are describing wondrous new powers that they believe are emerging in the human psyche. They herald new consciousness, new ways of perceiving reality, and so on. This is heady stuff. It is the kind of optimistic dream-spinning that drew me, as a young college teacher, out of the biological sciences and into the humanistic science of persons. However, if this capacity for wonderment is not to lead to a fool's paradise, or worse, I think we need to remind ourselves and each other that such openness also has its pitfalls. A short review of some of what we know about ourselves psychologically might illustrate just how vulnerable to perceptive errors we really are.

If I hadn't believed it, I wouldn't have seen it

Our experience of reality can never be entirely accounted for by stimulus alone. It is always a construct based on our perceptions and interpretations of things—not the things alone....

Probably everyone has had the auditory hallucination of hearing a phone while in the shower, for example. The components of this hallucination are twofold. One element is the perceptual set—the web of memories, concepts of reality, imaginations, and expectations connected to any experience—the other is the actual here-and-now sensory excitation due to the effect of sound vibrations on sense organs. Part of our perceptual set might be the belief that someone 'always calls when we are in the shower' (Connor, 1984). It is created through a combination of folklore and a process of paying more attention to experiences that conform to our beliefs than those that do not. We register hits and ignore misses. (In science-dominated, technological societies like ours, for example, 'folklore sets' are frequently solidified by claims that there is 'scientific' evidence for the phenomenon.)

It is not carelessness. Our perceptual capacities are designed to single out what is interesting and to ignore what isn't. They are also designed to construct coherence, predictability, and reasonableness out of ambiguous or chaotic stimuli. The sound of running water has sufficient ambiguity that the mindset can prevail over the physical stimulus and can create a ringing out of the frequencies present in the sound of running water. If one's folk belief is influenced by Alfred Hitchcock, the mind has no difficulty creating the sound of approaching footsteps out of the same water!

I clearly remember once as a child, the whole of England agonized for almost two weeks over the fate of Captain Carlson on the bridge of his badly listing S. S. Flying Enterprise. One evening on the way home from school the cumulus clouds above me seemed to me to be an exact replica of the doomed ship. I watched it fascinated, and when the cloud slowly rolled over in the sky I wept, 'knowing' that Captain Carlson had perished. I learned on the next newsreels that he in fact had been saved, but my experience had been so strong that I was unwilling to believe this good news.

The perpetuation of the 'Hundredth Monkey' phenomenon myth within the New Age community gives another wonderful illustration of this process.

At the time the story first appeared, there was already a widely held pre-existing folk belief that we were witnessing the dawn of the New Age of Aquarius, in which minority ideas might become universally accepted once a certain number, called a 'critical mass', had been converted.[5] Then along came Lyall Watson, supposedly producing objective scientific evidence of such a phenomenon in monkeys. His 'scientific data' were used to bolster the collective perceptual set. Wherever groups of folks with New Age inclinations met, whether at an EST seminar, an encounter group, a New Age gathering of some sort, and if those assembled came to a consensus (a highly prized situation for most of them) and began to feel or think the same way about something, someone in the group would likely recount the monkey story. The group would count a 'hit' and believe they now had more evidence for the 'reality' of the phenomenon. All counterexamples would be ignored or rationalized, and other ambiguous stimuli—i.e., situations that are complex enough to read anything into—would be interpreted as examples of the phenomenon.

It should be easy to see how, if you take as your 'field of data' something as vast as 'modern culture', and if you come at it with a strong mindset, you will be able to discern some kind of 'new process paradigm' for which you can find 'supporting evidence'. Only of course you didn't find it—you produced it!

We are all aware of how eyewitness reports of accidents or crimes vary a good deal (Loftus, 1979). There is also evidence that what is remembered of an accident will be greatly influenced by subsequent suggestion. In one experiment, when an interviewer suggested to witnesses of an accident that a blue car had been present, subsequent eyewitness descriptions included the blue car. In another experiment, graduate students were shown videotapes of a group meeting in which participants appeared only in silhouette. When they thought participant 'Lou' was the only Black in an otherwise White group, raters said Lou was very active, almost to the point of domination; when observers believed the group to be racially balanced, however, nothing unusual was noticed about Lou. This kind of 'singling out the token' has been confirmed for other minorities and women (Kanter, 1975). Observations are usually biased in the direction of whatever belief the observer has about the situation.

We are easily fooled both by others and by ourselves. Professional magicians will tell you that the more intelligent a person is, the more easily he or she can be fooled. When you point your finger, for example, an adult will look away from the finger to the point indicated, but a child and a dog will look at your finger. The magician's ability to fool the spectator lies in 'leading his audience down a (conceptual) path but not going there himself' (Ganoe & Kirwan, 1984, p. 133).

Another well-documented characteristic of the human mind is that, if presented with a conceptual or perceptual field with gaps in it, we will fill in the missing elements and we will believe that we have seen them.

This is especially true of bright and agile minds. An agile mind will make connections where none is actually given. This is, of course, the basis of all creativity. The artist and scientist may begin with only the rudiments of an idea and be able to see within it the reality of the finished work. It is also the basis of much psychotherapy. Therapists help clients pull out seemingly disconnected images and memories which, at a moment of insight, suddenly become reorganized and elaborated into enlightening new understandings about their whole life predicament.

If a mindset is very strong, it may even prevail over contradicting information that is not at all ambiguous, as shown in a recent experiment with students at California State University at Long Beach (Singer & Benassi, 1980–1981). To examine the willingness of people to accept claims of paranormal or psychic powers, two researchers had a young amateur magician perform for their class a short magic routine containing some of the standard 'psychic' illusions—metal bending by mind power ('telekinesis' in the psi world), reading numbers while blindfolded (clairvoyance), and materializing sacred ashes from the palms of a young woman. Half the classes were told the magician was a conjurer who was going to perform magic tricks and who wanted to get feedback on his act. The other half were told he was a psychic and wanted feedback about his psychic powers. Singer and Benassi (1980–1981) were stunned to find 77 percent of the students believed the magician's claim to be psychic on the basis of three simple magic tricks. They were even more stunned to learn that 65 percent of those who had been told Craig was a stage magician doing conjuring tricks still were convinced he was psychic.

In the success of charlatans, fakes, quacks, and conjurors—whether consciously perpetrated, as with professional con-artists and entertainers, or innocently promoted by people who genuinely believe they are in the possession of special powers or have witnessed or discovered new realities—the greatest ally is the fallibility of human consciousness itself.

Openness—The good news and the bad news

We have very strong social needs to trust other people. As children, we must learn from others. Vulnerable creatures like us could never learn all we need to know quickly enough to survive in a hostile environment were it not for trusting others to pass on what they know and believe. We are, therefore, especially open to people who create an aura of trustworthiness. Psychotherapists, physicians, educators, and parents all rely on trust to do their work. Successful psychics, telepaths, mediums, pseudoscientists, magicians, and con-artists also present the appearance of being trustworthy. Many are also very bright, handsome, and charismatic. The air of trustworthiness is often bolstered by biographical material indicating altruistic motives, aligning themselves with 'good works' and keeping a financially modest profile, at least at first.[6]

Folks who are drawn to New Age ideas are unusually trusting people. They have enormous goodwill, believe themselves to be nonjudgmental, and express faith in the basic goodness of people.[7] Implicit in their positive regard of human nature is the obvious imperative to place a high value on acceptance, open-mindedness, and willingness to give others the benefit of the doubt, especially those who bring good news. This creates a wonderful environment for trial balloons, where new ideas—whimsical, serious, inspirational, foolish, trivial, and important—can be generated, entertained, and explored. New Age gatherings are hospitable to all kinds of new ideas. A list of conference speakers and workshops sponsored and promoted by the Association for Humanistic Psychology over the last 25 years, for example, will reveal just how hospitable.[8]

While acknowledging its positive aspects—who can say anything against tolerance?—there is a major problem in being so undiscriminating. Without reliable, agreed-upon criteria with which to test and evaluate these trial balloons, potentially valuable ideas and innovations cannot be sorted from those without merit. After a while, trial balloons become simply balloons—pretty but disposable. This puts anyone seriously interested in furthering studies in humanistic psychology between a rock and a hard place. Some choose to avoid the mess by invalidating the whole field, declaring humanistic psychology dead, killed off by the 'New Age' fringe within it. This is the choice being made by more and more of the established graduate schools of psychology as they turn back to psychoanalysis and ego-psychology in the clinical schools and to cognitive and behavioral psychology in the research schools. However, those who, like me, still believe humanistic scholarship has something significant and distinct to contribute to the search for understanding and knowledge of the human condition and who wish to ask the kind of questions only the humanistic movement within psychology has addressed, there is no current alternative but to be willing to swallow an awful lot of chaff along with our wholewheat.

Science and certainty

When I speak at gatherings of humanistic psychologists, I usually encounter considerable anti- and pseudo-scientific sentiments. I frequently find myself having to explain to the New Age contingent of my humanistic brethren what 'science' really is. The image of the mainstream scientist held by most New Agers is of a person, usually a White male, with no feelings, no spiritual yearnings, and who is probably oblivious to both the darker applications of his craft and the magical possibilities of the human mind. The image of 'science' is of a completely rational, reductionistic power-trip where 'linear or left-brained thinking' and closed-mindedness predominate. At times, the New Age response to science can become downright hostile. On a telephone call recently, one New Age advocate, wanting a place in a conference I was working on, called me a narrow-minded dogmatist; my attitudes, he felt, were divisive and demonstrated dangerous elitism.

Nothing could be further from the truth. Science, as a way of apprehending nature, was invented for people exactly like today's seekers by people like them. Folks who wish to understand their world, to look beyond the present limited visions, who wish to open themselves to novelty and to creative achievement, to dream of new worlds and then work to bring them about, need some kind of science. We humanistic psychologists and New Agers need it precisely because of our openness and because, like all agile-minded people, we can be so easily fooled. If we are not to exist in a confusing 'Alice in Wonderland' world of uncertainty, where real and imagined are interchangeable, where we are, like the schizophrenic, at the mercy of our imaginations, prejudices, and ignorances—as well as of those who would bamboozle us for their own purposes—we need a way to separate what might possibly be true from what is actually true (Jacob, 1982).

This problem of uncertainty as to what and what is not 'real' has been with us since the dawn of culture, but before the rise of modern science. The problem was taken care of for laypeople by varied priesthoods, vested with the authority to speak for God and to declare truth for everyone else. Entry to a priest class was always closely restricted by the ruling classes, and access to their knowledge was jealously guarded. In Christian Europe, for example, where scholarship was restricted to monasteries and Christianrun universities, no infidels or women needed apply!

With the Copernican revolution, this began to change. Over the 300 or so years since the beginning of the scientific revolution, there has been a steady erosion of priestly authority in matters of what is true, natural, preternatural, supernatural, and divine. We have seen in its place the rise in secular authority in general and of scientific authority in particular. The will and courage to doubt—often at great personal cost, both social and psychological—that lies at the heart of the scientific quest led to the development of processes with which to systematically question and evaluate the grounds for beliefs, collect evidence, suspect one's prejudices, hypothesize, test and theorize, and so on, all the processes that we now recognize as comprising the scientific approach to the quest for knowledge.

Authority to name truth was wrested away from dogmatism and papal fiat with the hope that universal, impersonally derived, abstract principles—some kind of litmus test for truth—could be discovered that would, on the one hand, free us forever from the priestly tyranny of, say, an Inquisition, Khomeini's Iran, or a Stalin's Soviet Union—worlds of 'one truth'—and protect us, on the other hand, from the terrifying uncertainty of a world of hopeless subjectivity with authority vested nowhere.

This quest for a value-free science was so spectacularly productive for almost three centuries that by the late 19th century, scientific truth was popularly considered to be synonymous with 'reality'. By the 1920s, we had gone full circle from faith in papal infallibility to a hope of infallibility for scientific objectivity.

We are all now well aware that events in subsequent decades of this century have scuttled this positivist project, especially—but not only—in the social sciences. Undermined by discoveries in physics, mathematics, thinking in history, philosophy of science, and discoveries in the social sciences, especially psychology, claims that science can deliver absolute certainty have turned out to be overstated. We now know that there is no way to escape uncertainty in any fundamental sense. Having grown beyond childlike reliance on priestly guidance and reassurance, having discovered our hopes in positivist science were exaggerated, our vulnerability is once more exposed. Only this time it is worse, since not only do our ultimate questions remain unanswered but we have lost faith in our faith. Theodore Roszak has suggested that by its phenomenal success, science robbed modern people of their age-old access to the sacred, via the great religions, but failed to fill the void as 19th-century scientific optimism had promised. We hunger to feel at home in the universe and find that neither traditional religion nor modern science can help (Roszak, 1981).

Mythmongering in uncertain times

It is in this abyss of uncertainty—which most of us find profoundly anxiety provoking—that the pseudopriest and the pseudoscientist find a ready audience. It is no coincidence that within a community like the consciousness movement, which had its origins in a period of history in which all established authority was suspect, and which elevated subjectivity almost to sacredness, that both pseudoscience and pseudoreligion flourish. Nor should it surprise us that within the movement and within the broader society in general the most successful delusions are those that claim to draw authority from both traditional religious and scientific sources. Parapsychologists, UFO believers, Scientologists, esties, spiritists, creationists, new-paradigmers, aquarian conspirators, and mythmongers of all stripes can be easily identified by their generous citation of scientific authorities—preferably physicists or Nobel Laureates—and of sacred texts—preferably oriental. They can also be identified by their wholesale disregard for the basic principles, tenets, disciplines, and axioms of the very traditions from which they borrow authority, and by their willingness to support their claims by selecting disembodied bits and pieces of evidence from very wide ranges of sources that neither they nor their audiences are in any position to evaluate. This form of intellectual sleight-of-hand identifies the 'pseudo' status of many writers popular with New Age adherents.

In both science and established spiritual disciplines, adepts rarely wander far from their own disciplinary neighbourhood. They are too well aware of how hard it is to remain current in even a small area of study. The fabric of a broad discipline such as biology, for example, is made up of a patchwork of overlapping competencies with folks in neighbouring patches perhaps able to engage in fruitful dialogue. Those in more distant areas have no choice but to take the pronouncements of other scientists on a kind of faith. For the whole thing to hold together and for real research to proceed, it must be possible to trust the integrity of countless unknown others. Unburdened by the disciplinary realities of ever doing any real research, pseudoscientists feel free to wander far and wide, to cite willy-nilly from fields as different as physics, astrology, and embryology. They strip knowledge of both its context and its concreteness, turning it into 'data' or bits of information that can be recombined without regard to any disciplinary integrity, rules of evidence, attention to questions of logical coherence, validity, or counterevidence.

The work of New Age or 'Aquarian' author Marilyn Ferguson is a good example of what might be called 'recombinant information'. In her keynote speech at the San Diego conference of the Association for Humanistic Psychology, she said that she doesn't take advice—she takes information (Ferguson, 1986). What she appears to mean by this is that she strips the statements others offer her of their moral and purposive contexts and transforms 'advice'—a human value-ladened proposition—into 'data'. That was one of the scarier things I had heard in a long time! With this much freedom, creatures with minds like ours—who can make a telephone ring out of running water or a psychic out of an amateur stage magician—should be able to come up with any position we want. And, of course, we do. Ferguson's book, *The Aquarian Conspiracy*, and her magazine, *Brain/Mind Bulletin*, are nothing more than pastiches of such 'data' arranged in accordance with whatever idea she wishes to promulgate.

It was Ferguson's *Brain/Mind Bulletin*, in fact, that brought wide New Age attention to Lyall Watson's story about the 'Hundredth Monkey Phenomenon'. The magazine's report referred to Watson as a biologist, when in fact he was known for his books on the occult. The *Brain/Mind Bulletin* writer also omitted, from an otherwise verbatim quote from *Lifetide*, a statement by Watson that he was basing his ideas on speculations, as 'those who do suspect the truth are reluctant to publish it for fear of ridicule' (Watson, 1979, p. 148). Ferguson is obviously more excited by bold ideas that can be fitted directly into her millennial vision than by scientific truths corroborated by careful lab work. She seems quite willing to erase the line between science and fiction and, what is worse, does not seem to recognize the sinister possibilities of such suspension of disciplined thought. Nor, it seems, do her enthusiastic audiences of New Agers who, in San Diego at least, roared their approval. In her disregard for traditional methods of inquiry and basing her assertions on some individualistic view of reality, Ferguson is clearly an heir to the antiauthoritarian push for the 'personal' that has characterized at least some of the humanistic movement in psychology. This endears her to many in the consciousness movement who regard her confident self-assertion as a sign of intellectual courage and creativity.

Subjectivity and power

In their legitimate rejection of the pursuit of a kind of dehumanized 'objectivity' in the study of human beings, psychologists like Abraham Maslow and Carl Rogers stressed the crucial importance of phenomenological analysis of subjective experience—an 'insider's view'—in what they hoped would be a 'new science of persons'. When they decided it was time to abandon their attempt to gain scientific legitimacy for psychological research by aping the methods of physics or biology, they embarked upon a radical project to create a whole new psychology based on holistic phenomenological studies capable of apprehending the glorious complexity of authentic human existence. They struck a culturewide nerve of alienation in the American psyche. Their bold, rebellious words and their antiauthoritarian methodologies were taken immediately to heart by a generation that was refusing to be 'folded, spindled, or mutilated'.

Discussion of the social and historical contexts of the campus movement in the 1960s are beyond the scope of this chapter, but we should remember here that a large proportion of the people who today strongly identify with New Age ideas were on college campuses during this time. At a stage in their lives when their minds were at their most awake, when the 'learning curve' was at its peak, this generation was being urged by its leaders to 'question authority', not to 'trust anyone over thirty', to 'lose their mind and come to their senses', and to 'turn on, tune in, and drop out'. They were told the only trustworthy authority was individual authority and the only reliable truth individual truth. They read books with titles like *If You Meet the Buddha on the Road, Kill Him!*, *Burn This Book*, and *The Politics of Experience*. They were challenging (with justification) academic curricula that defended a worldview dominated by White middle-class males and pressuring colleges and universities to establish women's and ethnic studies departments.

There was much talk of 'becoming a person', much experimentation with 'peak experiences' as first college students, then others, hungrily gobbled up the outpourings of books, seminars, and workshops designed to realize human potential. The idea took hold in the popular psyche that we were all being held back from our true possibilities by oppressive systems of education, cultural practices, and mores, by sexism, racism, and 'left-brained linear thinking' in the form of big science, big government, and militarism. Since the whole established culture was deemed tainted by the vested interests of the 'oppressor', the only standards upon which we felt we could base our sense of 'truth' or 'reality', or determine our decisions and actions, became our own, inner, private sense of rightness. This internal or (as it was called) 'intuitive' sense of truth was no longer just an important source of data among many, but in a world in which every other authority had been discredited it had become the only source. Whether this source was reliable or not, and I hope I have shown that it often was not, was beside the point, since by this time no other acceptable basis for certainty existed.

What none of us foresaw in our enthusiasm to proclaim the personal, however, was that in a world where an insider's view becomes the only view, when each individual's private truth is considered to have the same status as everyone else's, when we ignore the problem of false consciousness, then there is, in fact, no truth at all. There is only power—power of the press, of persuasion, coercion, and ultimately of force.

To show what I mean, let's imagine a society where there was the kind of merging of science and religion hoped for by many New Age believers. How would such a community approach the problem of AIDS, for example? One person might promote the 'virus' idea, another the 'God's curse' idea. Someone else might learn in a dream that AIDS is caused by an energy imbalance, another that it was brought in from some other planet as a vehicle by which to learn something very profound about the relationship between human sexuality and 'life beyond the body'. If, in our mythical New Age community, everyone's individual truth is equally valid, how would the group go about deciding how limited resources would be spent in response to the epidemic? What would happen in such a community, of course, is that the idea with the most politically powerful adherents would prevail. So, let's say that in this community it is the 'channelers' who have the most respected place. They have learned from their spirit sources on a far-off planet that AIDS symptoms occur only in those earthlings who have low consciousness and who are prone to 'negative thoughts'. The community resources are to be mobilized to provide 'positive thinking' workshops for every man, woman, and child and to reprogram the sick. The 'virus' proponents, in turn, would try to amass 'evidence', but no one would know what to make of it. Who has ever seen a 'virus'? How could something as cosmically beautiful as lovemaking be responsible? Eventually the virologists might become fanatical, take to the labs, and wait out the inevitable (in their superstitious eyes at least) demise of the channelers. They would teach scientific thinking and practice to their children and hope that one day they might be part of a 'paradigm shift' in the direction of rational thought. They would probably dedicate themselves to finding ways to discredit the channelers and to weaken their power.

To some degree, the modern world already shares some characteristics with our mythic community. The ideal of one absolute truth has given way to the idea that different spheres of life and different communities can base their understandings and explanations of things on differing 'stories' that give coherence to their experience. However, coherence is not the only necessity of a system of thought. At some point we need to be able to select from alternative stories, stories that—as far as we can tell—correspond to realities we have no part in creating. Call them 'facts', call them 'universal realities', call them 'truth', call them what you like, but some realities exist outside of subjective experience and some stories are truer than others. We have no way of separating those independent realities upon which we can base public actions from private intuitions other than by a system of collective critical and public evaluation of all claims on our belief. If we want a world—as I do—in which we can all be open to the whole of creation, to let the universe speak to us directly, and in which each person can become a vehicle for truth, an ideal I also share with New Agers, then we will need to be able to separate mythic truth from scientific truth.

It is not at all clear that New Agers will be able to do this. The problem they face is that they have no obvious theoretical way to go about this, and the further away New Age thinking gets from its origins in philosophy and research-based psychology, the more difficult becomes the task.

In the early days of the human potential movement, the individual and social levels of human life were examined together. Much energy was devoted to considering the personal effects on public life as well as the effects of larger social systems and structures on intrapsychic experience. The slogan of the times was 'the personal is political'. As early as 1972, however, when I was beginning my doctoral studies in clinical psychology, a schism was already appearing between 'politicals'—those influenced by Marx and Hegel, who saw private consciousness as the product of social realities like sexism, racism, economics, and so on—and the 'experientials'—influenced by Kierkegaard, Freud, Rogers, and Maslow—who felt that societies are reflective of the individual consciousness of their members. The 'politicals' believed if we made laws that changed the structure of society so that the poor would be fed and the oppressed emancipated, a New Age would be upon us in which individual and collective consciousness could flower. The 'experientials', on the other hand, believed that if we were all to resolve our internal conflicts, expand our consciousness through psychotherapy, meditation, or some other consciousness discipline, we could transcend fear and negativity. This approach would foster the growth of individuals who could parent better, teach better, manage better, and govern better, and reset social priorities so that the poor would be fed and the oppressed emancipated.

Yet another issue upon which people with a humanistic vision differed—and still do—is the question of whether or not human nature is essentially good. One view—represented in recent dialogues by Carl Rogers (May, 1982)—holds that human nature is basically trustworthy. If left alone, the theory goes, humans will move toward health, growth, wholeness, and altruism. Evil, in this view, is seen as an unfortunate maladaptation to a society that fears human possibilities and so represses them. An opposing view, represented in the dialogue by Rollo May (1982), argues that human nature is neither good nor bad per se. May's view follows more closely the existentialist position that human consciousness (as compared to non-human) implies free will and the necessity of consciously choosing good over evil, by embracing Being rather than nihilism. Combinations of these views can be summarized in the grid below (Figure 12.1).

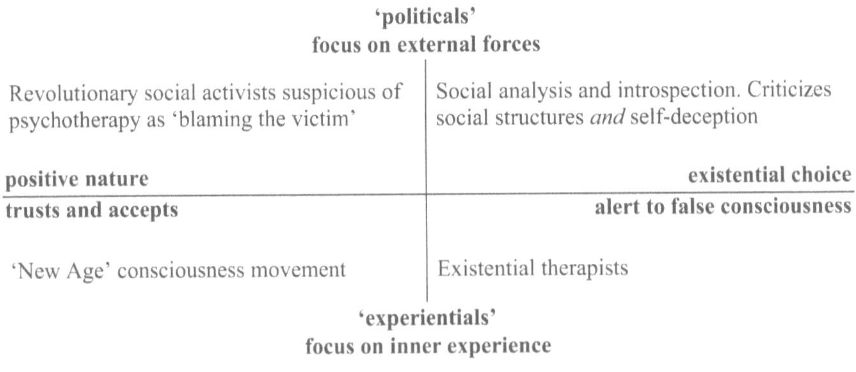

Figure 12.1 Viewpoint constellations

When the 'essentially positive and trusting' view of human nature is held together with the inner directed 'experiential' position, as is the case for most New Agers, the whole belief system folds in upon itself and ends up in a state of acritical solipsism. There is simply no need, if you are a believer, for any form of self-doubt, for external verification of personally held truth or for social structures and institutional practices that would contain, regulate, or arbitrate individual consciousness or actions based in it.

Within the Association for Humanistic Psychology in particular, and within the broader social movement it helped fuel, it seems the 'experientials' have won out over the 'politicals', and the 'trust human nature' belief has won out over the position of existential choice. Certainly, if we look at who draws the biggest crowds at conferences and which books are the most widely read, it is clear that the New Age voices predominate. (Revolutionaries, by the way, have long since left for more fruitful fields, like Critical Theory, and are now nowhere to be seen or heard in humanistic psychological circles.)

Throwing out the bathwater and cleaning up the baby

Is there any way the humanistic vision can be rescued from these built-in tendencies toward hopeless solipsism? By virtue of human nature and the ideals of our culture we are prone to all manner of self-deception, illusion, and quackery, and we have been encouraged by history to look beyond traditional authorities and orthodoxies for knowledge. Does that leave us in such conceptual murkiness that we must finally admit, as many critics claim, that the humanistic vision has been irrevocably compromised by the New Age movement and is intellectually bankrupt? Should we follow the universities and return to the apparent solidity of psychoanalysis (despite its obvious theoretical difficulties for women) or to empiricism (despite its emphasis on behavioral control)? Should we accept that we are all individually lost and turn to those charismatic speakers and personalities among us who give the appearance of knowing what is going on? Or perhaps we should simply withdraw from philosophical discussions of truth and declare everything metaphor. If deception works to achieve the ends we want, shouldn't we use it?

No doubt some people will follow each of these options, but when we consider the example of our mythical New Age community facing its AIDS epidemic, it should become clear that not all of these options are equivalent and none of them would be much help in the face of a real problem like the one we consider. Our community needs some way for the truth about the epidemic and its viral origins to surface and prevail against majority prejudice and vested power. It needs to know—with as much confidence as possible—the basis upon which precious resources should be spent. It needs processes that can be seen to be more or less impartial—however imperfect that impartiality turns out to be in practice—and that can be seen to have validity outside of and across differing belief systems, so that even communities who base their worldview upon different articles of faith are willing to give them credence. In other words, the community needs some form of established science.[9] It also needs democratic institutional structures that can protect minority constituencies from groups with bigger sticks so that unpopular views can get a hearing.

A volume like this one may be part of such a path out of the murkiness, and in my view, it offers a great deal to the cause of humanism. It represents a willingness on the part of the writers to seriously evaluate the claims and aspirations of all—including New Agers—who feel in their souls that something is very wrong with the world we have created and so explore new realms of consciousness and new possibilities for our global collective.

However, at the same time, it also recognizes that in a world in which the search for externally located absolute truth has given way to an intersubjective, cogenerated view, criticism and debate are perhaps the only ways we have to separate show from substance.

I have been a strong advocate for recommitment, in humanistic psychology, to an ideal of disciplined scholarship. While I agree with those who caution against reactionaryism and locking ourselves into an empty (and dehumanizing) search for scientific certainty, I nonetheless believe we need to cultivate what may best be described as a scientific attitude. In addition to our justified suspicion of reductionism, our prizing of openness, creativity, and curiosity, we must also develop competency in logic, criticism, and evaluation that are suitable for our field. Open-ended investigation of something like 'channelling', for instance, may reveal unfamiliar dimensions of consciousness, altered states of awareness, or deep psychological realities. We might gain understanding of the phenomenon as a response to social pain, a legitimate (yet futile) revolt against nihilistic forces at large in mechanized society, as a symptom of alienation of people stripped of any other sources of self-affirmation. Whatever approach we choose—whether phenomenological, interpretive, or experimental—we need to ground our investigations in thoughtful and healthy scepticism.

I would like to see us rededicate ourselves to an unfinished task, one that is (however distorted and derailed it has become) at the heart not only of the New Age vision but of the American democratic ideal: the creation of a world in which individual persons can be nourished and cherished by a society whose basic sustaining beliefs, structures, and institutions strive to support its multiple and varied constituencies in ways that are just and nonexploitative with regard for both persons and nature wherein—in the long run at least—the ideal of truth, however imperfect, will have a chance to prevail over prejudice, however comforting.

I firmly believe that progress will not come from as-yet-unknown magical powers, from messages 'channelled' from dead people or extraterrestrials. If progress comes at all, it will come from the concerted actions of countless ordinary folks on this planet struggling together with the concrete dilemmas of existence.

From our deeper, perhaps inarticulate—some might say religious—selves may come visions of imaginary futures wherein suffering ends, death is conquered (or its sting soothed), joy and plenty are universal, and wherein each person born may live a fully human existence. However, if we are to bring these imaginary worlds into reality, it will take more than visions—it will also take well-articulated ideas based in sound research. We would make a good start by telling the pseudoscientists, con-artists, mythmongers, and other silver-tongued snake-oil salesmen we don't need them and by bidding them a tolerant but final adieu.

Notes

1 When this was originally published, Maureen was a practicing psychotherapist and a professor of Women's Studies at San Diego State University. The ideas in this chapter were first presented to the members of the Association for Humanistic Psychology at its annual meeting in 1986.

2 From Walter M. Kotschnig's Smith College Armistice Day Speech on November 8, 1939.

3 The term New Age is somewhat vague, but since I use it throughout, I want at least to sketch a broad description if not a precise definition. New Age thinking is a fundamentally optimistic set of beliefs that focuses on questions such as expanded consciousness, human transcendence, ecological awareness, and global peace. It particularly emphasizes the possibility (some would claim inevitability) that human consciousness is in the process of undergoing a 'paradigm shift', in which old ways of knowing—identified as rational, Newtonian, capitalistic, competitive, violent, left-brained, masculine, and materialistic—will give way to a new world where there is integration of masculine and feminine, which is cooperative, nonviolent, intuitive, Einsteinian, and spiritual. Its view of human nature is essentially positive, attributing evil deeds to maladaptive responses to an oppressive culture. People who hold New Age beliefs tend to be interested in extraordinary human capacities like ESP, psychic phenomena, and mediumship. They embrace and go far beyond Maslow's ideal of a fully actualized person, or Rogers' 'person of tomorrow', believing that enormous new powers—especially of the mind—are about to become manifest as humankind makes a large evolutionary leap. New Agers tend to hold a combination of religious beliefs, such as reincarnation, karma, Taoism, Zen, spiritism, animism, and shamanism; yet, they reject Christian fundamentalism, Catholicism, and Judaism. Books and authors recently influential among New Agers include Marilyn Ferguson's *The Aquarian Conspiracy*, Shirley MacLaine's *Out on a Limb*, Fritjof Capra's *The Tao of Physics* and *The Turning Point*, Gary Zukav's *The Dancing Wu Li Masters*, Ken Keyes' *The Hundredth Monkey*, Rupert Sheldrake's *A New Science of Life*, Ken Wilbur's *Up From Eden*, and Jean Houston's *The Possible Human*, among many others.

4 The main thrust of the hypothesis proposed that once 'a form' (a term that for Sheldrake encompassed things as different as a five-digit vertebrate limb, an architectural design, a molecular structure, and an ideology) has occurred, it is more likely to occur again. This is due, according to Sheldrake, to subtle nonenergetic forces that he calls 'morphogenetic fields' (after a concept in embryology), which directs nature down already trodden paths by a yet-to-be discovered process of resonance with forms already in existence.

5 We had experienced the 'Summer of Love' and the musical 'Hair'; encounter groups were ubiquitous. The educated middle class was flocking to Esalen, following the Maharishi, listening to John Lennon, and reading Carlos Casteneda. Marilyn Ferguson had published *The Aquarian Conspiracy*, in which she promoted the idea that there was a global movement of 'New Age' consciousness. Baghwan Rajneesh was proclaiming the end of culture and the birth of an entirely new form of human. Werner Erhardt was promoting the idea of 'critical mass' in est's 'Hunger Project'. Fritjof Capra, in *The Tao of Physics*, had suggested some kind of equivalence between subatomic physics and

human consciousness, and Gary Zukav's *The Dancing Wu Li Masters* had given the general public the idea that Werner Heisenberg's principle of uncertainty implied that thought transfer across space and across time was within the realm of scientifically established possibilities. Terms like 'critical mass' were taken out of the specialized language of nuclear weaponry and into the language of the 'New Age'. Thomas Kuhn had introduced the concept of 'paradigm shift', supporting the idea that modern science of mind might be in a 'pre-paradigmatic' state. All these cultural elements were quite familiar to those in the 'consciousness movement'. We were eagerly expecting news of a 'paradigm shift'.

6 This might be changing in the 'go for it' 1980s, where financial success itself is often regarded as a sign of credibility. New Agers did not seem to begrudge Baghwan Rajneesh his Rolls Royces, and, recently, Shirley MacLaine has made it part of her pitch that in her personal struggle between spirituality and materialism, she has come down on the side of materialism. This echoes the direction of the flock of New Age evangelist Terry Cole-Whittaker, who can be identified anywhere in San Diego county by their bumper stickers proclaiming 'Prosperity—Your Divine Right'.

7 Critics of the New Age often point out that this tolerance and faith does not seem to extend to scientists and technologists, militarists, Republicans, and the religious right.

8 Conferences have included gestalt astrology, Scientology, 'past-life regression', 'Lunaception', 'tantric medicine', a West African voodoo healer, rebirthing, spirit-painting through a medium, Rajneesh body-work, ARICA, 'crystal healing', aura-reading, shamanism of all sorts, 'trance-channelling', as well as work that, while on the fringe at the time, it was first presented, has subsequently become integrated into more mainstream psychological and medical practice, such as bioenergetics, acupuncture, psychodrama, gestalt therapy, Tai Chi and Akido, humanistic education, relationship enrichment, stress reduction through meditation, and many health and nutrition approaches that have stood the test of subsequent scientific evaluation. In the early days, for instance, conferences like these were the only places to get a hearing for suggestions that mood and attitude may have clinical effects on the immune system.

9 About the word science. I am aware that there are very good arguments for leaving the word to those disciplines and questions in which the ideals of objectivity, replicability, quantifiability, and predictability are appropriate and finding another word for the project of human inquiry. I personally lean towards this position, preferring words like 'studies', 'inquiry', or 'scholarship'. I leave this important discussion for some other occasion.

Chapter 13

Is it time for clinical psychology to deconstruct constructivism? (1995)[1]

Maureen O'Hara[2]

I revisit the debates over absolutism versus relativism, freedom versus determination, objectivism versus subjectivism, representationalism versus nominalism, determinacy versus indeterminacy, and other manifestations of the realism versus constructivism debate in psychology. I consider the advantages and drawbacks of both extremes and suggest that although as a critique of mainstream scientific psychology, the postmodern discourse has been fruitful for clinical theory and practice, at its extreme it undermines its own claims as a basis for healing because it denies the legitimacy of any authority. Referring to recent thinking in cross-cultural psychology and neuroscience, I suggest that there may be certain universal givens that form limiting constraints on how far psychologists can take indeterminacy. I suggest that psychologists hold a double vision, using each end of the realist–constructivist spectrum of positions as a limiting frame for the other.

Situating the discussion

Let me begin in good postmodernist form by situating myself with regard to the postmodern psychological debate. I suppose I was destined to be drawn into the postmodern questions about the relationships between context and meanings. More than 20 years of practice as a multiply hyphenated psychotherapist (person-centered-gestaltfeminist-emancipationist) has meant thousands of hours in deep, often emotionally and intellectually intense conversations with diverse people. I have participated in therapeutic dialogues with Ivy League intellectuals, southern California suburbanites, British factory workers, urban Japanese bureaucrats, illiterate *favelados* (inhabitants of shanty towns) in Latin America, rural aristocrats in Italy and Brazil, and college students in many countries. I have been given privileged access to the inner worlds of heterosexuals, lesbians, gays, and bisexuals; young people and old people; and members of dominant classes and oppressed classes. Over the years, the enormous range of life stories, told in the voices, languages, and narratives of such a variety of people, coupled with a Rogerian/Freirian position of attempting to indwell as far as possible in the client's phenomenal life world, has inevitably forced me to evaluate critically or deconstruct my

DOI: 10.4324/9781003519454-17

own working-class European modernist worldview and see it for what it is—one among many viable ways of understanding and making meaning of the world. Although such a pluralism of experience has required that I take a postmodern view, it has also reaffirmed my belief that people arrive at mutual and shared meanings more often than not. For this reason, I wonder if it is now time to deconstruct constructivism.

Another look at the perennial paradoxes

There is nothing new about the constructivist debate. Some form of it has been a perennial theme in conversations about reality throughout history. It is a play with many names: absolutism versus relativism, freedom versus determinism, nature versus nurture, objectivism versus subjectivism, realism versus constructivism, and representationalism versus nominalism are only some of its Western names. It is a play that has engaged erudite philosophers as well as cynical con-artists.

In our own generation, this age-old discussion has once again become intensified. It has been spurred by the enormous success of critical intellectuals—many from within previously culturally marginalized groups and disciplines—in demonstrating, both empirically and philosophically, the ideological origins of many seemingly solid tenets of established knowledge. From within frames of reference classified as 'other' by the dominant discourses, they have been spectacularly successful in identifying the hegemonic properties of many of the so-called objectivist disciplines. This intensification of the realist–constructivist argument has been highly (but it is important to point out, not exclusively) visible in the social and psychological spheres. Science historians (Gould, 1980; Keller, 1985; Laqueur, 1990; Showalter, 1985), feminist psychologists (Belenky et al., 1986; Chesler, 1972; Gilligan, 1982; Hare-Mustin & Marecek, 1990; Maccoby & Jacklin, 1975; Weedon, 1987; Weisstein, 1971), antipsychiatrists (Laing, 1967; Szaz, 1970), psychologists (Gergen, 1991; Maslow, 1966; Rogers, 1961/1967b), sociologists (Berger & Luckmann, 1966; D. E. Smith, 1990), and countless others have critically reexamined classical psychological claims and made strong cases illustrating the built-in biases, social fictions, and powerful selective frames that have been erected by specific social groups, some of which have been maintained through language and traditional practices over long periods of intellectual and social history.

Women's imagined inferior capacity for moral reasoning is but one of many well-known examples, traceable as it is through mythic, ecclesiastical, political, and scientific discourses from Biblical accounts of Eve, through St. Augustine and Freud, all the way to the moral development studies of Lawrence Kohlberg in the 1960s. A claim that had once been considered solid fact, with confirmatory evidence putatively piled up in many disciplines, finally melted away once women scholars began asking the questions and, more importantly, gained access to scholarly publications (Gilligan, 1982).

Pluralism within the constructivist conversation

Within American psychology, the constructivist discourse is by no means a monolithic movement. It has emerged as a collection of several different perspectives. Philosophically descended from Kant, through Hegel, Marx, Gramsci, and Foucault, entering the world of psychotherapy through the work of Kelly, Bateson, Lacan, Laing, Maslow, the later Rogers, radical and feminist therapists, ethnotherapists, and, recently, the family therapists, with more than a little influence from Zen Buddhism and Sufism, the constructivists have made the repudiation of 'representationalism' (Gergen, 1994) their distinguishing claim. They argue that what humans refer to as reality, including their own private 'inner' psychic realities, are fictions. Human experience consists of the stories humans make up and tell themselves and each other.

I do not believe that many in psychology still doubt that some of humanity's cherished ideas about itself are culturally and historically situated social constructions. Neither, I imagine, are there many left who would deny the importance of context, particularly the social contexts of language, discourse, and tradition, in the making of meaning. Like it or not, we have all entered the world of indeterminacy.

How far shall therapists take indeterminacy?

The dilemma for the constructivist psychologist, whether clinician or scientist, lies in how far to take the indeterminacy. Even if he or she admits, with Kelly (1969), that anything that can be construed can be reconstrued, the question remains as to the degree to which people are free to, or for that matter need to, reconstrue the world unfettered by any constraints at all given by natural endowments.

Constructivists are not all alike. Among the psychological constructivists, there are two distinct voices. One group—who might be called the strong-form constructivists—argues with the post-structuralists that psychological realities and meanings may be endlessly deconstructed, reframed, and reconstructed. Strong-form constructivists are antirealist and take the position that there is no reality either beneath or beyond linguistic constructions (Held, 1995). Psychotherapy is seen as conversations for the purpose of dismantling dysfunctional linguistic constructions and as a vehicle to teach clients the dialogical skills they need to skate from context to context, responding flexibly and improvisationally to each emergent situation. What people take as experience is nothing more real than the constructions produced in the process (Efran et al., 1990; Gergen, 1991; Hare-Mustin & Marecek, 1990; Hoffman, 1988; Kristeva, 1980).

There is another, more moderate constructivist camp, who might be called the weak-form constructivists. They acknowledge that consciousness consists of constructions, but they see these constructions as surface clues to deeper, more essential, and more universal experience. Psychotherapy as a form of inquiry aims to look through these clues to find potentially universal or meanings or givens (Gadamer, 1975; Giddens, 1991; O'Hara, 1986; Polanyi, 1969; B. M. Smith, 1994; Taylor, 1990).

To the strong-form constructivists, what people refer to as selves or 'subjectivities' are nothing more than the free play of emergent improvisations, products of specific dialogical contexts. Change the discourse and you change the self. Weak-form constructivists take the position that even though selves are far more flexible and variable than any self-respecting (no pun intended) modernist rationalist would be willing to tolerate, organismic, existential, or spiritual givens exist that form limiting boundaries within which selves are experienced and then conceptualized.

At times, as an emancipationist-feminist, I find the radical indeterminacy and limitless potential for self-recreation offered by the strong-form constructivists a powerful and liberating concept. Nevertheless, I now believe that no matter how productive it may have been in the humanities, strong-form constructivism is seriously limited as a basis for clinical psychological practice. It is even more limited, perhaps even fatally flawed, as a public politic, but I leave that discussion for another occasion.

Constructivism as clinical psychology

Modernist genesis of clinical practice

The limitations of constructivism for clinical practice are both epistemic and pragmatic. Clinical psychology, after all, is a quintessential modernist project. As a discourse, it draws its authority from the self-confident modernism of its 19th-century origins. It is a tacit, often explicit, given of clinical psychology, part of the contract between the therapist and the client that sets up the terms and frames of reference of therapy, that therapeutic conversations are meaningful, purposeful, and a valid activity that leads somewhere—somewhere better and somewhere real.

For psychotherapy to be effective, it is necessary for the people who engage in it, both the therapist and the client, to believe that all is not random and arbitrary, that although perhaps out of sight at present, coherence exists, and causes, meanings, and remedies for suffering can be found. If this tacit assumption is, like any other assumption, radically deconstructed and exposed as representing merely the collective investments of established psychological elites, it is fair to say that justification for the practice of clinical psychology evaporates, except, as radical critics have charged, as means of either cynical commerce or coercive social control (Chesler, 1972; Foucault, 1965; Laing, 1967; Szaz, 1970; Weedon, 1987).

Some strong-form constructivist psychotherapists seem to be able to square themselves with continuing to practice even after they have concluded that ultimately no therapeutic claims can be justified. Is this really tenable?

Assumption of coherence and meaning

As Polanyi (1969) points out, the willingness to have faith in some greater coherence is the sine qua non of both the scientific and psychotherapeutic enterprises. Recent accounts of the evolution of mind suggest that the need to assume coherence may be more basic to human psychological processes even than that. Allman (1994), for instance, argues that the human psyche might never have evolved at all were it not for the need to know—with reliability—what is going on in the minds of other members of the community. If people were to remain focused at the level of surface signs, abandoning any faith that they point to deeper, coherent realities, they would become flooded with undecipherable sensory inputs and lost in endless, meaningless, and maddening surface incoherence. Without 'universal intent'—people's shared belief that their utterances point to something beyond themselves or, in other words, mean something—the practice of deconstructionist psychotherapy, far from leading to greater levels of sanity, as promised, leads to cynicism and eventually to madness.

It turns out that there is good reason to believe that there is more than good fictions that holds human psyches and communities together. There also may be reasons to believe that at least some inner psychological realities map rather reliably onto a real world. There may also even be good reason to believe that human languages—mathematics, narratives, and other social constructions—are creative expressions of both deeper and wider truths that speak, albeit cryptically, to some shared universals about life in human bodies on this planet.

Givens and universals in psychological life

This is not the place to elaborate all the evidence for the existence of universals that both are affected by and provide limiting boundaries for socially constructed realities. A few selected examples will have to do.

- Depression-negative cognitions, hopelessness, a preoccupation with death, flattened affect, intense concern for suffering, and a sense of ultimate meaninglessness are considered an illness in the upbeat West. In Buddhist cultures, however, such a condition would be cultivated and seen as a sign of a superior mind (Obeyesekere, 1985). Serotonin reuptake inhibitors may be indicated in either case (Epstein, 1993).
- The meaning of colours is to some degree culturally relative, but every culture knows at least black and white; if a culture knows three colours, red is the third; if four, yellow-green is the fourth. Cultures with multiple colours share about eight basic recognized colours (Lakoff, 1987).
- Cross-cultural studies and studies comparing the facial expressions of blind children with those of sighted children reveal that there are about six basic human emotions that are recognizable and perhaps universal among human beings (Ekman et al., 1982).

- Concepts of living and not living, good and bad, here and there, this and that, food and not food, stop and continue, are all universally known.

New research on the brain suggests that at least some of humanity's categories of reality, which show up in its social constructions as 'symbols', even 'concepts', may exist as chemical and topological information within the human brain structure. Arguing almost the complete reverse of the social constructivists, Gazzaniga (1992) suggested that what is out there is very real and that humans' own organismic evolution, including consciousness, has been emergent from and in terms of that real stuff. Humans' social constructions, even mathematics, the products of 'in here', map onto the world as well as they do because what is 'out there' is also 'in here' as both fixed and modifiable patterns of neurological connections and firings, selected for, over evolutionary and biographical time scales, by experience with the world. Such a view was already evident in the work of the early 20th-century zoologist D. Thompson (1917) and is supported by more recent studies, such as those by Melzack (1990) on the phenomenon of the phantom limb. Melzack points out that the existence of phantom limb experiences, even in persons born without limbs, suggests that having come as far as human beings, evolution has hardwired many important experiences and activities of mind. Allman (1994) has recently argued that the extant human psyche—its intellectual and emotional investments; its understandings of the natural and interpersonal world; and its capacities for art, language use, and meaning-making—evolved in response to the human's life as a social primate in which the meanings of others in the social group had life-and-death significance.

In the realm of social reality, despite the frequent hilarious and tragic misunderstandings, people more or less are able to understand each other's constructions. I submit that this is because social constructions, whatever their idioms and nuances, are produced by the same kind of beings in response to a world that presents similar biological, existential, and spiritual demands on all.

All of this means, I believe, that clinical psychologists must refuse the radical indeterminacy of strong-form constructivism.

However, I do not suggest that clinical psychologists abandon constructivism altogether and settle for some form of primitive determinism, either scientistic or mystical. Rather, I think they should consider the possibility that there might be something (dare I say it?) universal about the issue itself. Is it possible that the question of, for example, absolutism versus relativism is debated because both qualities exist as intrinsic properties of both mind and matter?

Essential tensions—Avoiding the extremes

When constructivists argue that abandoning certainty will permit tradition-bound modernists to enter the free play of novel social improvisation and that this might hold hope for a brave new postmodern world in which old exploitative power structures might be replaced by those that permit a wider access to the benefits of civilization, they are surely right. But so, too, may be neurologists who attribute at least some aspects of psychological life—cognitive style, some gender differences, patterns of family life, and archetypal imagery, for instance—to inherited and perhaps shared neurological endowments.

It is when therapists take either the determinist or constructivist position to its extreme that they run into trouble. Regardless of which extreme the approach, all grounds for vitality and individuality evaporate. Taking an absolutist determinist position, be it that humans are determined by genes, by inbuilt cognitive patterns, by Oedipal longings, or by self-actualizing tendencies, leads to a view of human beings driven by lifeless, repetitious, and robotlike compulsions. Human will, as an expression of human agency, disappears. If they take the extreme postmodernist/relativistic view, where all contexts become contexts for other contexts, human agency again disappears, and individual existence has no meaning except that granted it by others or by circumstance. As a psychology, either extreme leads to emptiness and despair.

Thankfully, this bleak view does not appear to be the norm. Humans seem a creative, playful, relatively stable, coherent, and expressive lot, who seem to enjoy life whenever they can and who seem never to tire of asking impertinent questions designed to overturn previous certainties—even about uncertainty. It seems reasonable to speculate that the age-old philosophical dilemmas may not be resolved in the abstract but may be resolved only in the concrete hurly-burly of a lived human life, which, despite what philosophers would like to believe, goes on with or without philosophical clarity. Clinicians, who, I presume, also inhabit the hurly-burly, must learn to be at home in the paradox. It may be useful to take more absolutist positions about some kinds of psychological realities, such as the centrality of infant–parent early bonding in the development of consciousness, and more relativist positions about others, such as the meaning of religious experience. However, for the most part, I think psychologists must be willing to inhabit more than one discourse community. Instead of looking for psychology's equivalent of physics' grand theory of everything, practitioners must learn to take a double both/and position and try to chart a course between the Scylla of absolutism and the Charybdis of paralysing relativism, and to avoid forcing themselves or each other into choosing either extreme, letting the existence of each position provide an interpretive challenge for the other. By holding such a dialogical double position, they can, for instance, interpret biological knowledge through the world of meanings and social contexts, and vice versa, and can let each provide a limiting boundary for the other.

With pretensions of universality

Presumably, human emancipation is still in progress, and mind and consciousness are still evolving. It seems reasonable to speculate that the world's evolution from tribal to global village will place new demands on humans' psychological and social abilities. Humanity's successful handling of the absolutist/contextualist paradox has brought consciousness this far, and I believe there is good reason to believe it is worth continuing to hold this double position. However, along with Polanyi (1969) and Gadamer (1975), I believe that although people hold this double position heuristically, they hold it with universal intent, believing—yes, believing—that by continuing to look beyond surface appearances, they may approach shared universals. I argue for at least 'the pretension to universality in the act of understanding and speaking' (Gadamer, 1975, p. 493) and for continuing to believe that because knowledge is never fixed but always in process of becoming something new, 'the possibility of reaching an agreement between reasonable beings can never be denied' (p. 180). Even while humanity acknowledges the deconstructability of master narratives, it should not abandon the search for noncoercive ways of arriving at mutually shared meanings at the same time it accepts that the experience of the voyage itself is far more important than the arrival.

Notes

1 Based on a paper presented at the 102nd Annual Convention of the American Psychological Association, Los Angeles, CA, August 1994.

2 Maureen was based at the Center for Studies of the Person, La Jolla, California, USA, when she originally wrote this.

Chapter 14

Reflections on Maureen O'Hara's writings on third force science

Maureen O'Hara and Keith Tudor

Keith: By now, the reader of this book will understand that you are a scientist, and as such, I am delighted that we have included three papers on your contribution to the articulation of humanistic psychology as a science, a perspective and paradigm that all too easily gets lost.[1] As the first paper, 'A hundredth monkey myth' (Chapter 11) was written as a rejoinder to a response (Flasher, 1983) to an earlier paper (O'Hara, 1983a), can you give us a brief description of the myth and of the context of the discussion?

Maureen: Debunking the hundredth monkey myth and the surprising response to it changed the direction of my thinking from a focus on person-centred practice with individual persons to trying to understand the way social narratives drive consciousness at personal and collective levels. I first encountered Imo, the eponymous hundredth money in an encounter group. At a moment of group resonance, when everyone was feeling attuned—as sometimes happens in groups—a participant pulled the book *The Hundredth Monkey* (Keyes, 1982) from her backpack and proclaimed excitedly, 'We are having a hundredth monkey experience'. Keyes' astonishingly successful book was based on a story by pseudoscientist Lyall Watson (1979). Watson reported on what he claimed was the achievement of telepathic capacity in a troop of macaque monkeys on Koshima, an island in Japan. Scientists there had observed that Imo, a lead female, had learned to wash her sweet potatoes to get the sand off them. One by one other monkeys imitated her and gradually others in the troop were washing their potatoes—behavioural propagation per usual. Initially. The graph of numbers in the troop who over time began washing their food indicated that uptake of the behaviour was slow and gradual. Then scientists recorded a sudden spike in numbers of washers. According to the myth promulgated by Watson and Keyes this was because, once a certain number of monkeys had learned the behaviour—say 99—with the addition of a hundredth something new happened, and suddenly all the monkeys were washing potatoes. Even

DOI: 10.4324/9781003519454-18

more surprising, according to Watson and Keyes, even monkeys on neighbouring islands with no contact with the Koshima troop were washing their food, thereby demonstrating, according to the myth, that once a 'critical mass' of individuals had caught on, a kind of telepathic collective consciousness occurs. As I explain in the article, the actual explanation was far simpler. The spike was due to a biological reality not a metaphysical one. After a while, the washers began to have offspring and whereas adult-to-adult transmission was slow, parent-to-offspring transmission was immediate and near universal. And the neighbouring islands? Films exist showing of monkeys regularly swimming from island to island.

What interested me about the story was not the behaviour of the monkeys but the behaviour of the humans who were so ready to believe the idea that once something is true for a critical mass of people, it will become true for everyone—and more than believe it, many members of the human potential movement welcomed it as a means by which cultural transformation might occur. This seemed to me to be a conspiracy theorist's road map to social control, cult formation, and tyranny, and it gave me the creeps.

After the publication of this paper, I received letters from several prominent humanistic psychologists thanking me for arguing for a return to critical thinking and disciplined scholarship. They were from leaders in the movement, namely, Rollo May, Walter Truett Anderson, and Donald N. Michael, and included an invitation to join an ongoing seminar at Rollo's home. The group of practitioners and theorists was exploring the implications of a postmodern information age where established sources of authority were losing credibility and where the necessary and legitimate critique of the ideal of objective truth along with championing radical subjectivity might be inadvertently setting the stage for a world where power replaces truth and 'might makes right'.

Keith: Thanks for this, Maureen. It provides a clear background to and summary of the problems you address, not only in that paper (Chapter 11) and another you published on the subject (O'Hara, 1985b), but also in your other papers in this part of the book (Chapters 12 and 13). I love your challenge regarding the burden of substantiation and the importance of backing up passion; your reference to Martin Luther King's concrete examples of injustice as well his dream; and your juxtaposition of teaching and *learning*. Thinking about juxtapositions, I would parallel your concern that the collective mind is wise with a similar concern that the individual mind is equally wise, not least as I share your concern about conspiracy, social control, and so on. When I hear colleagues being critical of 'group think' (Whyte, 1952), I often want to balance that by raising the problem of what I would call 'individual think'.

Maureen: Yes, I see a real danger in any kind of knowledge or truth that fails to recognise the limits as well as the promise of ideas no matter how appealing. All ideas are both expressions of personal interpretations of embodied experience and of the contextual landscapes which provides the framing. One without awareness of the other is at best only partial, at worst delusional. In these times of massive information overload without a commitment to reflection on both the personal and collective agendas at play in any policy decision, for example, leaves us vulnerable to manipulation.

Keith: I'm interested that you were on to this, again relatively early on in the history of humanistic psychology. Your call, in 'Science, pseudoscience, and mythmongering' (Chapter 12) on humanistic psychologists to 'take a hard look at our gullibility' (p. 107), your critique of the status of the 'individual's private truth' (p. 116), and of 'acritical… and hopeless solipsism' (p. 119), and your assessment of the dominance of 'the "experientials"… over the "politicals"' in humanistic psychology (p. 119) are all well-made and, sadly, with rare exceptions,[2] still relevant. I also note your comment about the more revolutionary thinkers in humanistic psychology having left for critical theory, which makes sense to me.[3] However, on re-reading this paper, I must admit to having some ambivalence. On the one hand, I really appreciate your focus on making humanistic psychology a genuine third force science (and hence the title of this part of the book); on the other hand, it appears that (at least here) you're more critical of humanistic psychology than you are of the other forces of psychoanalysis and behaviourism and their science—and pseudoscience.

Maureen: I can see how it might appear that way, but I ask you to consider that I was making my critique as 'an insider, sympathetic—even enthusiastic—to the broader aims of those involved with humanistic approaches' (Chapter 12, p. 107). I was trying to make my case within a specific community of practice. There were plenty of folks mounting critiques of the other forces and I myself made a pointed critique of 'scientism' (O'Hara, 1989a) which I wish was more widely read. My concern was that some of the radical observations about human potential coming to light in humanistic encounters across the diverse worlds of practice were not being captured and evaluated. Though they were having a culture-wide impact in the United States and the developed world and were spreading across a public hungry for paths to greater self-fulfilment, knowledge gained through these human potential experiences was not making its way into codified collective knowledge. It was being ignored and even denigrated by both psychoanalytic and behaviourist voices. I wanted to make sure that what we were learning about the transformative power of learning in large group encounters, for instance, could provide the basis of a new paradigm for social change. I was frequently dismayed by the easy resort to stories about spoon bending, the hundredth monkey, and contact with aliens in order to make social transformation sound magically easy and thus obviating the need for any disciplined systematic exploration of events. I believed—and still do—that humanistic psychology was onto something transformative in the history of ideas. I celebrate the inclusive and expanded view of human potential emerging from underneath the weight of repressive ideas that for centuries have undervalued human *beings* as creative agents. But I believed then, and now, that if we forgo a critical approach to separating reliable knowledge from wishful thinking, delusion, and deception and if we don't submit our knowledge to disciplined inquiry to separate what we can rely on from what we might hope for but can't yet verify, we squander an immense opportunity for learning. Humans are trusting beings, especially when together in intense experiences with others who share their values and beliefs; so if we want to make a sustained and trustworthy claim for a collective consciousness based in humanistic ideas and practice, we will need to adopt both an appreciative and critical stance to our efforts.

Keith: Thanks, and so to your paper on constructivism, which is another lovely example of the clarity of your thinking and writing. I'm not sure I share your assessment or optimism that not many in psychology (still) doubt that ideas are 'culturally and historically situated social constructions' (pp. 125). I have too many experiences and examples of psychologists, psychiatrists, and psychotherapists being uncritical of empiricism as the only valid form of knowledge and basis of scientific enquiry, the (Western) medical model of human health, and cognitive behavioural solutions to human dilemmas and suffering—and, worse, of universal knowledge and models. Nonetheless, I appreciate your analysis and summary of the different perspectives in constructivism, which, as I have noted before about your work, is still relevant.

In the paper, you make an important point about constructivism, which I think has serious implications for third force science, on which, as this is 'another occasion' (p. 126), I'd like to invite you to elaborate. It is that that strong-form constructivism is 'fatally flawed' as a public politic—in this context—with regard to science and, specifically, as you suggest, to the practice of clinical psychology.

Maureen: I still believe that granting epistemic validity to subjectivity as does humanistic psychotherapy and engaging in critical examination of the ways diverse human realities are constructed, by whom and for what purpose as do feminist and critical therapies is an emancipatory project. Critical consciousness of the pragmatics of knowledge generation at personal and social levels can help people suffering many kinds of psychological pain recognise that their pain may originate in oppressive social systems. It may also help them find ways to free themselves and others caught in those systems. At the same time, though, I have found myself at odds with what I call a strong form postmodern position that denies the possibility of objective reality that can be known and shared beyond individual subjectivity. As Rogers (1980/1995b) puts it approvingly,

> The only reality I can possibly know is the world as I perceive and experience it in this moment. And the only reality you can possibly know is the world as you perceive and experience it in this moment. And the only certainty is that these perceived realities are different. There as many "real worlds" as there are people.
>
> (p. 102)

I think Rogers and others who extrapolate their experience from within the special case of psychotherapy to the larger social context are mistaken and, far from offering a solution to antagonisms among groups, this highly individualistic idea actually provides justification for polarisation, alienation, and misunderstanding. My thinking on this question has been greatly influenced by the work of philosopher of psychology Barbara Held who for years doggedly countered claims made by strong-form constructivist psychologists (she uses the term 'constructionist'), including cognitivists, postmodernists, feminists, and family therapists by pointing out the fundamental contradiction in this position. She writes: 'The discourse of postmodernism *proclaims with a unified voice the context-dependence or knower-dependence, the relativity or subjectivity, of all truth claims*' (Held, 1998, p. 193; my emphasis). This is a universal claim, and it holds that there can be no knowledge that is independent of the knowers. This is an anti-realist position where any claim of fact can be undermined by suggesting that facts are constructions that reflect the interests of the proposer and so can be countered by those with other interests. The proposition of the postmodernists is that different interpretations can be reconciled through dialogue which, as in that in encounter groups, conforms to certain ideal conditions that prevail, i.e., logic, reason, mutual respect, empathy, and freedom from coercion.

I was attracted to this idea as it aligned with our experience in encounter groups in which persons in conflict with each other could arrive at a new mutual understanding when they practiced person-centred approaches to dialogue. I recognised, however, that establishing such conditions in a group was challenging and, outside person-centred practice, rare. I was concerned at the time about the potential in other group situations that did not establish person-centred norms for interminable polarisation and even aggression where each side believed their view was real, any other mere 'spin', and no mutually respected referee existed. I feared that, in a world of radical subjectivity and rejection of any shared sense of ultimate givens as was being championed by postmodernists, people would face levels of existential uncertainty and anxiety that would be intolerable. They would become vulnerable to demagoguery, cult leaders, and state propaganda that would offer—and eventually impose—an official reality on everyone.

My early concerns are being borne out. At this point in history, we are seeing what this process looks like on a socio-political scale. We are living in a world turned on its head without reliable touchstones to distinguish fact from fiction. The population is fed a steady diet of what one of Donald Trump's advisors, Kellyann Conway, famously calls 'alternative facts', and news outlets and internet influencers pour out a deluge of fake news, anti-science fantasy scenarios, and anti-public health disinformation. Conspiracists spin outrageous lies about their enemies and no counter facts are accepted as valid. Even courts of law can now be dismissed because of claims by those indicted that they have been 'weaponised', and the facts bent to serve political agendas. It is epistemological warfare where what counts as truth is determined by those with the power and calls for justice are met with the rejoinder 'whose justice'?

While at first the constructivist voice came mostly from the political left, now the right has appropriated its revolutionary potential with a vengeance—and I mean that literally. Republican states in the United States justify extremist policies such as censorship of any books or materials that discuss changing social norms as eradicating the 'woke'.[4] Women's studies, African American studies, and human sexuality programmes have been dropped, and the teaching of critical race theory is banned in some states even at universities, with courses on American patriotism put in their place. At the same time, legislators insist that textbooks include sections that claim slavery had positive effects because slaves learned usable skills, and they insist that this slander be taught in schools as a fact. The backlash accelerates: school curricula are reviewed by right-wing politicians aiming to eliminate what they argue is indoctrination of children by woke and queer academics: data about the climate emergency are now routinely dismissed by the right as a hoax; public health officials are accused of poisoning people and endure threats of violence; libraries remove books when even one parent objects; the account that White supremacy is real and is to blame for violence against Blacks is a divisive 'fake narrative'; drag performances draw armed vigilantes; and providing medical care to transgendered people is criminalised. The through line to all these moves is they represent a wholesale roll-back of social progress of disadvantaged groups based on empirical evidence of constructed systems of injustice and supported by critical theories about race, sexuality, and physical ability that the right dismisses as the 'woke agenda'.

In a fact-free world based on a strong form of postmodernism where any truth is only as valid as the power of those who assert it, those with the power over the channels of information and mythmaking—benign and malignant—will determine what is taken as true. No critique will be more than just one more opinion or agenda. Not only does strong-form constructivism destabilise and overthrow collective norms that in democratic societies maintain individual freedom and social order, it also renders pointless any attempts to find a greater truth that is generalisable and independent of the knower. Science stops; and power and finally tyranny fill the vacuum. We are back where we began, only now without grounds for hope that truth, reason, justice, freedom, love, or personhood have any reality worth striving for, and with the stage set for autocracy and fascism. My point is that human progress towards a world in which all persons are free and supported to fulfil their calling requires critique of systems of knowledge that impede such progress—but, if we are to avoid sinking into a *Mad Max* world of all-against-all, our critique must be aimed towards a social consensus, however locally construed, about our shared human reality upon a finite planet.

Keith: Thank you so much for that elaboration, Maureen. I agree that we face an epistemological war—which is why I appreciate it when you talk about epistemology. Sometimes when I hear the (pseudo) justification of feelings as/being facts, I want to remind people of Popper's (1967/1972) useful distinction between different worlds—or realms within the known universe.[5] Perhaps we might get back to that as a way of going forward? In any case, I think we should let your powerful critique of strong-form constructivism stand as a good place to conclude this particular reflection on your consistent and significant contribution to a genuinely third force science of humanity.

Notes

1 My own contribution to this was when I was the director of the postgraduate programme (in Person-centred Psychotherapy & Counselling) at Temenos in Sheffield, UK (2004–2009) (see https://www.temenos.education/), and we approached Middlesex University to validate the programme, which it did—as a Master of Science.

2 See House et al. (2018).

3 See Tudor (2015).

4 Woke is an adjective derived from African American vernacular English, meaning 'alert to racial prejudice and discrimination'. From the 2010s, it encompasses a broader reference to awareness of social inequalities such as racial justice, sexism, and LGBTQI+ rights.

5 Popper distinguished between a realm of states and processes studied by the natural sciences (world 1); that of mental states and processes, based on the emergence of living organisms (and thus including animals and humans) (world 2); and that of the 'products of thought', which encompass a wide range of entities such as scientific theories to works of art, laws, and institutions (world 3). Thus, facts, such as the statistics of discrimination based on sexism and racism, belong to world 1, whereas feelings about marginalisation belong to world 2, and discussions about different forms of constructivism belong to world 3; and we confuse them at our—and others'—peril.

Part IV

Client-centred therapy

Chapter 15

Feminist 'postmodern' analysis of a session of psychotherapy between Carl Rogers and a woman client volunteer 'Sylvia' (1996)

Maureen O'Hara[1]

> *Psychoanalysis is the creation of a male genius, and almost all those who have developed his ideas have been men. It is only right and reasonable that they should evolve more easily a masculine psychology and understand more the development of men than of women.*
>
> (Karen Horney)[2]

Introduction

All through the time I worked closely with Carl Rogers, first as a graduate student, and later as a colleague and a friend, I had the profoundest love and respect for both the man and the work. This respect deepened over the years as I saw him, in countless and varied situations, apply in the flesh the same principles he had outlined theoretically in his writings. Over the same years, my own developing intellectual work took me into arenas of thought and practice that constantly challenged me to examine and reflect upon the ideas I held about human nature, the process of therapy and growth, and my own place in the world where I acquired my own set of lenses, filters, and frames of reference with which to 'read' or 'listen' to Carl's approach to facilitating the growth process of others, whether as a therapist, teacher, group facilitator, parent, friend, or colleague.

From the beginning, our relationship was yeasty and passionate. We had innumerable discussions, dialogs, and plain old fights about our different frames of reference and different 'constructions of reality'—although we wouldn't have known to name it such in those days. Our differences were very often productive for both of us, sometimes cutting through each other's ossified conceptualizations with the analytic precision of the diamond cutter's knife. Other times reformulations of conceptual schemas or 'truths' came about gradually, more like the way the florist creates a bouquet from the assortment of flowers and foliage at hand.

Carl was always open to new ideas and new ways of looking at things. We read many of the same books, admired many of the same people, worked harmoniously side-by-side, saw eye-to-eye on many of the social, political, and spiritual issues of the times. On many occasions, our discussions would result in both of us seeing things anew; seeming differences were vigorously explored only to dissolve in a greater shared perspective.

DOI: 10.4324/9781003519454-20

But as the years went on, it became clearer that our most fundamental and troubling differences came not from some intellectual disagreement in things such as theories of personality, techniques of therapy, or even commitments to person-centered therapies. No, the genesis of our difference had to do with the position in the universe each of us occupied. There were times when not even the empathic genius of Carl Rogers could bridge the gap and reconcile the fundamental differences in 'worldview', 'perceptive sensibility', 'construction of reality', 'knowledge claims', 'knowledge interests', 'way of knowing', or 'paradigm' between Carl—a famous, powerful, successful, upper-middle-class, White American male, and Maureen—a young, unknown, immigrant, working class, White English female. It was maddening to want desperately to arrive at a consensus or agreement, and to discover that the deeper we dug, the further away from each other we got. It was all the more frustrating because at the time both of us were laboring under the positivist notion (I would now say illusion) that if we could find it, somewhere beneath our misunderstanding was a more fundamental truth that would be true for both of us. Thoroughly acculturated, as we both were, in a Western scientific tradition, neither of us was ready for a poststructuralist world!

Not surprisingly, the gap between us was most obvious when we came to issues of power, authority, inclusion and exclusion, and political realities such as sexism and racism. On the one hand, I did (and still do) see client- and person-centered approaches, both theoretically and in practice, as providing support for an ideal of 'full personhood' and empowerment for each and every individual. I have written elsewhere about what I have taken to be profoundly emancipatory aims of person-centered therapies (O'Hara, 1989a) I saw, both in his writings and in his practice, Carl's deep-felt belief in the essential worth of all people. It was for this above all else that I valued person-centered therapies and based my own work as a therapist on these ideas. On the other hand, though, as the years elapsed and as my consciousness as a woman began to evolve through my own experience in the world, in dialog with feminist and non-feminist women, disenfranchised peoples of color, lesbian women and gay men, oppressed classes from countries in Latin America, and the working class of Northern England, I began to see another side to the story of person-centered approaches.

Despite the powerful emancipatory promise in person-centered therapy, there are aspects to the approach that, whether consciously or unconsciously, served to preserve, maintain, and protect the interests of the Eurocentric, patriarchal, Judeo-Christian world. Illustrating the principle, Karl Mannheim describes, 'If one were to trace in detail… the origin and the radius of diffusion of a certain thought-model, one would discover the peculiar affinity it has to the social position of given groups and their manner of interpreting the world' (Mannheim, 1936/1997, p. 247). Carl's own place in the world is firmly embodied in his theories. In the same way as Freudian psychoanalytic theory and method both challenged and reproduced the conditions of 19th-century Vienna (Showalter, 1985), Rogerian person-centered therapies both critiqued and perpetuated the conditions of mid-20th-century North

American culture. Although certainly not entirely or exclusively, that culture was, and is, still sexist and racist.

In this discussion, I want to take up these points and, by reference to the session as text, reflect on both the content and the process of the interview with a view to gaining a greater understanding of some of both the power and limitations of person-centered therapy as an emancipatory strategy.

It should be noted (and never forgotten) that my reflections will also illustrate Mannheim's thesis. A similar interpretative analysis of *my* reflections would likewise reveal the biases and particularities of my place in the universe. I will be satisfied if the following permits a deeper appreciation and understanding of Carl's contribution to our ongoing search to understand ourselves and our relationships.

Analysis

Self as knower

At the outset of the exchange, Sylvia says that she wants to share. With this use of the word 'share', she signifies that she sees the process as one of mutuality and that she does not want to take a subordinate position in the exchange. This seems to foreshadow what will become a major theme in the session—her growing sense of personal empowerment as a woman. She goes on to discuss her experience of herself as a learner and the sense of achievement she feels about that. 'It's a big deal!' she tells Carl.

In their work on women's development, Belenky et al. (1986) identified as a major developmental turning point the moment when a woman's view of herself shifts from seeing herself as part of the world of the ignorant to seeing herself as part of the world of the 'knowers'. When a woman who has been disenfranchised and silenced first discovers she is capable of learning, her consciousness of herself makes a quantum leap. Sylvia, who had always felt herself outside the community of learners, now discovers herself a member. Significantly, Carl seems to recognize that the moment is significant, marking it by stepping out of a purely reflective empathic stance and directively asking Sylvia to say more about herself as a learner.

Self as mother

It is illuminating from a women's development standpoint that the sphere of knowledge which Sylvia claims first is her mothering. This was also true for many of the women in the Belenky study mentioned above. Sylvia tells Carl that she has become stricter with her children. She has taken charge of them where before, we gather, she has not. And even in the face of her children's resistance, she has the confidence, the sense of 'knowing better', to insist on her parenting program. She has reclaimed her authority as a mother.

Feminists and ethnic scholars have long argued that one of the most oppressive aspects of the White patriarchal (alternatively called Eurocentric–androcentric) worldview is the way it marginalizes, devalues, and even pathologizes the knowledge of subordinated groups (Weedon, 1987; Weisstein, 1971). Their experiential knowing is not seen as a valid 'other perspective' but instead is seen as trivial, erroneous, seditious, or not seen at all. Mothering (mothering here is used to mean both sex-exclusive childbirth and nursing as well as nurturance and care of children, which is overwhelmingly although not exclusively done in our culture by women) is a complex, dense, web of skills, knowledge, ways of responding, acting, speaking, and feeling, that has evolved through the concrete experience of raising children in a particular context. The authentic authorities on maternal knowledge are the people who do the mothering (Ruddick, 1980). The problem is that in a world where only women take care of children and where women's work is seen as trivial and 'natural', i.e., not real 'expertise', then the knowledge she acquires in the course of her work is devalued by her society and therefore by her. She cannot use it as, say, an attorney might, to strengthen her sense of herself as a person who has valuable knowledge. When Sylvia reclaims her maternal knowledge, she gains a sense of herself as a knower, and, with that, power and self-esteem.

Carl's response to this is interesting and revealing. He interprets Sylvia's experience as feeling more 'grown-up'. The implication here is that he ('grown-up' is Carl's word not Sylvia's) sees Sylvia's previous sense of lack as immature. In this choice of image, Carl expresses the familiar tendency of dominant groups to see dominated groups as 'children'.

Carl could have drawn upon any number of other words or concepts. He could have suggested Sylvia had become more 'empowered', 'authoritative', 'emancipated', 'secure', and so on. Such language could allow for the possibility that Sylvia's lack of confidence is not a dispositional problem but is situational, i.e., is a consequence of living in a world which systematically devalues women's knowledge. By making it a personal developmental issue that she can 'grow' out of, Carl's language obscures the possibility of social origins of Sylvia's psychological experience. In other words, it blames the victim.

Sylvia goes on next to describe her increasing sense of empowerment with regard to her sexuality, not coincidentally perhaps, another area of women's lives where the weight of male dominated society comes down heavily. Women's sexuality has always been subjected to restrictions, taboos, controls, and prohibitions. Until very recently and even now in all but a small segment of contemporary society, women's sexuality was/is the exclusive property of men. The idea that a woman can express her sexuality for her own satisfaction has been universally condemned by patriarchal institutions as 'sinful', 'unfeminine', 'unnatural', 'pathological', and, at worst, the work of Satanic forces.

Sylvia says that she is no longer looking to therapists, books, or other people for wisdom about her sexual life. She has stopped looking for knowledge 'out there' and begun consulting her own lived experience as a guide to what pleases her. She has begun to base her sexual reality on an experiential, body-based knowledge rather than on theoretical or abstract bases. Her use of the word 'risk' in this context, however, suggests that she sees her desire to be sexually authentic as problematical.

What does she mean here by the use of the word 'risk'? Clearly, she is not talking about the risk of pregnancy or disease. She suggests that it is her own fear that has been a barrier to her authenticity. Her language is the language of individual pathology rather than societal oppression. She too (as do most of us raised in this culture) shares the androcentric view of female sexuality, even her own. My interpretation is that she is referring to feelings of anxiety she encounters when she wants to act spontaneously upon her sexual feelings. It is not her sexuality per se that is 'risky', but it becomes so in a world where sexuality, especially female sexuality, is subject to social control. In attributing her sexual reticence to her own fears without acknowledging or understanding why she experiences fear at being sexual, I believe Sylvia mislocates the origin of the problem.

Carl also picks up and focuses on the word 'risk' and goes on to reiterate this concept several times. By doing so, both he and Sylvia create a shared belief that Sylvia's previous sexual experience had been limited because of her own unwillingness to take risks—once again a dispositional or intrapsychic explanation.

Reframing this situation from an emancipatory feminist perspective might include an exploration of where the sense of danger Sylvia experiences comes from, what kind of danger she envisions and so on. This might serve to shift the sense of danger away from her own sexual inclinations, which can then be seen as authentic and whole, and onto patriarchy's interest in the control of female sexuality. Instead of seeing her own impulses as dangerous, she may come to see that how much a patriarchal world is afraid of her sexual authenticity—an altogether different reality. (I was made aware of this kind of conceptual 'mislocation' of the source of danger when a woman client of mine reacted to my use of the terms 'risk' and 'courage' in her decision to separate from a misogynistic partner. As we explored her reaction, it became clear that the 'risk' or 'courage' was in remaining in an abusive situation for the sake of the two children. Packing up her kids and leaving was an act of nurturance and self-assertion. By accurately locating the source of danger, her actions on her own behalf felt as she put it, 'More like rolling down hill than pushing up hill'. This conceptualization constructs an image of authenticity as far less grueling than is created by the use of words like 'risk'.)

In the commentary, Carl also uses the word 'risk' to describe several of Sylvia's recent behaviors. How much more empowering would it be, one wonders, if he saw not 'a lot of risking behaviour' but a lot of self-assertiveness, self-confidence, authenticity, or politically revolutionary behavior?

Gaining a voice

There is a strong theme in Sylvia's description of her process of what Belenky et al. (1986) have termed 'gaining a voice'. Her insistence on 'sharing' rather than seeking help is the first clue to this. She goes on to tell Carl how she is gaining her voice as a mother. She is gaining new significance in her role of raising children who are acceptable to the world, and she is now willing to give voice to her knowledge.

Sylvia also demonstrates a keen sense of the important relationship between gaining a voice and the development of self. She explicitly acknowledges that speaking out loud, in the form of making the film, serves to give weight and importance to her growth. It makes both her progress and her self more real. Clinchy and Belenky (1987), in their work with poor rural women, use tape recorders in a similar way to enable women who have previously felt silenced to learn from their own and others' stories. The simple act of recording their words and playing them back so others may learn from them, gives both the words and the speaker a greater significance. Sylvia recognizes that the power of words is in making them public.

Separateness or connection: conflicting views of maturity

After a whole series of statements about Sylvia's growing sense of autonomy and empowerment, Carl reflects what he has heard saying that he feels her to be more 'self assured'. Interestingly, Sylvia seems to resist this idea. She responds by backing away from this view of herself. She begins at once to talk about her 'immaturity'. She seems confused about whether she is immature or mature. As she says more about this, we get the idea that to Sylvia 'maturity' means independence, separateness, self-sufficiency, and not needing any help from anyone.

In the past 20 years, it has become clear that this view of maturity is an essentially Anglo-Saxon and masculine view. In the field of psychology, it is derived from developmental research using predominantly middle-class White male subjects. When the development of other cultural groups (Shweder & Bourne, 1982) and the development of women and girls is examined (Gilligan, 1982), we find a somewhat different pattern. The work of feminist psychologists and others has revealed that in the lives of women, connection and relatedness are essential aspects of maturity (Belenky et al., 1986; Gilligan, 1982; Jordan et al., 1991). Only when compared against models of maturity based on maps of White male development would Sylvia's wish for connection, support, and nurturance from Carl be seen as signs of pathology or 'dependent personality' as Sylvia herself labels it. Sylvia, like so many women who have been exposed to a malebased psychology, has internalized its myths and is now using them against herself.

Here we see a crystal clear illustration of the way Sylvia's own sense of herself has become 'pathologised' as a consequence of the introjected values of an androcentric view of development. Sylvia believes that there are only two possible positions for her to be in, in her relationship with Carl. She can either be 'mature' and strong, in which case she must be self-sufficient, or she can be 'immature' or helpless and not in control, in which case she can receive something from her connection to Carl. The dilemma here is obvious—strength is equated with separateness and closeness is equated with loss of control and helplessness. Sylvia feels she must choose between a version of empowerment which severs her connections or a connectedness which renders her powerless. (She may in fact be correct in her assumption. In traditional patriarchal societies, male–female relationships are situations where connection means subordination. Patriarchal concepts of masculinity see men as 'protectors' and 'providers' and women as 'dependents'.)

At this point, one of the limitations of a strictly reflective, empathic therapy emerges. Carl's response here is to support Sylvia's view of her predicament. He does try to reframe her self-label 'dependent' by the use of the word 'vulnerable', but her core belief that in order to learn she must give up power and control, goes unchallenged. This could mean that subsequent concepts will be built upon this erroneous conceptual 'foundation' locking her into a disempowering view of the learning process.

A more actively dialogical therapy such as feminist therapy would permit Sylvia's potentially self-defeating conceptual schema to be challenged. A feminist therapist might point to Sylvia's own earlier statements as a way to draw new awareness from her own experience. She had told Carl that she was 'learning' as a mother and about her sexuality, not through therapy but as a consequence of her own empowered action in the world. She might come to see how her belief that she must surrender power to the male authority in order to gain from the relationship is perhaps driven more by patriarchal mythology than her own experience. She may also come to realize that in relationships that are free from the exploitative elements of sexism, closeness and mutuality do not come at the expense of one's personal power but are enrichments of it.

As it happens, Sylvia's actions are more self-assertive than her beliefs! She does not, in fact, surrender to Carl but actively reaches out to make the kind of contact she wants. She takes hold of his hands. And in yet another demonstration of the importance of connection and mutuality in the growth and therapy of women, it is in the context of this closer connection that more conflictual feelings emerge.

Internalization of culture: the socially constructed 'self'

As the session proceeds, Sylvia's struggle for authentic identity—her self—becomes the dominant theme. After establishing a physical connection with Carl, she confesses to him that she is attracted to Black people, and she feels ashamed and embarrassed about it. Using harshly evaluative language, she labels herself 'crazy', 'neurotic', and 'sick'. She experiences the conflict on multiple levels. At the intrapsychic level, she experiences shame; interpersonally, she suffers her family's and friends' disapproval; and at the societal level, she confronts a racist culture.

In their exploration of her experience once again, both Carl and Sylvia are trapped by their Eurocentric–androcentric ways of thinking. Sylvia looks for a psychological explanation of her attraction. Interestingly, she does not to seek to explain her embarrassment! Neither she nor Carl addresses the societal issues of racism and sexism. Both deal with the problem as an intrapsychic issue. (This is not to say that Carl, when confronted consciously with relationships between people who are assigned to different race categories in Eurocentric thought, would disapprove or be unsupportive. Carl's history of work toward ending sectarian and racial violence and injustice is well known. The bias I am referring to here is at the deepest levels of the structure of thought, conceptual habits, and linguistic constructions, much of which we are not ordinarily conscious of.) But, we should ask, where do her feelings that a White woman's attraction to Black people is sick or crazy, originate? Once again, Sylvia mislocates her problem. She is so thoroughly colonized by White racism, even in her inner psychological world, that Sylvia has made a complete inversion!

Here we get a glimpse at the way social, cultural, and linguistic habits construct inner psychological reality. French deconstructionist feminists such as Julia Kristeva and Luce lrigaray have attempted to demonstrate that even at the level of desire—let's say sexual desire for a particular person—we learn from birth the expectations, interests, taboos, and values of our culture such that all future psychic reality will be experienced, interpreted, and constructed in terms of these primary elements. Established in the body, before the development of language (and later symbolized by it), the embodied attractions, revulsions, and antipathies feel 'natural'. (I am deliberately sidestepping the issue of 'first causes' here—the determinist vs. free will—religious arguments as to whether or not our interests are biologically determined, reincarnated from previous lives, or created *in toto* from our experiences in the world. What matters from a therapeutic point of view is that phenomenologically we can experience what we call our 'authentic self' and that this can change during our lifetime. What may have felt 'not me' two years ago may feel like 'me' today and what I would have sworn by before I now reject.) We feel no need to explain desires which are consistent with this felt natural sense. In this way, the culture is carried in the 'selves' it creates and is reproduced by raising children in its own image. (For a community to be stable, it must be able to reproduce itself in each succeeding generation. Mores, values, and 'reality stories' must seem 'natural' and as 'the way things are'. To the extent that its values are life-enhancing, this process may drive healthy communities, and to the extent that they are life-negating, they may drive cultures of oppression. The goal of emancipatory therapies (or philosophies, pedagogies, or politics) is to identify the unconscious internalized values that dehumanize, and to replace 'unconscious' patterns of life with conscious 'fully human' processes. The ultimate goal is the co-creation of a world in which one group's (or person's) wellbeing does not come at the expense of another's.) Only when there is absence of desire in the 'right' direction or presence of desire in the 'wrong' direction do we experience anxiety and look for 'reasons' (Toril, 1987). Without following Kristeva or lrigaray into the labyrinth of Lacanian–Marxist–deconstructionist assumptions about the presence or absence of a phallus as the primary psychic organizer, we can nonetheless use these ideas in order to examine the way Sylvia has mislocated the pathology.

Sylvia experiences desires that are at odds with the interests of White racist society and its ideas of 'normalcy', so she feels anxious. Her desires are not mirrored by either the micro-culture of her family or the culture at large and she labels her feelings pathological.

As I said, it is not her anxiety that puzzles her but her attraction. (She completely misses the import of her own observation that her Black friends see nothing to be explained in her attraction.) Despite the fact that we might consider her embarrassment and her critical self-judgement as a form of internalized racism, in fact, from an emancipatory therapy perspective at least, Sylvia's desire system must already be more 'colour-blind' or emancipated than that of most Whites, for Sylvia actually experiences her fascination. Most of us are not so open as Sylvia. Her anxiety has not been sufficient to actually extinguish the fascination but only to burden it with shame—the introjected censure of White racist society.

What Sylvia does psychologically here reveals the enormous potency of cultural attitudes like racism and sexism. Sylvia turns upon herself and labels her pain as her own pathology. She is blind to the way in which her inner psychological process serves not her own authentic interests but those of the dominant class. In the private recesses of her own mind, she has become an agent of White racist society in the service of her own oppression! But none of this can emerge from the dialog between Sylvia and Carl. On the contrary, Carl participates in keeping the focus intrapsychic.

Sylvia seems to conceive of her task as one of gaining a stronger sense of individual identity. She also seems aware that if her identity is too deviant, too out of step with her community, it will be hard to maintain her sense of authority. Once more linking voice with self, she makes active use of the medium of making a film with Carl Rogers as a way of amplifying her own voice and of counteracting the critical voices of her society. It is probably also true that Carl's non-judgmental position and her search for 'other women who feel the same way' can all be seen as attempts to minimize the discomfort she experiences in the tension between being and belonging. As we shall see, even this, apparently, is not enough.

Being or belonging: the struggle for authentic relationship

What happens next is very interesting and even more revealing of how essentially conservative consciousness often is. After exploring her 'deviant' desire system, she begins to disconnect from her own words. She has a sense of 'talking away her feelings', and says she feels she 'didn't hear what she said very well'. Carl's interpretation is that the disconnection is a defence against changing too fast.

We may ask, what is the danger in changing too fast? To answer this, we need to ask two more questions; the first, what 'change' will her new awareness bring about, and the second, what are the perceived consequences of such a change? The answers to both questions are given in the text.

Sylvia is moving from seeing herself as voiceless and powerless, with attractions which are shameful, to seeing herself as empowered, envoiced, and willing to own her attraction even if it means her society's disapproval. By working toward an understanding of her authentic knowledge and inclinations, she is involved in a personal revolution against her culture. At this point in her journey toward a fuller humanness, Sylvia encounters in her own psychological defensive process the existential conflict between connection and freedom, between being and belonging. As Sylvia sees it, she is in a lose–lose situation. Authenticity brings freedom but it also brings rejection and isolation, societal conformity brings guilt and shame. She is in a state of cognitive dissonance in which a coherent sense of self is at odds with her sense of social integration. This predicament is especially anxiety provoking for women. As already mentioned, the work of feminist researchers suggests for most women identity development is inseparable from their sense of embeddedness and connection in mutually affirming relationships. If Sylvia openly acknowledges to herself the reality emerging from her exploration with Carl, she must face the prospect of losing her social connections with friends, family, and culture. When anxiety (in this case we might call it existential anxiety) becomes overwhelming, she can defend herself either by ignoring her new awareness (by dissociation and denial) or she can expand her map of reality and reach some new level of cognitive (and emotional) development which can support her new self-concept.

It seems that Sylvia's first inclination is to 'deny' her experience—to not 'hear' her own words, to discount them as 'jabber, jabber' and to turn upon herself once again. This time Carl does not follow her into the intrapsychic battleground but instead assertively disagrees with her self-assessment. Paradoxically, he counters Sylvia's self-discount by discounting her reality! In his exquisite interpretation of her words, Carl gives real weight to them, making denial more difficult and advancement of consciousness more possible. The emancipatory potential for the client of deep, empathic listening by the therapist—the *sine qua non* of person-centered therapies—is clearly demonstrated by the way Carl's reiteration helps Sylvia deeply listen to herself, and in so doing, take her own words much more seriously.

Carl's willingness to listen carefully and to enter the relationship in a real way (by disagreeing with Sylvia) also serves to show Sylvia that there is an alternative to her lose–lose scenario. Carl's attention and focus upon her words offer her a new connection—with him and people who have the values he does. She may become alienated from groups who reject her new identity, but she may discover new connections with people who are willing to listen to her with respect and to enter into mutually affirming contact. The possibility exists that she will not have to choose between being and belonging. As she realizes this, she relaxes and reengages with the learning process.

Retreat from reason: the personal not the political

Discussions as to whether or not person-centered therapies are apolitical have been a long-standing tradition. Within the ranks of those who call themselves client- or person-centered therapists, there is a general acceptance of the view that these approaches are profoundly political. Indeed, much of Carl's later work was in the public, political arena, working as he did in South Africa, South America, Eastern Europe, and the Soviet Union. On the other hand, critics like feminist Miriam

Greenspan (Greenspan, 1983) have argued that in their focus on the intrapsychic levels of reality and in the emphasis of feelings over thoughts and analysis, client-centered and other humanistic therapies actually keep the oppressed from an adequate understanding of the social sources of their pain and in so doing become part of the problem rather than part of the solution. I have also discussed this in other writings (O'Hara, 1989b). An examination of the final interchange between Sylvia and Carl points to some of the difficulties with client-centered therapy as an emancipatory therapy.

After Carl's reiteration of her words, what strikes Sylvia is her realization that there is a part of herself which she simply does not understand. Carl adds to her statement, 'You have to have reasons'. He seems to imply from his tone of voice here that perhaps reasons are not necessary. Sylvia picks this up and says, 'So it seems like I don't have to have a reason'. Carl supports this by stating, 'So maybe intellectual understanding isn't as important as you thought it was'. Sylvia concludes, 'I think the acceptance is what's most important'. In the voice-over commentary, Carl makes it even clearer that he sees Sylvia's analysing as unnecessary. He says to Sylvia, 'If I could accept it, I wouldn't have to understand in the sense of knowing the reasons'.

I think this passage makes it very clear that Carl is looking at Sylvia's struggle from a strictly psychological point of view and a very narrow, intrapsychic, emotional version of psychology at that. By creating a false dichotomy between reason and acceptance, he implies that acceptance could never come from intellectual understanding. Here he returns to the position he held throughout his career that interpretation and insight are of very doubtful usefulness in therapy. I believe there would have been far more to gain, both politically and psychologically, if Carl had been able to help Sylvia explore the connection between understanding and acceptance. A powerful illustration of the way analytical, intellectual knowledge supports the psychological can be seen, for example, in work with women who have been molested or raped. In addition to the pain of their trauma, these women are often wracked with guilt because they have internalized societal myths that somehow they had caused what happened. Understanding the way sexist society sets up women—all women—for such trespass upon their bodies is frequently the most significant therapeutic intervention, permitting self-acceptance and self-comforting to occur.

Beyond the obvious problem of the false dichotomy, there is another perhaps more serious problem in the interaction. Sylvia says she does not have 'to explain it to anybody'. Carl suggests that in her imagination. she is trying to explain it to someone. Sylvia sits for 25 seconds in silence. Then she says it seems she will 'never understand it. So [she] can make life a lot easier for [herself] by not trying'. In this interaction, Sylvia is being supported by Carl to see her struggle both as an entirely personal issue and one that is not worth the trouble to figure out. His support of her defeat and the suggestion that it is not so important for her to understand as to accept, has a ring of 'don't worry your little head about this'. The two of them agree to reduce the whole struggle for her emergence as a woman to an intrapsychic struggle for self-acceptance. They tacitly agree to ignore entirely the therapeutic potential for Sylvia and the transformative potential for the whole society if Sylvia were able to understand and explain, not only to herself but to her society, her predicament, its origins, and her successes in the direction of her liberation. What if Carl had asked her, in the directive way he had asked her questions about her learnings, 'To whom do you want to explain?' or 'Who do you think could benefit from your experiences if you were able to explain them?' and so on? At this point, it might have been clear to both of them that in exactly the same way that Sylvia's inhibited self bears the traces of her development in a world that is racist and sexist, sharing with others her emancipation from those cultural introjections could be part of a revolutionary creation of a new culture that is less sexist and less racist. By reducing her work to the private sphere, Carl, in the tradition of White patriarchal culture, keeps Sylvia politically impotent. When she asks Carl if he ever looks for reasons to justify himself, his answer, 'I suspect we all do', is strangely coy for a man who has had a major transformative impact on his culture by doing just that!

Conclusion

In comparing person-centered approaches to therapy to the pedagogical strategies outlined by Paulo Freire in his *Pedagogy of the Oppressed*, I enumerate the significant ways I consider person-centered approaches to be emancipatory in the broadest sense.

> The work is... aimed directly at the uneven balance of power... the disparity, between the individual and... family, community, culture.... The work involves re-examination of introjection and the way the individual is diminished and limited in expression of full humanness.
>
> (O'Hara, 1989b, p. 19)

In affirming the dignity and worth of his clients and, by extension, the worth of every individual, in the theory and practice of person-centered approaches, Carl Rogers' ideas take their place alongside the great ideas of Western liberal humanistic tradition. That this humanism is emancipatory when compared to other views of the human condition, such as totalitarianism, fascism, feudalism, and other ideologies of subjugation, cannot be disputed. But for all that, the interview with Sylvia shows us that there are serious limitations, both theoretical and practical, which must be addressed if the full potential can be realized for person-centered therapies as emancipatory strategies for the disenfranchised.

Perhaps the most important is the recognition that the approach was formulated prior to the emergence of what is now variously called the constructivist, poststructuralist, deconstructionist movements in epistemology. (It may be possible to argue that in its insistence on unconditional acceptance of the client's internal frame of reference that person-centered approaches verge upon being postmodern without the implications of this for the theory having been yet elaborated.) Rogers lived his life in a world with a unitary reality. He believed that it was possible for the therapist to arrive at a level of understanding where they could accurately know the world of the client. He says the therapist must assume

> the internal reference of the client, to perceive the world as the client sees it, to perceive the client himself as he is seen by himself, to lay aside all perceptions from the external frame of reference while doing so, and to communicate something of this empathic understanding to the client.
>
> (Rogers, 1951, p. 29)

Postmodern thinking puts the therapist in an entirely different relationship with the client. If we accept the postmodern proposition that the knower is inseparable from what is known, that perception itself is a creative process, then we must also admit that empathy as described by Rogers in the above quotation is not possible. It is not possible for us to set aside our own subjectivity in this way. Furthermore, any claim that we have done so blinds us, more than our own subjectivity could ever do, to the ways in which our own biases and interests are embodied in all our understandings of the world, all our expressions of our own world, and in all our questions.

Postmodern epistemologies make it necessary for us to reconsider what we mean when we speak of empathy. Dialog, like that between Sylvia and Carl, is seen more as a mutually intersubjective conversation in which Sylvia explores her inner and outer reality and the world in which that reality was forged, as Carl allows himself to be involved, touched, and moved by her story. Empathy becomes a term for how one person's life can be touched, illuminated, and affected in connection with another's. Like a hermeneutic reading of a sacred text, we understand another's world by way of, not despite, our own subjectivity.

Carl demonstrated on many occasions, and here in this interview, what an extraordinary 'reader' he was. Over the years I worked with him he got ever better. This is not because he was better able to put his own subjectivity aside but rather the reverse. He had, by his countless deep readings of others' lives, expanded his own inner landscape so that, in somewhat the same way that someone experienced in many languages has a better chance of decoding ancient scrolls, Carl's enormous wealth of experience enhanced his ability to understand the meanings offered in the expressions of his clients.

Not less self then, but more—but still self. And this brings us to the issue of blindspots and biases and that leads us back to Mannheim.

We must now admit that Carl does not achieve his stated ideal of laying aside any outside frame of reference. Nor could he, for in order to hear another we must already have a language to hear them in. With that language comes myriad cultural associations and meanings which describe and define the way of life of those who share the language. As I have illustrated, the language and values of client-centered therapy are the language and values of its creators—White middle-class male North Americans. It could not be other and there is nothing inherently disempowering in that situation. The problem comes in the failure to recognize the inevitability of bias. By denying that all 'listening' implies interpretation, that we hear what we expect to hear, that what we are aware of and what we say reveals our own construction of reality, the client-centered therapist runs the risk of engaging in covert 'reality making' for the client. That this goes unacknowledged makes it all the more insidious and potentially oppressive, as we have seen in Sylvia's interview. On the one hand, realities that are very important for her and for women in general are missed, misunderstood, minimized, or distorted due to Carl's own biases and blindspots, and on the other hand, he offers (entirely unknowingly) subtle pressure to conform to a Eurocentric, androcentric *status quo*. Perhaps if Carl had not been such an extraordinarily open man, so flexible in his point of view in comparison to most other men his age and class, his biases would have been seen more clearly earlier. Perhaps if he had not been such an exquisite therapist, the structural and theoretical limitations of client-centered therapy might have been more obvious. Until feminists and others began to elaborate the new postmodern critique, there has been no language in which to adequately discuss these problems. But if client-centered therapy is to survive and thrive in this new postmodern world, it will need to incorporate these multiple 'other ways of knowing'.

Notes

1 When Maureen originally wrote this, she was based at the Center for Studies of the Person, La Jolla, CA.
2 Horney (1926, p. 324).

Chapter 16

Relational empathy

Beyond modernist egocentricism to postmodern holistic contextualism (1997)

Maureen O'Hara

In the beginning is the relationship.

(Martin Buber)[1]

Aims of the chapter

The chapter is intended to contribute to the fast-growing discussion of the limits of the indigenous psychology of the Western world in addressing the relational needs of its members. In particular, it will examine the limits of modernist individualism as a paradigm for understanding human experience, and to bring into focus some of the ways Western psychological understandings of empathy have obscured some of the important ways empathy functions in human relationships. I also intend to show that, because of its position as a modernist, objectivist discourse, Western psychology has been slow to recognize how its modes of enquiry and expression have limited our understanding of relational realities. I want to extend our understanding of empathy beyond its present role as the 'royal road to understanding' of individuals by using somewhat different frames of reference from those traditionally characteristic of psychological discussion. Although my main goal will be to expand understanding of empathy as a therapeutic process, I hope to reach further. As our world undergoes what some consider to be the birth pangs of its first truly 'global civilisation', in which national, ethnic, religious, gender, and class boundaries are shifting on unprecedented scales (Anderson, 1990), all of us will need new postmodernist psychologies with which to navigate. The ability to empathize with other individuals and other groups may become the most important interpersonal and even political competence. Increased attention to mutual empathy could lead those of us in Western societies to recover some of our sense of connectedness to each other, our communities, and our world, a recovery which, given the West's current disproportionate impact on global realities, may prove vital to future survival.

DOI: 10.4324/9781003519454-21

Western indigenous psychology

The modernist worldview

In recent years, a strong case has been made by many scholars that the worldview which frames mainstream Western psychology is culturally and historically situated, representing the interests, investments, and experiences of participants in a world dominated by particular ways of thinking and living (Bellah et al., 1985; Berman, 1989; Gergen, 1991; Giddens, 1991; Levin, 1987a; Shweder & Bourne, 1982; Taylor, 1989). This worldview—referred to as modernity—has been shaped by 'the Copernican revolution, Newtonian physics, Cartesian epistemology and metaphysics, humanism and its political revolutions, and the beginning of the technological, industrial and commercial transformations of society' (Levin, 1987a, p. 2). The view of the person at its centre also reflects the major philosophical commitments of modernism. The idea that people have something inside called 'a self' or 'the Self', which contains a deep interiority which is contacted through introspection, self-examination, or some other form of 'inward vision' would have been incomprehensible to Europeans before St. Augustine. It still is to some peoples from non-modern societies untouched by the Western worldview.

Western psychology, particularly clinical or applied psychology and psychiatry, is a quintessential modernist enterprise. It is based in modernist views of the nature of human reality which appeared first as scientific rationalist epistemology and became culturally institutionalized though socializing processes. Its origins were the Italian Renaissance and came of age during the 19th and 20th centuries in Europe and North America (see, for example, Berman, 1989; Cushman, 1992; Gergen, 1991; Giddens, 1991; Guisinger & Blatt, 1994; O'Hara, 1984a; Showalter, 1985; Shweder & Bourne, 1982; B. M. Smith, 1994; Taylor, 1989). Participants in the process of psychotherapy in Western societies, whether clients or psychotherapists, perceive and experience themselves in terms of an indigenous Western psychology. They see themselves as distinct, autonomous agents, separated from other individuals by a whole array of boundaries of identity. Whether as the European self, full of dangerous tensions between aggressive and sexual drives barely contained by the rational will, or as the American self, enthusiastic, achievement-oriented, and transcending its animal baseness through hard work and religious commitment, Western modernist society has valorized individual experience and has placed at its centre a monadic, decontextualized person who is virtually unencumbered by any a priori external constraints (Cushman, 1992).

Shweder and Bourne refer to the Western modernist self, at the centre of its own worldview as *egocentric* to suggest its individualistic, abstract, and decontextualized paradigm. They contrast this with a quite different psychology found in premodern Europe and in non-modernist societies like India and Mexico, which they term *sociocentric*, to describe a frame of reference that sees personhood as deriving from participation in the world holistically, concretely, and contextually (Shweder & Bourne, 1982). I shall use Shweder and Bourne's language here.

In egocentric cultures, people tend to think of themselves as possessing a self within, which they speak of in terms that are both context-free and abstract. Ideal human relationships are seen as voluntary contractual agreements between two or more individual and autonomous agents. People in America, for instance, where the individual is supraordinate to any social role or obligation, will say that they *have* a family. In sociocentric India, the hierarchy of who belongs to what is reversed, and people say and feel at the deepest levels that they *belong to* their families.

In egocentric cultures, people take it for granted that there is a split between their inside self and the outside world. The view of the self-as-monad becomes everywhere projected outwards, idealized, and codified. Once institutionalized in parenting habits, in religious, educational, and political traditions, or incorporated into art, language, and other symbols of consciousness, this monadic self is then re*internalized* (a very modernist word). It becomes the experienced reality, the master narratives, the automatic social patterns, and habits of life in that society. Situated within such an all-encompassing milieu, where everything mirrors the conceptual and perceptual effects of modernism, inhabitants of 20th-century Western democracies come to take this mechanistic and egocentric, atomized world as 'the way things are', and it is very difficult, if not impossible for us to imagine how it could be otherwise. We highly prize values such as the sovereign rights of individuals, celebration of individualism, egalitarianism, glorification of the solitary hero, tolerance for difference, protection of freedom, encouragement of individual creativity and expression, and the idealization of reason and objectivity. At the same time, threats to sovereignty, or demands made upon one solely by dint of birth, social context, or other non-chosen circumstances makes Westerners very uncomfortable. To have one's unique inner subjectivity dismissed, violated, expropriated, or, as the French psychoanalyst Henri Wallon says 'confiscated', is experienced as an almost unbearable psychic loss (Berman, 1989, p. 36). Some have suggested that this self-versus-other dichotomy has led to a chronic vulnerability in the Western psyche, leaving it with an insatiable need for psychic affirmation from significant others, debilitating shame if the object of insult, rejection, or abandonment, and an almost inconsolable longing for recognition and connection with significant others. The prevalence of neurotic illness, narcissism, depression, self-disorders, relationship breakdown, and addictive disorders has been linked by many authors to this fundamental rupture between selves and their contexts (Levin, 1987a).

The rise of mechanistic psychiatry

Psychiatry and its descendants became a prominent aspect of Western medicine contemporaneously with the rapid and brutal industrialization of Victorian life. The exponential rise of psychiatry from the mid-1800s to the present day can be seen as a response to an epidemic of madness which Victorian psychiatrists believed to be occurring in dark irrational counterpoint to the unprecedented advances in political, scientific, and technological achievement. It should not surprise us, then, that at a time when mechanistic thinking was resulting in engineering feats the likes of which the world had never seen, that when medical men—and they were men—turned their attention to psychology, they would see human experience as a matter of *mechanisms* and would seek 'to apply rigorous scientific methods to the study of insanity rather than rely any longer on... vague humanitarian sympathies... of their predecessors' (Showalter, 1985, p. 104). Henry Maudsley (1835–1918), editor of the *Journal of Mental Science* and founder of the psychiatric Maudsley Hospital in England, asserted in 1874:

> Lunatics and criminals are as much manufactured articles as are steam engines and calico-printing machines. They are neither accidents nor anomalies in the universe, but come by law to testify to causality; and it is the business of science to find out what the causes are and by what laws they work.
>
> (Maudsley, 1874, as quoted in Showalter, 1985, p. 104)

With its emphasis on individualism, rationalism, objectivism, and instrumentalism, an emphasis which as we shall see continues to the present, modernist Western psychology overwhelmingly views human life from within a mechanistic psychology of individuals. To modernist psychologists, the clear identification of boundaries separating classes and categories of nature is vitally important, nowhere more so than in the categories which separate health from disease and rationality from irrationality. To the founders of modern psychiatry, the most important therapeutic skills were diagnostic objectivity, analysis, and instrumentalism. By contrast, subjectivity, sensitivity, and compassion were seen as soft, even feminine, placing the doctor at risk of being drawn across the boundaries separating him from his patient.

Even though it might have been 'just what the doctor ordered' for people suffering psychic disconnection, empathy had no place in such a psychology. Indeed, there was not even the word *empathy* in English until 1912. The opinion held by the Victorian founders of Western psychology was that it was dangerous for the healer to come too close to the patient, threatening the physician with contamination by those afflicted patients who inhabited the 'borderlands' or who had traversed the boundary between sanity and madness (Showalter, 1985, p. 120).

Empathy in egocentric psychologies

Empathy, the *Oxford English Dictionary* tells us, 'refers to the power of entering into the experience of or understanding objects or feelings outside oneself'. Originally coined as the English equivalent of the German word *einfuhlung*, when it first appeared in English, empathy had nothing to do with psychotherapy. Rather it was an epistemology—a way of knowing—and referred to the process by which artists and poets gained access to their subjects. John Keats' empathic ability to merge the boundary between himself and his subject matter is legendary (Rollins, 1958). When first discussed as 'the process… which plays the largest part in our understanding of… other people' (Freud, 1920/1955, p. 110), a scientifically valid method of observation by which psychiatrists could gain understanding of the inner world of their patients, it was highly suspect.

As Herbert Feigl (1959) explained:

> We recognize that, especially in the psychology of human motivation, and in psychodynamics generally, empathy is an often helpful and *important heuristic tool* [emphasis added]. But we realize also that empathetic judgements can go woefully wrong, no matter how strong their intuitive conviction. Empathy may be a source of knowledge, in that it suggests hypotheses. But it is not self-authenticating.
>
> (p. 119)

Gradually, however, within the field of clinical if not experimental psychology, empathy came to be highly valued as a 'source of analytic data' (Levy, 1985), a means of learning about the contents of other minds, particularly in client-centered therapy, psychoanalysis, and other depth psychologies.

Early conceptions of empathy have a decidedly modernist egocentric feel. Freud describes empathy as a 'mechanism by means of which we are enabled to take up any attitude at all toward another mental life' (Freud, 1920/1955, p. 110). Of what he called one of the 'necessary and sufficient conditions' for personality change in psychotherapy, Carl Rogers (1959) states:

> The state of empathy or being empathic, is to perceive the internal frame of reference of another with accuracy, and with the emotional components and meanings which pertain thereto, as if one were the other person, but without ever losing the "as if" condition. Thus it means to sense the hurt or the pleasure of another as he senses it, and to perceive the causes thereof as he perceives them, but without ever losing the recognition that it is as if I were hurt or pleased etc. If this "as if" quality is lost, then the state is one of identification.
>
> (pp. 210–211)

At first, Rogers was the consummate modernist (O'Hara, 1995a). He saw empathy as an instrument. The therapist gained access to the inner meaning world of the client in order to reflect these meanings back to the client for use in reconfiguring their authentic sense of self. He believed that empathy, like any other reality, existed in some quantity that could be accurately and quantitatively measured. The image of a clearly bounded individual discerning the inner world of another without becoming contaminated by whatever is found there, clearly echoes earlier Victorian nervousness about blurring important boundaries. Truax and Carkhuff, students of Rogers, took objectivism even further and developed the widely used scale for quantifying the ability for empathic understanding. The 8-point scale measured how skilful people were in paraphrasing another's statements (Carkhuff, 1969; Truax, 1961). More recently, client-centered therapists have attempted to take Rogerian empathy beyond formalizable operations to include 'emergent modes of empathy'. However, the frame of reference is still individualistic, and atomistic. Bozarth states that therapists must 'develop idiosyncratic empathy modes predicated upon the therapist *as a person*, the client *as a person*, and the *therapist–client interactions* [emphasis added].' (Bozarth, 1984, p. 69). Mechanistic metaphors feature prominently. One writer suggests 'the therapist's understanding depends on his sensory perception of the signals the client relays' (Vanaerschot, 1990, p. 278). Whatever the metaphor, characteristic of early Rogerian conceptions of empathy is an egocentric image of two separate individuals wherein one—the therapist—attempts to discern something happening within the skin of the other—the client.

It is not only Rogerians who have described empathy in egocentric terms. In recent years, empathy has taken centre stage among psychoanalysts, particularly the object relations analysts. Greenson describes building up of a 'working model of the patient' (Greenson, 1960, p. 421), and Buie (1981) suggests that 'the empathizer compares... behavioral cues with one or more referent in his own mind which could be expressed by similar behavior. He then infers that the inner experience of the object qualitatively matches that associated with his referent' (p. 305). The work of Kohut has been particularly influential. At first, Kohut too regarded empathy as a heuristic tool, as a means, along with introspection, of knowing and understanding the inner motivations and intentions of his patients. Empathy, he said, 'is the capacity to think and feel oneself into the inner life of another person' (Kohut, 1984, p. 82), and more recently Kohutians Rowe and MacIsaacs have defined empathy as the 'analyst's attempt to experience as closely as possible what the patient is experiencing' (Rowe & MacIsaacs, 1991, p. 16). In obvious attempts to avoid charges of being 'soft', non-scientific, or non-objective, writers about empathy go to great pains to emphasize that 'empathy is neither a mystical, artistic or innate ability' (Levy, 1985, p. 373), and to distinguish between pathological and healthy forms of therapist–client connection (Buie, 1981). Concerned with protecting the ability to move into and out of an empathic state, early on, Kohut resisted suggestions that empathy should be used to gratify a patient's longing for reconnection to the mother-bond, and emphasized the importance of analytic neutrality (Kohut, 1959). Later in his career, however, he conceded that it was 'normal' for the analyst to prize the patient the way a mother might prize her infant (Kohut, 1984). As if suspicious of any psychic organization not based upon the modernist ideal of individuation, psychologists from analytic, existential, and humanistic traditions have characteristically insisted that empathy be clearly differentiated from the more regressive process which Buie calls 'merging'.

The pervasive bias in Western modernist psychology in favor of objectivist-materialism and instrumentalism has obscured the extent to which the psyche in egocentric contexts differs from that of people in sociocentric societies. Such a bias significantly limits access by Westerners to realms of empathic knowing beyond the customary limits of objectivism.

Sociocentric psychology

Self-assertive and self-transcendent states

There is good evidence that people are not all in the world in the same way and that the way people experience themselves and their phenomenal world has differed historically across time and still differs from context to context. In familial, tribal, or communitarian cultures, such as Indian people of South America, and Indians from Asia, consciousness of self is more holistic, contextual, and concrete (Shweder & Bourne, 1982). Similar observations have been made about women in North America, whose sense of self is more holistic and concrete than American men (Belenky et al., 1986; Clinchy & Belenky, 1987; Comas-Diaz & Greene, 1994; Gilligan, 1982; Jordan et al., 1991; Surrey, 1991). Similar differences have been noted for Africans and for African Americans (Jones, 1991).

Connected consciousness

It is through the work of artists and poets that we can best grasp the differences in consciousness between sociocentric people and Western modern people (Romanyshyn, 1982). The yarn paintings made by Huichol Indians of Mexico, the ephemeral sand paintings by North American Navajos and Tibetan Buddhist lamas, the arabesques of Islam, the calligraphy of Taoist penmen, and Australian Aboriginal art reveal a way of being in nature in which the categories, distinctions, and discontinuities common to Western consciousness are nowhere to be seen.

Such imagery provides us with an inside view of what Shweder and Bourne mean by sociocentric or holistic consciousness. It conveys the organic connections and shifting interpenetrated realities where boundaries, if they exist at all, are shown as fuzzy, and situational. This is a world where reality is experienced as an emergent process, not a clearly delineated stable product. This is a fluid, sensuous, undulating world in which the mind moves from place to place, and figure and ground continually shift in response to its own particular priorities.

Attention is self-transcendent or holistic—directed outward beyond the skin of individual persons to involving itself in the group, community, and natural world. Viewers, like the artist, are drawn into the imagery and find themselves drawn beyond their own skin, dwelling in the swirling interconnected world. Such a state of mind, in which familiar ego boundaries are loosened, may be referred to as self-transcendent or holistic consciousness. It is not limited by fixed boundaries of time or space. Long dead relatives or folks across the globe are as real and as palpable as some solid object held firmly in hand. Self-transcendent consciousness does not experience itself standing apart from the world but as constituent parts of yet larger wholes.

The art most highly revered by modern Westerners, by contrast, strikes one immediately as far more self-assertive. From the Renaissance onwards, we see distinct images of recognizable individuals, their faces bearing the hallmarks of a complex and unique interiority. The self-portraits of European masters look directly out at the viewer as if to say, 'Here am I', conveying an impression of a consciousness which pays attention to unique personhood, and identity. Modernist consciousness sees itself self-assertively—as foreground—the rest of creation set behind—as background.

We are describing here more mere difference in conceptualizations about universal realities, but different phenomenal worlds are so differently structured and populated as to constitute differently lived versions of reality.

Empathy through a sociocentric, holistic frame

Now, in the last decade of the 20th century, it is clear that the extreme of Western modernism in psychology is coming under scrutiny, driven largely by cross-cultural and 'cross-general' critiques of mainstream thought.

Beginning in the mid-1970s, Carl Rogers' work began to shift in a sociocentric direction, as his interest moved beyond its earlier individual focus to the workings of relationships, groups, communities, and ultimately societies (Bowen et al., 1979; O'Hara, 1983a, 1984a, 1989b; Rogers, 1977, 1980/1995b). It was this work which compelled us to rethink traditional Rogerian ways of understanding empathy.

In 1977, five members of the Center for Studies of the Person of La Jolla, California, myself and Rogers among them, were invited to convene a large community workshop in Brazil (Bowen et al., 1979). On that trip, we were plunged into intensely intimate engagement with people whose worldview was far less egocentric than ours. When we presented our ideas, we were chided for what Brazilian participants experienced as our exaggerated individualism. This cultural collision made it necessary to acknowledge the limitations of the egocentric worldview for addressing relational realities. Our understanding of empathy in particular became greatly enlarged.

Empathy as contextual awareness

Empathy has a more respected role in sociocentric human relations than it typically does in egocentric cultures. Not seen as poor relation to objective interpretation, many non-Western societies encourage the development of empathic skills and consider the ability to empathically apprehend realities—activities like meditation, astrology, poetry, the Yogas, and so on—as an essential element of adulthood and an indispensable part of a leader's education. The Japanese *omoiyari*, for example, is characterized by a heightened sensitivity to and concern for the feelings, and thoughts, needs, and moods, of subordinates in hierarchical relationships such as psychotherapy (Roland, 1988). The Japanese take it for granted that those in authority will have *omoiyari* toward subordinates. Indigenous American tribal people also consider modernist Westerners somewhat handicapped by their limited empathic abilities.

It was decidedly humbling for the Rogers team attempting to transfer to non-Western societies the importance of empathy in client-centered psychotherapy, to discover that workshop participants in sociocentric cultures were routinely more empathic than we were—sometimes to a startling degree. Time and time again people—therapists and lay-people—were able to sense feelings, thoughts, movements, and dynamics of both individuals and groups with astonishing perceptivity.

I suggest that the highly developed empathic abilities of people in sociocentric cultures are a new kind of empathy for Westerners, a full understanding of which requires a shift from egocentric to sociocentric thinking. It requires a shift from over-reliance on abstract, analytic, contractual thinking to a consciousness that is more contextual, holistic, and synthetic.

Relational knowing

Within a sociocentric frame of reference, it becomes possible to understand empathy as a state of consciousness. It is a way of perceiving and knowing and a way of being connected to other consciousnesses, by which individual human beings gain access to the inner worlds of other individuals and to the workings of relationships, and whole ecologies, of which they are but parts. It is also a way through which relationships as entities, including groups, and communities can themselves become aware of themselves as wholes. Often this is accomplished through myth, ritual, and other holistic forms of knowing.

Let me give an illustration: in one Brazilian workshop, the community-building process had bogged down in a tension-filled impasse as the group tried to come to a consensus about whether Carl Rogers should make a formal presentation of his ideas. There were many strong and conflicting feelings. Some felt Carl owed them a presentation. They had paid for the workshop so that they could hear him speak in person about client-centered therapy. Others argued that a formal presentation was a poor substitute for a lived experience of Rogers' work and wanted the unstructured process we were engaged in to continue. On the surface, the conflict could have been easily resolved. The group could have voted on it and abided by the majority. Or those who wanted a presentation from Carl could have heard him by themselves while everyone else did something else. However, the group saw itself *as a whole* and could not agree to either of these positions. People resisted any moves to fragment the group. Just when one person would seem to be suggesting a reasonable solution, someone else would point out what was wrong with it. This commitment to a somewhat chaotic and frustrating process of hearing everyone out, of staying open to the participation of even the small inarticulate voices or those who spoke in poetry and metaphor starkly contrasted the problem-solving focus more typical in groups of Europeans or North Americans. Rogers worked tirelessly to empathize with each of the individual participants, often capturing the meanings of people speaking a foreign language with exquisite accuracy. However, even this was insufficient to break the impasse.

The second night people went to bed exhausted and angry. They were becoming disillusioned with the much vaunted 'person-centred process'. The following morning, three individuals described dreams they had had during the night. All three dreams were similar and obviously referred to the impasse within the community. One featured a battle between a white polar bear and a Brazilian *mãe do santo* or shaman. The shaman, a priestess of the Afro-Brazilian religion Macumba, was refusing to let the polar bear pass into her house. She finally consulted *exu*, a powerful spirit entity who according to Macumba tradition guards crossroads and doorways, who told her that as long as she gave *exu* his usual ration of *cachaça* (Brazilian rum), the polar bear could pass safely into her home.

All the Brazilians agreed that the reason for and the solution to the impasse was obvious. We Americans, especially big white bear Rogers, were trying to penetrate Brazilian society with our ideas. The shaman was there to help mediate the passage by insisting that traditional sensibilities be honored and that the local gods were given their due. The Brazilians interpreted the dream sociocentrically, as providing information in symbolic and metaphoric form which could be used as a guide for community action. That evening a local *mãe do santo* arrived at the workshop, presumably invited by one of the participants, and the whole company participated in a ritual of passage, giving *exu* his *cachaça* and tobacco and invoking the help of the various Macumba entities in unlocking our community's impasse. The ceremony went on well into the night.

The next morning, the community meeting began a little later than usual. The change in atmosphere within the group was apparent at once. In place of tense competitiveness, people were laughing and joking. Even Rogers, who until then had been a little uptight and stiff, was visibly looser and more playful, seated less formally, obviously enjoying his physical closeness [to participants]. People talked about their experiences of the Macumba ceremony and as we approached lunch, the group had come to an agreement about Rogers' presentation. There was a clear consensus that nothing Rogers could say in a formal presentation could come close in richness to the experience of the last 48 hours.

When we first had experiences like these, we did not know what to make of them. At first mysterious, we gradually realized that they represented holistic ways of knowing, which were commonplace among many of the world's inhabitants. The dreams and their interpretations by group members revealed an awareness of the community's 'group mind', caught in a group-level identity conflict. We gradually came to see this, and other experiences similar to it, as evidence of a form of group-level empathy that was symbolic, holistic, and trans-individual. The level of action based upon that empathy was also holistic, involving participation, symbol, and myth or story and ritual.

To us, this was a new form of empathy, which occurred on conscious and unconscious levels. It provided complex, subtle, and *reliable* knowledge in an imaginal, metaphoric, and narrative form, about the community as a whole that could inform appropriate, coordinated, and graceful action by the whole.

Conscious groups—groups in which many people are aware of group-level phenomena—seem also to produce more than the ordinary share of exceptional individuals, suggesting to us that when a person can align themselves with the movements in the larger context without losing their unique perspective, they appear to 'know' more and perform better than they ordinarily do. When a mediocre basketball player plays on a team which is flowing, they can play far beyond their own personal best. Collaborative learning can lift an individual student's performance several levels higher than usual; actors perform better when the audience is with them. It may also account for such frequently observed (and often trivialized) phenomena as 'women's intuition', when a wife may have knowledge of her partner's extramarital affair even though he is going to great pains to conceal it. In one organization I consulted with, a car with Texas license plates in the company parking lot resulted in highly secret reorganizational plans being sensed by the whole organization seemingly at the same time. One employee told me, 'Everything had been very normal, too normal recently. Everybody knew something was up, but nobody knew what. When we saw the Texas Lexus, we figured out we were on the auction block'. A month later, the company was bought out by a Texas conglomerate.

Different communities understand such phenomena in different ways. In our Brazilian group, explanations would have included the activity of the spirits of the departed. My own British grandmother would have attributed such knowings to a 'sixth sense'. Organizational psychologists believe this to be a somewhat regressive state which recapitulates experience in the family. The group becomes 'mother' and individuals merge with the group the way the infant merges with the human mother (Schein, 1985). Polanyi differentiates between focal awareness and subsidiary awareness. When we are focally aware of a whole, we are subsidiarily aware of its parts. When we focus on a part, we are subsidiarily aware of the whole. In Polanyi's view, modernist overemphasis on attention to the parts has led to a disregard for the skills required for tacit knowing of the whole. He suggests that knowledge breakthroughs are made when scientists or poets who have retained their ability to 'indwell' in the fuzzy world at the boundaries of consciousness and are able to dissolve their attention past the focally apparent particulars to gain a glimpse of some until-now unapprehended greater whole. In moments like these we know more than we believe we know because it is possible to shift attention from the parts to the larger whole if we believe there is a reason to do so (Polanyi, 1958).

This ability to shift attention back and forth between the parts and the wholes to which they pertain might account for some of the seemingly magical and even *paranormal* breakthrough events that occur in psychotherapy, such as when the therapist and client simultaneously share the same image, when the therapist makes an 'out of the blue' statement that proves to be profoundly appropriate, or when the therapist knows in advance that the client will soon begin share some until now hidden story. A sociocentric view would explain this not by suggesting that the therapist is 'inside the skin' of the client, but inside the skin of the relationship, of which he or she is a part. Bozarth has referred to this phenomenon as 'emergent' empathy (Bozarth, 1984). I prefer the term relational empathy, to signify the sociocentric, relational nature of the process.

A relational worldview

Relational empathy

When looked at through a sociocentric lens, empathy provides a means of knowing relationships not only egocentrically in terms of its particulars, but also holistically as wholes that are more than the sum of their parts. In their groundbreaking work examining the role of empathy in the psychological development of women, Stone Center theorists have recently shifted descriptions of empathy in a sociocentric direction by referring to it as the *relational* skill par excellence (Jordan et al., 1991).

Holism, sociocentric awareness, and transindividual empathy

For psychology to make a shift from an egocentric to a sociocentric understanding of empathy requires new holistic language. Holistic thinking distinguishes between those characteristics and behaviors which give something (entity, object, thing, category, being, etc.) 'wholeness', and those associated with its 'partness' (Koestler, 1987). For example, a football quarterback, when known as a whole would be known in terms of features unique to them such as personal biography, a sense of humor, talent, speed, throwing accuracy, and stamina: those qualities they exhibit as an individual. They can, however, also be known as a *part* of the team. In this case, qualities such as being able to get along with teammates, engendering team spirit, planning plays within the abilities of their team, loyalty, and displaying the ability to inspire other players would be important. One familiar way to speak about this distinction in Western psychology would be to distinguish between their 'self' and their 'role'. However, in both cases, they are obviously them*self*. The difference is between the aspects of self we see when we look at them as a whole and those we see only when we pay attention to the way they function as a part. For instance, their performance can be measured in terms of their individual statistics—the usual American way—or can be assessed in terms of how well their performance contributed to the performance of the whole team—the sociocentric cultural preference. Furthermore, their unique individual characteristics, as seen egocentrically, may be true of them in any context, whereas the characteristics they demonstrate as 'part' will change from context to context as a function of the wholes they are a part of. A careful analysis of how they act in one context—say on the field—will be a poor guide to how they might be in others, like at home or in church. The same distinction can be made about the team itself. How it will play against another team will be a function both of its own limits and the opportunities provided by the context.

Koestler (1987) calls those states of mind and activities that have to do with a sense of one's wholeness *individualistic* or *self-assertive*, and he calls states of mind and activities that have to do with the sense of participation and becoming one with a larger reality, *self-transcendent* or *integrative*. Wholeness is associated with sovereignty—individual identity, self-expressiveness, initiative, integrity, aggression, uniqueness, discrimination, delineation, clarity, separateness, analysis, either/or thinking, competition, distinction, specificity, and boundedness. Partness or integrative behavior is associated connection—self-transcendence, empathy, listening, understanding, synthesis, cooperation, oneness, merging, diffuseness, participation, integration, belonging, both/and, generality, love, and intuition. For any human entity, be it person, group, family, community, or tribe, both partness and wholeness are two faces of being. Like the two-eyed Buddha, who has one eye facing inward to itself as a whole and the other facing outward to the cosmic whole to which it belongs, human consciousness knows itself both atomistically or self-assertively and relationally or self-transcendently.

Relational knowing

Human knowing is a *relational* activity. It implies both a *knower* and a *known*—we are always conscious of something, or better yet with something. It includes sensing, recognizing, and making sense and above all *meaning* of experience. Consciousness implies both self-transcendent and self-assertive states of mind. It requires the ability to discriminate between bounded categories and among entities, and it requires the ability to synthesize and integrate. It involves awareness of oneself in the process of knowing—how one's knowing is influenced by the contexts in which one is knowing—and it involves being swept away, out of oneself into the expanded contexts of life. By a continuous process of selection, categorization, organization, and synthesis, consciousness weaves ongoing representations of reality out of symbolic interpretations of inner and outer worlds and the dynamic relations between them.

Individual sovereignty versus group think

Participatory or relational consciousness, where individual selves are known more through the way they participate in larger wholes than as unique individuals, worries many Westerners. The idea of shifting attention away from individuals—decentring to postmodernists—looking at them only as clues to the workings of larger systems—raises fear that the intrinsic worth and sovereignty of individuals might diminish. Well-known examples of the dehumanizing effects of perverted collective consciousness such as Fascism, Communism, the Salem witch trials, or the Inquisition, provide historical evidence of the dangers of 'group think', and support for the importance of creative egocentric individualism. More recently, feminist critiques of the hegemonic patriarchal worldview, ethnic critiques of Eurocentrism, post-structuralist critiques of master narratives in general, and Kuhn's demonstrations of the conservative nature of scientific paradigms, offer further caution about the hegemonic properties of collective thinking. Psychologists, too, resist sociocentric consciousness when they feel it disregards the need for people to individuate and be cherished as beings for themselves. Client-centered psychologist Barrett-Lennard (1984), for instance, despite having focused his work on families and communities, shares what he calls his 'prejudice', when he admits that he has 'largely by-passed' the bulk of the systems theory discussions because he fears that 'the subjectively experiencing person [may be] lost or underemphasized, in terms of agency' (p. 241).

Such critics are right. If consciousness is limited to its wide-angled, sociocentric state, the only aspects of a person's being considered important are those having to do with their participation in larger contexts, and human beingness reduced to serving as mere clues to the workings of larger orders, then unique, creative selfhood and the view of self as an autonomous agent, may indeed become invisible. People raised in sociocentric communities are not immune from pain at having their individual needs ignored. The *ie* stem family system of Japan requires that individual selves, so sacred to participants of Western democracies, become submerged in order to take their place in a larger, interpenetrated kinship system. Japanese psychologists report considerable psychic costs, seen in paralysing guilt, repressed hostility, and other psychological disturbances, that can be directly correlated with the submersion of individual expression (Roland, 1988). Across the world, practices such as arranged marriages, obligatory veiling of women, forced political re-education, censorship, ritual genital mutilation, and many others, while certainly providing a sense of psychic coherence for sociocentric peoples, strike individualistic Westerners as unbearable assaults upon self.

This tension becomes resolvable not by taking exclusively either egocentric or sociocentric positions but by thinking holistically and by striving to understand persons neither as abstracted from their contexts nor as subordinated to them but as both whole unto themselves and active participants and cocreators of the contextual wholes that they inhabit. Furthermore, every situation is unique, every context providing novel and endlessly permutational possibilities that may, in turn, also be known uniquely by different individuals.

What any particular person is aware of, and the degree of focus or expansion of their awareness, will depend upon processes (physiological, neurological, conceptual, emotional) going on within that individual, and upon processes occurring within the larger context impinging upon them. It will also depend upon on relational conditions existing at the boundary between the individual level and the higher relational level. For example, if I am physically well, alert, safe, beloved, and accompanied, I might have awareness of myself both egocentrically and sociocentrically. I may be conscious of myself as a unique individuated centre of knowledge and agency. I know what I am striving for and the meaning it has for me. At the same time, I am aware of the way I am interacting with others. I can also be aware of how others are experiencing me. I may even understand relational movements in my marriage, the organizational dynamics at work, and the political or cultural movements in my community all at once—life as a fully experienced whole. However, if I am afraid, in pain, or ill, my attention may be focused upon myself, even on some isolated body part, to the exclusion of all other dimensions. This shrunken awareness might be due to dysfunctions in the larger system—such as family or political oppression, or to dysfunctions within me—such as a biochemical disorder or previous psychological trauma.

Psychological wellness as a function of degree of appropriateness in focus or inclusiveness of consciousness

This leads us to the possibility of looking at psychological functioning of an individual or group not only in egocentric structural terms but also in relational and contextual terms.

Healthy functioning implies that consciousness will include all contextual dimensions of concern within a given situation and at a given moment. Additionally, if we are not to become overwhelmed by endless contexts, we will exclude those elements that are irrelevant to present purposes. Much pathology or dysfunction is due to awareness that is either inappropriately shrunken or restricted—a person sees only fragments but not the whole—or inappropriately inclusive, and attention is too global and life becomes overwhelming. The relational therapist's function is to help clients learn how to let their awareness focus or expand as their unique contextual situation demands.

When conflicts exist at an intrapsychic level, and many of them do, focusing consciousness at this level is appropriate in that it may yield solutions to situations of concern. However, not all psychological conflicts or difficulties exist at this level. Nor do all resolutions. The individual psyche may not always be the relevant level for therapeutic attention. Some have suggested that excessive attention by psychotherapists on these intrapsychic levels of awareness has contributed to the rampant narcissism and other problems of contemporary Western life rather than their solution (Bellah et al., 1985). The following example reveals the limitations of the traditional egocentric psychological worldview for addressing relational needs.

A single father recently disclosed to his therapist that a few years earlier he had been intensely shamed by a psychologist who had interpreted as 'inappropriate' his decision to cancel three weeks of twice weekly therapy appointments to drive his 18-year-old daughter across country to begin university. The trip represented an enormous sacrifice in terms of time and money for the father and he felt intense grief about losing his daughter—although he was proud that she was to attend his Ivy League alma mater. He was inexplicably anxious about spending so much time alone with his daughter. The daughter, on the other hand, was very enthusiastic about the trip and was making elaborate plans. The psychologist suggested that the father was 'co-dependent and controlling' and that his anxiety was a clear signal that he was unconsciously aware that he was being drawn into something that was not good for him. He also indicated that there might be some incestuous seductiveness on the part of the daughter in wanting to 'pal along with dad' instead of taking herself off to college in an 'age-appropriate' way. The psychologist tried to persuade the father that he should heed his discomfort and in the interests of his daughter's individuation and his own psychotherapy, cancel their plans, and insist the daughter take a plane. The trip proved difficult for the father, although he was glad he'd done it. However, his experience of humiliation and anxiety at what the psychologist had said was so intense that he was unable to return to psychotherapy.

The psychologist in this case was obviously interpreting the client's actions from within the egocentric bias of his training. To him, it was virtually axiomatic that interrupting psychotherapy for a month reflected resistance, that fathers and daughters do not behave as friends, and that psychological maturity required separation and individuation. A relational sociocentric perspective enables us to look at this situation quite differently, looking at the father's decision in context. Despite some uneasiness, both father and daughter felt somehow moved to make the trip across country together. To both of them, it represented an almost mythic rite of passage. After raising her since childhood, the father was seeing his daughter finally moving out into the world, and both he and his daughter wanted their final three weeks to be a time to allow their relationship to make the transition to its new adult–adult configuration. They were both naturally anxious and uneasy about how this would play out on the trip.

Although no doubt empathically accurate about the father's discomfort, what the psychologist missed, which thankfully neither the client nor his daughter did, were the needs of the relationship. Only from a relationally empathic vantage point within that specific father–daughter dyad could the relational needs be known. For some other father–daughter relationship, perhaps allowing the daughter to go it alone would have been the relationally appropriate thing to do.

Psychotherapy is a joint project of at least two participants. In holistic terms, it is a multilevel relational situation. There are *whole* individuals and there are participants in *relationships*, *dyads*, or *groups*. These levels are also parts of larger configurations such as professions, families, classes, cultures, and genders. Attempting to understand larger system problems only from within an egocentric individualistic frame more often than not results in 'blaming the victim'.

The origin of a client's difficulty may be on any level. The holistic psychotherapist needs to be able to bring a repertoire of techniques—from the free association of psychoanalysis and the social activism of feminist therapy to spiritual practices like Macumba, meditation, or prayer—to help bring into awareness all the components of experience relevant to a predicament.

Empathy, in both egocentric and sociocentric modes, is an essential skill of both therapist and client in this process. Egocentric empathy permits the therapist to know the client as a unique whole individual. Sociocentric empathy provides the therapist with ways of knowing the relationships in which their clients participate, including the therapeutic relationship.

Relational psychologists may have an even more important contribution to make to the larger culture, by helping society bring into consciousness and develop the necessary skills to effectively deal with higher-order relational realities so long ignored by Western cultures. Futurists are warning that many of the complex problems facing postmodern global societies will not be solved by individual genius, but instead will need the coordinated efforts of diverse and creative groups (Dubos, 1981; King & Schneider, 1991). It is commonplace to suggest that nothing is so powerful as an idea whose time has come, but rarely do we consider how it is that an idea's time arrives. Our experience with relational empathy suggests that new and important ideas exist in groups in holistic, perhaps even holographic, forms as emergent properties of group consciousness. On those rare occasions when group members are empathic not only with each other, but with the group itself as a conscious entity, then vague inchoate inklings just below the surface of the group mind may crystallize into clear ideas. As the idea is articulated by one of its members, the group as a whole becomes instantly conscious of the new reality.

Empathy reconsidered

At this point, it is possible to consider empathy from outside the modernist discourse and look afresh at this ubiquitous human activity from within a relational frame. From this new vantage point, empathy ceases to be seen as the highly skilled instrumental activity of one autonomous individual—the therapist—intervening in the life of another—the client—while themselves remaining separate and unaffected. Instead, empathy becomes understandable as an essential feature of human relational connectedness, an expansion of a person's consciousness to include in the perceptual field the other as an individual and the relationship with the other of which they are a part.

Empathy is probably one of the oldest—both phylogenetically and ontogenetically—ways of orienting to self and others, predating symbolic language in both prehominid and prelinguistic human infants. One can speculate that for social primates without symbolic language, the empathic ability to sense the feelings and intentions of others and accurately read the cues provided in the complex interpenetrated webs of actions of social groups would have given enormous advantage to those that excelled at it. Cross-cultural studies of contemporary tribal people show that for people who live in highly structured interdependent communities, such abilities are still needed and highly valued. Symbolic and linguistic skills, as well as more recent technological advances in communication, while providing greater opportunities for complex social life, have not superseded more basic means of orientation. In fact, this may have simply added other, larger contexts in which sociocentric empathy is required. Western culture has for centuries gone to great lengths to socialize children toward egocentrism. This is in marked contrast to sociocentric patterns of childcare. Brazilian rainforest Indian women hold their babies close to their own bodies 24 hours a day. They continue this close connection for the first two years of life. Every breath the mother takes, every movement, aroma, or word, occurs as part of the experiential field of both the mother and the infant. This shared experiential reality is in stark contrast to the first experiences of infants in Western technological societies where babies are frequently enveloped in sterilized clothing and placed for long periods in solitary cots. Indian babies know nothing of separation and separateness until well after language develops, while a Western baby may be detached from physical contact with its mother within minutes of birth. Such contrasting early developmental contexts provide quite different psychological challenges to the child's evolving consciousness.

Some writers have suggested that individuals socialized for egocentricity make poor therapists for clients from more sociocentric communities, such as females of Asian, African, or Latin-American descent (Chin, 1994; Comas-Diaz & Greene, 1994). Fortunately, though, for those egocentric Western therapists who wish to develop more relational forms of empathy, it appears the relational competences can be regained, even in adulthood. By the end of his career, 'big white Polar Bear' Carl Rogers, after over 50 years of tuning in to the world space of others—the last 15 years or so frequently immersed in non-Western contexts such as Africa, Russia, Japan, and Latin America—said this about himself:

> When I can relax, and be close to the transcendental core of me, then I may behave in strange and impulsive ways in the relationship, ways I cannot justify rationally, which have nothing to do with my thought processes. But these strange behaviors turn out to be right in some odd way. At these moments it seems that my inner spirit has reached out and touched the inner spirit of the other. Our relationship transcends itself and has become something larger.
>
> (Rogers, 1986a, pp. 130–131)

Mutual empathy

The discussion so far has been aimed at a better understanding of empathy as a way of relational knowing, a way of, in Polanyi's (1958) words, 'indwelling' in the experiential life world of individuals and groups. However, there is still more that Western psychology can gain by moving beyond modernist views of empathy.

Empathy provides more than just information *about* relationships. It is an expression of *being in* relationships. It is not just a means to a better healing relationship, but because it recenters relationship as a central organizing feature of psychic life, empathy itself is healing. The experience of being known and accepted deeply by another, being aware of another being aware of you, what Jordan calls 'mutual empathy' (Jordan et al., 1991), is among the most psychologically important human experiences. There is ample evidence that without a clear sense of connectedness, human beings, especially infants and children, cannot thrive. It is through mutual empathy that we develop a sense of ourselves in relationship, the security of knowing that we belong, the knowledge of who we belong to, and how we must participate if we are to be loved and recognized by our community.

Although much easier to come by in sociocentric cultures than in egocentric ones, a sense of belonging is a sine qua non of healthy psychological functioning everywhere. Such a sense, beginning in infancy and continuing throughout life, comes about by experiencing mutual empathy and by sensing oneself as part of a whole, which recognizes and accepts that one is a member.

Relational empathy in an era of globalization, narcissism, and industrialized health care

The healing benefits of empathic connections are not something that the therapist can provide for the client, the way the physician gives medicines. For the full healing potential of therapeutic relationships as contexts in which human beings can heal and become fully themselves to be realized, relational empathy must be two-way. A common mistake made by egocentric therapists is to provide an empathic setting for their clients and interpret empathic attempts by clients as transference or as attempts at manipulation. People frequently leave therapy still operating from an egocentric frame of reference, wanting others to be empathic with them but having developed few or no relational competencies of their own. If people are to function well in the multiple relational contexts of their lives, clients need to learn how to enter self-transcendent states, to develop the capacity for egocentric and sociocentric empathy. This is best developed in a therapeutic relationship that is itself relational and in which mutual empathy can be achieved. Creation of mutual empathy takes trust. It takes commitment to creating conditions which permit emergent forms of consciousness to develop. It takes effort and time.

Ironically, and potentially disastrously, it is precisely these aspects of psychotherapy which are the first casualties in the massive changes in health care presently underway in the United States. The industrialization of health care, although intended to create economic gains for both employers and workers and to make mental health care available to a wider population, may accomplish this by forcing a return to the individualistic mechanistic paradigm of earlier periods of psychological history. Such retrograde developments may wipe out recent progress toward more holistic and relational frames of reference in psychotherapy and result in a greater emphasis on a one-size-fits-all modernist reductionistic behaviorism and on psychopharmacology. The role of empathy might conceivably return full circle to become reduced to a role only in the data gathering and hypothesis building stage of diagnosis. Its potential to heal disconnections and alienation and to provide access to ever wider pluralistic realms of knowing may be left unrealized. Worse yet, through the global reach afforded by Western technology, as other societies wrestle with the demands of the new competitive global marketplace, we might export our alienating practices to those still uncommitted to modernism.

Postmodern possibilities for a relational psychology

Psychology has much to gain by resisting these pressures to shrink ourselves into isolated egocentric bubbles. Now is the time to help midwife a new postmodern psychology able to meet the demands of our emerging postmodern world. It is time to reach beyond our isolated and individuated selves into the infinitely interpenetrated relational world. If able to learn more about the workings of conscious groups and how to help them form, psychology might be standing on a new threshold of knowledge. The British biologist J. B. S. Haldane (1954) suggests a non-mystical way to understand such expansion of consciousness beyond modern individualism when he states:

> If the cooperation of some thousands of millions of cells in our brain can produce our consciousness, the idea becomes vastly more plausible that the cooperation of humanity, or some part of it, may determine what Compte calls a "Great Being".
>
> (p. 24)

Relational empathy permits individual and collective access to the wisdom contained in higher-order shared contexts and nurtures the ground out of which new creative possibilities might emerge. A new generation of Western artists are already pointing the way.

British artist David Hockney's photo collage, *My Mother, Bolton Abbey, Yorkshire Nov. '82*, is of the artist's mother within the ancient ruins of a Cistercian abbey. The picture is composed of multiple shots, multiple camera positions, and an idiosyncratic, irregular frame. It contains an unmistakable reference, in the form of a shot of the artist's own feet peeking into the bottom of the picture, to the subject-to-subject relational connection among the artist, Mrs. Hockney, and us, the viewers. Hockney, inspired both by the work of 20th-century physicists and 14th-century Chinese scroll paintings, strains to render the images of a reality yet to be created. We need, he says, 'to break down borders, to entertain the interconnectedness of things and of ourselves with things; the notion… that it is no longer possible to have ideas about reality without taking our own consciousness into account' (Hockney, 1988, p. 87).

Should psychology choose to go in this direction and develop a greater understanding of relational empathy, as a way of knowing and as a way of being connected, and should psychology learn more about the contexts in which relational consciousness can be developed, and how to create communities which permit both being and belonging, psychology might yet offer some grounds for optimism in an increasingly alienated, fragmented, and pessimistic society.

Note

1 Buber (1923/1970).

Chapter 17

Moments of eternity

What Carl Rogers still has to offer brief therapists (2002)

Maureen O'Hara[1]

Introduction

As far back as I can remember, I have been a scientist. In nursery school, I collected bugs and slugs, put them in jars, and lost myself for hours watching them go about their 'bugging' and 'slugging'. This rapt fascination with the world, which I still experience each time I encounter an unknown creature or listen to my son describe his adventures in molecular genetics, has been a reliable source of pleasure, inspiration, and revelation. However, all along my love of science has been combined with something not usually associated with scientists.

Although I hesitate to say it out loud, I have also been something of a mystic. Not an upper-case Mystic, who talks to God, has grand visions, writes inspirational texts, or even professes any particular religious faith. Rather, I have been a sort of street mystic, always taken a little by surprise by glimpses of the divine in the ordinary daily-ness of life. I started my career as a biological researcher, but even from the start there was a difference. The Professor (Chair) of my department, Dr. Irene Manton, one of the few women Fellows of the Royal Society, was a world-famous microscopist. She took me under her wing and resolved to teach me the basics of being scientist. I didn't realize until much later that she was no ordinary scientist. She too was a mystic.

One day we were gazing into a very high powered microscope, as she tried to show me the fine structure of a particular subcellular organelle that she had identified. For a very long time, I looked desperately at the field of random squiggles, but despite all my efforts, I could make out absolutely nothing. I wanted to give up, cursing the 'bloody thing'. Finally, Professor Manton said gently, 'Dear girl, if you don't love it, you won't see it. You cannot force the universe to do your bidding. You have to wait until you are ready for it, and it is ready for you'. I took a deep breath, relaxed, and began to look at the specimen with a much softer gaze. A few minutes later, in a blink of an eye, the amorphous puzzle on the screen took shape, and with something approaching bliss, I began to see the structures which no one before her had ever seen, and which a few moments before I had doubted even existed.

DOI: 10.4324/9781003519454-22

As an apprentice in her lab, I came naturally by the notion that the scientific attitude is indistinguishable from the mystical. Both require discipline, self-preparation, and openness to experience and a willingness to dwell in mystery. At the center of both the mystic's life and the scientist's is a faith that the universe has an implicate order, a desire to encounter this reality in greater depth and complexity, and to be transformed in the encounter. Not all scientists, but certainly a far greater number than will admit in public, are, like mystics, fired by a spiritual longing to indwell in the mysteries of existence in an attempt to get closer to the divine.

With this kind of early training, it was inevitable that when I shifted careers from biological researcher to educator and psychotherapist, I would be drawn to the work of another scientist–mystic—Carl Ransom Rogers (O'Hara, 1995a; Van Belle, 1990; Van Kalmthout, 1995). From the first exposure to his written work, through 17 years of personal relationship as a graduate student and later as a colleague, I saw his approach to therapy and growth in clients, groups, and communities as another path to deepening my exploration of the enigma of Being—my own, and my clients, and of the contexts in which we found ourselves.

The evolving Rogerian tradition in psychotherapy and counselling

Carl Rogers, the inventor of person-centered therapy (first called 'non-directive therapy', later 'client-centred therapy', and finally 'the person-centred approach'; although the Rogerian community is not all in agreement on this, in this chapter, I will use them synonymously), is arguably the most influential American psychologist and perhaps the least understood. His work spanned 60 years, from the late 1920s to the late 1980s, and participated in three radical philosophical shifts that occurred in 20th-century psychology—leading one of them. As a college student, he had first thought he would study agriculture. After that, he entered the seminary to become a Protestant minister. He attended an ecumenical religious gathering in China in the 1920s and on the six-week sea voyage immersed himself in Chinese religion and philosophy. He began his studies of psychology at Teachers College, at Columbia University in New York, and at first considered himself, and was acknowledged by his peers, as a positivist empiricist scientist (O'Hara, 1995a). His driving passion was to discover the 'necessary and sufficient conditions' that if applied would lead to psychological healing and growth. During this first phase, he succeeded in establishing the basic tenets of client-centered therapy, which eventually formed the basic ground rules for almost all species of effective 'helping' relationships (see below).

In his middle years—partly as a consequence of his disappointment with the dominant mechanistic paradigm for psychological research, but mostly because of what he was learning about human experience from his clients—his ideal of empirical objectivity in psychological research faded into the background (although he never lost it completely). Instead, he turned to the more subjectivist phenomenological approaches to research that he felt could better grasp the highly nuanced complexity of human experience as it was lived. He was attracted to the American transcendentalist and romantic traditions of Thoreau and Emerson, the pragmatism of James and Dewey, and to European existentialists such as Søren Kierkegaard, all of whom sought psychological truth in the deep interior world of individual subjective experience. He was also greatly influenced by the ideas of Otto Rank (Kramer, 1995) and the 'upper-case' Jewish Mystic, existential philosopher Martin Buber (Kirschenbaum & Henderson, 1989). He became increasingly interested in the interpersonal dimensions of life, enthusiastically embracing the encounter group movement. At this time, he expanded his goals beyond psychotherapy and aimed at discovering the basic rules governing all healthy human relationships.

During these middle years, he remained, however, strongly attached to what Gergen (1994) has called the romantic-modernist idea of a sovereign inner 'real self' to which, in the interest of mental well-being and self-realization, one must 'be true'. His early research on encounter groups focused on the ways in which groups aid the individual growth of participants. As the work developed, however, pulled once more by his desire to step out into unknown regions of experience, he was drawn out of the therapeutic context altogether, and into the messy waters of large-group community processes, cross-cultural communications, and diplomacy and peacemaking on a global scale. It was during this shift towards larger systems that I joined up with him and his colleagues in La Jolla.

The large-group work took him and his colleagues to Asia, South Africa, Latin America, pre-Perestroika Soviet Union, Northern Ireland, and Eastern Europe and increasingly focused on situations of serious inter-group conflict. In Northern Ireland, he worked with groups of Protestants and Catholics; in South Africa, he led a workshop that was half-Black and half-White; and in Rust, Austria, he and the members of the Carl Rogers Institute For Peace facilitated a group of diplomats and politicians from Central America and the United States who came together to discuss the conflict raging in Nicaragua at the time.

Listening to the world through the experience of people from many cultures and trying to understand the strange, nonlinear emergent processes that occur in these large-group contexts, demanded another paradigmatic shift. Confronted, in these poly-cultural experiences, by the realization that the 'essential self' at the center of Western psychology is an almost exclusively 19th- and early 20th-century male European construct, that it is the exception rather than the rule among most of the world's cultures (Geertz, 1979; O'Hara, 1996b), he was forced into a constructivist world of multiple contextual psychological realities.

In 1974, while meditating on a beach in Northern California, he wrote an article, 'Do we need "a" reality?' (Rogers, 1980/1995b), in which he concluded, 'The way of the future must be to base our lives and our education on the assumption that there are as many realities as there are persons' (p. 105). He proposed that the work of therapists and educators must be to nurture the birth of a culture and a psyche where human caring would not be conditional upon sameness, but on a celebration of difference. He had also loosened (but not quite abandoned) his moorings in the romantic-modernist view of the self, and was describing what he referred to as 'persons of tomorrow' who have sufficiently developed levels of consciousness as to be 'at home in a world that consists only of vibrating energy, a world with no solid base, a world of process and change, a world in which the mind, in its larger sense, is both aware of, and creates, the new reality' (Rogers, 1980/1995b, p. 352). He spent his last years attempting to put to use his learnings about the conditions which foster psychological growth and healing, trying to facilitate the birth of such a consciousness.

Rogers was among those humanistic psychologists who repudiated the instrumentalist, medical model of psychotherapy. In this model, the person seeking help is seen as suffering from some pathology, or as otherwise defective in some way. The effective therapeutic agent is thought to be the therapist-delivered treatment, applied in prescribed doses and according to pre-determined protocols to specific diseases or disorders exhibited by a 'patient' (Bohart & Tallman, 1999). In place of this 'allopathic' view of 'treatment from without', Rogers, along with many others—Milton Erickson among them—saw the client as an active agent in their own change and sought to align himself with the self-healing powers of individuals and groups. More radically, Rogers believed that this capacity for self-healing and creative agency is the human organism's local expression of an intrinsic evolutionary tendency in the universe impelling all of nature—from molecules to galaxies—towards greater complexity and expanded levels of consciousness. To align constructively with the formative tendency (Rogers, 1978) of the universe and with the self-actualizing potential of a particular person or a group is a far more ambitious project than the alleviation of psychological symptoms! In Rogers' view, and the view of those of us who worked closely with him on the development of what in 1975 we renamed the 'person-centred approach', to establish the kind of relationship in which people make an experiential shift towards greater awareness and higher orders of consciousness is to participate in some minuscule way to the process of matter becoming conscious of itself.

Necessary and sufficient?

> *Encountering another human being means being kept alive by an enigma* (Emmanual Lévinas)

When asked about the place of Carl Rogers' methods in his work, solution-focused brief therapist William O'Hanlon replied, 'That's the first five minutes. If you don't do that stuff, I don't think you are going to get anywhere' (O'Hanlon, 1993).

What 'stuff' is O'Hanlon talking about?

During the 1940s and early 1950s, Rogers and a large team of co-investigators systematically evaluated the therapeutic conditions under which clients progressed towards wholeness in psychotherapy and counselling. These studies, published in 1954 (Rogers & Dymond, 1954) established what he thought were the six essential conditions for therapeutic growth. He summarized the findings in the now classic paper, 'The necessary and sufficient conditions of therapeutic personality change' (Rogers, 1957), in which he states:

> For constructive personality change to occur, it is necessary that these conditions exist and continue over a period of time:
>
> 1 Two persons are in psychological contact.
> 2 The first, whom we shall call the client, is in a state of incongruence, being vulnerable or anxious.
> 3 The second person, whom we shall term the therapist, is congruent or integrated in the relationship.
> 4 The therapist experiences unconditional positive regard for the client.
> 5 The therapist experiences an empathic understanding of the client's internal frame of reference and endeavors to communicate this experience to the client.
> 6 The communication to the client of the therapist's empathic understanding and unconditional positive regard is to a minimal degree achieved (p. 96).

Going into the project, which lasted several years, the researchers had expected to identify key techniques and interventions that seemed to correlate with therapeutic shifts, and they hoped that this would provide a standardized approach to therapy and counselling. This was not to be. The further into their project the team got, the more audiotapes and session transcripts they analyzed, the more objective pre- and post-therapy tests they ran, the more they were forced to admit that what seemed to bring about significant shifts in therapy was not the technical expertise of the therapists, but a certain set of attitudes, values, and personal qualities, which Rogers (1980/1995b) later came to call 'ways of being' which they bring into their relationships. Central to these attitudes are two major positions: firstly, a faith that 'each person has within himself or herself vast resources for self-understanding and for constructive changes in ways of being and behaving' (Rogers & Sanford, 1989, p. 1493), and, secondly, that these resources can be released and realized when the therapist and client are in psychological contact within a relationship with certain definable qualities. These qualities are realness, caring, and a deeply sensitive non-judgmental understanding and the willingness and ability to enter into an experiential empathic connection with clients so as to sense the internal experience, the frames of reference, and flow of feelings and meanings as if from the point of view of the client.

Although these conditions were identified by Rogers as early as 1942 (Rogers, 1942), over the decades since then a wealth of outcome and process studies have been conducted by others on a wide spectrum of therapeutic approaches, including some that are conscientiously at odds with person-centered approaches—such as cognitive-behaviorist and psychoanalytic approaches—which have largely confirmed Rogers' discoveries (Luborsky et al., 1975; Seligman, 1995). The vast preponderance of the 'common factors' research points to the remarkable stability over the decades of Rogers' basic constructs. Even in non-client-centered therapies, client resourcefulness, agency, and capacity for self-directed growth, in the context of a relationship characterized by warmth and respectful and empathic understanding, overpowers any other variables such as technique, theoretical orientation, diagnosis, or experience level of the therapist (Bohart & Tallman, 1999).

It is ironic, then, that just as there seems to be a convergence of evidence that would support the person-centered approach as the basic therapeutic stance, the approach has been all but banished from the universities in the United States, and is rarely the therapy of choice with health maintenance organizations (HMOs), which appear to prefer any therapy with the words 'brief', 'short term', 'strategic', or 'medication' in its name!

A brief field study of brief person-centered therapy

> *If we can recognize this [time] limit, and refrain from playing a self-satisfying Jehovah role, we can offer a very definite kind of clarifying help, even in a short space of time.*
>
> (Carl Rogers, 1942, pp. 247–248)

In order to find out if this neglect of person-centered therapy is justified on grounds that such non-directive approaches, though effective, are too time-consuming and expensive in these cost conscious days, I conducted my own informal survey of person-centered practitioners around the world about therapy length. I belong to several global electronic listservs of humanistic and person-centered therapists, so I asked participants the typical length of therapy needed to arrive at a successful therapeutic outcome as identified by both client and therapist. I also asked them to share any research they had conducted or knew about on the topic, or any anecdotal evidence that could shed some light on the question of whether person-centered therapies could legitimately be considered 'short term' or 'brief therapy'.

The responses, which came from Latin America, Australia, Europe, and North America, from younger practitioners and old hands, revealed that most of the respondents had worked at least some of the time in settings where the number of sessions was tightly restricted. These settings included employee assistance programs, college and university counselling centers, on-call emergency psychiatric clinics, residential treatment centers, and HMOs.

Most respondents said that although they did not favor the artificially imposed limits imposed by extra-therapeutic factors, they nevertheless felt that under the right circumstances, even with externally imposed time limits, it was reasonable to expect positive results in several sessions (eight to twelve was the typical number); some reported significant effects in as little as three sessions (Mearns, 1994); and one reported positive changes after an allotted single assessment interview. Interestingly, others who were under no externally imposed time constraints, also reported that their typical number of sessions with clients was in the same range.

Some of these therapists, however, did report that sometimes clients remained in therapy up to fifty sessions and beyond.

Respondents were mixed in their overall assessment of the efficacy of short-term therapy. Several respondents had been much influenced by the radical ideas of Rankian social worker Jessie Taft (1933/1973), and saw the presence of an externally imposed time limit as a facilitative factor if it were made to stand for unavoidable existential limits within which we all must live. In a radical challenge to the endless psychoanalytic therapies of her era, social worker Taft argued that even one hour of therapy can provide the occasion for transformation.

> When he can take it [the therapy hour] and also leave it without denying its value, without trying to escape it completely or keep it forever because of this very value, in so far he has learned to live, to accept this fragment of time in and for itself, and… if he can live this hour he has in his grasp the secret of all hours, he has conquered life and time for the moment and in principle.
>
> (Taft, 1933/1973, p. 17)

From the earliest days, Rogers and colleagues were interested in time-limited treatment. These were the days of interminable psychoanalysis and years of in-patient sanitarium care and there was, as now, more readily accessible short-term care. Rogers believed that if the contact was to be short-term, non-directive therapy was especially worthwhile, but he did not expect any major personality restructuring. Short-term 'clarifying help' can 'enable the client to express his problems and feelings freely, and leave with a clearer recognition of the issues with which he is faced' (Rogers, 1942, pp. 247–248).

Early research suggested that the longer the therapy, the greater the gains, with 20 sessions being predictive of significant therapeutic gains when measured as a function of several outcome dimensions related to psychological progress, such as degree of personal integration of the client, life adjustment of the client, degree of satisfaction of client with the outcome of therapy, and therapist rating of outcome (Seeman, 1954). In another related study, Standal and van der Veen (1957) suggested that increases in the degree of personality integration seemed to be correlated with longer therapy (14 or more meetings) but other personality change variables seemed to be achievable in therapies lasting less than 14 sessions.

Shlien (1957) undertook a major study of time-limited client-centered therapy and concluded that brief time-limited client-centered therapy facilitated positive outcomes on several measurement scales but appeared to have some negative effects as well. He speculated, on the basis of deterioration in Thematic Apperception Test (TAT)[2] scores in the follow-up, that if clients perceived the termination as arbitrary and unwelcome and therefore experienced it as a blow to their desire for autonomy and self-direction, then actual harm might be done by premature termination. On the basis of his own study, which in some ways had set out hoping to validate Rank's and Taft's assertions about the positive effects of time limits, Shlien advised caution before endorsing time limitations more generally.

Since the 1950s until quite recently, person-centered therapists seem to have been less interested in further evaluating the effects of time limits. Recently, the issue has been raised once again, provoked, as it has been in other therapies, by externally imposed time limits to service. Brian Thorne, a leading person-centered therapist in the United Kingdom, described his own unexpected conversion to short-term therapy after completing a small pilot study. As the director of a university counselling service, he was under pressure to economize. After a census of client records revealed that many clients had arrived at satisfactory conclusions to counselling in as few as three sessions, he decided to experiment with a voluntary three-session service. Clients who wished to continue were to be referred to an ongoing group. Thorne concluded that very short term person-centered counselling can bring significant results with some self-selected and highly motivated clients (Mearns, 1994). My own experience is similar to Thorne's. With some clients, remarkable progress can be made in one or two meetings (see case material below).

From therapists working with people in all degrees of distress from chronically psychotic to situational crises, the consensus among person-centered therapists seems to be that the crucial variable is not length of time in therapy, but rather who it is that makes the determination about the duration of service and the agenda to be addressed in therapy. If these decisions are made externally to the therapeutic relationship, this violates one of the fundamental tenets of the approach—client self-determination. When they are made mutually by the client and therapist, and are in terms of the clients' understanding of their growth needs, then the length of therapy may be short (1–6 sessions), middling (16–25 sessions), or long term (30–70 sessions).

Another set of responses came from therapists who pointed out that in the intensive small- and large-group encounter settings, significant life-changing effects could be experienced in short-term encounters. During the large community group phase of Rogers' career, he described several such examples, including some with serious psychological difficulties (Rogers, 1977), and he has described the long-term impact of single sessions done as therapy demonstrations (Rogers, 1980/1995b; Rogers & Sanford, 1989). In a study co-authored with Rogers and others, we had reliable, independently corroborated reports of radical life changes that occurred for some of the participants of a two-day encounter with several hundred people (Bowen et al., 1979). Follow-up reports indicated that the changes persisted over time (Rogers, 1980/1995b).

It seems quite clear that person-centered therapy in its theory and as it is practised can legitimately be considered as a brief therapy. So why, in the light of this evidence—some of it anecdotal and some of it gained through exhaustive controlled research—do contemporary person-centered therapists, including myself, not identify with the brief therapy movement? Why are we not busily touting the person-centered approach to the managed care industry and financially strapped social service agencies as a cost-effective method of delivering short-term 'quality care' that research studies show (Seligman, 1995) have the added value of receiving high 'customer satisfaction' ratings?

It's the paradigm!

> *The single element that most sets client-centered psychotherapy apart from the other therapies is its insistence that the medical model—involving diagnosis of pathology, specificity of treatment, and desirability of cure—is a totally inadequate model for dealing with psychologically distressed or deviant persons.*
>
> (Rogers & Sanford, 1989, p. 1483)

Put simply, the reason person-centered therapists are not lobbying to be recognized as practitioners of one of the brief therapies is because most do not think of their practice in the terms of the contemporary medical discourse and especially not in the aggressively manipulative expert-focused stance of brief-strategic approaches (Cade & O'Hanlon, 1993). In the Kuhnian sense, they inhabit a different paradigm (Kuhn, 1970). The medical model focuses on what's wrong—the client's problems, symptoms, illness, dysfunctions, chemical imbalances—and invests all efforts in preparing therapist 'experts' to provide ever better solutions to these afflictions by refining techniques, strategies, and treatment protocols, and where the relationship between therapist and client is only important insofar as it facilitates the client's compliance with therapist interventions (Bohart et al., 1998; Bohart & Tallman, 1999). Practitioners of person-centered therapy believe they are doing something rather different.

Although described in different language over the years, person-centered therapists are attempting to make a soul-connection with their clients. Their goal is to, as far as possible, open themselves to be present to the mysterious enigma of Being, and to join with people called clients in ways that facilitate their achievement of the same kind of openness. They seek to stay close to the edge between the known and the unknown, of the moment between the already been and not yet become that is so pregnant with possibilities for both constructive and destructive action, and to stay alert to opportunities to be a force for constructive movement.

Rogerian therapy is based in faith. At the core of the tradition, as it has evolved over 60 years from non-directive counselling to client-centered therapy and student-centered teaching, to include experiential therapy, and its most recent iteration as the person-centered approach, is an invariant radical faith in a self-organizing emergent vector at work in nature. Rogers described 'an evolutionary tendency towards greater order, greater complexity, greater interrelatedness' (Rogers, 1980/1995b, p. 133). This faith leads to trust in the inborn desire and capacity of all human beings to choose relational mutuality over either isolation or relationships of exploitation and domination, to choose growth and wholeness over fear and disintegration, and to participate co-creatively rather than compliantly in the formation of larger conscious groups such as families and communities. Whether one believes such a faith is warranted or not—and clearly this moves into the realm of metaphysics—without recognizing the difference in their metaphysics, it is impossible to understand how radical the difference is between the person-centered tradition and mainstream medical-model psychotherapy. A fuller discussion of these differences can be found in O'Hara (1997a).

Moments of eternity

> *I feel continuous waves taking up every cell of me, transforming me "forever". They come as feelings, very pure, without words, as I seem to have forgotten what was said either by you or me or the others at the most significant moments. What is here, and is incredibly vivid, a thing of now, is what resulted in those moments.* (Participant in a person-centred workshop)

While mainstream psychotherapy trusts a mechanistic world of cause and effect, the person-centered therapist's focus is on developing ways of being in relational encounters with the Other and by doing so, open sacred space and time—moments of eternity—within which the self-organizing formative tendency in nature can become manifest and effective in the world. Whether with a single individual, a family, or a group and whatever the level of disturbance, healing becomes not a matter of what one does but of what and how one is in a relationship to the world, including the world of the Other.

Once this is admitted, then the nature of the encounter shifts. No longer I–It, as Buber (1923/1970) would say, but I–Thou, in which a true encounter between Beings of infinite complexity and infinite possibilities can occur. If it does occur, the next moment and all future moments are open. The work the therapist must do shifts from techniques to apply to the client to the development for greater capacities to be spiritually open.

In an interview late in his life, Rogers said he endeavored to be as much as possible in a state of 'openness' or as he described it, 'a continuing way of meeting life. This includes openness to the beauty of my fuchsias, as well to what is going on in me or what is going on in a relationship' (as cited in Harman, 1990, p. 251). Openness means adopting a learners' stance, what in Zen is called 'beginners mind', in meeting with clients. In this state of openness, all stereotype and pre-judgment—including diagnosis and prescription—are suspended, and in their place an empty mind waiting to be filled with the possibilities presented in the present moment. For Rogers and other person-centered practitioners, this accepting, non-judgmental, and non-directive attitude is the bedrock of their work, out of which comes the courage to listen deeply, to enter into an empathic attunement with the Other, to surrender separate individual consciousness, and enter the phenomenal world of the other. In doing so, they attempt to become one with the emergent edge between the known and the unknown. Wood (1997) describes the 'mediumistic' quality of Rogers' sessions from an early stage. Rogers and others came eventually to call the states (after Buber) 'presence' (Thorne, 1997). Rogers exquisitely captures this experience as follows:

> I find that when I am closest to my inner intuitive self, when I am somehow in touch with the unknown in me, when perhaps I am in a slightly altered state of consciousness, then whatever I do seems to be full of healing. Then simply my presence is releasing and helpful to the other. There is nothing I can do to force this experience, but when I can relax and be close to the transcendental core of me, then I may behave in strange and impulsive ways in the relationship, ways which I cannot justify rationally, which have nothing to do with my thought processes. But these strange behaviors turn out to be right, in some odd way: it seems that my inner spirit has reached out and touched the inner spirit of the other. Our relationship transcends itself and becomes a part of something larger.
> (Rogers, 1980/1995b, p. 129)

When clients or groups sense that they are being received with this kind of openness, they too are more willing to open up to the greater resources within them, within the relationship, and in the greater contexts of their lives. They discover, almost miraculously sometimes, new creative responses to what challenges them.

Moments like these seem to regularly involve altered states of consciousness—altered that is from the customary ego-bounded state that is valued in contemporary 'professional' Western scientific discourse, but entirely recognizable to shamans, hypnotherapists, ministers, poets, mothers, lovers, and other kinds of healers. Attention is more diffuse, however, rather than sharp, edges are fuzzy, thoughts are quieted, muscles relaxed, things come to consciousness as images, patterns, sounds, bodily sensations, and symbols more often than they come as words or ideas. The ordinary sense of time disappears and in its place a sense of timelessness. There is a sense of alert patience—waiting. (The origin of the word 'therapy' is to wait.) It is common at such moments to lose the sense of separation between self and Other and instead experience oneself and all other existence, as the same thing, part of one indivisible and endlessly generative whole. In wisdom traditions, these moments are sought as intimations of enlightenment, in religious traditions as glimpses of God, and in shamanic traditions as moments of healing.

Such states of consciousness are by no means passive, but the practitioner is wide awake, aroused, fully there, not thinking, judging, evaluating, diagnosing, but simply available. We wait until the spirit moves us and move us it will. We move towards or away, we hear a new note, we sense new symbols, we see an opening, we encounter a boundary, we are filled with pain, we are teased, we are swallowed up, we are seduced, repulsed, encouraged, and plunged into despair.

This kind of openness, especially in relationships with a person or situation which is chaotic or dangerous, is no job for the faint-hearted. To meet another available to be moved by their story means opening oneself to all the pain and nastiness that life can hurl at us (Neimeyer & Stewart, 2000). Murder, rage, greed, rape, trickery, madness, terror, despair, loss, confusion, incoherence, numbness, and death all move through us as if they were our own—because they are. Rogers himself describes one experience during his University of Chicago years that was so intolerably painful that he felt forced to abandon the client he was working with and take a couple of months away from practicing psychotherapy to get back his perspective and regain his sanity (Kirschenbaum, 1979; Shlien, 1997).

Therapeutic moments are like love—they catch us by surprise. They cannot be willed or 'performed' and cannot be domesticated and controlled. Love swells up from some hidden source and flows through us. We cannot hold onto it, it is beyond will, beyond volition. If we are available to it, it will move us to action that is natural and harmonious with the situation much in the same way the winds play music on a quiet harp. We become the instrument.

We are not needed to 'fix' anything, to perform, or to intervene. The research data are clear (Bohart et al., 1998). Whatever 'fixing' that will happen as a consequence of the meeting will be done by the client. Our clients need us not for what we do, but for who and how we are and for how we can be with them. They need us to bring to the encounter our hope, courage, energy, and love to accompany them in their journey, which for the moment is too hard for them to bear alone. Therapist creativity, knowledge of psychological processes, techniques for focusing and reframing experience, relaxation, trance induction, guided imagery, narrative restructuring, and so on may be of assistance to a client. So may aid in learning to think more critically or expansively. Honest feedback about behavior, even giving advice—all handy tricks of the therapist's trade, may, under the right circumstances, provide useful assistance to clients. They may also not. In any case, such resources can be accessed by the motivated client from many other sources, such as friends, self-help books, self-help groups, TV shows, workshops, spiritual retreats, etc. To what degree the therapist's experience and skills are useful remains up to the client. As Bergin and Garfield (1994) concluded in their recent volume on psychotherapy research, 'it is the client more than the therapist who implements the change process. If the client does not absorb, utilize, and follow through on the facilitative efforts of the therapist, then nothing happens' (Bergin & Garfield, 1994, p. 825).

Our significance to our clients, particularly those who are very troubled or very perplexed, is as constant and loving witness to their existence. They need us to stand alongside them as they struggle with the happenings of their lives, to love them, to be at least one significant Other who regards them in return—with all their difficulties and flaws—as a significant Other. In the mutual recognition of one human being for another comes the possibility to go beyond I–It, and even beyond I–Thou, to become a 'we' (Schmid, 1997). By being willing to risk even temporarily becoming a 'we', a new never-before-existent universe is created between therapist and client.

Friedman (1985) describes this process as the 'concrete unfolding of the "ontology of the between"' (p. 152). Never-before encountered or even imagined choices become available, and creative understandings and solutions to predicaments become possible. For those who feel separated and alone, cut off from themselves and from fellowship with the rest of the human race, the bridge back from exile, into a world of relationship and of infinite possibility, is what Gilligan calls 'sponsorship' or non-possessive love (Gilligan, 1997).

Transformational andragogy

Practitioners of consciousness traditions have invested centuries studying transformational moments, both the details of how they are experienced and how they can be facilitated. The Hindu yogi disciplines, Zen Buddhism, Tibetan Buddhism, Taoism, Sufism, Judaism, and Christianity possess centuries of accumulated wisdom on how best to help another enter transformational states and on the phenomenology of what happens when one does. Illness, in many of these traditions, is regarded as signs that people or systems are out of balance with the universal flow of Being. Consciousness disciplines such as awareness work, prayers, martial arts, calligraphy, poetry, philosophy, and meditation are regarded as educational practices developed to help people regain their balance and to realign with the life force.

Partly due to the West's obsession with objectivism, and partly due to American psychology's abandonment early in the century of William James' studies in consciousness in favor of experimental behavioral science, detailed exploration of inner psychological processes has been neglected until recently. The recent convergence of neuropsychology, mind–body interaction, phenomenology, existential psychology, cognitive psychology, developmental psychology, psychophysiology, epistemology, systems science, and complexity science, has revitalized interest in consciousness. It has also provided new non-religious (at least non-sectarian) languages with which to speak about the process of consciousness change and its facilitation.

Whether gradually over a period of time, or apparently in an instant, deep irreversible, transformational change occurs all through life in the way human beings experience their world, make meaning of it, and act in it. (See Alexander and Langer, 1990, for a review of recent studies.)

Case example (the biographical details are significantly altered, although the essential elements of the story are intact, and the quotes are her words):

When Jenny first came to see me, she was 40 years old, with a high school education. She was suffering from acute debilitating panic attacks of recent onset and complained that 'instead of getting more self-confident with age', she was 'losing ground'. She blamed other people for her difficulties—her father, who had abandoned her and a sister when he divorced their mother, her stepfather for being a 'drunk', her husband for being a 'workaholic', even psychologists for not having diagnosed her dyslexia as a child. Her thinking was one-dimensional, and she jumped around from topic to topic, never able to reflect on her story, only to recount it.

She was the mother of two teenagers—an older boy and a younger girl, the wife of a distant overworked physician husband, and she had a small, not too successful jewellery design business. She admitted that she was often close to despair and told me that she had flirted with a neighbor but backed off at the final moment. She was 'disgusted with herself', was feeling 'old, unattractive, and ripped off by life', and was contemplating divorce.

During the first two sessions, she spoke of her pent-up frustration; of her many attempts to solve her problems herself—self-help books, assertiveness training classes, journaling, Oprah, a women's support group, and so on; and of her self-diagnosis as a 'chronic under-achiever who had married out of her intellectual class'. She disclosed that as an adolescent she had been molested by her stepfather, and that her dyslexia had made high school a 'nightmare'. All this, she said, had left her alternately depressed and school-phobic throughout high school. She had married Mark as an escape. She was currently not sleeping well, had gained weight, and at times felt hopeless. As her sad story tumbled out, it seemed that we might be at the start of a fairly extensive process of psychotherapy, and at her initiative we even discussed her husband's suggestion that she take medication for depression. Disapproving of 'chemicals', she decided to hold off to see if therapy might 'work'.

For the third session, Jenny arrived in a highly agitated state. She had obviously been crying in the waiting room. She began to cry again as she started to speak. Her tears were angry. She was 'livid', 'incensed', and she would like to 'tear the face off' her son's high school principal, she exclaimed. Apparently, he had just announced a new policy that only students with grades B or better could play baseball. Her son Todd (also dyslexic), whose grade point average was a B−, had been kicked off the team and he was, in his mother's words, 'devastated'. This affected the whole family since she, her husband, and daughter were heavily involved with Todd's team. Jenny had wanted to storm off to speak with the principal on her son's behalf, but he begged her not to. This left her even more furious and impotent. At first, she ranted, alternately blaming herself, then the principal, then her son, then her husband. She felt completely stuck, overwhelmed by emotions, not knowing what to do. 'I'm damned if I do, and screwed if I don't'.

I simply listened—there was no need (or room) for me to say anything for quite some time. Occasionally I asked for clarification, expressed surprise, sympathy, or curiosity like any engaged listener would. Once, in frustration, she demanded angrily that I 'earn my fee' and give her some advice, 'Should I go see the principal even though Todd said not to?' she asked. 'Shouldn't a mother intervene for her son when injustice has been done?' 'Won't he be scarred by being rejected like this?' I responded quite honestly to Jenny's legitimate request for 'expert' advice by saying that I had more faith in her ability to work this through than I had in any counsel I might offer. Once or twice, I expressed my confidence in her and my admiration for her fierce support for her son. However, mostly I just listened attentively and appreciatively as she explored the multiple dimensions and meanings of her predicament. Gradually, she developed deeper and more nuanced understanding of the complex basis for her rage, the way it related to her own childhood experiences, separating these transferred feelings from the problem for her son, his need to not be seen as a mama's boy, her own feelings that baseball had been the reason her son was willing to try to succeed in school and her fear that he would now withdraw his efforts the way she had, her anger at her husband because 'as usual he won't do anything', her anger at male authority, and so on.

Eventually, the flow of her words slowed down. She began to listen to herself, and to correct herself as she did so.

Jenny: The principal's a fucking asshole. He's on a big power trip. (Pause) No, that's not really true, it isn't all the principal's fault, he has a job to do and he's probably under pressure to improve kids' grades so they can go to college. I seem to be looking for a villain. I am noticing now that I do that when I don't know what to do. That's what Mark always says I do. It really pisses me off when he says it, but he may be right. (She smiles, I smile back.) (Pause) Hmmm.

Sometimes there isn't one, right? No easy answers? Somehow that doesn't seem so scary at this moment. (Pause) This seems like a big deal, to be getting this after all these years of knocking my head against a wall.

Therapist: You are beginning to see just how complicated the situation is, not so easy to see what to do, but now you have noticed this pattern, you seem to be willing to go beyond your usual search for someone to blame. That seems like something important!

Jenny: Yeah, it does. Finding a villain only makes me feel like a victim. It's even worse when I decide the villain is me, then I just want to go away and shoot myself. It's like right now I can see it in bigger perspective, somehow. You know, when Mark would say 'you're losing perspective', I didn't really know what he meant, like there was right and there was wrong and you had do what was right. But it's not so clear, is it?

As Jenny's exploration of the issues continued, what began as a one-dimensional victim story gradually became elaborated into an entirely new and much more complex grasp of the situation. This understanding extended beyond herself to include empathy for all the participants, including the high school principal. As we approached the end of the session, she seemed different. She was more relaxed, she sat quietly, her face calm, and her eyes wide. She sat silently for several moments (the first long silence of the session), and then said:

Jenny: Something incredible has just happened. I don't feel angry anymore, I don't feel afraid, I don't feel inadequate. It's as if I am seeing all of this in a new way—like instead of it all happening to me, I am part of a whole lot of other people's lives and they're part of mine, and what I do affects them and what they do affects me. I suddenly feel a sense of confidence in my own position on this baseball and grades thing, I feel like I am a part of it all somehow, not just a bystander. I feel like an adult—like I understand why the principal thought it was a good idea. I just don't agree. And maybe Todd needs his friends' respect more than he needs baseball, and maybe he needs baseball so much because he thought it meant so much to his dad and me. I don't know, but I am going to talk all this over with him.

Between that session and the next, I was to learn, Jenny had conversations with her family and with Todd alone. With Todd's blessing, she paid a (calm) visit to the principal at which she expressed her disagreement with his educational strategy while affirming his responsibility to 'call 'em as he sees 'em'. She shared with me that her entire family seemed to be taking her more seriously and that her customary sense of dread had evaporated. She was laughing a lot more.

Jenny: In that last session, it was as if all these years of struggling to come to terms with my shitty life had come to a head over this one issue. I just couldn't hide behind the molest thing anymore, making excuses for not standing up for myself. Even as I talked, part of me knew more was at stake than Todd's baseball. I think that's why I came. I could either walk away from it and say it's too hard, like I have a thousand and one times, or I could face it and do something else. But now, I am seeing a whole lot of interconnecting lines going everywhere—to Todd, to Megan, to Mr. Boyd, to my dad—it's all one big bundle of people and everyone has their point of view. It could be easy to get lost, but somehow I seem to have my own opinions as well. I am still here, but somehow I'm in it as me.

Because you were so there for me… in a funny way you were more help because you didn't try to help, you never gave an opinion about what I should do, but you did seem genuinely interested in me and my situation. Usually, with Mark, he either takes over or won't get involved—so he tries to talk me out of my feelings. What you did and what you didn't do was just right. It gave me the space to see the bigger picture, I guess.

The next week Jenny arrived with a basket of vegetables from her garden and a decision to end therapy.

Jenny: I can do it myself, I think. You said you had confidence in me, and I thought when I got home, 'Heck, if she sees me like that, why don't I just do it'. So, I tried it, and it is working out. If I can't do it sometime, I'll come back. OK?

She didn't. She did, however, keep in touch by Christmas card and the occasional letter. Over the decade since I last saw her, she went to college, finished a fine arts degree, began to design for a major jewellery house, and rebuilt her relationship with her husband. Now at 51, she has a business making a good income and is close to her family in a way she had never been. She has not needed any further psychotherapy; she experiences occasional stage fright before making a major sales presentation, but otherwise is anxiety free. More importantly, she still feels 'like an adult'. She says she is 'a deeper person, somehow' and is beginning to think she is going to make a 'pretty awesome old lady one of these days'.

Jenny had a transformative experience—apparently in just four sessions—a brief therapy success. However, it wouldn't matter whether it had taken 10 sessions or even 30, as it was the quality of the change that marks it as significant. It would miss her achievement altogether to evaluate what occurred in reductionist terms as 'number of sessions', 'symptom reduction', 'problem-solving', and certainly in terms of the managed care industry's favorite standard, 'returning her to pre-morbid functioning', and it would miss the importance of the presence of a significant Other, to think of my role in this as provider of 'psychological treatment'.

In a very real sense, Jenny underwent an enlightenment experience. Who she was after the experience was qualitatively altered from who she had been just the week before and this change permeated her whole existence. She had not only changed *what* she thought about the situation she was facing, she had changed *how* she was thinking.

Jenny had been operating from within mental processing frameworks inadequate to the complexity of the situation she was facing. It was as if she was attempting to navigate the complex psychological terrain of adult life with the very primitive maps she had drawn as a teenager. Epistemologically, she was 'over her head' (Kegan, 1994). She herself realized that she needed capacities she did not (yet) possess and had worked furiously to find her own remedy. All those books, classes, talk shows, and her women's group had certainly expanded her repertoire of conceptual options in important ways, but had up until then added more to the 'quantity' of her knowledgebase, rather to the quality of how she processed it.

When faced with contradictory life challenges, such as her unsatisfactory marriage and her simultaneous commitment to being a good mother, in which several of her well-established but adolescent cognitive-emotive patterns were in conflict, it seemed to Jenny that any solution from within one pattern would violate the requirements of another. The crisis over Todd's baseball playing had kicked the whole dilemma into high gear. She had been running around in mental circles looking for ways out of the impasse and this had precipitated her anxiety attacks. Her level of physiological arousal had been raised significantly, and this had activated many if not all the mental possibilities she had accumulated over a lifetime of experience. At home, without a supportive context in which to permit this process to take its own course, she was flooded with unbearable anxiety, but within the special conditions of the therapeutic setting, where she experienced herself as being met in the appreciative context of an unconditionally accepting 'we', she was able to resist her impulse to retreat, and instead of another failure, she was able to find her way out of the impasse. It is crucial to recognize that all this learning would have been lost had she been either 'therapised or medicated' out of her crisis.

As artists, scientists, and mystics have long known, states of high mental arousal, when not accompanied by too much fear or sense of threat, permit us to bring into focus all at the same time, ordinarily disparate and disconnected fragments of knowing, state- and context-specific schemas, tid-bits, unrelated ideas, narrative repertoires, odd-ball possibilities, unconscious connections, strange and creative associations, and to make new connections. Neural pathways and cognitive subroutines, which develop separately at different stages of development and in response to specific experiential challenges, and which usually operate somewhat independently, become available to each other in such altered states. Emotional, cognitive, and even neurological reorganization can take place, and higher orders of mental functioning can be achieved. According to Pascual-Leone (1989), growth that creates advances in levels of mental functioning only occurs as 'a result of overcoming (i.e., reversing or accepting failure)' (p. 275) because (deep cognitive-affective) structures do not change unless change is required. By 'accepting errors' in her characterization of the situation, 'taking them as a challenge' (Pascual-Leone, 1989, p. 276), getting perspective on a broader more comprehensive level, and by becoming aware of her own existential involvement in the flow of her life, Jenny's breakthrough is archetypal of all higher orders of psychological growth.

Jenny is navigating a transformation from a way of being in which she is a passive recipient of life to one in which she is an active agent, from 'subjective knower'—where the only truth is her own personal feelings, to something approaching 'constructive knower', where reality is seen as a co-construction among multiple players (Belenky et al., 1986). In this one series of statements, we can hear her begin to see her connectedness to larger systems, her existential limits, and the dialectical relationships between the systems she is involved in. She can see the tension between Todd's membership in the family, his relationships with peers, and their relationship to the high school culture. Jenny begins to 'dis-identify' with her own emotional responses—'getting perspective'—which she can now see are contaminated by out-of-awareness associations from her own (very different) childhood. She also begins to see that she had choices in the way she construes the world—'no right answers'—and begins to accept personal responsibility for the way she sees things, while accepting others will make different choices. Whether such transformations occur through psychotherapy, education, the ordinary challenges of life, successfully faced, through participation in enlightenment traditions, rapidly during a crisis, or over the long haul is incidental; Jenny is on her way to becoming what Rogers calls one of the 'the persons of tomorrow' (Rogers, 1977, p. 263).

Rogers believed that unless prevented by overwhelming and aversive circumstances, leaps of consciousness such as these could be expected to occur in therapy, in encounter groups, in community workshops, at home, at work, or in church, temple, or mosque, because it is the *nature of Being to become*. Like the South African prime minister, Jan Christian Smuts, who in 1926, on the heels of a political defeat, originated the concept of holism, and physical chemist Ilya Prigogine, who pioneered research on self-organizing systems, and physicist David Bohm—all of whom he felt kinship with, Rogers believed that complex systems—especially living systems—do not obey the laws of entropy, but rather move towards higher levels of organizational complexity. In this view, the 'formative tendency' of the cosmos is eternally waiting for opportunities whereby the unseen, 'implicate order' (Bohm, 1980) of the not yet Being, can become.

Notes

1 I wish to thank the global community of client-centered and person-centered therapists for their generous help in the preparation of this [the original] article. In particular, I wish to thank John Shlien for kindly lending me a copy of his dissertation and for bringing the work of Jessie Taft to a new generation of therapists; Jules Seeman and Ferdinand Van der Veen for tipping me off to the original 'brief therapy' research they had conducted in the 1950s; Barbara Temaner Brodley for case material; Vera Cury for information about therapy in Brazil; and Brian Thorne and David Mearns for their contribution from the British Isles.

2 The Thematic Apperception Test is a projective psychological test developed during the 1930s by Henry A. Murray and Christiana D. Morgan at Harvard University.

Chapter 18

Reflections on Maureen O'Hara's writings on client-centred therapy

Maureen O'Hara and Keith Tudor

Keith: So, having discussed more about your contributions to the big picture, the macro level—the person-centred approach (Part 1), humanistic psychology (Part 2), and third force science (Part 3)—we now come to discussing your work on the micro level of clinical practice. The three chapters in this part are a small but nonetheless significant and representative sample of your contribution to the literature and practice of client-centred therapy. I was interested in these three contributions as, while they are concerned with practice, they retain some of the themes apparent in your work, evident in the chapters in previous parts of the book, namely, feminism (Chapter 15); context and postmodernism (Chapter 16); and philosophy (Chapter 17).

The first paper is a chapter that appeared in the book *The Psychotherapy of Carl Rogers* (edited by Farber et al., 1996). I mention this as the project of the book was to provide commentaries on some of Carl Rogers' 'cases', mostly recorded demonstrations for which the editors and now we have the transcripts to study. The book is divided into two sections: 'Rogers' therapy cases: Views from within' and 'Rogers' therapy cases: Views from within and without', i.e., within and without (or outside) with regard to the person-centred model. I refer to this as, perhaps somewhat surprisingly, your contribution and commentary appear in the second part, which raises the question of the extent to which a feminist analysis is or has to be positioned within and/or without client-centred therapy.

Maureen: You make a good point. The introductory comments to that section (Raskin, 1996) do imply that a feminism-informed analysis of the encounter between Rogers and the client Sylvia is 'outside' person-centred therapy. The other commentary on the same interview by Cain (1996) focusses on the granular level exchanges between Rogers and Sylvia and stays squarely within an intra- and inter-personal framework. Rogers did not see it this way. At the time this case was published, pushed by female colleagues and his feminist daughter Natalie, he was actively exploring ways to become aware of unintended

DOI: 10.4324/9781003519454-23

patriarchal and Eurocentric biases in his work. He was open to taking steps to undo his own privilege wherever possible and to be an ally to women in the struggle for social justice. In *Carl Rogers on Personal Power* he shared a small piece of his struggle when he wrote, 'I am totally in sympathy with the view that women are subtly demeaned by the use of a masculine pronoun when speaking in general of a member of the human species' (Rogers, 1976, p. ix). Rather than use what he felt were linguistically clumsy compromises such as he/she, or him or her, however, he opted to alternate by chapter the use of masculine and feminine pronouns. He was open to the experiences of women colleagues and workshop participants and responded to the suffering of his brilliant daughter Natalie. Working closely with him into his 80s I saw first-hand his willingness to open up to new iterations of the PCA and to take on board feminist ideas about the violence of patriarchal systems. He often said there were as many person-centred approaches as there are practitioners.

Keith: Thanks for that—and I appreciate the point you make (following Manheim, 1936/1954) about the impact of a person's, and, in this context, a practitioner's thought-model, which we might think about in terms of an internal frame of reference. As for the paper (Chapter 15) itself, I appreciate your analysis and the way in which you move from the micro or granular level of the choice of words Rogers uses to their significance at the macro level; your clear but respectful critique of Rogers' work, for instance, his overly psychological and intrapsychic focus; and the comparisons with feminist therapy and other ways of knowing—and being and interacting, therapeutically.

I was interested in your comment about how 'essentially conservative consciousness often is' (p. 149). I would have thought, not least from your other writing, that you would think that consciousness is constructed and, therefore not *essentially* conservative or, for that matter, feminist, or Marxist.[1]

Maureen: There is no contradiction here—only a specific use of language. I was using the term 'essentially conservative' not in an ideological or philosophical sense but from the vernacular meanings: 'essentially' to imply naturally, basically, or intrinsically and 'conservative' to mean aiming to protect and safeguard what already exists. The point is that the ordinary course of learning or growth is gradual. We add to what we already know by accretion and only when a new experience destabilises our accumulated conceptual organisation do we restructure or in more extreme instances transform, such as happened to me with Laing (Chapter 1) or might occur because of trauma and some moments in psychotherapy.

Keith: Thanks for the clarification, which, appropriately enough, brings me to a point at the beginning of your tour de force on relational empathy

(Chapter 16) in which you argue for a sociocentric rather than an egocentric empathy.

First, I want to acknowledge that, as I read this paper again in the context of this volume of papers, it is clear that it builds on your critique of modernism (as exemplified in Chapter 4), and your deconstructive views about concepts such as the self (Chapter 7), as well as your advocacy of holism (O'Hara, 1984a). Also, I was interested to read your account of Rogers' and Kohut's views on empathy (on which Rogers himself commented in an article published in the last year of his life [Rogers, 1986a]).[2] I agree with your critique of some developments of client- and person-centred approaches to this attitude and quality of the therapist, especially those such as Truax and Carkhuff, whose work misrepresents Rogers' original (1957, 1959) formulations, and has led to an oversimplification of client-centred therapy, and the kind of instrumentalism about which you write. In my view, the great strength of this paper is your development of client-centred therapy as an application of a sociocentric psychology.

Maureen: Thank you. Yes, I was—and am—attempting to capture the sense of the client–therapist encounter as a relational entity that cannot be reduced to Newtonian billiard balls. When we see the world transactionally (as your paper illustrates) so much of what happens between us is invisible and we are left with an oversimplified mechanical understanding rather than a more expansive holistic awareness of the potentially cosmic significance of our encounter.

Keith: There's one other point I'd like to pick up from the beginning of this paper (Chapter 16) when you refer to the 'indigenous psychology of the Western world'. I know this is a debate in the field of indigenous psychology and there are some who claim that all psychologies are indigenous. However, given that many psychologists, including Rogers, develop(ed) their psychology and therapy in lands and contexts to which they and their ancestors were not indigenous, I wonder about the veracity and usefulness of this claim, especially in the context of our interest in client-centred therapy being a therapy that accounts for the context of the person of the client.

Maureen: This is another complex topic that again brings up the question of changing language and the history of ideas. At the time I was developing the ideas that I articulated in this paper, I was in dialogue with Art Warmoth, a student of Abraham Maslow and founding Dean of the Institute for Humanistic Psychology (now Saybrook University) and Chinese philosophical psychologist Louise Sundararajan who went on to create the Task Force on Indigenous Psychology (IP) as a project of the Division of Humanistic Psychology of the American Psychological Association (APA). What we meant by 'indigenous' at the time was only to signify 'of the place where it originated'; thus, the eucalyptus trees along the Pacific Coast Highway in California are indigenous to Australia; Buddhism is indigenous to India. Warmoth's position, which he stressed to his students, was that all psychologies are indigenous. There is no psychology from nowhere or no-one, and so any claims made by the psychologists who are the gatekeepers for what is normal, healthy, and universal such as journal editors, accreditors, funders, health care agencies, governments, and the dominant media, simply represent hegemonic power moves that put Western individualist positivist psychology in the centre and define any other framework as 'other'. We were part of a committee attempting to persuade the APA that its accreditation standards were based on a particular view of psychology which, while claiming universality, was in fact a psychology that reflected the local values, patterns of life, mind, and cultural investments of the descendants of the European Enlightenment. Our committee was made up of representatives from clinical psychology programs that were based in third and fourth force psychology paradigms and reflected the then new conversations about social constructivism and post-positivist human science. Our arguments rested on the mounting evidence from multiple directions that there is more than one 'psychology' and that all are adapted to life in particular circumstances. The psychology of many of the world's peoples is based on premises that, while markedly different from Euro-American assumptions with respect to ontology, epistemology, and metaphysics, are nonetheless coherent, realistic to the communities who hold them and adaptive to the needs of particular communities.

In the last few decades, as the voices of previously invisible persons are finding ways to be heard in academic and political spaces, there has been an evolution in the use and meaning of the word 'indigenous' and 'indigeneity'. While originally used to signify where and among whom a psychology emerged, more recently 'indigenous' has taken on an emancipatory role within psychological conversations. It has come to signify distinct peoples who existed in a particular place and culture before any colonists arrived and connotes a shared affiliation and political solidarity with other groups with similar histories of colonial oppression. This is the meaning best known outside academic conversations in the 21st century. Were I writing this today, I would likely not use the term indigenous for Western psychology in general but refer to the 'psychology which emerged among elites (principally males) in Western European societies, their diasporas, and former colonies'. Of course, this does not really solve the problem of what to call the diverse psychologies of Confucian cultures, Marxist societies, or the multiple cultures of India or the Middle East.

Keith: Thanks for this, Maureen. I really appreciate your explanation(s) which both acknowledge the original context of your writing, and give us an insight into how you have kept in touch with—and, indeed, been a part of advancing—different and developing analyses.

Moving on, I was particularly keen to include your paper on brief therapy in the book (Chapter 17), particularly given our mutual interest in the subject.[3] I think it's important in a number of ways, but wonder, and especially looking back on it, what you consider its importance and/or relevance today?

Maureen: I think the focus on the potential for transformative learning in a short encounter might be even more relevant today. As I write this there is ongoing hot war in Ukraine that kills dozens and traumatises thousands of civilians every day. Two months ago, the entire city of Lahaina on the Island of Maui burned to the ground destroying cultural sites and leaving hundreds dead and thousands homeless and just today (October 7, 2023) Israel declared war on Hamas in response to a brutal invasion that has already cost the lives of over a thousand Israeli and Palestinian civilians. Hundreds of Israelis—many of them children, teens, and elders—have been taken hostage to be used as human shields. The immediate and long-term psychological costs of such catastrophes is incalculable occurring as they routinely do within a global social environment that, as the COVID-19 pandemic revealed, is polarised, incoherent, and unprepared. The relentless deluge of information on official and unofficial sites reveals extreme levels of disorientation, anxiety, and depression on a scale beyond what existing cultural capacities handle (Chapter 19).

As described in your book *Brief Person-Centred Therapies* (Tudor, 2008), it was obvious even in the 1950s (Shlien, 1957) that the need for psychological care, even in affluent populations and especially for the poor, far outstripped the availability of professional psychotherapists. This is still the case with recent mental health statistics revealing that almost one in four people will experience mental distress that would warrant a medical diagnosis within a medical framework. This has not changed over decades despite the exponential growth in mental health budgets. Some of these people will have access to therapy of some kind and, as illustrated in the collection of articles in your book, even brief person-centred approaches can be effective but most will not. Instead, clients will be thrown back on their own resources if and wherever they can find them.

After following mental health trends for decades, it is my conclusion that, despite increasing attention to mental suffering, the gap between need and availability of effective help has not narrowed. The pain is personal certainly, but it is also cultural. If, as a world society, we are to attend to the massive levels of psychological suffering, we will need to rethink what psychologists can usefully offer that is both healing for persons under stress and capacity-building for whole societies. I do not believe that the solution is to try to apply existing forms of psychotherapy to more people no matter how effective and valuable they are on an individual level. Of course, interventions in acute crises, traumas, and extreme psychotic conditions will continue to warrant the application of traditional and innovative therapies when available but there will never be enough. We need new paradigms that build on what we know about well-being, psychological growth, and healing with individuals and in group encounters but take that knowledge outside the medical context and introduce it at institutional and cultural levels. We must create new (and reclaim old) spaces where collective healing and transformation can occur. In our book *Spaces for Growth* (2022), Graham Leicester and I describe examples of such spaces and identify some of the conditions that facilitate transformative change.

In this paper (Chapter 17), I am trying to make the case that such a new paradigm exists in the theory and practice of person-centred therapies. I hope that this chapter makes clear that what enabled Jenny (my client) to make such a transformative expansion of her capacity to handle her life more competently was very human and quite simple. It did not entail the use of sophisticated techniques, hours of one-to-one therapy based in esoteric theories. It required only that Jenny and her partner—in this case a therapist—created a relational space characterised by a few key attitudes that enabled Jenny to access her inherent capacity to self-right and change her perspective. Though core to person-centred approaches, these attitudes or ways of being are found in most human societies and are widely known to facilitate healing and growth with or without a trained professional. Jenny was in a state of distress. She was psychologically ready to be met by another person who showed she cared that she was hurting. She felt received unconditionally, authentically, and empathically. Most importantly, she felt trusted by the therapist who by her willingness to listen but not advise communicated that Jenny had the inherent capacity to find her way through. As she said:

> [I]n a funny way you were more help because you didn't try to help, you never gave an opinion about what I should do, but you did seem genuinely interested in me and my situation… What you did and what you didn't do was just right. It gave me the space to see the bigger picture, I guess.
>
> (p. 190)

I have come to believe that the ability to be with another who is in distress, without taking over or minimising the situation but simply being present in these times is a basic human literacy that we all need to acquire in our early years in the same way we expect all children in schools or at home to learn basic skills like reading and taking turns. That's the easy part. The harder part will be to convince leaders, policy makers, and the professionals currently responsible for mental well-being to trust the self-healing capacity and intrinsic resilience of persons and their communities and support rather than direct the creation of spaces that nurture transformative growth.

Keith: Thanks, Maureen. I think you've summarised the chapter well—and I couldn't agree more!

Notes

1 For an articulation of which, see Séve (1974/1978).

2 Elsewhere, I analyse Rogers' changing views on empathy in terms of Stark's (1999) taxonomy of one-person, one-and-a-half, and two-person psychology, with my own addition of a two-person-plus psychology (Tudor, 2011); thus, 'I and my colleagues realized that this empathic listening provided one of the least clouded windows into the workings of the human psyche, in all its complex mystery' (Rogers, 1974/1995a, p. 50) (one-person psychology); empathy 'involves a continuous process of checking with the client to see if understanding is complete and accurate. It is carried out in a manner that is personal, natural, and free flowing: it is *not* a mechanical kind of reflection or mirroring' (Raskin & Rogers, 1989, p. 189) (one-and-a-half person); 'Empathic understanding—understanding with a person, not about him' (Rogers, 1952/1967a, p. 332) (two-person psychology); and, empathy is 'in itself a healing agent. It is one of the most potent aspects of therapy, because it releases, it confirms, it brings even the most frightened client into the human race. If a person can be understood, he or she belongs' (Rogers, 1986a, p. 129) (two-person-plus psychology).

3 See Tudor (2008), a book for which Maureen wrote a generous endorsement (O'Hara, 2008).

Part V

Psychology futures

Chapter 19

Alternative psychological scenarios for the coming global age (2001)[1]

Maureen O'Hara

Introduction

When considering the likely future effects of contemporary trends and events, most futurists focus on the macro level. A general consensus exists among futurists that when viewed from this level, the world is experiencing an era of increasing turbulence that is expected to create unprecedented political, economic, technological, demographic, and cultural changes (Anderson, 1990; Rosenau, 1990). However, whatever the effects on the macro scale, it is on the level of the lives of individual people and their families that the human effects of these changes will be experienced. If history is any guide, we can expect that a cultural transformation of this magnitude will also bring changes at the psychological level—the meso level of the psychodynamics of institutions and organizations and groups, and the micro level of the psychology of individuals (Taylor, 1989).

It is now uncontroversial among psychologists that in terms of both mental 'content'—cognitive schemata, mental routines, and representations of reality—and mental 'process'—perception, mental operations, and conceptual strategies—the individual and collective consciousness develops as a function of an ongoing dialogical interplay between the organismic givens and challenges made by the physical environment and the human-made cultural environment. The specific kind of mental organization developed by persons in any particular context is the emergent result of the history of the organism–environment dialogue. It is to be expected, then, that any massive transformations on the environment side of this interactive equation will bring with it corresponding changes in the inner world of the human psyche.

Changes can be expected to occur in the typical patterns of mind, shared expectations of what is acceptable behavior, how a well-adjusted person should behave, what is worth striving for, and what are the most important psychological strategies for survival and self-realization. Much of this change or learning is gradual and cumulative, adding to experience and consolidating prior knowledge. However, it is crisis situations—situations which cannot be addressed with the knowledge, mental skills, and emotional equilibrium currently available—which lead to the largest and most radical shifts in mental structuring and processing. When

DOI: 10.4324/9781003519454-25

people are confronted with a challenge for which they have not yet the capacities required to resolve, a situation of cognitive dissonance is provoked.

In psychological emergencies—whether personal or cultural—psychological and physiological arousal increases, leading to an increase in mental activity. There is an internal push to resolve the crisis and return to a state of equilibrium as quickly as possible. In communities dominated by a Western scientific worldview, this push is often referred to as 'anxiety'. Both individuals and collectives develop culture-specific strategies through which to contain this anxiety and prevent it from overwhelming essential functions or undermining psychological stability and coherence. When the traditional 'psychic containers' are adequate, threats to individual or group stability posed by challenges to habitual routines can be neutralized. When they are not, stability is compromised, and radical and discontinuous change is likely.

Whether that change is healthy and growthful or pathological and destructive will depend to a large degree on the support systems available at the time. Support may be in the form of economic resources—in general, wealthier people survive crisis better than those in poverty; psychological resources—well-adjusted people are more resilient in crisis than those who are psychologically vulnerable; and cultural resources—those who can draw on intact cultural traditions, religious institutions, family, and kinship systems are more adaptive to crisis than those who are more disconnected.

Growth and transformation

When adequate internal and environmental resources are present and the higher levels of arousal can be tolerated long enough for new capabilities to be discovered and developed, the response can be a movement toward higher levels of functioning. At the lower end of the growth continuum, there is an increase in experience, and enlargement of available mental repertoire and consolidation of prior learning upon which future experiences can be based. At the most expansive, however, there may occur a qualitative shift such that not only the contents of consciousness expand but the way in which experience is processed shifts to a higher order of complexity. Previously established routines and response patterns, accumulated knowledge, problem-solving strategies, and conceptual and epistemological frames of references become re-ordered into a more highly complex mental capacity. This has been referred to by me and by others as the *transformational response* and it can occur in both individuals and groups (Kegan, 1994; O'Hara & Wood, 1983).

Reactionary defence

In the felt absence of the necessary conditions to support psychological growth or transformation, defensive efforts—both conscious and unconscious—will be mobilized to maintain equilibrium and the status quo. Defence strategies are as varied as they are essential, but they share one common feature, namely they are the individual's or community's attempts to avoid having to change in the face of some new complexity and to avoid a felt threat of annihilation and identity disintegration. Denial, avoidance, reaction formation, alienation, distortion, displacement, compulsion, obsession, dissociation, and simplification are all special cases of psychological processes aimed at limiting the psychic threat attempting to limit awareness of novel challenges through simplification. While normal, creative, and adaptive, when used to avoid unnecessary disturbance of previously successful routines, if the pressure to change remains constant, then resistance eventually becomes a liability.

These reactionary efforts are costly in terms of individual and collective resources and frequently lead to high levels of stress, reduced vitality, diminished creativity, and increased hostility. Enormous amounts of effort are sometimes required to bolster defences in the face of sustained psychic emergency. In individuals, misused defensive strategies may lead to psychological symptoms. More serious individual effects might include psychological illness such as depression, personality disorders, narcissism, anxiety disorders, attention deficit disorders, and identity diffusion. In groups and communities, reaction takes the form of repressive social processes aimed at maintaining the existing social order. These processes often include intolerance of difference, political repression, social scapegoating, fascistic social movements, fundamentalism, an emphasis on enforcement of 'law and order', intergroup prejudice and conflict, and political and institutional conservatism. When the forces driving change reach a point where resistance becomes self-defeating, repetitive use of defensive strategies can be seen as a 'neurotic' response (Levin, 1987a, 1987b; O'Hara, 1998). An important exception to this must be made when considering resistance to oppression or perceived injustice. In such cases, even long-term and severely self-damaging refusal to change would not be characterized as neurotic. The distinction lies in the fact that such resistance is conscious and choiceful rather than compulsive and automatic.

Chaotic breakdown

When psychic arousal is extremely high and there is insufficient capacity for either transformational change or maintenance of the status quo through 'neurotic' suppression of the drivers of change, complete and catastrophic breakdown may occur. The psychic containers disintegrate leading to chaos and madness. In these 'psychotic' states, anxiety is neither transformed nor suppressed, but instead explodes in an orgy of cathartic expression, the purpose of which is the release of tension and annihilation of the offending threat even if it means self-destruction. Psychotic states are incoherent, nothing makes sense, there is no perceivable order, and no recognizable relationship between ordinary consensual reality and the inner psychic maps of individuals.

The deeper news

The radical shifts now occurring in the environmental contexts in which contemporary consciousness must survive and people thrive clearly present an intensifying challenge to all existing patterns of mind. The experiential world of a child who learns about the rainforest by navigating the logic of their personal computer is qualitatively different from that of their mother who read books and watched films, and different again from the child who lives in the forest and learns about it through navigating the logic of the forest itself. Life for the Oaxacan immigrants in New York City makes radically different developmental demands than does life in their village in Mexico. Migration back and forth between the two makes yet another kind of psychological demand. As the global change process accelerates and its influences widen to embrace the lives of everyone everywhere, individuals, groups, and whole societies are being pushed beyond their previously established equilibrium and are being forced to respond. From those responses, repeated over and over again throughout a lifetime, it is likely to come not only superficial changes in externalized actions, but in the deep structural mental patterns of how reality is experienced and how the self-concept is constructed.

Global identity crisis

All societies develop their own traditional forms of life and social institutions through which people are successfully socialized to be at home in those traditions. These processes, which include child-rearing practices, family and kinship patterns, education, work, religion, architecture, epistemology, forms of logic, metaphysics, cultural narratives and myths, approaches to medicine, and relationship to the natural world, lead to the development of particular forms of local psychology that may be highly adapted to particular lifeworlds but quite maladaptive elsewhere. In his groundbreaking research comparing the psychology of people from different cultural contexts, Shweder (Shweder & Bourne, 1982) demonstrates that there are deep differences in both self-concept and conceptual practices across cultures.

In an earlier work (O'Hara, 1997b), I summarize reports of characteristic self-configurations that, while certainly not the case for every individual, are nevertheless more or less modal for what Shweder (1991) terms 'sociocentric' people—those who live in tribal or non-industrialized ways of life, and for 'egocentric' people who inhabit individualistic, urban, and industrialized worlds that have characterized Europe and European-dominated cultures since the 18th century (see Table 19.1).

Radical change in the lifeworld inevitably results in the opening of an experiential gap between the existing sense of self and what is being demanded by the new world, frequently provoking an identity crisis for individuals and groups affected. Whether the crisis is caused by forced dislocation of people from their familiar surroundings and traditions—as in the case of refugees, migrants, victims of war, occupation, or conquest by foreign forces, or from voluntary changes in that society as happens as a consequence of political, philosophical, technological, or social revolutions—the changed lifeworld demands reorganization of the inner psychological world. The greater the discontinuity from familiar patterns, the greater the degree of required change and the greater the anxiety to be managed.

Table 19.1 Sociocentric psyche vs. industrialized psyche

Tribal or socio-centric psyche	*Modernist/industrialized psyche*
• Embedded in contexts and tradition	• Innovative—overthrows traditions
• Accepts multiple realities but 'ours is better'	• Recognizes one 'reality'—others are 'belief systems'
• Located in time and territory	• Mobile 'home is where the job is'
• Relational/sociocentric	• Individualist/egocentric
• Perceives patterns and gestalts	• Perceives linearities and parts
• Ethics based on 'preserve and care'—conservative	• Ethics based on 'universal principles'—liberal
• Non-historical—'timeless wheel'	• Historical—'progressive'
• Holistic thinking—symbol, metaphor, and allegory predominates	• Atomistic thinking—analysis and reduction predominate
• Reasoning synthetic, narrative, and recursive	• Reasoning abstract, deductive, and theoretical
• Organic explanations preferred	• Mechanistic explanations preferred
• Trusts the body—no 'mind–body' split	• Distrusts body—splits 'mind' from 'body'
• Trusts intuition as much as rationality	• Distrusts intuition in favor of rationality
• Empathic with human and non-human worlds	• Empathy not a high priority, objective distance preferred
• Collaborates with kin but competes with 'others'	• Competes with friends and 'others' and collaborates strategically
Anxiety containment	**Anxiety containment**
Preferred strategies emphasize art, magic, tradition, story, ritual, attunement with nature, repetition, community, conformity	Preferred strategies emphasize reason, predictability, power, control of nature, self-mastery, science, order, entertainment

The psychological, social, political, and economic demands of the emerging global information society are so radically different from any to which either tribal or industrial peoples are accustomed, the rate of change is so rapid and the process so turbulent, that neither existent culturally specific self-configurations nor established socializing institutions can adequately prepare people to be at home in the new emerging contexts. The worlds we are collectively creating intentionally and unintentionally can no longer be navigated successfully, using the representations, epistemologies, patterns of life, ways of thinking, and sense of self that we have aimed to develop in our various cultures.

Neither the tribal nor the modernist psyche seems particularly well suited to the new postmodern world. According to development psychologist Robert Kegan, the kinds of capacities required to hold a job in today's business environment, or successfully balance the world of work with the world of family and community life, for instance, do not feature particularly prominently in the modal modernist psyche aimed at in American education and socializing practices (Kegan, 1994). From factory floor to board room, employees are routinely expected to be 'self-starters' yet highly relational and collaborative, assertive yet empathetic, comfortable with 'multiple tasking' but able to focus and meet deadlines, be at home in racially and gender-diverse work groups, be able to cooperate and collaborate, evaluate their own work, keep company secrets, cross boundaries, cope with rapid change, know how to create emergent creative processes in groups, have an internal sense of ethics and work standards, and so on. Even in advanced democratic societies, psychological demands have outstripped the modal level of psychological capacity. For dislocated tribal people, the situation is even direr. We are all, as Kegan puts it, 'over our heads'.

According to research conducted by Kegan's group, two-thirds of late 20th-century Americans have not achieved the levels of mental capacity required by life in the late 20th century. Mental distress is already extremely high, and every indication suggests it is climbing. By 1987, over 18 million or 7% of Americans per year sought treatment for mental distress, and recent figures suggest that by 1998, that figure had grown close to 11% (Rabasca, 1999). Rabasca quotes one clinical psychologist who specializes in phobias and other anxiety-related disorders who estimates that 'as many as one in every five Americans experience symptoms of anxiety' (p. 1). At least some of this increase can be directly correlated with macro-level events. In the same article, Rabasca reports an increase in people developing phobias and anxiety-related symptoms stemming from fears about the so-called 'millennium bug'. In the industrialized nations, leaders have not even begun to think about what happens to a society in which large numbers of the population have not the requisite minimal mental capacities to navigate the challenges of daily life, and there are neither formal nor informal systems by which these capacities might be deliberately developed. Historical evidence and reports from tribal peoples from many parts of the world suggest that the consequences can be catastrophic (Tuchman, 1978). In the case of tribal peoples, dislocation from ancestral lands, disruption of traditional ways of life, and exposure to the alien worlds of contemporary urban life have been devastating. The annual 'Conference on Suicide Prevention among Indigenous Peoples' draws participants from all around the globe (Osava, 1998).

In the high-tech world of cybernation and in the rainforests of South America, people are confronted with the same dilemma—how to cultivate in the population at large the higher orders of mental capacities and habits of mind required to thrive in the totally new contexts of the 21st century and how to design social processes through which the new self-configurations might become institutionalized. There are no experts here—no global shamans or psychotherapists who know what will be needed in the new reality. Whether village person or urbanite, we are all strangers in a strange land facing the same dislocation from our historical and contextual roots, and the same individual and collective anxiety and the same challenge of inventing healthy rather than pathological responses to it. It is important to say, however, that we face them with vast inequality in economic resources at our disposal.

A new psyche for new times

If it is true that both the tribal and modernist forms of psychology are ill-suited for the new era, it might be useful to consider what kind of psychology might be more suited. One obvious necessity is flexibility. In a rapidly changing context, firm

Table 19.2 Emergent transmodern psyche

- Innovative and conservative
- Multiple truths lightly held
- Lives, thinks, and acts locally and globally
- Embraces spirituality
- Thinks holistically and systemically
- Tolerates ambiguity and difference
- Reflexive learner
- Contextual 'self-in-process'
- Ethics—'Right action' over fixed principles
- Assumes personal responsibility and accountability
- Particularist and generalist
- Reasons abstractly and narratively
- Trusts body—no 'mind–body' split
- Multi-epistemological, respecting rational non-rational ways of knowing
- Boundary crosser
- Collaborates and competes in the service of whole
- Empathic with self and 'others'

Anxiety containment

Relational connections, flexible social systems, relevant rituals, self-mastery, art and science

commitments to any patterns quickly become anachronistic and self-defeating. The ideal of a stable sense of identity or self, whether tribal or individualist, seems to be ever less viable anywhere. In its place, a new kind of person might be emerging who can respond to the turbulence, complexity, and large-scale cultural changes by developing new and multiple sources of identity and creative strategies for success. There is at least anecdotal evidence that a new kind of hybrid 'both/and' psyche might be emerging that is more fluid, emergent, contextual, and relational than the modernist ideal and more individuated than is typical in tribal selves (Anderson, 1997; Gergen, 1991; Giddens, 1991; see Table 19.2).

This 'transmodern' psyche—which is neither Western-modernist nor non-Western-tribal, neither sociocentric nor egocentric—is inventing new hybrid ways of being that balance the kind of psychological strategies appropriate to a technologically mediated world of 'individual rights and responsibilities' with the more basic needs for relational continuity, community, spirituality, and connection to the natural world characteristic of non-modern consciousness. Although probably in short supply, these 'persons of tomorrow' may be more numerous among those who have learned to live in more than one world—refugees, colonized peoples, and immigrants, people marginalized from the mainstream culture for whatever reason, as well as those who deliberately practise consciousness-expanding disciplines such as Sufism or Zen meditation, psychotherapy, or philosophy, or who through advanced education have become 'multi-epistemological', or those who have experienced life-changing crises and have been able to mobilize the psychological resources necessary to achieve a transformational rather than a neurotic or psychotic response.

This leaves a vast number of 'people of today' who we can expect will be less adaptive to the polyglot worlds of tomorrow. It seems reasonable to assume that as the pressure from the macro level intensifies pressures on meso and micro levels, we will see a rise in both neurotic and psychotic responses. The worldwide rise in fundamentalism of many kinds and the explosive nightmares such as those in Northern Ireland, Uganda, or Kosovo represent these pathological responses.

This is a moment that is pregnant with possibility and the emergence of a new transmodern psyche might be the first signs of a further step in the evolution of consciousness (Csikszentmihalyi, 1993). More pessimistic observers warn that there are other more alarming signs that might signal a decline of consciousness and descent into a new dark age (Kaplan, 1996). Whatever scenarios unfold—they are almost sure to be plural—they will make their demands on social resources and the collective imagination. In the coming decades, one of the most pressing tasks will be to help people recognize the dialogical links between the macro level of large-scale social changes, the meso level of organizational and group psychology, and the micro level of individual psyches. We urgently need to identify effective strategies and mobilize the necessary resources for ensuring that as many people as possible develop the psychological capacities to maintain their equilibrium in the changing contexts in which they will find themselves.

Part of that task is to invent and encourage the use of social forms that can serve as cultural containers to prevent the inevitably elevated levels of anxiety from turning destructive as they so often have done in the past. This will require the development of new transmodern governance structures, legal systems, educational processes, management approaches, art forms, and spiritual and secular rituals. If these can be developed on a wide enough scale and in locally appropriate ways, it is not inconceivable that psychological transformation might occur. In any case, however, the need will be urgent to develop new culturally appropriate approaches to mental health services for those who fall victim to the times. Investment in psychological services for casualties will have to be made not only for humanitarian reasons but also to head off the possible social catastrophe that could ensue should either the neurotic or psychotic scenarios predominate on a cultural scale.

Note

1 Presented at the Annual Convention of the American Psychological Association, 2001.

Chapter 20

Another inconvenient truth and the developmental role for psychology in a threatened world (2010)[1]

Maureen O'Hara[2]

> *The new age which knocks upon the door is as yet unknown, seen only through beclouded windows... But whatever the new world will be, we do not choose to back into it. Our human responsibility is to find a plane of consciousness which will be adequate to it and will fill the vast impersonal emptiness of our technology with human meaning.*
>
> (May, 1969, pp. 308–309)

Friends, preparing for this address, I spent some time reviewing what has excited me about the humanistic tradition in psychology, my own professional history, and the people and ideas to which I have been exposed and have shared with students over the past 40 years. Once again, I was taken by the power and timeliness of the core ideas of this tradition in psychology. Re-reading the words of the likes of Abraham Maslow, Carl Rogers, Erich Fromm, and Rollo May, I was renewed in the belief that as the human species faces what could conceivably be its last-chance encounter with destiny—the challenge posed by the threat of planetary catastrophe in the wake of global climate changes—these core humanistic ideas about our inborn capacities for self-righting and self-healing, empathy, authenticity, for mind-boggling innovation and creativity, and for solidarity with those in need and suffering—still have enormous relevance. Better still, they can yet provide grounds for hope that we can address these challenges before it becomes too late. If the worldview, values, and associated ways of being and being with each other, outlined by humanistic psychologists over the last half-century, were to become part of the shared story of how humans might journey through the next critical period in our history, this might provide a philosophy and praxis for the development of a new psychology suitable for a sustainable and liveable global society. If the prognosticators are right about the coming threats, as I believe they are, we have little time to waste and I want to argue today that, as ethical psychologists, this must be the overarching focus of all our efforts. Anything less is fiddling while Rome burns or rearranging chairs on the deck of the Titanic—choose your catastrophe metaphor.

It seems to me that over the past decades, American clinical psychology has lost its way. It has focused too much of its energies on building its financial stake in the

DOI: 10.4324/9781003519454-26

illness-focused health care economy. Psychologists spend time defining so-called mental illnesses at ever finer levels of distinction such that there are now hundreds of diagnostic labels, each with its own insurance code and justification for treatment. The American Psychological Association and pharmaceutical companies who manufacture psychoactive drugs have, between them, spent millions of dollars seeking additional diagnostic categories to justify insurance reimbursement, parity with medicine, and lobbying for prescription power (I won't call them privileges). This hand-in-glove mutual aid scheme is intended to secure a piece of the 'big-pharma' pie and a first-class seat on the health care gravy train for psychologists. For the pharmaceutical industry, it aims at direct access to a huge population of psychologist drug dispensers to peddle their wares. For psychiatrists and psychologists, it promises millions more potential patients.

A place in the health care industry was never the goal of humanistic psychologists. Indeed, virtually from the outset, humanistic psychologists have mounted a vigorous critique of the medical model of mental life that reduces communities to *demographics*, persons into *patients*, suffering into *symptoms*, and healing and recovery into *treatments*. Where medicalized psychology has been reductionist, the humanistic tradition in psychology has always been about the much bigger cultural stories—about individual fulfilment, the avoidance of war, a saner society, the well-being of humanity, and about ensuring a more humane future for all. From its emergence in the 1940s, humanistic psychology was offered up as an alternative to the disease-oriented focus of existing psychology and sought in its research and practice to affirm human possibilities and explore the growing edge of human potential. Rogers' core conviction that clients had within them the capacity to change and the inherent drive for greater wholeness that could be relied on to direct the course of therapy revolutionized the fields of counselling and psychotherapy. Early humanistic thinkers saw this new positive voice in psychology as providing a counterweight to the then dominant theories of human motivation offered by Freudian psychoanalysis and behaviorism. Instead of understanding human behavior as either controlled by unconscious drives or external stimuli, the founders of the humanistic movement in psychology believed that such notions sold the human capacity for awareness, creativity, responsibility, and free choice grievously short.

Beginning in the 1930s, humanistic psychology's chief founder, Abraham Maslow, hung out in the emigre-enriched psychological community of New York City. He met regularly with Adler, Horney, Goldstein, Fromm, and other psychological intellectuals who had fled the darkening clouds of Hitler's Germany. The 1941 attack on Pearl Harbor brought the war home to American territory, and from that day, too old to serve in the military, Maslow dedicated his efforts to putting psychological knowledge to the service of improving the world. Maslow said:

> I had a vision of a peace table, and people sitting around it, talking about human nature and hatred and peace and brotherhood… I realized that the rest of my life must be devoted to discovering a psychology for the peace table.
>
> (Hoffman, 1996, p. 148)

Maslow and those who joined him in the new humanistic psychology movement, including Carl Rogers, Erich Fromm, Rollo May, Clark Moustakas, Gardner Murphy, and anthropologists Margaret Mead and Ruth Benedict, saw themselves as involved not only in an academic discipline, but in a psychologically informed, but explicitly moral, social movement that sought to prevent repetition of the monstrous behavior that had just occurred on a global scale. With the images of mushroom clouds haunting the popular psyche, in the 1950s humanistic psychologists wanted to prevent nuclear holocaust and to develop a psychology that was up to the twin tasks of healing those who were casualties of both violence and neglect, and, at the same time, creating the cultural and interpersonal conditions that would lead to greater social justice and expanded opportunities for human fulfilment and advancement of consciousness.

It is fair to say that many of their hopes have been realized, due both to their direct contributions to the collective psychology, and to the work of many others also aligned with a basically humanistic worldview. The world is a different place in 2009 than it was in 1948. The UN's *Universal Declaration of Human Rights* (1948), a radical affirmation of human dignity, was held for 60 years, and, over the decades, has become real to ever more people: women and minorities have been gradually gaining their voices and have made progress towards social and political equality (uneven though it be); almost all children receive some level of education; infant and maternal mortality rates are down overall (though this too is uneven); average life expectancy has increased; and the notion that environmental sustainability is essential for human well-being is now universally acknowledged. Maslow's Being values (1962) are showing up in international policy documents. The four pillars of learning that are the universal aims of education identified by UNESCO, for instance, include 'learning to be' and 'learning to be with', in addition to learning to know and to do (Delors et al., 1996, p. 19). In the world of business, there is hardly an organizational trainer who does not quote Maslow's pyramid or hierarchy of needs. Companies and organizations within civil society all recognize the value of empowerment, networks, flattened hierarchies, democratic participation, good communications, listening, systems thinking, authenticity, and transparency, to a degree unimaginable in the 1960s. (Granted that, in many cases, these innovations in management are as much style as substance [Potterfield, 1999].) But the fact that these core humanistic values are credible and so widely employed across many fields of human endeavor surely reflects the heightened expectations of today's employees that they be treated with dignity as competent and whole persons. When a few years ago the *Harvard Business Review* selected articles for its 15 classic articles series, they selected a 1952 article on communication by humanistic psychologist Carl Rogers with Fritz Roethlisberger (Rogers & Roethlisberger, 1952). Perhaps even more indicative that deep cultural change that reflects core humanistic values has occurred, in his book, *The Audacity of Hope*, President Obama (2006) explicitly introduced the idea of the importance of empathy, authenticity, and caring when it comes to leadership, governance, and even foreign policy. And so far, no nuclear war. A lot of human progress since 1945!!

But I am pretty sure that if Rogers and Maslow were alive today, they would be disappointed in our movement and how we seem to have turned ourselves inward and toward the concerns of individuals, and away from the huge looming issues facing humanity as a whole. They would be looking with alarm at the global juggernaut bearing down on a psychologically unprepared world, and asking if and how humanistic psychology might help to address or mitigate the challenges before us. They would be seeking to liberate the power of human creativity, capacity for empathy with those who are suffering, and capacity to innovate and learn, to address the coming crisis and turn it into opportunity for growth and learning. They would want humanistic psychology to be at the centre of research and praxis about new forms of social intervention based on a more accurate, more inclusive, less ethnocentric view of human potential. They would be looking at the global changes underway and aiming themselves squarely at the coming global humanitarian crisis. They would understand that the context of all our lives—whether rich or poor—is now threatened, and they would want to do anything they could to be part of the solution, not part of the problem. They would, I am sure, recognize that the future is made by decisions made in the present. As psychologists with a keen grasp of the relationship between the inner world and the outer context, they would be reminding everyone that what we see as possibilities for the future is a direct result of both the kind of world we inhabit today and, above all, the psychological capacities we cultivate and nurture in our human community.

I ask you today to join with me in reclaiming the social transformation agenda that was so important to the founders of our discipline. I do so because, in my view, humanity is facing challenges that are radically altering the context and prospect of human existence; challenges that, if not addressed, threaten wholesale collapse of civilizations. In privileged places in the United States and Canada, the signs of this coming crisis are not yet so obvious in our daily lives. But any newspaper, web search, or TV channel offers plenty of evidence for those who are awake that just beyond our still-comfortable horizons, a great unravelling is well underway and signs are everywhere that we are involved in a life or death struggle for the future of civilized life and, perhaps, the global ecosystem. Though mostly framed as challenges for governance, technology, and economics, I want to argue that all of these rest on the question of mental capacity or consciousness.

We humans operate within a web of interconnected physical, biological, and human-made realities, and it is within this web that we, as conscious beings, live out our short lives. Psychologists often refer to the *biopsychosocial context* of individual's lives. In my view, this is not a good term, failing, as it does, to capture the dynamical interplay among multiple levels. We need a more holistic term that can encompass the vastly complex interplay among stable and fluid elements, organic and inorganic, symbolic and systemic, interactive processes that make up the experiential context of human consciousness. My candidate is a new term, *psychosphere*. By analogy to the concept of *ecosphere*, which describes complex physical and biological environments, *psychosphere* refers to the holistic, interconnected, interpenetrated, mutually influential system of narratives, symbols, images, representations, languages, metaphors, patterns of life, values, epistemologies, cognitive habits, rituals, religions, power relationships, sports, forms of commerce, governance, metaphysics, art, and technologies that, together, provide the raw materials of identity and the psychological context of individual and group life. A mouthful, I know, but a radically important concept for us to comprehend for, at any moment in a human life, all these dimensions of reality (and maybe more that are unseen) form the substance of consciousness and through human action alter the world.

Psychospheres are more than cultures. Referring to objects, concepts, and processes, psychospheres provide the basic ingredients of conscious life and influence neuronal pathways in the brain, individual and collective memories, cognitive habits, language, artefacts such as art, video games, and the content of libraries and TV shows, patterns of family life, drug use, all the way to political agreements and social arrangements. What these days we speak of as *consciousness* comes into being, exists and evolves within this vast interwoven and holistic context.

For any discrete society (from sports team to tribal band, to global corporation, to nation state) to be stable and to be able to maintain sufficient levels of social harmony to permit successful identity formation, psychological resilience, and social well-being, they must share a coherent collective psychosphere. Though psychospheres vary widely, they must always give satisfactory answers to the core existential questions that all people must address, such as where do we come from, why are there haves and have nots, what distinguishes *our people* from *their people*, what is our relationship to nature, and what is the relationship between the individual and the group? In stable communities, answers to these questions must make sense to most and be widely shared (Shweder, 1991; Taylor, 1989).

Changes in the psychosphere can be disturbing and anxiety-provoking. They disrupt routines, upset certainties, and make collective meaning-making difficult. But as long as changes are gradual, the inevitable anxiety generated can be managed within the existing psychological structures, narratives, and structured institutions. When change is gradual, people work through their disturbance over a myriad of conversations that explain the changes from within existing shared narratives. The change can be explained and understood not as a break with the old but an expansion, innovation, or improvement to it.

When Western narratives about women and Blacks changed in response to civil rights struggles and feminism, for instance, previously segregated institutions eventually accepted women and Blacks by arguing to themselves that this did not destroy the original mission (identity) of the university, but simply extended it to a wider population. Struggle, strikes, demonstrations, and even riots—but no culture shock, no collapse of life as we know it. Though in the turbulent 1960s more than a few feared cultural breakdown, enough social glue was in place in Western democracies to hold collective anxieties in check; preventing them from erupting into chaos long enough to work through the transition. This capacity to incorporate and adapt to change without collapse makes coherent cultures resilient and resistant to fundamental or revolutionary upheaval, and has led to the success of human communities over millennia. The human mind cannot tolerate having to reinvent every wheel, every day. From an evolutionary perspective, it takes too much energy. We need most of the basic functions that keep us alive to run automatically, without any attention from us, so we can focus our cognitive and emotional capacities on new challenges. We do better when change comes slowly and with good believable explanations that might embellish or expand but don't challenge our basic taken-for-granted storylines. Though a few casualties inevitably occur, given adequate time to work the new into the old, communities and civilizations can adapt and remain vital over very long periods (Toynbee, 1972).

Rapid and radical change is, however, another matter. When change occurs too fast, on too many fronts, or too fundamentally, established institutions often are unable to cope. Institutional ways of addressing difference and dissent, for instance, may be inadequate to restore life as we know it. In such cases, anxiety may rise to unbearable levels. Examples throughout history suggest that, in these cases, societies and whole civilizations can collapse into violence, chaos, and sometimes disappear. In the introduction to his translation of Lucretius' *The Nature of Things*, R. E. Latham observes that as the Hellenistic psychosphere disintegrated, the mismatch between inherited wisdom of Aristotle and Plato resulted in 'disillusionment, skepticism, and fatalism' (Lucretius, 1951, p. 7). Rollo May's interpretation of the psychic breakdown was that the 'myths and symbols had broken down… and the human being does not know where in the world he is' (May, 1969, p. 295). Historian Barbara Tuchman's (1978) portrait of the 'violent, tormented, bewildered, suffering and disintegrating age' (p. xiii), that was the 13th and 14th centuries in Europe, describes a 'period of anguish when there is no sense of an assured future' (p. xiv). In 1920, American sociologist Westfall Thompson compared this same chaotic period to the aftermath of the Great War, where a 'whole population is suffering from "shell shock" from frayed nerves [leading to a] semi-hysterical frame of mind throughout Europe' (J. W. Thompson, 1920, p. 570). When empires conquer and occupy, when nation states are defeated by invaders, when religious reforms contradict stabilizing belief systems, or when political revolutions sweep away kings or regimes, it may take generations of violence, disorder, and brutal repression before stability is restored and new coherent psychospheres are established (Toynbee, 1972).

In the West, the unquestioned value of change is core to our psychosphere. It is common for political platforms, both Left and Right, to promise change. It is hard to imagine a successful campaign in the progressive West that would promise more of the same. But human beings are slow to learn from history and are often blind or amnesiac about the darker side of cultural change.

American college students are taught that the European Renaissance, for instance, was a time of great breakthroughs in art, science, and political processes—the 'rebirth' of classical culture in which 'laid the groundwork for modern civilization in political and social relationships as well as in the arts' (Cantor, 1970, p. 61). We reflect mostly on the gains, and our textbooks point to the immense social and cultural transition out of the chaos of medieval era as a story with a happy ending.

In the vernacular telling of history, we disconnect the undisputed cultural advances from the darker realities that went along with the changes such as millions massacred (perhaps as many as four million deliberately and sadistically murdered as witches and heretics), lost communities, pandemic plagues, and endless wars. A deeper reading of history suggests that the psychosphere we now call modernity that results in a psychology identified as 'normal' by American psychologists, and familiar to all of us in the Western world, was not stabilized overnight—nor without victims. It took almost three centuries of turbulence, during which time accepted assumptions about reality were gradually overthrown through a laboured process of social learning, new conceptual insight, argumentation, scientific treatises, poetry, storytelling, architectural shifts, as well as internecine fights, epidemics of madness, bitter and brutal conflict, persecution and oppression of dissident views, including indigenous folkways, Islam, and Judaism—all this before the modern mind and modern ways of life became established as the way things are. Psychospheric change is not smooth, not anxiety free, not fast, and rarely happy.

You and I, and most certainly our children and grandchildren, are living at a time of unprecedented psychospheric upheaval cultural change on a scale and at a speed beyond anything humanity has faced before. This time, the disintegration of existing psychospheres is pandemic, simultaneously reaching the furthest tributaries of the Amazon and the rarified science labs of the West. It is not at all clear that we know how to navigate our way through this.

Driving this great unravelling is a combination of many factors. Chief among these is the process of globalization which includes destruction of local cultures and intensification of Western hegemony; innovation in technology (genomics, robotics, informatics, and nanotechnology); accelerating urbanization—largely in slums; shifting age demographics—aging population in the West and Japan, and drastic reduction of the median age in much of the rest of the world; radical changes in geopolitics—end of the cold war, disintegration of the old Soviet Union, emergence of an enlarged European Union, the rise of China and India; a shift from an energy-based industrial economy to a knowledge society; travel, migration, and an explosion of the number of refugees; the rise in expectations and demand for economic and political justice; the rise in fundamentalism and intensified religious fervour; instant and unmediated communication bringing information overload and incoherence; unbridled consumerism and extra-societal corporate domination of mass culture; degradation of human beings who are reduced to role of consumers, rather than citizens; and exacerbating environmental pressures, including population increases and climate change.

The combined result of this era of a thousand revolutions is that long-standing frames of perception, cognition, and patterns of life—through which individual and group identity is preserved, and existential anxieties managed—are literally breaking down on a global scale. Stable psychospheres are hard to find, and within a single generation a mismatch has opened between inherited local psychologies and the demands of the world we now must inhabit. In this *futureland* which is emerging, we are mostly immigrants, and many of us are refugees.

Across the world, individuals and societies are trying to make sense of what is happening, trying to hold on to whatever coherence they can, even while all about them life becomes more confusing all the time. This cognitive challenge is creating what amounts to a global conceptual emergency (Leicester & O'Hara, 2009), and with it rising uncertainty, high anxiety, even panic—that becomes increasingly dangerous.

The human mind did not evolve in such an incoherent context. For most of our 300,000 years of human evolutionary history, change occurred slowly, over multiple generations, not in a single lifetime. We became human in this apparently timeless relationship between us and the natural world. Our collective psyches had time to adapt to slow-moving cultural shifts that happened without our awareness. But now that has changed. Humanity must adapt within single lifetimes to evolve, in short order, new kinds of persons who are at home in this totally new world and who can tolerate and even thrive in levels of complexity and change what our grandparents, and a thousand generations before them, would have experienced as intolerable.

One can argue that history seems to indicate that humanity has faced challenges like this before and though civilizations have come and gone, humanity as a species has endured and, from the point of view of progressive Western thought, advanced.

However, I submit that this time is different. Even if the global conceptual emergency were not enough to cast doubt on whether, as a species, we have the capacity to successfully learn our way into the new, all-connected, boundaryless world, the survival stakes have just been dramatically raised. Thanks to the efforts of our best and brightest scientists, who provide us with information about planetary changes in the far past, the present, and likely futures, we now become aware of threats and opportunities our ancestors had no way to perceive (W. T. Anderson, personal communication, November 5, 2009). Our monitoring technology makes it clear that we face self-created, whole-system perils that, if not addressed, may put an end to all life as we know it. *I am talking about the threat to the sustainability of the planetary ecosystems due to climate change and the prospect that we may have damaged the earth's self-regulating mechanisms beyond its capacity to self-repair.*

Former US Vice President Al Gore's film *An Inconvenient Truth* (Guggenheim, 2006), brought this inconvenient truth to the broader public, breaking through the collective denial about the impending global catastrophe that global climate change could bring. Since then, the scientists have refined their data, and the picture becomes worse and more acute. At this point, there are no scenarios being created by climate experts that, in the near and midterm future, do not include extreme challenges to the inhabitants of planet Earth, no matter what we do. Let me repeat that, *no matter what we do*. The die is already cast. Temperature increase occurring in 2009 is the result of human activity in 1980, when our carbon emissions were lower than today. We will not feel the effects of what we are doing today for at least another 30 years. In the meantime, things will continue to heat up from what we have done since 1980. Information from many sources shows that we have pumped so much carbon into the atmosphere that we have already set in motion climate changes that will inevitably result in a 1.5–2.0 degree rise in global temperatures.

The good news, if you can call it that, is that if the planet warms less than 2.5 degrees in the next 25 years, though provoking extreme events for those in already hot areas, including massive species die-off, famine, drought, pandemics, and more mega-storms, human beings, the world's advanced civilizations, and the planetary ecosystems that support us can probably eventually adapt. Massive levels of suffering will be unavoidable (and, indeed, is already reality from many people beyond the privileged safety of the technologically developed world) but, eventually, a new homeostasis could be established that is sustainable.

The darker news, however, is that if temperatures rise to more than 3 degrees above preindustrial levels, a cybernetic engine is unleashed that triggers accelerating warming to over 10 degrees above acceptable targets (Dyer, 2009). These levels mean irreversible environmental collapse. No longer a fanciful doomsday scenario providing fodder for special-effect-laden disaster movies, planetary death is now being openly discussed in scientific meetings around the world. Geo-engineering proposals such as artificial sky darkening and deep-earth carbon sequestering—a sort of Army Corps of Engineers meets environmental activism—are now showing up in articles in science journals (Wigley, 2006), conversations among White House advisors, and DARPA (Defense Advanced Research Projects Agency; Kintisch, 2009) and the British Royal Society (Shepherd, 2009).

If the nightmare scenario occurs, observers like Dyer (2009) say, 'Humanity will in all likelihood be headed towards war: war over access to water, over arable land, over dwindling resources' and distracting us from the urgent job of discovering the escape route into a sustainable future. In his book's final chapter (which he pointedly entitles 'Childhoods end'), Dyer argues that in the long history of the evolution of consciousness, successful avoidance of nuclear annihilation in the 20th century was humanity's midterm exam—which, according to him, we passed. But we are so far into the destruction of the planet's capacity to restore itself that if we do nothing, planetary destruction of habitat for more advanced life forms will be unavoidable. Dyer is not alone in this conclusion. In fact, climate scientists who look at this problem agree that simply reducing the rate of increase in carbon emissions, which is the most those negotiating international treaties like Kyoto are talking about, is already insufficient. We need to stop further carbon dioxide emission, and actually remove some of the carbon that we have already released. We, as a species, have so changed the ecology of the planet and damaged Gaia's capacity to heal herself that, whether we like it or not, responsibility for the continuation of planetary life is now in human hands—yours, mine, our children and grandchildren's. Business as usual is not a survival option (Gribben & Gribben, 2009).

Geo-scientist Paul Crutzen (Crutzen & Stoermer, 2000) believes we have entered a new geological epoch, for which he offers the name *Anthropocene*, where human activity is the main contributor to global geological changes. During the 3.5-billion-year journey from *cyanobacteria* to the whole of the Earth's current flora and fauna, including us, natural evolutionary processes gradually created the ecology upon which we and all other complex life forms rely. In a few short centuries, however, in order to enhance our own survival chances, we humans have so disturbed the balance of this ecology that if we are to survive, we must govern evolution (Anderson, 1987). To avoid irreversible collapse, taking most of the more complex organisms with us will require that we successfully steward the planetary life support systems long enough to mitigate and reverse some of the effects of our 200 years of burning fossil fuels and find renewable forms of energy to replace them. Dyer (2009) writes, 'Now it's the final exam, with the whole environment that our civilization depends on at stake. It's not just about knowledge and technical ability; it is also about *self-restraint and the ability to cooperate. Grown up values if you like* [emphasis added]' (p. 244).

I agree with him, but values are psychological phenomena—they speak to what is psychologically important to us—and like almost all those writing about the coming global catastrophe, Dyer says *absolutely nothing about how self-restraint and cooperation and 'grown up values' might be developed.* This neglect of the psychospheric dimensions of the impending crisis is common. For instance, a colleague of mine noticed that in a recent series of meetings of the World Business Forum on Sustainability, which was convened to create scenarios for the year 2050 to aid business in its long-range planning, there appeared a distressing blind spot in the proceedings (B. Horn, personal communication, May 15, 2009). The project was convened to identify the key issues that are likely to be facing humanity 40 to 50 years hence. Working groups of experts deliberated at length on the technical challenges: economics, energy, health and disease, immigration, and other aspects of the imaginable future. Each group drew up detailed elegant scenarios. But according to my colleague, who was one of the experts, when describing what would need to happen for worst case scenarios to be avoided, these specialists usually ended with a statement to the effect, 'behaviour and values will have to change'. When asked to imagine how this shift in human consciousness might occur, few ideas were offered. It is significant to me, a psychologist, that among the experts carefully recruited as participants, there was not one psychologist. Al Gore has begun to recognize the pivotal importance of consciousness in how the various scenarios will play out. In his latest book, *Our Choice: A Plan to Solve the Climate Crisis* (Gore, 2009), he has taken time to talk with neuroscientists about how the human brain processes short-term and long-term threats. What is missing, though, and this is more psychology's failure than Al Gore's, is consideration of how we translate psychological knowledge from the micro scale of brain processes to the scale of personal and interpersonal behavior and macro scale of political action, governance, and collective human behavior and, of course, vice versa.

This brings me to my main point. Another inconvenient truth is that, in all likelihood, the most difficult challenges faced by planet Earth in the 21st century are not technological but *psychological*, and involve a simultaneous confluence of a whole gamut of challenges to human consciousness on a global scale.

We are, in my view, facing two very messy challenges to consciousness that intersect and exacerbate each other. One is the worldwide disintegration of established coherent psychospheres described earlier, where the resulting incoherence creates uncertainty, divisiveness, and drives up anxiety levels that frequently gets expressed in individual and societal pathologies. The other is that action based on a realistic understanding of what we face, making the necessary sacrifices, accepting finite limits, requires a new global psychology and psychosphere that will create it and sustain it.

In my view, surviving this next period in history may depend upon enough of us being able to tolerate the inevitable anxieties and social disruption ahead without turning on each other in hatred and violence, and instead of sinking into self-destruction and despair in ways societies have in previous times of cultural disturbance, finding a transformational response to what confronts us. And this is why psychologists—in particular humanistic psychologists—must enter the story, and we must do it now.

In the longer term, survival of predicted disruptions in the physical world will require scientific advances and technological inventions. But it is our collective response to disruption and disintegration in the *psychological* environment that will be even more critical in the shorter term. The biophysical effects of climate change will be gradual—over a generation or two—but psychic collapse can occur much more rapidly. The psychic destruction of indigenous peoples everywhere has occurred in a few decades. Within only 20 years after the calamitous Great War, Germany once again descended into cultural psychosis and the Holocaust, chaos followed the breakup of the former Yugoslavia in just a few months, and in Rwanda the total collapse of the rule of law resulted in the deaths of over a million people (half of them Hutus and half of them Tutsis) in an orgy of rape and slaughter within a period of days.

In my view, if those two great American humanists, Maslow and Rogers, were alive today, they would not be focusing energy trying to marginally improve psychotherapy outcomes for Americans, debating whether psychologists should prescribe drugs or whether one kind of therapy treatment is marginally better than another. Their agenda would be far bolder. They would frame the current mental health crisis not in terms of individual diagnoses and the need for better therapist driven treatments—but as symptoms of a broader cultural crisis. They would be focusing on helping humanity develop the psychological ideas and social practices that can help us (and all other life forms) develop the necessary capacities and resilience to make it through the coming crisis. They would be urging us to put psychology at the service of the final exam to emerge from the current mass denial about how serious the threat is and to try to prevent the end of life as we know it. They would draw upon the transformational power of hope, creativity, and intelligence in order to learn, expand our consciousness, and grow our way out of the current crisis. They would be reminding us of the unfinished work of ushering in a new stage of evolution where, for instance, *us* is defined as all of life, and *other* is seen not as a threat to be avoided or subjugated, but as a valued opportunity for innovation and learning. They would be urging us to search for sources of meaning and fulfilment within relationships based on mutual respect and love, and to find satisfactions at consumption levels the planet can sustain. In other words, as Dyer (2009) suggests, developing grown-up values.

Carl Rogers explicitly sought what he hoped might be law-like behaviors that would enable us to avoid alienation, nuclear war, genocide, and ecological devastation and to align with a transformative trajectory—formative tendency—that he believed existed in nature, extending from the outer reaches of galaxies to the inner reaches of the human heart (Rogers, 1980/1995b). Maslow proposed that we need a new enlightenment to develop our capacities for aesthetics, compassion, creativity, ethics, love, and spirituality (Goble, 1970).

It is long past time to recall this fierce commitment to peace and social justice that propelled the early thinkers of the human potential branch of psychology and rescue their cultural leadership project. There is no time to lose. The signs are everywhere that the mental health 'industry' is close to collapsing under its own ineffectiveness, and can no longer cope with the level of mental anguish that people feel. Across the spectrum—from left to right and from consumers to presidents—people are crying out for innovation in how we address the psychological well-being of individuals and communities without going bankrupt. The gravy train that fuelled the rise of professional psychology in the 1980s and 1990s, and made our compromises lucrative, if not wise, is running on empty and if we are to avoid escalating suffering on a massive scale, we need new ways of thinking about psychological health. Business as usual is no longer adequate and new ideas are in short supply.

And here comes the good news—or at least some grounds for hope. Psychologists and teachers know that it is often at the points of greatest confusion, cognitive dissonance, and high anxiety that breakthroughs occur and new levels of consciousness are achieved. In a long-forgotten volume that had a huge impact on me (and incidentally on Carl Rogers), Stavrianos (1976) reminds us that when empires come to an end, the collapse is never total. Humankind has answered previous threats to survival by grit, invention, and creativity. Historians like Toynbee and Tuchman also believe that there is nothing inevitable about human history and that the quality of human aspiration plays a central role in whether civilizations decay or remain vital. If history and psychotherapy provide any guidance to times of anxiety and threat, it might be in the observation that when people can contain their anxiety long enough to tolerate and actually face the dissolution of past certainties, they can often find the growing or emergent edge of insight and innovation. If, instead of denial or collapse, individuals and collectives can expand their awareness and allow themselves to clearly see what confronts them, they can rise to the occasion and become more than they were before.

In my view, the most important work that Maslow and others who saw the need for a humanistic voice in psychology started back half a century ago, is not yet done.

The contemporary 21st-century psychosphere is more nihilistic than inspirational, more encouraging of self-indulgence than sacrifice or self-transcendence, more focused on aggression than on love, and framed more as *me and mine first*, rather than a psychology for the well-being of all of humanity and other life forms. A psychology of resilience and transcendence is not yet what our parenting and education cultivate in our children and the highly developed mental capacities needed be at home in our vastly complex world, is not what we yet expect of our citizenry.

But that could change. And because, as we know, consciousness is a nonlinear process, it could change quickly.

So here comes the good news. People are waking up to the need to reframe the problem of health. In a recent workshop with health care workers dealing with a funding crisis in a metropolitan mental health system run by the International Futures Forum (www.internationalfuturesforum.com), facilitators asked participants the question, 'What are we all pretending is true that we know in our hearts is not?' (P. Hennigan, personal communication, October 15, 2008). The collective answers shook everyone and revealed a disturbing level of complicity in a failing system. Answers ranged from 'pretending a 5 minutes med check is sufficient to establish trust and figure out what's wrong'; 'people from the mildly anxious to the acutely psychotic need the same expert care'; 'there is a correlation between years of training and practitioner effectiveness'; that 'the despair we see every day is due to "illness" that we can "treat" with cognitive behavioral therapy (CBT) and drugs, when we know it is the result of poverty, deprivation and abuse'; and 'what I do as a counsellor will lead to a better outcome for a homeless client than a job, a friend and what they can do for themselves even though evidence points in the other direction'. Even more shocking for a group of mental health professionals was that they volunteered that they believed the mental health care system contributed more to the well-being of providers—in salaries, status, and professional identity—than it did those seeking help, who were often subjected to dehumanizing revolving-door pseudo-treatment and subtly encouraged to become dependent on counsellors, therapists, welfare workers, rather than empowered participants in their own recovery.

So let me propose an agenda for mental health educators to prepare practitioners for these new realities. We must, at a minimum:

1 Frame mental health as inextricably linked to, and co-existent with, cultural health and individual psychological structures and processes as part of a holistic *open system* that includes the rest of organic and physical reality.
2 Provide preparation for our graduates to assume creative leadership roles in new forms of practice for the coming challenges. We need leaders, administrators, program designers, managers, and team members for new kinds of systems of care. And we must make sure they are able to work as teachers in the diverse new BA and MA programs that will be needed.
3 Prepare people to work in multidisciplinary teams with diverse professionals, clients, and lay people. Mental health practice will come from unexpected and unlicensed places.
4 Provide training for working with people who are displaced, violated, unschooled, traumatized, and destitute across the globe.

5 Collaborate with Master's-level educators and practitioners. Most psychotherapy will be done—if at all—by Master's-level practitioners—at lower market rates.
6 Cut the cost of training or find funding for students. With many leaving private graduate schools with as much as $150,000 in debt, we owe it to them to be honest about what their employment prospects are.
7 We must Globalize our psychology—recognizing that, as it has been taught thus far, psychology as a discipline is narrowly ethnocentric, does not reflect other psychospheres or psychologies, or the diverse world it strives to serve has suddenly changed.
8 We need to Focus our research and our students on theories and practices that can help create the new global psychosphere. We are now a global society, but with a collective psychology that is incoherent and at risk of being dominated by hegemonic societies like the United States. We may live in locally specific environments—a Sudanese desert demands a different psychology than does suburban Minnesota. But though locally specific, we are all now aware that humanity's destiny is shared. We need a new psychology that takes this shared future as its core assumption. The United Nations' (1948) *Universal Declaration of Human Rights*, for instance, must become part of everyone's world, taught to every child, and respected by every community—including psychology. The Western enlightenment paradigms must be put in context—as one among many—and now subject to dialogue and engagement with other forms of knowledge, other wisdoms, and other ways of life. Our students must be opened to the resources of other cultural assumptions about psychological life.
9 Humanistic psychologists must Develop new Master's degree programs that are compilations of existing and new knowledge, skills, and attitudes that more directly address contemporary concerns. We need to merge disciplinary boundaries, between education, psychology, sociology, social transformation, community organizing, media, and communication. Needed specialties will include prevention through effective parenting and early interventions to building resilience, elder wellness, client self-care, community organizing, immigrant integration, facilitation of the creation of civil society initiatives for housing, conflict resolution, trauma care, childcare, spiritual comfort and guidance, and a host of other human-to-human activities. These new areas of expertise should not be additions to the curriculum studied after students have mastered the diagnostic categories of the *Diagnostic and Statistical Manual of Mental Disorders* (DSM) and principles of psychopharmacology, important as these are, but should *be* the curriculum.
10 Teach students how to participate in policy making. We could be a very powerful voice in policy discussions such as those surrounding the future of health care, now so tragically impoverished by too many years of reductionist, top-down, command, and control thinking. Policy makers are looking for new ideas—let us provide some. We may be able to persuade those making funding

> decisions to focus on approaches that liberate the self-healing potential of clients and put the professionals in the role of educators and facilitators who are there to give psychology away. In my view, it's a win–win. People are helped to access resources for self-healing, health care costs come down, and the population becomes more empowered (but watch out for the resistance from special interests—such as other psychologists who want their share of those dwindling health care dollars).

As Maslow said, the whole of humanity is our client (Goble, 1970). The human community stands at a tipping point, and it looks like it needs our help to work through its conceptual emergency and to grow up.

Like the founders of humanistic psychology, I think those of us who care about the future have an obligation to put transformative psychology to the service of a world in peril. Though humanistic psychologists may have strayed from the emancipatory project envisioned by Rogers, Maslow, Fromm (and compadres such as Paulo Friere, Ronnie Laing, and Leo Basaglia), we nevertheless have much accumulated knowledge and practice experience to offer if we so choose. In Rogers' last book, he wrote:

> If the time comes when our culture tires of endless homicidal feuds, despairs of the use of force and war as a means of bringing peace, becomes discontent with the half lives that its members are living-only then will our culture seriously look for alternatives... When that time comes they will not find a void. They will discover that there are ways of facilitating the resolution of feuds. They will find there are ways of building communities without sacrificing the potential creativity of the person. They will realize that there are ways, already tried out on a small scale, of enhancing learning, of moving towards new values, of raising consciousness to new levels. They will find that there are ways of being that do not involve power over persons and groups. They will discover that harmonious community can be built on the basis of mutual respect and enhanced personal growth. As humanistic psychologists with a person-centered philosophy—we have created working models on a small scale which our culture can use when it is ready.
>
> (Rogers, 1980/1995b, p. 205)

We are way past ready. It is surely time for us to return to this social transformation agenda and the development of a humane praxis—for humanity's sake and for the sake of the world.

Notes

1 Division 32 Presidential Address, presented at the Annual Convention of the American Psychological Association, Toronto, Canada, August 8, 2009.

2 When Maureen originally wrote this, she was based at the Department of Psychology, National University, La Jolla, California, USA.

Chapter 21

Reflections on Maureen O'Hara's writings on psychology futures

Maureen O'Hara and Keith Tudor

Keith: In your paper on moments of eternity (Chapter 17), you acknowledge that, for as long as you can remember, you have been a scientist (a theme that runs throughout this book), and also name, albeit more hesitantly, that you are something of a mystic. Although you don't claim any capitalised Mystic status in terms of 'grand visions' (p. 175), I do wonder whether your utopianism (to which we both referred in Chapter 10) has, alongside your passion for a better present, driven your interest in and vision for the future?

Maureen: Another story. I remember exactly the moment I began to get serious about the future. I was 12 years old, on a school field trip to York Minster. The highlight of the visit was a climb to the roof (no longer allowed mercifully). I refused to go as I was afraid of heights and chose instead to remain at ground level and visit the breathtaking 13th century stained glass window *The Five Sisters* which in 1925 was dedicated to the women who had died serving as nurses in the First World War. It was near closing and our class was the last group; so, while my classmates climbed the tower, I sat in the quiet of the almost empty chapel and looked up at the window. As I gazed at the massive yet delicate columns of medieval glass, I experienced an overwhelming sense of gratitude: first for the nurses who perished, their names engraved in the chapel, and then for a cascade of architects, artisans, glassmakers, and a multitude of generations of custodians who over the centuries had been part of creating and preserving their beauty. Although it took me years to work through the impact of that moment, even then I realised I was part of a centuries—maybe millennia—long community of human beings I would never know who worked on that exact spot for something beyond themselves, whose lives were dedicated and some sacrificed so that the world would go on, with beauty in it and that the human spirit might be elevated. I also came to recognise that as much as the legacy was a gift for the ages from the past it was also a responsibility to the future that whether we accept it or not we all share. This sense of purpose has been my moral compass all my adult life and animates my intellectual inquiry and drives my activism.

DOI: 10.4324/9781003519454-27

On reflection, I see three major influences which together define my quest for a more just and sustainable future. First was the environmental movement that emerged after the publication of Rachel Carson's *Silent Spring* (1962). Then came the human potential movement, especially the work of Carl Rogers who saw humanistic education in general and encounter groups in particular as sites for nurturing 'persons of tomorrow' (Rogers, 1980/1995b). Finally, came my connection through the Association for Humanistic Psychology with futurist Walter T. Anderson who happened to be close friends with Rollo May. After I published the Hundredth Monkey paper (Chapter 12), Walter invited me to join an interdisciplinary group of highly regarded futures thinkers with decidedly humanistic values he set up to explore the humanistic implications of the cultural upheaval underway. For the first time in that company of highly regarded scholars and researchers, I was able to bring together my critical science background, my postmodern, transformative viewpoint, and my feminism unapologetically to explore scenarios for a more humane future for the world that were grounded in real evidence. I was in heaven.

Keith: Thanks for this story—and for all your stories. They provide me/us the personal to the psychological, and the passion behind your position(s). It also reminded me of what Rogers (1980/1995) writes about having a keen interest in the future.

The first paper in this part of the book (Chapter 19) addresses the micro level of the likely future effects of contemporary trends and events, and, as such, encompasses the personal and intrapsychic responses to growth and transformation in terms of defences and breakdown, crises of identity, and anxiety. I particularly appreciate your discussion of consciousness, not least as it addresses a point we discussed in one of our earlier dialogues (Chapter 14), as well as your description of a new psyche for new times. In doing so, you appear to develop Rogers' (1980/1995) description of the qualities of 'the person of tomorrow'. Was that in your mind as you wrote this?

Maureen: I was building on Rogers' (1969) idea of persons of tomorrow, but I came at this from women's psychology and postmodern concepts of constructivism. I was able to fill out Rogers' framework drawing on advances in understanding of psychological development ushered in by feminist, cross-cultural, African American, historical, and post-structural studies that exploded in the 1990s that demonstrated that psyches and cultures are reciprocally co-created. At the same time, I was learning from my futures studies colleagues that the concrete conditions of life were changing for everyone at such a pace and at such depth that the future was in effect a new culture for which a kind of mind or consciousness adapted to that world would be needed—and fast—yet I saw very little attention being given to the task by psychologists.

That is still true today with meteoric advances in artificial intelligence (AI) threatening or promising to usher in a brave new world based on superhuman data processing capacity and instantaneous access to the accumulated knowledge of humankind. We are utterly unprepared for what is already happening.

In the last decades, I have been working with colleagues of the International Futures Forum, a Scottish 'think and do tank' founded in 2001, whose mission is to explore what is needed to take effective action in a world we can no longer understand and cannot control. While most books dealing with such big-picture questions usually offer lists of skills, tools, and strategies, that is not what we have learned. In our observations of persons who are thriving in today's context of complexity and rapid change outlined in our book *Dancing at the Edge* (O'Hara & Leicester, 2019), we found that what makes the difference is not ways of doing but ways of being and the ways of being that are the most useful for both external action and inner well-being look an awful lot like those speculated on by Rogers as 'persons of tomorrow'.

Keith: I appreciate the analysis you offer in this paper as it brings the social (analysis, world) into the psychological, for instance, your idea of the reactionary defence, in a very open and non-defensive way, for instance the non-neurotic resistance to oppression. One of the things that I notice in your writing and, more so, as we engage in these dialogues, is your attention to language and your refusal, resistance even, to giving away words such as resistance. This reminds me of Speierer's (1990) point that 'what is considered by a therapist as resistance is… due to temporarily a lack of empathy on the part of the therapist' (p. 343).

Maureen: Over decades living in more than one culture, each with its own language and conceptual frameworks, I have become adept at decoding what feminist sociologist Dorothy E. Smith (1991) identifies as the 'conceptual practices of power'. The words we use connote a deeper, tacit universe of assumptions. We can't avoid that if we are to speak at all, but we can—and in the postmodern complexity I would say must—be mindful of how language not only describes the social realities we live in but also constructs and maintains them. The use of concepts in psychotherapy such as 'resistance' carries codes defining power relations where one person's movement is deemed legitimate and the other's not only different but also less agentic. When Mr Trump refers to Democrats as vermin and insurrectionists as patriots the metaphors signal an entire worldview within which violence can be legitimised. Increasingly, commentators are helping the population become aware of these gambits but, at the same time, forces that would capture power are working feverishly to ban emancipatory pedagogies with the intention of keeping their power moves hidden.

Keith: I agree—and I love your phrase 'tacit universe of assumptions'.

I think perhaps the key point you make in this paper, which is still relevant nearly a quarter of a century later, is that 'Neither the tribal nor the modernist psyche seem particularly well suited to the new post-modern world' (p. 207). I tend to agree and, while I want to think that what you refer to as the 'transmodern' psyche can manage our post- or even trans-modern world, I'm not so sure. What do you think?

Maureen: I'm sure that a new psyche is emerging that is adapting to 21st century circumstance, but I'm not sure if this represents transformation or accommodation—probably both. Experience in our International Futures Forum 21st century competence labs suggests that there are many people among us who successfully integrate capacities that are characteristic of the modern psyche with ways of being anchored in older mental capacities and this flexibility serves them very well. We do see them as persons of tomorrow. In an article I wrote with Walter Anderson, 'Divided we stand' (O'Hara & Anderson, 1996), we tell the story of a Mexican American woman who had grown up as the ninth child of an indigenous Oaxacan family and was now a senior government official in California. When I met her, she was struggling to feel legitimate in her career because she often found herself at odds with her Euro-American colleagues; and, when in Oaxaca, she often chided herself for acting submissively with her family as an expression of filial piety. She finally resolved her dilemma when she realised that each way of being was adapted to particular webs of human experience and, as a 'hybrid' (her term), she could draw on both sources of knowledge when circumstances called for it. In our workshops we find that the younger participants can move between worlds with grace and humour, and this seems to give them a resilience in the face of novel challenges like the COVID-19 pandemic. As we describe in our book, they dance at the edge (O'Hara & Leicester, 2013).

Keith: That's both poignant and interesting. I, too, have been involved with colleagues who claim and explore hybridity.[1]

Your reference to Mr Trump reminds me of a phase in your second paper in this part of the book (Chapter 20) about our (species) facing its 'last-chance encounter with destiny' (p. 211). Apart from the obvious capitalism, sexism, racism, and other forms of oppression manifested by Trump and those he represents, I am profoundly worried about the damage he and others are causing to what we might think of as epistemology, i.e., how we know what we know. When feelings become facts, and alternative facts become 'reality', we're lost, and I know I can feel hopeless, so perhaps this is a good point to ask you how you feel and retain hope. When you say 'American clinical psychology has lost its way'—and I would apply that to clinical psychology and other 'psy professions' in most if not all other countries in the world, how do you hold hope as you do?

Maureen: Big question! I share your concern about the damage the assault on truth and truth systems—logic, rationality, science, expertise, authority, the rule of law, myth, religion, and folklore—is having, particularly on the inhabitants and institutions in technologically developed societies. Many of my futurist colleagues believe we are now well into a period of civilisational disintegration not unlike what happened in the 14th century in Europe with calamitous results (Tuchman, 1978) when any statement about truth can—and will—be challenged and deconstructed. Some of this is emancipatory, breaking up established hegemonic frameworks which have provided the justification to the powerful for their exploitation and dehumanisation of the powerless, and allowing transformative innovation to emerge in new social spaces. Innovation may not necessarily be benign from a humanistic perspective, however. Much of the global epistemological meltdown going on today is anything but emancipatory and in some ways amounts to epistemological warfare. Positions about anything are so irretrievably polarised as to threaten societal collapse. Playing on the anxiety accompanying rising levels of uncertainty, those with a nihilistic bent seek to take advantage of the breakdown to gain power. Trump's advisor Steve Bannon has often said his aim is to 'flood the zone with s***' such that ordinary people can no longer tell fact from fiction so as then to be able tell them what Trumpists want them to believe. It works. Today, months before the 2024 US presidential election, a recent poll found that 28% of Republications believe President Biden stole the 2020 election and that Donald Trump is a victim of leftist conspiracies. They see him as a Christ-like figure innocent of wrongdoing despite 91 felony charges, and that retribution through political violence is legitimate. So, in the face of the apparent success of disintegrative forces it is fair to ask what my hope is based on.

At a theoretical level, it is based on faith in what Rogers called the 'actualising tendency': the inherent movement in all life forms, including human beings towards greater levels of complexity and integration. Like Rogers, I hold a view that the universe is purposeful and, though far too vast and unknowable to prove by positivist science, there is as much evidence of a vital force in all nature as there is that we are merely dead chemicals deteriorating into chaos. But my hope is more practical than that and it rests on the evidence of human history which has countless examples of how, despite periods of darkness, human beings as individuals and societies have responded by making transformative leaps in consciousness and social capacity. I believe we are living once again in such transformative times that in a presentation to the World Association for Person-Centered and Experiential Psychotherapy in Vienna in 2018 I referred to as an insurgency of hope:

> Despite the looming threats which often appear to block out the light of hope, we are in fact witnessing an insurgency of hope at the core of which is a new consciousness. There are 'persons of tomorrow' everywhere engaged in large and mostly small creative and effective initiatives addressing the multiple challenges humanity faces in the 21st century. There are transformative projects currently being done by people in this room that include theatre productions, projects to end gun violence in Texas, facilitator development for peacemakers in the Arab–Israeli conflict, helping elders in care create empathic conversations, adolescent counselling, drop-in counselling in Rio's favelas, and empathy circles on the streets of Oakland California.
>
> (O'Hara, 2018)

In societies across the globe, there are quite literally millions of humanitarian groups filled with persons who see the needs of a world struggling with its existential moment and, instead of exploiting it for their own benefit, have chosen to be on the side of healing and growth. When human beings focus on their calling to serve others, they become connected through the work and differences that may divide at a theoretical level become less important than the shared commitment to get things done. Of course, the future is radically open—we have no guarantees—but when taken as a testament to humanity's collective creative drive, it provides ample support for radical hope.

Keith: Thanks, Maureen. There's a lot in this to which I relate, not least in terms of local organising and moments and well as movements of resistance, and my own experience of hopelessness,[2] but I'm more than happy to leave this reflection on futures with your view and vision of radical hope.

Notes

1 See Grennell-Hawke and Tudor (2018), McCann and Tudor (2022), and Hill (2022).
2 See Neville and Tudor (2024), Chapter 8.

Part VI

Education

Chapter 22

The challenge for education in uncertain times (2005)[1]

Maureen O'Hara[2]

Maybe the time has come in our civilization for a period of creative suspension. True creativity appears when we stay within the tension of a question or an issue and do not rush to assuage our insecurity with easy solutions. We are all essential parts of this modern world and must exercise our collective creativity to discover orders beyond, new forms of action and exercise our ability to hold a variety of viewpoints in creative tension and mutual respect.

(David Peat)[3]

The test of a first-rate intelligence is the ability to hold two opposed ideas in the mind at the same time, and still retain the ability to function.

(F. Scott Fitzgerald)[4]

I believe we... need a revolution. We need a mindset change if we are to attain a just and sustainable future. And the revolution must be in our thinking. As Einstein has said, 'We cannot solve the problems of today at the level of thinking at which they were first created'.

(Anthony D. Cortese)[5]

An educated person has the ability to appreciate, learn from, and embrace contradiction, even when we might prefer closure.

(Peter Salovey)[6]

Introduction

We are living in a period when foundational givens of thought are on the move and when the cosmology that has framed experience in Western societies is unraveling. This is creating a shift in our understanding of reality so fundamental that it undermines many of the bedrock assumptions on which Western consciousness is based.

After an almost 500-year march from medievalism to modernism, during which time we in the West have addressed our desires for knowledge and eased our existential anxieties through a variously titrated mixture of metaphysics, superstition, natural science, alchemy, theory, and practical knowledge, the world is changing so fast around us that our minds cannot keep up.

DOI: 10.4324/9781003519454-29

It is hard to overemphasize the implications for knowledge in the conceptual revolution that is underway. In the sciences and technology, this shift from a world of Newtonian certainty and predictability to one of quantum uncertainty and chaotic unpredictability comes largely as the logical consequence of discoveries in theoretical physics at the opening of the 20th century and to the development of the mathematics of nonlinear systems in the 1950s. Taken together, these intellectual developments represent a fundamental shift in our way of understanding the world, and as Peat says, 'puts an end to that Enlightenment dream of conquering the world through pure reason' (Peat, 2002, p. 5). It also reopens the possibility of dimensions of realities not apprehensible through rationality and objectivity.

There are many ways to think about this great unravelling, with significant implications for scientific research, ethics, and philosophy of science, for instance. I would like to explore it as a psychological event and discuss the simultaneous danger of mental distress and opportunity for consciousness breakthrough or growth. Further, I would like to propose some steps that those of us in the knowledge business—whether inside the academy or outside—might take to avoid possible cultural and psychological meltdown, and instead to enhance the likelihood that humanity will find ways to embrace the learning opportunity offered by its collective existential predicament and cultivate the necessary capacities of mind to live well in an unavoidably uncertain world.

The missing elephant

In the familiar Sufi tale of the blind people groping to try to understand what they have in hand, the point of the story is that the blind seekers can transcend their own partial knowledge and understand the totality of the elephant—the mysterious whole—only if they recognize the partiality of their viewpoint and can pool their various local knowledge of the parts toward an understanding of the whole. The story presupposes, however, that there is a position—that of the storyteller—from where it is possible to know the whole. Furthermore, it presupposes that there is already a whole to be known. For reasons much more situational than ontological, we now face a world as Donald N. Michael once observed, where the elephant is missing (Michael, 2000). Or more accurately, there are an infinite number of elephants, chickens, spirits, rainbows, concepts, music—potential patterns to be recognized or produced, each an emergent phenomenon of particular participant–subject relationships. And furthermore, the cosmos may well be more vast than we can ever really know.

Lost at sea

No matter the issue—global warming, terrorism, famine, avian flu, the nature of love, the location of a housing development, the existence of being after death or care of the aged, once you begin to include into your thinking all the information that could potentially illuminate your subject, you find you must look at technology, science, sociology, folklore, religion, psychology, anthropology, media, personalities, politics, big picture, up close, history, current events, future predictions, and so on out into an ever-expanding universe of relevance. Before you know it, you are awash in a sea of information where the more you learn, the less you understand. And despite the availability of sophisticated data-mining techniques and ever more intelligent search engines, the sheer volume of information—good, bad, and ugly—coming at us from everywhere, at accelerating speed, in different languages, epistemologies, assumptive frames—sometimes contradictory, sometimes complementary—means that even if we had the most super-duper pattern-recognizing-mega-computers and data-mining techniques with which to process it, we could no longer hope to separate signal from noise to make the kind of sense we used to refer to as truth.

We experience information overload, yet at the same time there is a widening realization of how much we don't know. We need information to understand our information, we don't agree on priorities, discipline, epistemology, metaphysics, metaphors, and values. Is global warming a technical problem, moral problem, or a social psychological problem—or no problem at all—and who decides? How much of the context do we include—too much and the signal disappears, too little and we can't join up the dots—in either case, we miss 9/11, and so on. Just a few years ago, the favorite metaphor for life in the age of hyper-rapid information flow was 'white water rafting'. Increasingly, it is 'lost at sea'.

Uncertainty as the new existential given

Such a world is a fundamentally uncertain world. Gone forever is the security that for every question there is a single simple answer—even one, as Mencken quipped, that is wrong. Our relentless search for new answers is itself a source of new ignorance, undermining old certainties at the same time as it creates new ones, only to have them disintegrate, in turn, in the face of new knowledge. Our irrepressible curiosity has brought us finally to a place where we can no longer hope to comprehend our world as a whole and to where we no longer have a basis to trust what we once trusted. Should we trust science, for instance? Our doctor? Priest? Tarot reader? Fox News? Al Jazeera? Dreams? Intuition? Logic? Wikipedia? Me? And if so, why?

Powerful times

Cultural psychologist Richard Shweder has observed that stable communities derive their stability in part from a shared 'cosmology'[7] (or 'grand narrative'), which coherently and convincingly explains to their inhabitants why things are the way they are (Shweder & Bourne, 1982). This cosmology includes the interpenetrated and culturally embedded stories, symbols, language, metaphors, beliefs, epistemologies, morality, view of reality, and cognitive and emotional routines that make any particular culture. It defines what is sane and what is crazy, what is mature, smart, foolish, good, evil, beautiful, worth striving for, worth living for, worth dying for, is the right way to think, perceive, feel, and act. It is the role of the socializing institutions—schools, families, churches, governments, media—to inculcate these ideas and values into the population. When the cultural consensus breaks down, societies and the individuals in them come unglued.

A shift in cosmology on a scale implied by the end of the Enlightenment dream, taken together with an awareness brought to us by ever-present global media, that our cosmology is actually just one of any number of reasonable stories to live by, is highly destabilizing. In the emerging global context, where previously trusted authorities and sources of knowledge must compete in the information marketplace with literally countless others, we are left with radical uncertainty not only as a theoretical reality, or as a technological limitation, but as an *existential reality*. For a great many of us, this presents us with a serious psychological challenge. As any psychotherapist can attest, an existential challenge can be both threat and opportunity, a source of anxiety and defeat or a spur to transformational learning.

Capacity gap

Peat (2002) argues that the fundamental complexity and uncertainty of our times require us to understand that 'we are all essential parts of this modern world and must exercise our collective creativity to discover orders beyond, new forms of action and exercise our ability to hold a variety of viewpoints in creative tension and mutual respect' (p. 5). If he is right, and I think he is, we must ask if we are psychologically prepared for such a task and if we are not, what can and must we do to become so.

As a clinical psychologist and educator, my look at the evidence suggests that while some small percentage of us may have achieved the level of psychological development implied in Peat's statement—which is actually pretty sophisticated—most of us have not and by a long way. We are mostly over our heads, where many of the challenges we face every day require levels of consciousness, habits of mind, and ways of being that are beyond the level of psychological development at which most people are operating (Kegan, 1994).

And I think the evidence suggests that a great many of us are not all coping well with being out of our depth. It is generally accepted in world health circles, for instance, that we are experiencing a global mental health pandemic. The World Health Organization (WHO) reports of 2001 and 2002 reveal mounting evidence of the global burden of psychological distress and violence. The WHO suggests that by 2020, depression will be second only to heart disease as a source of illness in the world (2001, 2002). This shows up in individuals in symptoms of anxiety, depression, and self-destructive and violent behaviour, and it shows up in communities as marginalization, alienation, hopelessness, and extremism. Though much of this is due to such factors as war, poverty, and other problems, even in advanced and economically privileged societies, mental illness is on the rise. At the level of nations, the unravelling shows up as failing states, civil war, and repressive regimes.

The Nuffield Trust's UK review of policy futures for health examined the deterioration in 'the social context for healthy living', pointing out how stretched people feel when there is 'no time for life, no partner for life, no job for life' (Peckham, 1999, as cited in Hanna, 2008, p. 2). In the United States, the *9/11 Commission Report* sees people turning to fundamentalism as a source of stability in a world in which many have lost their bearings (National Commission on Terrorist Attacks Against the United States, 2004). The report notes Osama Bin Ladin's appeal to 'people disoriented by cyclonic change as they confront modernity and globalisation' (p. 48). Palestinian psychiatrist and human rights activist Eyad Sarraj, describes the evolution of what he calls 'a paranoid culture' in the Middle East, where older cultural coherence was destroyed by colonial actions in the region and nothing coherent replaces it (Benjamin, 2015). In its *Readiness for the Future Index* of 2001, the World Economic Forum states that 'social harmony' in a nation is necessary for sustainable competitiveness, but notes that this is deteriorating in many countries (World Economic Forum, 2001).

Perhaps we should not be surprised about how unprepared we are for the new context of complexity and uncertainty in which we find ourselves. After all, in the West, socializing institutions, especially our educational institutions, are still mostly designed with the Enlightenment dream in mind. For all the usual reasons—entrenched interests, bureaucratic inertia, established hierarchies, revered tradition, ideology, and so on—the educational establishment has been highly resistant to fundamental change in its basic commitment to the Western scientific canon and over the last decades and science and engineering rule the roost. This is especially true of the universities and colleges that are often 'prisoners of their own legacies… trapped in long-established procedures and norms' (Kelley, 2005, p. 212) and where legitimate concerns for quality and accountability approached through the frames of the Enlightenment dream have led to an exaggerated focus on metrics, the unintended consequences of which is to freeze innovation and to overload teachers.

Increasingly, higher education as a socializing institution is seen to be failing its students and the societies that support them. P. Smith (2004) has suggested that in large measure this is because the curriculum increasingly misses concerns of a generation already living in a post-Enlightenment world, that our schools are organized for failure, and that our 'industrial model' does not work for the 21st century. In the United States, less than 50% of young people actually enter college and only 50% of those leave with a completed degree. The figures for Blacks and Latinos are even more distressing. Even those who do graduate do not develop the needed competencies for success in today's work force or for life. In particular, according to employers, they lack the higher order mental capacities such as critical thinking, imagination, analysis of ideas, creativity, expressive skills, and social skills that are now required for success in most jobs. This misalignment between the curriculum within the academy and the world outside it will become all the more salient in the not so distant future in which China and India—exposed to European thought relatively recently, and after millennia of seeing the world through radically different frames—become the dominant economies. Inadequate capacity to deal with the inevitable uncertainties of life in a world where Eastern modes of thought have equal standing alongside Western, for instance, will leave the West vulnerable; yet in the West, we continue to construct educational programs as if no other forms of thought even exist, let alone have epistemic legitimacy. If a student brings up questions from outside the Western canon, such as questions about talking to ancestral spirits or other non-material beings, for instance, they are still likely to be ridiculed. Singapore, in contrast, has already realized that to be successful in the emerging future, a new commitment to mental formation of its young is required where a far more expanded conception of consciousness guides learning programs. In 1997, the Prime Minister launched the *Thinking Schools, Learning Nation* initiative, where emphasis is placed on the ability to function in ambiguous situations, with problem-solving skills, creativity, flexibility, new literacies, and self-motivation (Ministry of Education, Singapore, 2021).

From these and many similar indicators, it seems obvious that we have come to a place in our development where the inherited ways of thinking and knowing are inadequate to the task at hand.

New minds for new times

In a recent presentation, Walter Anderson quoted Stewart Brand, who suggested that since we now possess the power to destroy worlds or to transform them, 'We are Gods, and we might as well get used to it' (Anderson, 2005). If this is true—and I assume he means by this that we now have the kind of responsibility for the future of the planet that was once thought to belong to beings of a higher order—then it seems to me urgent that we consider what kind of education this unprecedented level of responsibility requires.

Questions arise. What would ensure that enough of us across the various world cultures develop the capacity to hold not just two opposing ideas at the same but many, and to resist the desire for easy certainty and premature closure? What kind of socializing experiences can we invent so we learn to see the world through new eyes and to take in its complexity without becoming overwhelmed by it? What will help us stay 'within the tension of a question or an issue' and live in the messiness for longer than is comfortable in order that creative new forms can emerge? What do we need to learn to live in peace and with respect for those we have been taught to see as the 'other'? In a rapidly moving technology landscape, what do we need to teach so that we develop 'just in time' technical and content experts who are willing to let go of obsolete information and to continuously learn? What kinds of experiences would help people steward our natural resources, protect the ecosystem that we are part of, while at the same time feed the next few billions of additional people? Can we reclaim lost capacities such as 'dream time', communication with animals, and connect to the spirits of a place?

Education for uncertain times

The mental capacities aimed at in the Western canon reflect those which generations of academicians believe are necessary for success in the industrialized world—objectivity, reason and rationality, linear logic, critical thinking, radical scepticism, secularism, a focus and clarity, either/or dichotomies, sensitivity to difference, preference for fixed categories and sharp boundaries, empiricism, analysis, quantification, self-mastery, and enough certainty for confident agency. Obviously, these capacities remain highly relevant in the emerging new world and need to remain a focus of socialization attention—in schools and outside. In the new world of uncertainty, the Enlightenment culture does not evaporate, but rather becomes subsumed within the new worldview. The modern, science-dominated world will be with us for the foreseeable future, and we can safely assume that as the developing nations enter the industrialized world, they will ensure that some part of the acculturation will involve learning to think in these ways (Schofer & Meyer, 2005).

But the new context of complexity and uncertainty calls for the cultivation of levels of consciousness and habits that go far beyond this and success will require new modes of consciousness. Let me briefly, and with some trepidation, describe what some of these dimensions of consciousness beyond the modern might be.

We must *learn*, or rather *relearn*, to view ourselves as subjects in a world of other subjects. Though as part of the methodology of science and technology subject–object thought has been immensely productive, it has arguably also brought us to the edge of destruction. With its arms-length relationship to the world, it has severed the deep empathic links our ancestors had with the earth, and with their kin and with other beings. We must reconnect. We need to cultivate intuition and appreciation of the non-rational; not as substitutes for reason and scepticism, but as a complement to them. We need to cultivate both/and thinking, enhance our capacity for holistic perception, gestalt awareness, network logic, and pattern recognition. Along with a capacity to focus, we need to be at home with fuzziness and a wide-angle view. We will need to balance a fear that we have not enough information with the problems of having too much. People will need to become comfortable in a world of fluid boundaries, understanding the world as a continuous web of relationally connected integrities. We will need to be able to work at the places where knowledge domains and interests overlap and interact. To make all this work, and to actually be at home in the creative tensions posed by a world in transformation, we will need to make explicit the importance of psychological self-care, emotional maturity, and the nourishment of the soul. This means we must recognize *and honor* the important place in most people's lives of what is called religion or spirituality.

If these are the ends to which we strive, what might be some of the approaches to learning and knowing that could provide the means?

There are four holistically interrelated dimensions which educational institutions must rethink—a new mission, new curriculum content, new pedagogy, and new modes of inquiry.

1 **New mission**

- First, education at all levels needs to rethink its mission in light of the emerging connected world. This mission must go beyond simply providing workers for the global economy. We also need to make it a high priority to cultivate the kinds of people—individuals and collectives—with the necessary scope of awareness and level of mental development to create sustainable systems in which human beings thrive and can co-exist on a fragile planet. *We must aim at an expansion of or evolution of the modal consciousness of our species.* Anything less is whistling past the cemetery. Unless we evolve our ways of thinking to embrace a wider sense of responsibility not only for self, or tribe, but for the entire planetary system, including its people and other creatures, nature may well decide that its experiment with *Homo sapiens* should be abandoned.

2 **New content**

- It is obvious that science and emerging technologies will remain crucial. Even in the unlikely event people say no to such galloping technological innovation—which I doubt—we will still need the knowledge to maintain our tools and toys and sustain and improve our quality of life and our environment. But given the rapidity with which old knowledge becomes obsolete and new discoveries are made, curriculum must be more process focused and content needs to be 'open source' and updated constantly in response to feedback from a changing world.
- New literacies must be added to the existing canon—eco-literacy, information literacy, visual literacy, cultural literacy, spiritual literacy, and epistemological fluency are all core capacities in the new context.
- Curriculum must be globalized. This means more than simply learning about other societies. As long as people beyond one's own national boarders are considered 'other', vital perspectives on human possibilities will be hidden from view. Global citizens must enlarge who they think of as 'we'. This will mean learning to put local knowledge into larger perspectives and bringing a global and multi-perspectival approach to local knowledge.
- Given the inevitability of the 'law of unintended consequences', consideration of possible futures must become part of everyday thinking not just of futurists but of everyone who must make decisions—in other words, most of us. Futures studies must become a core element of all education and must include awareness of, and responsibility for, the short-term, medium-term, and long-term future.

3 **New pedagogies**

Not only what we learn but *how* we learn will need to adapt to the new agendas.

- We must make a shift from a content focus to process focus. From a focus on knowledge as a noun to a focus on learning as a verb. Expertise will still be needed, but the ephemeral nature of information, and the speed with which we must act, means that learning how to harvest information from multiple sources as needed will become more important than accumulating a body of knowledge. Discernment and critical and appreciative appraisal of knowledge all become essential skills.
- Whole person pedagogies will have to be developed that involve experiential activities where theory can emerge from practice.
- If we are to keep our heads in the dizzying world of contradiction and complexity, 'inner work' that leads to psychological maturity needs to be part of all learning environments. Mind development approaches such as yoga, psychotherapy, the arts, creativity, meditation, contemplation, and self-reflection will all be important elements in learning.
- In curriculum, most make room for love, emotions, creativity, spirituality, and aesthetics, because these all influence how sense is made, how priorities are set, and how the world is interpreted. The Singaporean education ministry mandated a 30% reduction in 'required curriculum' to permit learners and teachers time to think and to process their experience. They believe that if they are to remain innovative, this will require openness to unpredictable, uncontrolled, and emergent experiences.
- More attention must be given to learning about human relationships, group dynamics, and unconscious dimensions of behavior. Since most projects will require collaboration with others who are different, high levels of social competence become essential.
- Education must be problem-embracing and case-based, and knowledge and learning derived from attempts to solve real problems.
- We need to provide 'cognitive apprenticeships' where learners can be socialized into the tacit dimensions of emerging fields by those who are already in them.

4 **New modes of inquiry**

- The context of complexity means that we must wean ourselves from our overdependence on positivist science as the only acceptable form of knowledge, and reclaim qualitative, more holistic, and even contemplative modes of inquiry.
- We need to emphasize systems inquiry not so that we can control systems, because most of them are too complex to be controlled, but, as Donella Meadows puts it, to 'dance with them' (Meadows, 2005).
- We need a new emphasis on pattern recognition, learning how to distinguish 'signal from noise' and how to navigate the exploding world of 'open source' information—Wikipedia, blogs, etc.

- We need to go beyond quantification with expanded emphasis on the human sciences such as phenomenology, hermeneutics, appreciative inquiry, action learning, contemplation, scenaric inquiry, ethnography, reflective practice, journalism, symbology, critical inquiry, discernment, and meditation.
- We need to further develop approaches to what Nicolescu has called trans-disciplinary knowledge production (Nicolescu, 2002; Nowotny, 2003) in recognition of the fact that in complex problems research is increasingly conducted in its application and its application frequently involves teams from many disciplines, as well as practitioners and lay people. The kind of open process learning referred to as 'Atelier learning' (Brown, 2005) can provide a safe space where errors are embraced and where practical applicability trumps theory.

Age of innovation

My colleague Eamonn Kelley has said that the world may be entering a 'Cambrian explosion' of innovation and experimentation in education and learning (Kelley, 2005). We are gaining knowledge of the brain and cognitive and emotional functions at an astonishing rate and this knowledge is already being used in instructional design to enhance learning and performance. We will see 'transhuman' mind enhancement through drugs and various implanted technological mental add-ons very soon (Hughes, 2005).

Announcements about innovations in educational delivery models arrive every day. Reports on new ventures—distance learning bringing classes to remote Indian villages by satellite, new business–academy partnerships, Barefoot academies, service learning that takes the academy into the world, apprenticeships, and corporate training that tack back and forth between academy and workplace. The boundaries between the research universities and commerce have all but disappeared; prestige institutions band together to create joint programs to satisfy the massive appetite for learning in societies like China and sub-Saharan Africa.

At lower-grade levels, educational innovation abounds. Even though hobbled by gargantuan bureaucracies and political wrangling, innovative teachers are gradually introducing systems thinking, group techniques such as 'sharing circles' and creativity labs, classes in eco-literacy, digital media production, and contemplation (though you cannot call it meditation!) and are increasingly employing the latest research from cognitive science in their instructional design. Adventurous youngsters too, are also part of the innovation—they are blogging, creating their own multimedia of high quality, doing simulations, and participating in online role-playing games with thousands of players worldwide. Many of these games expand the imagination, requiring intense participation, long attention spans, and the development of sophisticated mental strategies.

Humanity—or at least large parts of it—has faced such inflection points before, where new forms of consciousness have been called for—the shift from the medieval to the modern world, for instance, and then later as a result of the industrial revolution. Some societies have thrived, and others have disappeared. The response to the present conceptual crisis must be to embrace the adventure and harness the potential for transformative learning that is implicit in such uncertain times. The stakes are high: if we fail to learn fast enough the world could, as it was in the 13th century, be cast into a *Mad Max* world of violence, craziness, and despair. But, however, and it is here that we must aim our efforts, the potential exists that we might use the challenge of these times to learn our way into the future.

If we can provide the supporting structures in education and other socializing institutions to permit us to live in the creative tension of unanswered questions and emergent possibilities, and if new or reclaimed capacities become integrated into our existing forms of knowledge, we may, as Peat suggests, '*discover orders beyond*'. This could conceivably result in a new stage of human evolution. It seems to me that this should be the goal of education for the global 21st century.

Notes

1 Presented at the General Assembly of the World Academy of Arts and Sciences, Zagreb, Croatia, November 2005, in the session 'From Certainty to Uncertainty: Thought, Theory and Action in a modern world' (Chair: David Peat).
2 At the time this was originally written, Maureen was the President of Saybrook Graduate School.
3 Peat (2007, p. 928).
4 Fitzgerald (1936/2017, para. 2).
5 Cortese (2003, p. 16).
6 Salovey (2005, para. 5).
7 I use the word 'cosmology' to refer to the totality of worldview, narrative frames, symbolic landscape, meaning frames, language, logical forms, cognitive schemas, and epistemologies that provide the taken-for-granted assumptions of life in that society.

Chapter 23

Frames and games

Hard science vs. difficult science in psychotherapy training (2010)[1]

Maureen O'Hara[2]

This presentation was given as part of a symposium organized by Division 32 for Humanistic Psychology at the 2010 convention of the American Psychological Association. The symposium was a response to a much-discussed paper by Baker et al. (2008) published by the Association for Psychological Science suggesting that the field of clinical psychology was at best pre-scientific and at worst hocus-pocus and urging that clinical psychology be limited to evidence-based techniques and that clinicians be trained as science-based medical practitioners.

Baker et al. (2008) and journalist Sharon Begley (2009) are shocked and dismayed that a study of clinical practitioners found that most do not rely much on the latest scientific evidence to support their practice. They suggest that 'ambivalence' toward science, de-emphasis of scientific training in graduate curriculum, and dumbing down of admissions' standards are largely to blame. The PsyD program in stand-alone professional schools, particularly for-profit schools, is figured as being largely responsible for this downward spiral. As we know and I don't need to repeat, Baker et al. (2008) want to create a new improved accreditation agency that will distinguish those clinical psychology doctoral programs that are science-based, from those that are not. Advancing arguments that have changed little since the American Psychological Society (APS) first separated from the American Psychological Association (APA) 25 years ago, that APA's view of psychology is not 'scientific' enough, and they imply that the current APA accreditation criteria for scholar–practitioner programs are inadequate and allow charlatans to become qualified.

Though my co-authors on the panel will each present their different takes on the issue, I will use my time to argue that this initiative and the rhetorical framing used in the announcements about it may be understood as symptoms of deeper cultural anxiety emerging within academic elites that coincides with massive societal changes underway in how we understand (and mostly don't) life in the new global context. I will also argue that such moves, however wrapped up they are in high-minded language about 'providing high quality services to the public', are nothing more than an old-fashioned turf battle over an ever-decreasing patch of grass waged through the instrument of propaganda. It begs the question of its basic assumptions, and at the end of the day, such a move and the counter moves by

DOI: 10.4324/9781003519454-30

APA or any other professional organization, though understandable from a guild preservation perspective, in light of the broader cultural shifts underway, and in the face of the looming issues that now confront a global society, may have little more effect on the future of mental health than rearranging the deck chairs on the Titanic would have in preventing it from hitting the iceberg.

As social psychologist Don Michael observed, we are living in the world of the missing elephant (Michael, 2000). Using the Sufi tale of the blind men, he pointed out that scientific and academic culture used to be guided by the belief that if each researcher investigates their own piece of the elephant, and if the holders of the various pieces share their knowledge, we might one day understand the whole elephant. However, though the academic enterprise still continues as if this is the case, this assumption no longer holds. We are living at a time where the conceptual frames by which we perceive and interpret our world are in motion. After a three-million-year history living in small, related groups who had similar experiences, making shared coherent understanding of things relatively easy, the modern world—including the scientific world—is increasingly fragmented and incoherent (Leicester & O'Hara, 2009). Human communities—including academic communities—now pretty much live in their own rather small discourse silos, have vastly different experiences, and have multiple ways of understanding themselves and their diverse interests. Knowledge—even scientific and technical knowledge—is widely dispersed across multiple spheres and disciplines, and knowledge from one section of the so-called 'academic community' is not easily shared with experts from another. Even in closely related fields—like the different divisions of APA—taken for granted assumptions in one area might be reasonably contested in another. When we move beyond the academic world, complexity expands exponentially. Relevant and meaningful knowledge may come from myriad sources, using different methods of inquiry, based in diverse epistemologies, and understood from within the conceptual practices, narratives, and metaphors that derive from culturally diverse views of the world.

The dominance of Enlightenment-based science

Nowhere is the problem of conceptual coherence more salient than in those professions that are outgrowths of the scientific and technological exuberance that characterized the German research institutes of the late 19th century. Enshrined at the core of these institutions and those university departments in the United States that emulate them is the Enlightenment emphasis on certainty, prediction, and control, and the advancement of human well-being through the methods of the natural sciences. The sought-after elephant was a world without suffering, disease, injustice, and war. A very humane vision.

However, the Enlightenment enterprise had another perhaps less virtuous agenda—the imposition of a secular worldview that denied the existence of non-material realities, such as spirituality, aesthetics, morality, and consciousness. In order to clearly separate psychology from philosophy, religion, and the arts and humanities, which for centuries had been the disciplines of choice for those seeking to understand human experience, a form of scientific fundamentalism arose in American psychology that vigorously rejected the claim that any disciplined consideration of the non-material was valid (O'Hara, 1989d). Introspection, empathy, intuition, discernment, dialogue, ritual, meditation—paths to knowledge that had effectively guided humans from the savannahs to complex civilizations—were discredited, and experts in their use dislodged.

These values have defined academic psychology for the last century. Though allowing for some philosophical diversity in clinical psychology programs, the APA Commission on Accreditation (COA) vigorously promotes a scientist–practitioner model. Science-based content and research methodology are a *sine qua non* of its accreditation standards.

Also institutionalized has been systematic and sometimes strident trivialization and disparagement of those psychological researchers and practitioners who are interested in moral, philosophical, socio-cultural, and pragmatic concerns (Miller, 1992). As those of us in the humanistic tradition know from almost 50 years of such disparagement, there is nothing new in Baker et al.'s assertion that clinical psychologists should be natural scientists, and that those who are not are probably charlatans and quacks.

However, the times are changing. The global climate change debate makes clear that Western science is increasingly recognized as a social construction situated within its own particular culture, with its own frames, values, and political and economic investments. Cross-cultural studies in psychology reveal that across the world's communities, constructions of reality define how we understand the world and our actions in it.

Some of the challenges to the authority of received paradigms of 'normal science' have come from subcultures *within* the scientific establishment itself. It is now openly admitted by scientists and policy makers looking at complex systems and problems that are high stake, overdetermined, and involve the subjectivities of diverse stakeholders—problems like the HIV/AIDS epidemic, global climate change, poverty, and so on—normal science *alone* cannot deliver (Funtowicz & Ravetz, 1990).

Challenge also comes from an increasingly sceptical and anti-science public. Some of this stems from the fall-out from scientific abuses that have come to light in the past decades that are increasingly understood not as the aberrant actions of a few rotten psychologist apples, but as evidence of psychology's Faustian bargain. Examples include studies on condemned concentration camp prisoners, conversion therapy for homosexuality, the Tuskegee experiments, forced electroshock of women, overmedication of children and older adults, and psychologist participation in torture, to name just a sample of procedures undertaken in the name of 'science'.

Scepticism also comes from people of faith who find the idea of their suffering being addressed by techniques born of a secular view objectionable. Religious people question a science that dismisses their prayers and rituals as placebo, or their therapist's compassion 'bedside manner effects', as it is by Baker et al. (2008). Psychological life is inextricably linked for many—the overwhelming majority across—with their existential, spiritual, and religious lives. So, the spiritually inclined public is suspicious of science without a soul.

Judging from the *Mental Health Services Act* (2004) that recently became a law in California, it appears that the general public has rejected the pathology-focused model favored by science-based clinical psychology. This legislation guides public spending on mental health services and training, and requires that services 'include prevention [and] emphasize client-centered, family focused and community-based services that are culturally and linguistically competent'. This approach has already made its way into the required curriculum for master's level practitioners in California. Though training in 'evidence supported treatment' is required, so is training in 'best practices', with a 'recovery vision' that offers 'hope, personal empowerment, respect, social connections, self-responsibility, and self-determination'. It seems that regardless of how much they are suffering, most human beings have a real aversion to being predicted and controlled even in the name of treatment.

Which brings me to another aspect of today's psychological landscape—the proliferation of professions trained to offer mental health services to the public, that, as Baker et al. (2008) complain, are 'crowding out' psychologists. A report by the University of California San Francisco listed ten different mental health practitioner professions (not including specialist nurses). In California alone, there are approximately 71,330 mental health providers, whose services are reimbursable by insurance.

We can add to this ever-growing list of services from life and career coaches, pastoral counsellors, psychic healers, and grief and bereavement counsellors all offering some form of psychological practice.

At the same time that this differentiation in the mental health marketplace is occurring, public trust in any kind of expertise is eroding. The Googlified world provides instantaneous access to specialized knowledge once the exclusive domain of highly paid professionals. A quick search of my iPhone apps turned up a *Depression Fix It App* for 99c, a *Live Happy App*, and a *Stop Smoking Now* program for free. As search engines become more sophisticated, people are cutting out high-priced middlemen and seeking their own solutions to what they have themselves have identified as their problems.

So, to sum up this part of the story, multiple cultural factors now converge with such force that the boundaries of even robust institutional entities are being undermined. Innovations often begin at the transgressive margins, but as they gain public acceptance can come to displace the fields they diverged from.

The result of this 'perfect storm' is that established professions like clinical psychology find their authority challenged, their legitimacy questioned, their power eroded, and, I submit, their identity and even survival threatened. They are facing what divinity schools, the humanities, and the arts departments in universities faced a century ago.

I submit that what is driving the APS initiative is a professional identity crisis. Moreover, as we existential psychologists know, people and institutions facing threats to personal or professional identity will go to considerable lengths to restore their sense of coherence and control.

In 'powerful times'—as Machiavelli referred to the cultural unravelling in the 15th century—the battle to name and frame what is real, legitimate, and valued and distinguish it from what is spurious or even heretical intensifies. There are many historical examples of battles for conceptual authority—many of them resulting in acts of oppression, persecution, and extreme violence. As cognitive linguist George Lakoff and political analyst Karl Rove have demonstrated, those who control the frame, control the game.

The recent moves by Baker et al. (2008) and the APS's tacit endorsement of them, though offered as a supposedly values-neutral logical argument, are actually moves in a conceptual power game, the purpose of which is to discredit those with whom they differ and establish their authority to name psychological truth and gain professional dominance. They are responding to a general erosion of professional credibility by attempting to capture what has been the most powerful legitimizer in a technological age—the mantel of science and technology. They seek to establish their control of psychological education and definition of clinical psychological services not through direct appeal to people's own choices, but through power—through creating a new regulating process claimed to be 'scientific'.

Baker et al. (2008) claim that their ultimate goal is the improvement of American psychological services. Who can object to that? However, the rhetorical devices used throughout their paper suggests an additional motive that harkens back a century or more—to discredit and demonize other discourse communities, to insinuate that other positions are suspect; their methods of inquiry ineffective and ethically indefensible, with a view to establishing normal science as the sole legitimate definer of reality when it comes to clinical psychological services.

Let's look at their rhetoric. The overarching frame—the one picked up by *The Washington Post* and *Newsweek*—contrasts 'scientific' approaches with those deemed 'prescientific'.

Graduates of programs accredited by APA are described in the paper (Baker et al., 2008) using words like 'ambivalent', 'dubious', 'charlatan', 'impressionistic', and 'strikingly deficient'. Clinical practice is 'mired in an experiential and intuitional quagmire' (p. 86) and clinical psychology today is like medicine in the 1900s, mentioning in the same breath, 'bleeding, blistering, purging and puking' (p. 78). At the same time, they select words like 'principled', 'rational', 'valid', 'effective', 'high quality', 'exacting standards', 'plausible', and 'sophisticated' in reference to the approaches to be taught in the programs they seek to accredit.

Raskin and Leitner (2010) correctly identify the category error (though in my view it is a strategic framing choice than an error) of considering psychotherapy a form of medical treatment. I say framing choice rather than error because for Baker et al. psychological suffering is the sign of a medical problem. Baker et al. inhabit a discourse community—medical psychology—where issues that are the focus of psychological attention are logically and ethically framed as 'illnesses', what clinical psychologists do as 'diagnosis' and 'treatment', and where the methods and standards for evaluation of outcomes are the same as those for other medical conditions. Debate about the pros and cons of this choice of a medical frame is a well-worn territory within the field of clinical psychology and so do not need to be repeated here (Bohart et al., 1998; Elkins, 2009). The point I wish to make here is not that the medical model is invalid or illegitimate, but rather that it is but one legitimate framing among many that have been demonstrated effective in helping people resolve psychological problems, even by the standards of the science Baker et al. would like to privilege. However, Baker et al. (2008) are not interested in validating other ways of understanding psychological life and considering their paradigm being one among others. They make their claims hegemonically—as if their particular framing is the only one that is logically, empirically, and morally defensible. The weakness of this position is illustrated by their own example, the treatment of tobacco addiction, in which they fail to include relevant factors that fall outside their medical viewfinder. In terms indistinguishable from those that would be used to describe the use of a drug or a surgical technique, they claim that science-based treatments show good cost-effective results. There is no mention of (or calculation of the cost of) the shift in public opinion about smoking brought about by antismoking campaigns, rising taxation on tobacco, legislation, the shift in US values toward health, iPhone quit smoking apps, or chat show coverage of celebrities who've quit as non-specifiable contextual factors contributing to someone's success in quitting smoking. Instead, they make the reductionist claim that their success is due to their use of science-based interventions. They dismiss therapist concerns raised from within other frames—such as the complexity of psychological problems that many clinicians help clients with, or the demonstrated importance of general or non-specific factors not as therapeutically important realities being raised by colleagues who are experts in other discourses, but as 'scientific ambivalence' or even 'insouciance'.

In a democratic society, Baker, et al. (2008), and those members of the APS who support their efforts, have every right to mount an attack on other centres of authority within American psychology, such as the APA. They also have the right to claim that normal science-based medicine is the only frame through which services should be offered and advise people to accept help only from those they have authorized. They have the right, but I would like to argue that this is a tragic and unnecessary mistake.

On Tuesday this week (August 10, 2010), a news report about the devastating floods in Pakistan reported that the Taliban have advised the government to refuse help from Western sources (NPR News Hour, 2010). They would apparently rather see millions suffer than compromise with those whose basic worldview they do not share. I see the moves by Baker et al. (2008) and the APS's complicity as a similar move.

What these authors do not appear to recognize is that as we move into an era of mounting global threat, the categories of reality defined by the values, conceptual frames, investigative methods, and systems of education that arose from the

European Enlightenment project, though of great value, may even be necessary, but are no longer sufficient. Despite all the astonishing advances that have come to us through modern science, the regions of our ignorance are still vastly greater.

Living in ignorance is a far greater challenge than holding on to our own piece of the elephant. To navigate the next passage in human history, we need approaches to knowledge that can, in the immortal words of Gene Roddenberry, 'go where no one has gone before'. I suggest this requires us—as individuals and as groups—to develop a new pluralistic psychology for our 'powerful times'. The easiest and, so far, usual way to feel safe in an uncertain world is to create bright lines between 'us and them' and to establish hierarchies that can be defended against diverse 'others' by the use of power—conceptual, legislative, and ultimately military.

The more difficult way—but I suggest the only one with any hope of guiding us through the huge, multiple determined challenges ahead—is to establish a relationship of trust, respect, and appreciation of diversity of thought, in the service of mutual stewardship of the human and planetary future. This requires that we refrain from the kind of name calling that is in such evidence in the paper by Baker et al. (2008).

I will go further. I believe the future requires that we, as psychologists, play our parts along with other cultural leaders, in helping an increasingly polarized world live with its rising uncertainty without resorting to power plays and violence. The humanistic community within psychology over the years has developed many promising ways of approaching difference through respectful and empathic dialogue and collaboration and acknowledging the value of human wisdom in its multitudinous forms. Basic and applied normal science remains vital and advanced scientific training a cultural necessity, but so is advanced training in philosophy, the human sciences, non-Western knowledge traditions, the arts and humanities, and consciousness expanding spiritual practices. Not, as the APA sees them, as electives to a basic prediction and control curriculum, but as disciplined sources of important human knowledge. If we cannot create a space for appreciation of multiple wisdom traditions within psychology, what hope is there for the wider human community? As we know, this kind of work is not easy, but that does not excuse us from the need to try.

Notes

1 Given as a presentation (2010, August 12–15). In B. D. Robbins (Chair), *Science and politics of the APS accreditation initiative—a cross-divisional response* [Symposium]. American Psychological Association 118th Annual Convention, San Diego, CA.

2 Maureen was the Chair of Psychology at National University when this was written.

Chapter 24

Generation open

The future of higher education in a DIY world (2011)[1]

Maureen O'Hara[2]

I recently spent a highly engaging few hours with two groups of aspiring entrepreneurs whose ages ranged from 23 to 29. Meeting at the HUBs—San Francisco and Berkeley, hot new gathering places that provide networking, education, and some start-up resources for social enterprises, we came together to talk about their ideas about higher education—graduate education in business in particular. My colleagues and I wanted to know why they had not gone on to graduate school after their Bachelor of Arts degrees. As representatives of graduate schools ourselves, we were interested in what kind of program would attract them, if any. What follows is my takeaway from the conversations, with a few reflections of my own added in. Names and details of specific businesses have been altered considerably to disguise particular identities, protect their business ideas, improve readability, and to convey in abbreviated form the essence of the two-hour conversation.

This remarkable group was ethnically diverse and from a range of socioeconomic backgrounds. Most had graduated with BAs, some from elite liberal arts colleges, one from a British 'uni', and a couple from state universities but had not proceeded to graduate school (except one, who had completed a 'green MBA').[3] Nor had they taken jobs in the kind of large corporations or organizations that would have snapped them up just a decade ago. Instead, they had gone out into the world to create their own enterprises. The one thing they had in common was a burning desire to change the world and make a living doing it. Rebecca's (24) company was aimed at ethical food production. She has already persuaded some California producers that this should be part of their 'brand'. Kylie (27) has just returned from a stint in The Gambia working with HIV-AIDS prevention. She was talking to venture capitalists to create a cloud-accessed database to help other social innovators across the world. Josh (29) had just handed over to the United Nations an anti-poverty social enterprise he had started in Southeast Asia that built housing for poor people. He had returned to the United States to start another business and was looking around for somewhere his skills 'could help out'. Bo (24) works as a marketing consultant to local arts groups doing theatre with youthful offenders, and Danny is working with colleagues in Doctors Without Borders to develop a phone app for aid workers to access and share information via satellite-enabled smart phones in the crucial hours after a disaster. As an undergraduate, he had worked on a pilot project

DOI: 10.4324/9781003519454-31

during the Haiti earthquake. Adam had already sold one start-up company and is now part of a collective creating online educational content for 'green' business programs and Amy's small consulting company develops bioethics and mediation programs for medical schools. Emily had recently completed a research study for a large foundation on Gen Y's attitudes, values, and aspirations. Other interests in the group included alternative currencies, human rights advocacy, and the 'Long Now'—thinking with a 10,000-year horizon. This group is not a representative sample of their generation, but according to Emily, her survey data support many of the attitudes expressed over the two-hour conversation. My colleagues and I very much appreciated their giving us this illuminating glimpse into their thinking.

View of the future

These young people have a somewhat ambivalent view of their future. On the one hand, they look with deep anxiety and apprehension at the immense challenge their generation faces. They have grown up hearing dire warnings about what is in store if we don't address the looming issues barrelling down on them—climate change, environmental degradation, overpopulation, war, disease, and the ever-expanding number of apocalyptic horses. There were no 'deniers' in this group. On the other hand, they are energized by the challenges and see in them almost unlimited opportunity, hope, creativity, and expanding space for their imagination and innovation. They are clearly called to make a difference, but they have little faith in 'big' anything—government, business, or non-governmental organizations (NGOs)—and so do not expect anyone but themselves to provide a better future for them. This is a 'light a candle does not curse the darkness' group. They believe the future is up to them.

Relevance is key

It was obvious at once that despite the fact that they all had succeeded as undergraduates, they had opted out of continuing education toward an MBA or PhD because they questioned the relevance. 'I loved being a student', said Bo, 'but I was in a bubble, separated from the real-world problems that people face every day'. 'I am not sure I need another degree full of courses that though perhaps relevant at one time, no longer fit the different business context', was Danny's concern. They believed they needed a different kind of education for a different kind of world and even more uncertain future and did not see it in the schools they had looked at.

Return on investment/debt

It was also clear that after their experiences in the field, they doubted that the cost and time for an MBA or other advanced degree would deliver enough return on investment. They had all borrowed money to get their undergraduate degrees. One described her tuition debt as her 'education mortgage'. 'We are already buried in debt. I can't afford to take on more'. Adam explained that his choice of social enterprise rather than the usual non-profit NGO world was partly economic. 'We can't work in low-paid jobs in non-profit organisations and pay back loans, so we need to combine our desire to fix the world with the capacity to make real money'. Adam had sold his business and was using his capital to pay off loans and invest in his next venture.

On-the-job training

The consensus in this group was that the situations and opportunities on the ground are too diverse for any single graduate program to prepare them for. 'Better to go out and get the experience and learn on the job', said Kylie, as she explained that while she was a Voluntary Service Overseas (VSO) volunteer in The Gambia, she was supposed to be collecting data for a health project. Instead, she found herself mediating disputes, organizing an evacuation effort after a natural disaster, substituting teaching as a replacement for an English teacher who had come down sick, and helping design an emergency delivery system for life-sustaining drugs after another international HIV-AIDS NGO pulled out. She asked, 'What graduate school would help me get all these skills before I graduated?' She also went on to explain that she had looked at MBA programs, but they all seemed too 'standardised' for her. 'Doing social enterprise in the developing world needs agility, engineering, and nursing skills as much as financial expertise and strategic planning'.

Technology

This was a tech-saturated group, and they were astonishingly adept at thinking up technological solutions for many kinds of problems. Most felt that the entrepreneurial sector was light years ahead of the higher education sector in its use of technology. One commented, 'universities are heavily bureaucratic. They are just not nimble enough'. Bo agreed, and added, 'They use technology to standardise and control. That's OK but it could do so much more. We here at the HUB use technology to innovate and find new opportunities. That's where the future is'. Everyone had a smart phone—iPhones. All had *Mobile-me*, cloud accounts, and saved everything to the cloud. They could (and did) create a Google group in minutes to continue their conversation. A couple of them were planning a gathering the following weekend and they had already 'viraled' an announcement to their HUB network. All stayed in touch through Facebook and Twitter, though there was some disagreement about whether they were drowning in the overload and becoming too scattered. Two participants of the group had created smart phone apps already, and the others were comfortable with digital information solutions. They deftly accessed information relevant to their interests on the spot. Danny, for instance, found articles (good ones) and blogs (not always good ones) as our meeting went on, adding colour and additional content to anything anyone was talking about. Someone mentioned 'alternative currencies', another asked, 'What's that?'

and within seconds Danny had an article by currency theorist Bernard Leitaer on his laptop. For them and their generation, technology is easy, and they see endless possibilities for practical solutions to difficult problems coming from a partnership between technologists and entrepreneurs like themselves. Kylie had linked up with an advanced database designer who had previously worked on space technology to develop search algorithms for social enterprises. 'I know about search as a consumer, but Ivo knows about the engineering, so we are a great team'.

Open source everything

This is Generation Open. 'Transparency' is their watchword. They are religious about Open Source everything, and connectivity is their holy grail of innovation. Through Facebook, tweets, websites, and blogs—and anything else that comes along—they stay up on what is happening in their shared learning spaces. They are big fans of the 'sharing society' and point to web resources such as shareable.net as examples. They embrace the 'swarm' mentality, where the flow of their interests, contacts, and resources flickers across their social networks day-by-day and sometimes hour-by-hour. Their conversation tended to swarm too. No dissertation talk here. There was some rapid fire back and forth on the economics of sharing, scrip systems, social justice, and broken world economic systems, before veering off into quality assurance in MBA programs and curriculum design. The HUB itself where we were meeting, itself a social enterprise, is a global network of nests of creative young people who share their talents, ideas, and energies to help each other get started and create change through social enterprise. Now on four continents with 12 HUBs full of 'diverse people doing amazing things', the HUB offers start-up resources and seed money for new projects on the condition that HUB members will be offered first crack at any employment that comes from it. One described a 'Transparency' conference in Washington, DC where over 12,000 young folk—high school and college age—collaborated on seminars, experiential training, and art sessions about everything from open government, open arts, and science and technology. All were fans of another open space phenomenon, the Burning Man festival, aligning with its values and philosophy, creative experience, and spirituality, and they share articles, forward TED links, consult with each other pro bono, or barter for expertise. They share whatever opportunities come along. The Idea Hive is a group of graduates of Bay Area green MBA programs collaborating on the development of intellectual assets, praxis innovation, and green business opportunities. They collaborate on international events like the SOCAP (Social Capital, for those out of the loop) conference in San Francisco. The 2010 conference was a gigantic success, bringing thought leaders and entrepreneurs together to change the world. The conference is now in its 15th year (https://socapglobal.com/events/socap23/). The conference moves to other cities such as Amsterdam and Malmö to carry the message of social capitalism wherever there is interest. Gen-Open expects its education to be 'open source' too. They are big fans of Anya Kamenetz's book, *DIY U: Edupunks, Edupreneurs, and the Coming Transformation of Higher*

Education. They are also fans of the open courseware movement such as Open Yale, MIT open courseware, and Webcast and Legacy Course Capture at UC Berkeley. Both Kylie and Bo had used Khan Academy (www.khanacademy.com) downloads as undergraduates to improve their math scores. It is important to add that this very well-educated group acknowledged the importance of the connections and networks they had developed as undergraduates. They were also cognizant of the realities of the talent marketplace where networks, contacts, and mentors are assets that are as important as credentials and wondered out loud about how this worked in a DIY system. Which brings us to their thoughts on the role of teachers.

Teachers

This was not an antiauthoritarian group, as many of their baby boomer parents had been in their youth. They respect expertise and wisdom and above all connections with the people this group referred to as 'wise elders'. The HUB is working on a project that will do just that. They were eager to learn but they were very clear that they wanted a different kind of relationship with teachers than the *in loco parentis* power hierarchy they had tolerated but resented as undergraduates. These people were independent learners, who can track down content whenever they need it. They don't need teachers for information. This is a generation that has more information available to it from more sources than any other in history. They see teachers as potential collaborators, as colleagues, not parent or boss substitutes. As Kylie said, 'teachers are way up on my asset map—but only if they can help me get my enterprise off the ground'. These young people want to work in social enterprises because they are ready to be masters of their own futures and run their own show. They want to learn from experts, but they want their own expertise to be acknowledged. They seek partnerships with teachers, not subordination. Josh said it simply, 'I created a company that constructed over 500 houses for poor people in Southeast Asia and I mostly learned on my own what I needed to know to be successful'. He does need guidance, though. 'At moments when things were unravelling, the two or three Skype calls I had with my old tutor from college pointed me in the direction of knowledge and expertise that helped bring things around and move us forward'. What Josh wants is a partnership with an academic community that would challenge his assumptions, point out where he needs to learn more, and help him integrate it into what he knows already. He also thinks scholars who know their discipline can help him separate the 'millions of pages on the web, from the hundreds that [he] can use to advance his mission'. 'In the world of action, it is what you can do that gets you respect, not how many credit hours you accumulate', Kylie said.

Networks

These young people would want to know before signing up for any degree program, 'Where are your networks?' They see this as the crucial ingredient in whether a degree is worth their time. They see their world as 'joined up everything', where boundary navigation is an everyday challenge.

Skills

This group knew what skills they wanted to develop and were all clear that before enrolling in any graduate program, they would be looking for the technical skills that they would learn. They were all plugged into the consulting worlds of Accenture, McKinsey, Deloitte, and Monitor, and knew that most of these companies have developed proprietary approaches to planning, management, leadership, business strategy, asset management, 'triple bottom line' accounting, design thinking, third horizon innovation, scenario planning, and vision management. They want to learn all this without working for McKinsey or Monitor and they want to apply these state-of-the-art methods in their small-scale start-ups. They wanted to learn organizational development and community organization skills, asset mapping, multiple stakeholder leadership, negotiating skills, cross-cultural dialogues, World Café convening, group facilitation skills, design thinking, and visual recording. As one person said, 'my classmates working for big companies will learn this at work. I want to learn what I need "just in time" as I go along building my enterprise'.

Soft skills

These young people represent a mind shift. Though they are ambitious to succeed in business, for them success goes beyond their own self-interest. They are more participatory, collaborative, connected, autonomous, idealistic, and impatient to see results, imaginative, creative, courageous, adaptable, and self-aware than previous generations. They want freedom and play as well as hard work and profit. Their heroes are Steve Jobs, Paul Hawken, Tim Jones, and Sergey Brin, not Jack Welch and Lee Iacocca. This, of course, makes them vulnerable—to blind spots in their emotional intelligence, to impulsivity, shallowness, distraction, disappointment, burn out, and organizational naivete. They blithely take on messy intractable problems like persistent poverty and Midwest urban decay that require complex capacities that ordinarily come with experience and wisdom. They can be unrealistic about issues such as finance and the challenges of scaling up their dreams. The good news is that unlike my own baby boomer generation, these young people know they will need more than 'love'. All of them said they felt their education had missed a crucial element—their emotional and social development. Two of them talked regularly to a coach and they all wished they had mentors and counsellors who would help them with the human skills needed for life in their super-fast, sometimes confusing, worlds. In Josh's words, 'in the end, this is about the meaning of my life—why I am here, what can I contribute. This requires me to know myself, to be able to access what is deepest in me and to follow my path, even when it seems pretty murky. To that I need more than better skills, I need the capacity to be fuller person'.

Take home

In the debrief session with my colleagues after these conversations, we all reported the same impressions. These young people were very impressive, full of energy, ambition, and noble vision. Our conversation suggests that higher education is going to have to make itself relevant to a whole new generation of learners in a different kind of way if it is not to be left behind by any one of any number of emerging innovations in the educational ecosystem.

Notes

1 Originally published on National University's website (no longer available) Eforum: Culture and Consciousness, node 29.
2 Department of Psychology.
3 Master of Business Administration.

Chapter 25

Reflections on Maureen O'Hara's writings on education

Maureen O'Hara and Keith Tudor

Keith: When I was thinking about the ordering of the parts of the book, I had assumed that we would end with your writing on psychology futures but, maintaining the organisation of the book by the chronology of your first publications on the respective topics means that we are ending with education, though interestingly what you write about education also has future-orientation. I have always thought of you as an educator, I guess, primarily as a result of your association with the work with Paulo Freire in the 1980s, and yet your first writing on the topic of education was not until 2010. Before reflecting specifically on the three papers that form the preceding chapters in this part of the book, I wonder if you would say something about the influence of Freire's ideas about education on you?

Maureen: I was introduced to *Pedagogy of Oppressed* (Freire, 1970) at almost the same time as I learned about Carl Rogers. In the orientation session for my doctorate, we were encouraged to explore the projects being proposed by other learners. Freire's ideas were introduced by a radical economist who planned to conduct a study of the ideas of Chilean president Salvador Allende about the kind of education needed in a newly democratic society like those emerging in Latin America at the time. The student explained the distinction Freire makes between education as 'banking' whereby the teacher deposits content (and habits of thinking) into the student's erstwhile empty mind—education to maintain the status quo—and education that emancipates and opens up creative space for transformation. By helping students explore the hidden curriculum of their oppression it sets them free to become subjects rather than objects of the educational process and active agents of their own learning. I recognised immediately that Freire's approach was ideally suited as an andragogy for human sexuality education. It allowed students to engage not only with the research content, which at the time was very limited, but also with their own experience and that of classmates as they explored their own sexual journeys. When I taught human

DOI: 10.4324/9781003519454-32

sexuality at Oberlin College in Ohio in 1972, this was the first time in the United States that academic credit had been allowed for this subject, thus providing both students and me as transgressive professor with an opportunity and a methodology to conduct a critical inquiry into the expanding horizons of a sexual revolution underway at the time. It also coincidently became the topic of my doctoral dissertation (O'Hara, 1976).

Keith: I'm so glad that you refer to andragogy (the teaching of adults). It always surprises me that educators and trainers in the field of psychology and therapy who are working with adult students use the word pedagogy (meaning the teaching of children) uncritically and without reference to its etymological origins. Anyway, tell me more about your contact with Freire.

Maureen: I worked with Freirians in Recife in 1978, who were using his ideas with sugar cane workers while he was still in Europe. They were far more sophisticated regarding the emancipatory agenda of literacy education than I was. I learned a lot about how consciousness develops through action and reflection working with groups to solve real life challenges. It was here the Rogerian faith in the client's reading of their experience became anchored in the real world. Later, around 1981, I was fortunate to have Freire join some sessions in a person-centred gestalt training program I ran in Sao Paulo. I also spent a day with him at his apartment in Sao Paulo where we vigorously debated whether American humanistic psychology was emancipatory or aligned with colonial interests. He got the better of the debate (O'Hara, 1982).

Keith: Thanks for sharing that. I came to Freire a little later, in the late 1980s, when I was studying radical social work and questioning the pedagogy—and it was pedagogy—by which we were taught the theory and practice of social work.[1]

One of the things that strikes me about your first paper (Chapter 22) is the epigrams which (as all good epigrams should) point to and prefigure the argument of the piece. In the ones you chose, I read the importance of a tension that gives rise to creativity; the importance of staying with process over outcome; and the ability to tolerate difference and even contradiction; the necessity of revolutionary, meta-thinking. I think these ideas or conditions are close to those of Rogers in *Freedom to Learn* (Rogers, 1969, 1983). Would you agree? I'm also curious that, in none of these three papers on education, you cite this book.

Maureen: You're right, there's a lot of resonance between my thinking on education and what Rogers explores in *Freedom to Learn* so your question makes me wonder why I don't refer to that work. It is even more puzzling when it was his chapter on student-centred teaching (Rogers, 1965) which prompted me to contact him asking him if he might become part of my doctoral committee. *Freedom to Learn* was a touchstone. I would explain it now as the result of my choice to follow divergent interests: women's studies; therapist training in Brazil; facilitating large group encounters and exploring their potential as a process for consciousness raising on a cultural scale; and exploring the emerging field of futures studies. Classroom processes faded from view. I was also heavily involved in humanistic psychology at a meta-level. I did a stint as President of the Association for Humanistic Psychology and later the Division of Humanistic Psychology of the American Psychological Association and I helped coordinate the Consortium for Diversified Programs in Psychology—a group of alternative educational institutions trying to break through the narrow accreditation standards that excluded humanistic programs. It wasn't until I was recruited to Saybrook Institute (now University) that the intersection of big picture challenges and what humanism could offer to the larger conversation came into focus once again.

Keith: Again, thanks for this. As for your papers on education, I am again struck not only by your humanism and radicalism, but also by their relevance to our contemporary world: uncertainty as an existential given; the reality and importance of acknowledging multiple cosmologies; the gap between our knowledge of what's needed and our capacity to meet the need; the need to develop new minds; and so on. Your four 'holistically related dimensions' for educational institutions are inspired and inspiring but I fear have not been adopted by any educational institutions in the 20 years since you wrote this paper—a point which appears close to the critique with which you open the second paper in this part (Chapter 23).

Maureen: This is a huge topic and with the entry of artificial intelligence into our lives just took a quantum leap in complexity. You raise what for me is the existential challenge of liquid times in which the old identities, rules, structures, and paradigms are unravelling but before new ones have emerged that can reliably replace them. In the interregnum that is post-modernity (according to Bauman, 2013), for instance, actions that were once transgressive and contested by the establishment such as distance learning or self-directed studies may now become normalised, and what were once core ingredients of educational programs such as geography or Latin become reframed, marginalised, or simply disappear. From 1996 to when I retired in 2022, I was part of accreditation teams evaluating diverse academic institutions. Over that period, it became clear that higher education in the USA was struggling to reconcile several powerful forces. Nevertheless, disintegrative processes that give cause for alarm may also contain the seeds of transformative growth, but, while we are up to our necks in the messiness, we struggle to distinguish real signs of hope from wishful thinking. I see a lot of progress on the four dimensions but much of it is happening in sites outside the established educational settings, such as schools and universities. I believe that the current battle over curriculum from the right, aimed at critical studies, gender studies, and a reckoning with America's history of brutal White supremacy and a slave-owning past illustrate both the transformative thrust emerging from the voices of those historically excluded and the backlash against it. I would also propose that the values and aspirations of 'generation open' indicate that whether inside formal education institutions or in the myriad learning opportunities in the informal sphere, the new consciousness is getting through.

Keith: I agree… which brings us seamlessly to the example of psychotherapy training or, more broadly, psychology training programmes (Chapter 23) and your point about frames and games, though I notice you don't say so much about the elements of games and the conceptual power game(s) or power plays. Before we get into some aspects of psychotherapy training, would you take this opportunity to say a bit more about this?

Maureen: By 'game' I mean any social activity where to complete its goal everyone involved must comply with implicit or explicit rules. The term comes from Wittgenstein but in this presentation, I was using 'game' as a metaphor for any rule-based social activity even if the rules are tacit. A flower arranging club, a university department, religious denomination, the US Congress, an outrigger canoe crew, are all games in this sense. They require participants to share the collective knowledge or canon of how their particular game is 'played'. In a complex game such as a psychotherapy training program, formal initiation and years-long training processes are usually required where newcomers learn what distinguishes their game from others and what is permitted by the rules and what is heresy. Games are more than amorphous or arbitrary social contexts as they usually have their own authority structures specifying—again tacitly or explicitly—who has authority to change, enforce, and interpret the rules. Though the term 'game' suggests something not serious, in reality they can exert a powerful psychological influence on players. Even for activities that appear inconsequential to outsiders, group recognition often brings psychologically satisfying rewards and, conversely, transgressions may come with crushing psychic costs thereby providing powerful inducements for compliance.

Keith: Thanks for this, that's really helpful. What you describe has echoes of how the term game (or 'psychological game') is used in transactional analysis (Berne 1964/1968) as well as Steiner's (1974, 1975a, 1975b, 1981) more radical contribution to this literature regarding the transactional analysis of 'power plays'.

So, to psychotherapy training. In your paper you make what I think is an interesting distinction between a category error and a choice about framing, and apply that to the well-worn—but, I would say, unresolved—argument about the framing of psychology in terms of the medical model. The implication of what you say about understanding psychological life, a paradigm, or even a discipline as being only one understanding suggests that the training or education of psychotherapists, for instance, needs to be or include a training in meta-analysis. Would you agree, and, if so, how do you think that's going?

Maureen: Most definitely it is needed but, except for a few boutique programmes that serve a small number of committed seekers, I think the mainstream programmes are responding to market demand for shorter and cheaper training.

We are living in a world where awareness of the relationship between consciousness and context is no longer debatable. Our sense of reality, perception, motivations, logics, beliefs, and conduct are created through interactions with our existential circumstances leading to neurological, conceptual, and social differences between us (Narváez, 2014; Narváez & Bradshaw, 2023; Nisbett, 2003; Shweder, 1991). Once we acknowledge that fact and we recognise the astonishing diversity that characterises the human condition, the ability to discern the meta-level dynamics at play in any context becomes essential. In the exchange between Jenny and me in Chapter 17 (pp. 189–190), it is when, with the help of a therapist attuned to the familiar power patterns in male–female relationships, Jenny becomes aware of how she plays victim and casts the school principal as a villain that she makes a conceptual and liberating leap. Rogers' session with Sylvia (which is the basis of my commentary in Chapter 15) shows what happens when the inability to read a client's framing and how it is different from her (older male) therapist's results in a missed opportunity for deeper exploration. In the session, Rogers' framing of Sylvia's struggle as one of 'growing up' catches my feminist attention as it reveals the familiar tendency of dominant groups to see dominated groups as 'children'. As I put it then:

> Carl could have drawn upon any number of other words or concepts. He could have suggested Sylvia had become more "empowered", "authoritative", "emancipated", "secure", and so on. Such language could allow for the possibility that Sylvia's lack of confidence is not a dispositional problem but is situational, i.e., is a consequence of living in a world which systematically devalues women's knowledge. By making it a personal developmental issue that she can "grow" out of, Carl's language obscures the possibility of social origins of Sylvia's psychological experience. In other words, it blames the victim.
>
> (p. 144)

You ask how training in meta-analysis is faring. From my situation here in the United States, given the diversity and professional levels of training offered, I find it hard to give a definitive answer. Training in psychotherapy varies from six-month addictions counsellor certificates, Associate Arts degrees, Bachelor's, and Master's. At the doctorate level, we have the Psychology Doctorate and Doctor of Philosophy. Degrees may be, in no particular order, in psychology, social work, behavioural science, counselling, nursing, education, coaching, and organisational development. More are added every year—evidence of the urgent felt need everywhere of ways to address the pain and disorientation generated by life in these tumultuous times. In my view, the unresolved tension you point to between a medical model framing and a growth model is only one of the tensions facing the would-be therapist. As I have discussed in several essays throughout this collection, the field of psychotherapy is shot through with epistemic fault lines that continue to go unresolved. This is too big a discussion for here, but I suggest that the fragmentation within the mental health landscape has been driven by a failure to reconcile fundamental philosophical differences among practitioners. In our book *Dancing at the Edge* (O'Hara & Leicester, 2012), we argue that being able to handle situations in which multiple paradigms are at play—riding more than one horse with one behind—as a necessary skill for survival in the 21st century but the multiple therapeutic communities seem to have defaulted to either epistemological Balkanisation in which each domain settles on its own framework, or the contradictions are simply sidestepped as irrelevant. So, right at the time when consciousness expansion is a matter of urgency, instead of helping our students transcend the limiting paradigms of modernity and helping the world learn to thrive in the kaleidoscopic global diversity, as therapy professionals we have withdrawn from the debate, opted for almost cult-like specialisations where we argue about orthodoxy, or we have surrendered to the legacy frames of the European Enlightenment and adopted the priorities of the healthcare industry.

Despite what I consider to be a capitulation to an outdated modernist hegemony among mainstream institutions in the marginal spaces around the bureaucratic centre, I nevertheless see pockets of resistance in the manifestations of a growth culture. In our programmes in the International Futures Forum, we find a lively debate between artists, therapists, coaches, and academics who are not ready to settle and who are seeking new frames and meanings that are more suited to a polyglot world remaking itself. A quick browse through the myriad websites offering human development resources reveals a vast ecosystem of persons and organisations outside the formal educational system pursuing personal and cultural transformation even in these turbulent times.

Keith: Thanks for this, Maureen. There's a lot in this with which I resonate, with regard both to your critique and to your hope. There's also a lot to think about and take forward but, at this point, this needs to be for another time, and, I would say, for others. Having taught—or facilitated the learning of—psychotherapy for many years in both private and public sectors, it does seem to be an impossible task for the impossible profession! At the same, I can't see not doing it… which perhaps brings me to ending this, our last reflection, with a point I raised at the beginning regarding the link between futures and education.

Maureen: Yes, as I see it, education, like parenting, is a quintessential 'futures' project. Unlike training, which teaches skills to be used in the present, education aims to prepare students for what they will encounter throughout their lives. In a rapidly changing world where today's skills are outdated often before they can be used, educational systems need to take on the role of not only teaching the collective knowledge of any particular society, but also help learners develop ways of approaching complex and uncertain futures that as yet are uncharted. When I took the position as president of a university and was immersed in the conceptual universe of higher education it became stunningly clear that most institutions were locked into ways of thinking that though suitable for a world that changed only slowly were utterly unprepared for the world that was coming—and still are.

Note

1 See Brown and Tudor (1981).

Epilogue

Keith Tudor and Maureen O'Hara

> *Rosalind. It is not the fashion to see the lady the epilogue; but it is no more unhandsome than to see the lord the prologue. If it be true that good wine needs no bush, 'tis true that a good play needs no epilogue. Yet to good wine they do use good bushes; and good plays prove the better by the help of good epilogues.*
>
> (Shakespeare, 1599/2021, Epilogue, lines 194–198)[1]

In this final contribution, we each reflect on the whole project of this book, our experiences of the dialogues, and what we're each taking forward.

Keith: Well, we made it—in both senses! We have literally made something, i.e., this book, which, for me, is very precious and, in terms of acknowledging your work, most well deserved. We also 'made it' in terms of completing it while you're still alive—which I mention in the context of my previous books with and/or about 'dead men' to which I referred in the Introduction.

Reflecting firstly about the process, I can say in all honesty that it has been easy and a delight—and, having has some difficult experiences in co-editing and co-authoring, I don't take that for granted. I have *loved* our engagement in the project. In his book on *Heuristic Research*, Moustakas (1990) writes about the first phase of heuristic enquiry being 'initial engagement', the task of which is 'to discover an intense interest, a passionate concern that calls out to the researcher, one that holds important social meanings and personal, compelling implications' (p. 27). For me, your work represents an intense interest and passionate concern that I have held for many years about the importance of social and the political as well as the psychological. So, while my initial engagement in the project of the book was less than a year ago, my engagement with your work has been much longer, over some 35 years, and has both informed and represents my engagement with psyche *and* society—and I certainly consider that your work has 'important social meanings' as well as 'personal, compelling implications'. As we acknowledged in the Introduction, our separate work, our previous contact, and our sense of each other as colleagues and comrades have created—or, more accurately, co-created—the relational space which has led not only to the editing and writing of the book but also to the tone and quality of our dialogues.

Secondly, with regard to the content, I have been both unsurprised and surprised. As someone who has followed and read your work over the years—and who has had the privilege of selecting the work to include in this volume—I have not been surprised about the content. At the same time, having re-read your work at greater depth, I have been surprised—or, perhaps more accurately, struck—by and appreciative of the range of your work (to which the six parts of the book attest) as well as the depth of your analysis; the clarity of your writing which provides access to the complexity of what you're often addressing; the consistency of your criticality and radicalism; your attention to language (here I'm thinking particularly about some of our exchanges in Chapter 2); your vision, which is still visionary and contemporary; and your provocations which, literally, 'call forth' the reader to think and act. Finally, as I've read through the book one last time in order to write this piece, I am struck by how many rich breadcrumbs there are for me and others to pick up and digest. In this sense, I think this book is not only a 'reader' but could and should be taken up as a handbook for psychosocial activists. You have indeed 'pushed the boundaries of received knowledge to find better ways of understanding the gloriously diverse manifestations of human being(s)' (p. 1) and I thank you for it, for being you, and for calling us to be more ourselves in the service of humanity—tēna koe, tēna koe, tēna koe. I thank you for learning from and representing the wisdom of ancestors such as John Bates, Irene Manton, Carl Rogers, and Paulo Freire; I thank you on my behalf as well as representing those who are present and still influenced by your work; and I thank you for the work you have done that will inspire future generations of thoughtful and humane psychologists.

Maureen: Pulling together a collection of work covering decades has been both a challenge and a gift, one that would not have happened without your initiative, encouragement, and sustained effort both as a gifted editor and a co-author. I am not a particularly disciplined archivist of my own work, preferring to focus on what I am currently thinking about rather than already published work. So, on revisiting the works selected, it was gratifying to discover that for the most part (with a few linguistic anachronisms such as references to a 'Third World'), when drawn into the present by your questions, the essays have stood the test of time and are still relevant to the times we are living in now. Your remarkable ability to see how the ideas fit together over time and across domains, identify the main themes, and select articles that carry the themes forward was a true gift, allowing me to see my evolution as a thinker and practitioner in a fresh way. As I reflected on what you resonated with, for instance, I began to see more clearly than I ever had before how my lived experience as a working-class girl from post-Second World War Yorkshire and educated as a scientist is foundational to how I perceive the world and construe reality. The tension between wanting to know myself as a conscious agentic *subject* at the same time as seeking to understand the ways social givens such as family, class, power, gender, and cultural norms shape how that subjectivity becomes realised animates much of my work—as it does my life. This dual focus has its costs as I sit somewhat marginal to both the depth psychologists and the social sciences—not integral to either. So, your appreciation of the philosophical positioning of my work and the proposal to produce this book came as quite a surprise, as you may recall. Reflecting together on the works even years after some were written, I was pleased to see that the issues raised over the decades continue to speak to the challenges and opportunities facing humanity in the 21st century.

Humanistic psychology was a response to the political and cultural turmoil in the 1960s that followed the Second World War when axioms such as the superiority of rationality and quantification—birthed in the Enlightenment—seemed no longer adequate for a world of nuclear weapons, environmental threats, and social justice demands of the oppressed and suppressed. Humanistic psychology was radically transgressive. It aimed to widen the aperture through which we came to know ourselves and reject scientific reductionism's shrunken view of human potential by embracing the humanities as well as the sciences. Exposure to Irene Manton's creative weaving, together with her love of modern art and her passion for disciplined scientific inquiry, convinced me that orthodoxy was overrated. Similarly, Rogers' courage to trust subjective ways of knowing as epistemically valid to the dismay of psychological elites appealed to the renegade in me as I sought more holistic ways of understanding psychological processes.

We are again living in darkening times when the gains in freedom and justice secured by decades of activists are now under siege by power elites seeking to re-establish an *ancien regime* with White heterosexual men of European descent in charge and their ideas dominant. Women are again prevented from making decisions about their own bodies and worse, people of colour and LGBTQ+ communities once more subjected to discrimination and violence; critical voices are silenced, their ideas banned from public libraries and erased from school curricula. This is all happening as antisemitic, anti-Muslim, anti-immigrant, and outright fascistic movements proliferate. I hope I have made clear however that authoritarianism, though understandable, is not the only response to the existential moment. As I describe in Chapter 24, there is a whole generation who have grown up in the fluid realities and uncertainties of the early 21st century who are seizing the opportunities presented by astonishing new technologies and in response to emerging threats are self-organising and are making new things happen.

Throughout my career as a therapist, teacher, executive, and community facilitator, I have taken seriously Rogers' hypothesis that persons and communities possess immense resources with which to creatively address the challenges life presents. I am with Bohart and Tallman (1996) in trusting that, when supported with authenticity, respect, and empathy, rather than directed or controlled, people in trouble can 'self-right' and go beyond their challenges. The overriding theme in these essays is that human beings are a creative species. Like any species, we face inevitable problems but, if conditions permit, we self-organise and innovate ourselves out of problems. Self-organisation doesn't always turn out as hoped for but in complex and unpredictable contexts such as those we are facing now, aligning public policy with the collective capacity of communities does better in the long run than top-down social engineering where power resides with leaders not in participants. Even when experiences are disappointing, the mere fact of active participation to try to change things for the better builds greater capacity for the future. In the face of a planetary future that is radically open, we had best admit our existential vulnerability, trust each other, and commit to learning our way forward together.

Keith: It is my privilege and pleasure to conclude this epilogue by facing outwards to you the reader, the audience, to say a few final words.

As long as I have been conscious of my interests, I have been interested in history, and as I have grown (and aged) so too has this interest. In terms of the discipline of psychotherapy, this has taken the form of researching the different traditions that have given rise to modern and postmodern soul healing,[2] acknowledging different traditions within branches of psychology and therapy,[3] and, more recently, writing with and about elders in the profession, not least to ensure their legacies.[4] These, however, are not historical projects that simply look back with nostalgia; they look at the past in the present to assure the future. This has been the purpose of this book: to present Maureen's work, in dialogue, to help us and future generations assure the future. Indeed, one of the many revelations of this book is precisely how future-focused Maureen always has been and still is. That work (of editing and writing the book) is now done. Now it's up to us—me, you, and others—to take it forward, with strength, understanding, compassion, and, of course, hope.

Notes

1 In the course of editing and writing this book, I discovered Maureen's love of theatre and her love of Shakespeare (Tudor, 2021), as a result of which I wanted to choose an epigram for our epilogue. Maureen also liked this idea and, separately and synchronistically, we both chose this from Shakespeare's *As You Like It*!

2 Tudor (2018b, 2018c).

3 Tudor (2022b, 2025).

4 Regarding Evan Sherrard (Tudor, 2017/2020), Claude Steiner (Tudor, 2020), and Bernie Neville (Tudor & Cornelius-White, 2025).

Appendix 1

Maureen O'Hara
A complete bibliography

Compiled by Maureen O'Hara, Bob Lucas, Keith Tudor, and Angie Strachan

Publication under the name Maureen Merrett

Merrett, M. (1969). Observations on the fine structure of *Chlamydobotrys stellata* with particular reference to its unusual chloroplast structure. *Archive fur Microbiologie*, *65*, 1–11. https://doi.org/10.1007/BF00412061

Publications under the name Maureen Miller

Wray, J. L, Reis, S. K., Filner, P., Miller, M. (1970). *On the mechanism of increase in nitrate reductase activity observed in barley shoots in response to simazine. AEC/Plant Research Report*. Michigan State University.

Miller, D. H., Lamport, T. A., & Miller, M. (1972). Hydroxyproline heterooligosaccharides in *Chlamydomonas*. *Science*, *176*(4037), 918–920. https://doi.org/10.1126/science.176.4037.918

Miller, M. (1973, February 2). The right to abortion. A personal, moral decision. *The Oberlin Review*, *101*(27), 3.

Miller, D. H., Mellman, I. S., Lamport, D. T. A., & Miller, M. (1974). The chemical composition of the cell wall of *Chlamydomonas gymnogama* and the concept of the cell wall protein. *Journal of Cell Biology*, *63*(2), 420–429. https://doi.org/10.1083/jcb.63.2.420

Villas-Boas Bowen, M., Justyn, J., Kass, J., Miller, M., Rogers, C. R., Rogers, N., & Wood, J. K. (1978). Evolving aspects of person-centered workshop. *Self & Society*, *6*(2), 43–49. https://doi.org/10.1080/03060497.1978.11086697

Publications under the name Maureen O'Hara (and Maureen Miller O'Hara)

1970s

Bowen, M., O'Hara, M., Rogers, C. R., & Wood, J. K. (1979). Evolving aspects of the person-centered approach. Newsletter of the Association of Humanistic Psychology, January, 11–14.

Bowen, M., O'Hara, M. M., Rogers, C. R., & Wood, J. K. (1979). Learnings in large groups: Their implications for the future. *Education*, *100*(2), 108–116.

1980s

O'Hara, M. M. (1982). Person-centered approach as conscientização. *Journey*, *2*(2).

Lucas, R. L. (1983). Conversations with Carl Rogers—video. (M. O'Hara, Moderator). Center for Studies of the Person, La Jolla, CA, USA.

Miller O'Hara, M. (1983). A consciencia do terapeuta [Therapist consciousness]. In C. Rogers, J. K. Wood, & M. Miller O'Hara and Afonso Henrique da Fonseca, *Em Busca de Vida: Da terapia centrada no cliente à abordagem centrada na pessoa* [In search of life: from client-centered therapy to the person-centered approach] (pp. 97–98). Summus.

Miller O'Hara, M. (1983). Introdução [Introduction]. In C. Rogers, J. K. Wood, & M. Miller O'Hara and Afonso Henrique da Fonseca, *Em Busca de Vida: Da terapia centrada no cliente à abordagem centrada na pessoa* (pp. 95–96). Summus.

Miller O'Hara, M. (1983). Psicoterapia centrada na pessoa: tecnologia da mudança ou busca de conhecimento [Client-centered psychotherapy: technology of change or a search for expanded consciousness]. In C. Rogers, J. K. Wood, & M. Miller O'Hara and Afonso Henrique da Fonseca, *Em Busca de Vida: Da terapia centrada no cliente à abordagem centrada na pessoa* (pp. 103–122). Summus.

Miller O'Hara, M. (1983). Reflexão acerca de um workshop centrada na pessoa [Reflections on a person centered workshop]. In C. Rogers, J. K. Wood, & M. Miller O'Hara and Afonso Henrique da Fonseca, *Em Busca de Vida: Da terapia centrada no cliente à abordagem centrada na pessoa* (pp. 123–134). Summus.

O'Hara, M. M. (1983). The hundredth humanistic psychologist. *Self & Society*, *12*(3), 126–131. https://doi.org/10.1080/03060497.1984.11084612

O'Hara, M. M. (1983). A hundredth monkey myth. *Association for Humanistic Psychology Newsletter*, November, 20–21.

O'Hara, M. M. (1983). Our foremothers as gurus. *Perspective: Association for Humanistic Psychology*, November.

O'Hara, M. M. (1983). Women's voice: Everyone's world. *Journey*, *3*(1).

O'Hara, M. M., & Wood, J. K. (1983). Patterns of awareness: Consciousness and the group mind. *Gestalt Journal*, *6*(2), 103–116.

Rogers, C. R., Wood, J. K., O'Hara, M., & da Fonseca, A. H. L. (1983). *Em busca da vida: Da terapia centrada no cliente, a abordagen centrada na pessoa* [In search of life: From client-centered therapy to the person-centered approach]. Summus.

Lucas, R. J., & O'Hara, M. (Producers). (1984). The family secret: Delivery of social services through community access cable T.V. [Video]. The Foundation for Community Television.

O'Hara, M. M. (1984). Person-centered gestalt: Towards a holistic synthesis. In R. Levant & J. Shlien (Eds.), *Client-centered therapy and the person-centered approach* (pp. 203–221). Praeger.

O'Hara, M. M. (1984). Reflections on Sheldrake, Wilber, and 'new science'. *Journal of Humanistic Psychology*, *24*(2), 116–120. https://doi.org/10.1177/0022167884242007

O'Hara, M. (1985). Comment on Carl Rogers's 'Toward a more human science of the person'. *Journal of Humanistic Psychology*, *25*(4), 25–30. https://doi.org/10.1177/0022167885254003

O'Hara, M. (1985). The 'hundredth monkey phenomenon': A look at the darker side of 'New Age' ideology. *Omni*, *8*(1), 22.

O'Hara, M. (1985). Of myths and monkeys: A critical look at a theory of critical mass. *Journal of Humanistic Psychology*, *25*(1), 61–78. https://doi.org/10.1177/0022167885251004

O'Hara, M. (1986). Heuristic inquiry as psychotherapy: The client-centered approach. *Person-Centered Review*, *1*(2), 172–184.

O'Hara, M. (1986). Of myths and monkeys. *The Whole Earth Review*, *55*, 30–34.

O'Hara, M. M. (1987, November). *Carl Rogers: Scientist and mystic* [Paper presentation]. Symposium honouring Carl Rogers, University of California Extension, Los Angeles.

O'Hara, M. (1988). Science, pseudoscience, and mythmongering. In R. Basil (Ed.), *Not necessarily the new age* (pp. 145–164). Prometheus.

O'Hara, M. (1989a). Constructing emancipatory realities: Towards a feminist voice in humanistic psychology. *AHP Perspective*, August/September.
O'Hara, M. (1989b). A new age reflection in the magic mirror of science. *The Skeptical Inquirer*, *13*(4), 368–374.
O'Hara, M. (1989c). Person-centered approach as conscientização: The works of Carl Rogers and Paulo Freire. *Journal of Humanistic Psychology*, *29*(1), 11–35. https://doi.org/10.1177/0022167889291002
O'Hara, M. (1989d). When I use the term *humanistic psychology*.... *Journal of Humanistic Psychology*, *29*(2), 263–273. https://doi.org/10.1177/0022167889292009

1990s

O'Hara, M. (1990). Humanistic psychology, co-constructionism and the global search for deep democracy. *AHP Perspective*, November.
O'Hara, M. (1992). If not now, when? Values for a pluralistic world. *Vital Speeches of the Day*, *59*(2), 41–45.
O'Hara, M. (Writer & Producer). (1992). *Myths that maim* [Video].
O'Hara, M. (1992). Relational humanism: A psychology for a pluralistic world. *The Humanistic Psychologist*, *20*(2–3), 439–446. https://doi.org/10.1080/08873267.1992.9986808
O'Hara, M. (1994). Relational humanism: A psychology for a pluralistic world. In F. Wertz (Ed.), *The humanistic movement: Recovering the person in psychology* (pp. 322–329). Gardner Press.
Lucas, R. J., & O'Hara, M. (Producers). (1995). *Journey into community* [Video].
O'Hara, M. (1995). Carl Rogers: Scientist and mystic. *Journal of Humanistic Psychology*, *35*(4), 40–53. https://doi.org/10.1177/00221678950354004
O'Hara, M. (1995). Constructing emancipatory realities. In W. T. Anderson (Ed.), *The truth about truth: De-constructing and reconstructing the postmodern world* (pp. 105–155). Jeremy Tarcher.
O'Hara, M. (1995). Is it time for clinical psychology to deconstruct constructivism? *Journal of Constructivist Psychology*, *8*(4), 293–303. https://doi.org/10.1080/10720539508405910
O'Hara, M. (1996). Feminist analysis of a session of psychotherapy between Carl Rogers and a female client 'Silvia'. In B. A. Farber, D. C. Brink, & P. M. Raskin (Eds.), *The psychotherapy of Carl Rogers: Cases and commentary* (pp. 284–300). Guilford Press.
O'Hara, M. (1996). Psychotherapy: Humanistic, experiential and relational approaches. In J. Jacobs (Ed). *The encyclopedia of alternative medicine* (pp. 148–155). Creative Enterprise Publications.
O'Hara, M. (1995). Streams: On becoming a postmodern person. In M. Suhd (Ed.), *Positive regard: Carl Rogers and the notables who knew him* (pp. 105–155). Behavioral Science Books.
O'Hara, M. (1996). [Untitled chapter]. In B. Mullan (Ed.), *R. D. Laing: Creative destroyer* (pp. 314–322). Cassell.
O'Hara, M., & Anderson, W. T. (1996). Divided we stand. *Family Therapy Networker*, September/October.
Bohart, A. C., O'Hara, M. M., Leitner, L. M., Wertz, F., Stern, E. M., Schneider, K., Serlin, I., & Greening, T. (1997). Guidelines for the provision of humanistic services. *The Humanistic Psychologist*, *25*(1), 64–107. https://doi.org/10.1080/08873267.1997.9986872
O'Hara, M. (1997). Emancipatory therapeutic practice in a turbulent transmodern era: A work of retrieval. *Journal of Humanistic Psychology*, *37*(3), 7–33. https://doi.org/10.1177/00221678970373002
O'Hara, M. (1997). Relational empathy: Beyond modernist egocentricism to postmodern holistic contextualism. In A. C. Bohart & L. S. Greenberg (Eds.), *Empathy reconsidered: New directions in psychotherapy* (pp. 295–319). American Psychological Association. https://doi.org/10.1037/10226-013

Bohart, A. C., O'Hara, M., & Leitner, L. M. (1998). Empirically violated treatments: Disenfranchisement of humanistic and other psychotherapies. *Psychotherapy Research*, *8*(2), 141–157. https://doi.org/10.1093/ptr/8.2.141

O'Hara, M. (1998). Gestalt therapy as an emancipatory psychology for a transmodern world. *Gestalt Review*, *2*(2), 154–168. https://doi.org/10.2307/44390671

2000s

O'Hara, M., & Taylor, E. (2000). Humanistic psychology. In A. E. Kazdin (Ed.), *Encyclopedia of psychology* (Vol. 4, pp. 186–190). Oxford University Press.

O'Hara, M. (2002). Emancipatory therapeutic practice for a new era: A work of retrieval. In K. Schneider, J. Bugental, & J. Pierson (Eds.), *The handbook of humanistic psychology* (pp. 473–489). Sage.

O'Hara, M. (2002). Moments of eternity: What Carl Rogers still has to offer brief therapists. In J. K. Zeig (Ed.), *Brief therapy: Lasting impressions* (pp. 337–366). The Milton H. Erickson Foundation Press.

O'Hara, M., & Wood, J. K. (2002). Transforming communities: Person-centered encounters and the creation of integral conscious groups. In B. Banathy & P. Jenlink (Eds.), *Dialogue as a means of collective communication* (pp. 105–136). Kluwer Academic/Plenum Publishers.

O'Hara, M. (2003). Cultivating consciousness: Carl R. Rogers's person-centered group process as transformative androgogy. *Journal of Transformative Education*, *1*(1), 64–79. https://doi.org/10.1177/0095399703251646

O'Hara, M. (2006). In search of the next enlightenment?: The challenge for education in uncertain times. *Journal of Transformative Education*, *4*(2), 105–117. https://doi.org/10.1177/1541344606287920

Cooper, M., O'Hara, M., Schmid, P. F., & Wyatt, G. (Eds.). (2007). *The handbook of person-centred and client-centred psychotherapy and counselling*. Palgrave-Macmillan.

Henderson, V. L., O'Hara, M., Barfield, G. L., & Rogers, N. (2007). Person-centered applications beyond the therapeutic context: Organizations, peace activism and creativity. In M. Cooper, M. O'Hara, P. F. Schmid, & G. Wyatt (Eds.), *The handbook of person-centred psychotherapy and counselling* (pp. 305–324). Palgrave-Macmillan.

O'Hara, M. (2007). Psychological literacy for an emerging global society: Another look at Rogers' 'persons of tomorrow' as a model. *Person-Centered & Experiential Psychotherapies*, *6*(1), 45–60. https://doi.org/10.1080/14779757.2007.9688427

O'Hara, M. (2007). Strangers in a strange land: Knowing, learning, and education for the global knowledge society. *Futures*, 39(8), 930–941. https://doi.org/10.1016/j.futures.2007.03.006

Schmid, P. F., & O'Hara, M. (2007). Group therapy and encounter groups. In M. Cooper, M. O'Hara, P. F. Schmid, & G. Wyatt (Eds.), *Handbook of person-centred psychotherapy and counselling* (pp. 233–235). Palgrave-Macmillan.

O'Hara, M. (2008). Foreword. In J. K. Wood (Ed.), *Carl Rogers' person-centered approach: Toward an understanding of its implications* (pp. iii–viii). PCCS Books.

Leicester, G., & O'Hara, M. (2009). *Ten things to do in a conceptual emergency*. Triarchy Press.

2010s

Leicester, G., & O'Hara, M. (2010). *WASC as cultural leader—Position paper*. WASC.

O'Hara, M. (2010). Another inconvenient truth and the developmental role for psychology in a threatened world. *The Humanistic Psychologist*, *38*(2), 101–119. https://doi.org/10.1080/08873267.2010.485915

O'Hara, M., & Leicester, G. (2012). *Dancing at the edge: Competence, culture and organization for the 21st century*. Triarchy Press.

Cooper, M., O'Hara, M., Schmid, P. F., & Bohart, A. C. (2013). *The handbook of person-centred psychotherapy and counselling* (2nd ed.). Palgrave Macmillan.

O'Hara, M. (2013). PCA encounter groups: Transformative learning for individuals and communities. In J. H. D. Cornelius-White, R. Motschnig-Pitrik, & M. Lux (Eds.), *Interdisciplinary handbook of the person-centered approach: Connections beyond therapy* (pp. 221–228). Springer.

O'Hara, M. (2013). Person-centered approach as a praxis for cultural leadership. In M. Cooper, M. O'Hara, P. F. Schmid, & A.C. Bohart (Eds.), *Handbook of person-centred psychotherapy and counselling* (2nd ed., pp. 483–495). Palgrave-Macmillan.

O'Hara, M., & Omer, A. (2013). Virtue and the organizational shadow: Exploring false innocence and the paradoxes of power. In A. C. Bohart, B. S. Held, E. Mendelowitz, & K. J. Schneider (Eds.), *Humanity's dark side: Evil, destructive experience, and psychotherapy* (pp. 167–187). American Psychological Association. https://doi.org/10.1037/13941-009

O'Hara, M., & Lyon, A. (2014). Wellbeing and wellbecoming: Reauthorizing the subject in incoherent times. In T. J. Hämäläinen & J. Michaelson (Eds.), *Wellbeing and beyond: Broadening the public and policy discourse* (pp. 98–123). Edward Elgar.

O'Hara, M. (2016). Making a difference: How humanistic practice makes a critical difference to humanity's future. *Psychotherapy and Politics International*, *14*(2), 107–119. https://doi.org/10.1002/ppi.1381

O'Hara, M. (2017). Humanistic psychology as praxis for a world in crisis. In R. House, D. Kalisch, & J. Maidman (Eds.), *Humanistic psychology: Current trends, future prospects* (pp. 75–86). Routledge.

O'Hara, M. (2017). Make it personal: International Futures Forum approach to community transformation. In R. Motschnig & D. Ryback (Eds.), *Transforming communication in leadership and teamwork: Person-centered innovations* (pp. 99–106). Springer.

O'Hara, M. (2017). Rising to the occasion: New persons for new times. *Estudos de Psicologia*, *34*(4), 454–466. https://doi.org/10.1590/1982-02752017000400002

O'Hara, M. (2018). Rising to the occasion: Personhood at the edge of an emerging civilization. *Self & Society*, *48*(2), 139–150.

O'Hara, M. (2019). Academies of hope: A transformative turn for person-centered practice. *Person-Centered & Experiential Psychotherapies*, 18(2), 139–150. https://doi.org/10.1080/14779757.2019.1618374

O'Hara, M. (2019). Empatia social: Encontrando a sabedoria comum. [Social empathy: Finding common wisdom]. In M. Tassinari & W. Durange (Eds.), *Empatia: A capacidade de dar a luz à dignidade humana* [Empathy: The ability of giving birth to human dignity] (pp. 105–118). CRV.

O'Hara, M. (2019). Prefácio: Abertura à empatia: Um modo de ser desvalorizado. [Preface: Openness to empathy: An unappreciated way of being]. In M. Tassinari & W. Durange (Eds.), *Empatia: A capacidade de dar a luz à dignidade humana* [Empathy: The ability of giving birth to human dignity] (pp. 15–22). CRV.

O'Hara, M., & Leicester, G. (2019). *Dancing at the edge: Competence, culture and organization for the 21st century* (2nd ed.). Triarchy Press.

2020s

Leicester, G., & O'Hara, M. (2021). *Spaces for growth: Learning our way out of a crisis*. Koreo.

O'Hara, M. (2022). Academies of hope: Making radical hope a reality. *Psychotherapy and Politics International*, *20*(1&2). https://doi.org/10.24135/ppi.v20i1and2.11

Di Malta, G., Cooper, M., O'Hara, M., Gololob, Y., & Stevens, S. (Eds.). (2024). *The handbook of person-centred psychotherapy and counselling* (3rd ed.). Bloomsbury.

Di Malta, G., Cooper, M., Gololob, Y., O'Hara, M., & Stephen, S. (2024). The person-centred approach today and tomorrow. In G. Di Malta, M. Cooper, M. O'Hara, Y. Gololob, & S. Stevens (Eds.), *The handbook of person-centred psychotherapy and counselling* (3rd ed., pp. 1–16). Bloomsbury.

Di Malta, G., Cooper, M., Gololob, Y., O'Hara, M., & Stephen, S. (2024). Preface. In G. Di Malta, M. Cooper, M. O'Hara, Y. Gololob, & S. Stevens (Eds.), *The handbook of person-centred psychotherapy and counselling* (3rd ed., pp. xvii–xxi). Bloomsbury.

O'Hara, M. (2025). *Selected writings of Maureen O'Hara on the science, art, and hope of humanism: Vitalising persons for turbulent times*. In K. Tudor (Ed.). Routledge.

O'Hara, M. (2024). Social change and cultural transformation. In G. Di Malta, M. Cooper, M. O'Hara, Y. Gololob, & S. Stevens (Eds.), *The handbook of person-centred psychotherapy and counselling* (3rd ed., pp. 463–478). Bloomsbury.

Schmid, P. F., & O'Hara, M. (2024). Working in groups. In G. Di Malta, M. Cooper, M. O'Hara, Y. Gololob, & S. Stevens (Eds.), *The handbook of person-centred psychotherapy and counselling* (3rd ed., pp. 123–137). Bloomsbury.

Tudor, K., & O'Hara, M. (Eds.). (2025). *Selected writings of Maureen O'Hara on the science, art, and hope of humanism: Vitalising persons for turbulent times*. Routledge.

References

Aanstoos, C. M., Serlin, I., & Greening, T. (2000). A history of Division 32 (Humanistic Psychology). In D. A. Dewsbury (Ed.), *Unification through division: Histories of the divisions of the American Psychological Association*, Vol. 5 (pp. 85–112). American Psychological Association. https://doi.org/10.1037/10356-004

Alexander, C. N., & Langer, E. J. (Eds.) (1990). *Higher stages of human development: Perspectives on adult growth.* Oxford University Press.

Allman, W. (1994). *The stone age present.* Simon & Schuster.

Anderson, W. T. (1987). *To govern evolution: Further adventures of the political animal.* Houghton Mifflin Harcourt.

Anderson, W. T. (1990). *Reality isn't what it used to be.* Harper and Row.

Anderson, W. T. (Ed.) (1996). *The truth about the truth: De-confusing and re-constructing the postmodern world.* Tarcher/Putnam.

Anderson, W. T. (1997). *The future of the self: Inventing the postmodern person.* Putnam.

Anderson, W. T. (2005). *Fragmegration, mystery and unity: Some thoughts on the global brain* [Conference presentation]. Tamkang University International Conference, Global Soul, Global Mind, Global Action: Futuring from Survival to Thrival, Taiwan.

Baker, T. B., McFall, R. M., & Shoham, V. (2008). Current status and future prospects of clinical psychology: Toward a scientifically principled approach to mental and behavioral health care. *Psychological Science in the Public Interest*, *9*(2), 67–103. https://doi.org/10.1111/j.1539-6053.2009.01036.x

Ballinger, L., & Wright, J. (2007). 'Does class count?' Social class and counselling. *Counselling & Psychotherapy Research*, *7*(3), 157–163. https://doi.org/10.1080/14733140701571316

Ballotpedia. (n.d.). *California Proposition 214, Healthcare Business Regulation Initiative (1996).* https://ballotpedia.org/California_Proposition_214,_Healthcare_Business_Regulation_Initiative_(1996)

Barlow, D. H. (1996). Health care policy, psychotherapy research, and the future of psychotherapy. *American Psychologist*, *51*(10), 1050–1059. https://doi.org/10.1037/0003-066X.51.10.1050

Barrett-Lennard, G. T. (1984). The world of family relationships: A person-centered systems view. In R. F. Levant & J. M. Shlien (Eds.), *Client-centered therapy and the person-centered approach: New directions in theory, research, and practice* (pp. 222–241). Praeger.

Bauman, Z. (2013). *Liquid modernity.* Polity.

Begley, S. (2009, October 1). Why psychologists reject science. *Newsweek.* https://www.newsweek.com/why-psychologists-reject-science-begley-81063

Belenky, M. F., Clinchy, B. M., Goldberger, N. R., & Tarule, J. M. (1986). *Women's ways of knowing: Development of self, voice, and mind.* Basic Books.

Bellah, R. N., Madsen, R., Sullivan, W. M., Swidler, A., & Tipton, S. M. (1985). *Habits of the heart: Individualism and commitment in American life.* Harper & Row.

Benjamin, J. (2015, July 29). *Acknowledging the other's suffering: A psychoanalytic approach to trauma in Israel/Palestine*. Tikkun. https://www.tikkun.org/acknowledging-the-others-suffering-a-psychoanalytic-approach-to-trauma-in-israelpalestine/

Berger, P. L., & Luckmann, T. (1966). *The social construction of reality: A treatise in the sociology of knowledge*. Doubleday.

Bergin, A. E., & Garfield, S. L. (1994). Overview, trends, and future issues. In A. E. Bergin & S. L. Garfield (Eds.), *Handbook of psychotherapy and behavior change* (pp. 821–830). Wiley.

Berman, M. (1989). *Coming to our senses: Body and spirit in the hidden history of the West*. Simon and Schuster.

Bernard, J. (1981). *The female world*. Free Press.

Berne, E. (1968). *Games people play*. Grove Press. (Original work published in 1964)

Blake, W. (1804). *Jerusalem, the emanation of the giant Albion*. W. Blake & Lessing J. Rosenwald Collection.

Bohart, A. C., & Tallman, K. (1996). The active client: Therapy as self-help. *Journal of Humanistic Psychology*, *36*(3), 7–30. https://doi.org/10.1177/00221678960363002

Bohart, A. C., & Tallman, K. (1999). *How clients make therapy work: The process of active self-healing*. American Psychological Association.

Bohart, A. C., O'Hara, M., & Lietner, L. M. (1998). Empirically violated treatments: Disenfranchisement of humanistic and other psychotherapies. *Psychotherapy Research*, *8*(2), 141–157. https://doi.org/10.1080/10503309812331332277

Bohm, D. (1980). *Wholeness and the implicate order*. Routledge.

Bowen, M., O'Hara, M. M., Rogers, C. R., & Wood, J. K. (1979). Learnings in large groups: Implications for the future. *Education*, *100*(2), 108–117.

Bozarth, J. D. (1984). Beyond reflection: Emergent modes of empathy. In R. F. Levant & J. M. Shlien (Eds.), *Client-centered therapy and the person-centered approach: New directions in theory, research and practice* (pp. 59–75). Praeger.

Bozarth, J. (1998). *Person-centered therapy: A revolutionary paradigm*. PCCS Books.

Bragg, B. (1984). *Between the wars. On brewing up with Billy Bragg*. Go! Disks.

Brilliant, A. (1979). Seeing is believing. *Pot-shots—Brilliant thoughts in 17 words or less*. www.ashleighbrilliant.com

Brown, J. S. (2005). *Learning in the digital age (21st century): Catalyzing creativity by artful making & by honoring the vernacular of today's students*. San Diego State University.

Brown, K., & Tudor, K. (1981). Social work education and practice: Reform and revolution—A theory for change. *Contemporary Social Work Education*, *4*(2), 101–112.

Buber, M. (1970). *I and thou* (W. Kaufman, Trans.). Scribner's Sons. (Original work published in 1923)

Bugental, J. F., & Bracke, T. (1992). The future of existential-humanistic psychotherapy. *Psychotherapy*, *29*(1), 28–33. https://doi.org/10.1037/0033-3204.29.1.28

Buie, D. H. (1981). Empathy: Its nature and limitations. *Journal of the American Psychoanalytic Association*, *29*(2), 281–307. https://doi.org/10.1177/000306518102900201

Cade, B., & O'Hanlon, W. H. (1993). *A brief guide to brief therapy*. W.W. Norton & Company.

Cain, D. (1996). Rogers and Sylvia: An intimate and affirming encounter. In B. A. Farber, D. C. Brink, & P. M. Raskin (Eds.), *The psychotherapy of Carl Rogers: Cases and commentary* (pp. 275–283). Guilford Press.

Cantor, D. W. (1990). I am not a dinosaur. *Psychotherapy in Private Practice*, *8*(1), 11–19. https://doi.org/10.1300/J294v08n01_03

Cantor, N. F. (1970). *Western civilization: Its genesis and destiny 1300–1815* (Vol. 2). Scott, Foresman and Company.

Caplan, P. J. (1995). *They say you're crazy: How the world's most powerful psychiatrists decide who's normal*. Addison-Wesley.

Carkhuff, R. R. (1969). *Helping and human relations, vol. I: Selection and training*. Holt, Rinehart, and Winston.

Carson, R. (1962). *Silent spring*. Houghton Mifflin.

Chesler, P. (1972). *Women and madness*. Doubleday.

Chin, J. L. (1994). Psychodynamic approaches. In L. Comas-Diaz & B. Greene (Eds.), *Women of color: Integrating ethnic and gender identities in psychotherapy* (pp. 194–222). Guilford Press.

Claiborn, C. D. (1996). Science for practice. *Contemporary Psychology*, *41*(11), 1100–1101.

Clinchy, B. M., & Belenky, M. F. (1987, August). *Women's ways of knowing: A theory and an intervention* [Presentation]. Smith College School of Social Work.

Comas-Diaz, L., & Greene, B. (Eds.) (1994). *Women of color: Integrating ethnic and gender identities in psychotherapy*. Guilford Press.

Connor, J. W. (1984). Misperception, folk belief, and the occult: A cognitive guide to understanding. *The Skeptical Inquirer*, *8*(4), 344–354. https://skepticalinquirer.org/1984/07/misperception-folk-belief-and-the-occult/

Cortese, A. D. (2003). The critical role of higher education in creating a sustainable future. *Planning for Higher Education*, *31*(3), 15–22.

Coulson, W. R. (1982, July). *Psychosalvationism in humanistic psychology* [Conference presentation]. First International Forum on the Person-Centered Approach, Oaxtepec, Mexico.

Covey, S. R. (1989). *The seven habits of highly effective people: Restoring the character ethic*. Simon & Shuster.

Crutzen, P. J., & Stoermer, E. F. (2000). The 'Anthropocene'. *Global Change Newsletter*, *41*, 17–18.

Csikszentmihalyi, M. (1993). *The evolving self: A psychology for the third millennium*. Harper Collins.

Cushman, P. (1992). Psychotherapy to 1992: Historically situated interpretation. In D. K. Freedheim (Ed.), *History of psychotherapy: A century of change* (pp. 21–63). American Psychological Association.

Daly, M. (1978). *Gyn/ecology: The metaethics of radical feminism*. Beacon Press.

Dawes, R. M. (1994). *The house of cards: Psychology and psychotherapy built on myth*. Free Press.

Delors, J., Al Mufti, I., Amagi, I., Carneiro, R., Chung, F., Geremek, B., Gorham, W., Kornhauser, A., Manley, M., Padrón Quero, M., Savane, M. A., Singh, K., Stavenhagen, R., Suhr, M. W., & Nanzhao, Z. (1996). *Learning: The treasure within. Report to UNESCO of the International Commission on Education for the Twenty-First Century*. UNESCO Publishing.

Douglass, B. G., & Moustakas, C. (1985). Heuristic inquiry: The internal search to know. *Journal of Humanistic Psychology*, *25*(3), 39–55. https://doi.org/10.1177/0022167885253004

Dubos, R. (1981). *Celebrations of life*. McGraw Hill.

Dyer, G. (2009). *Climate wars*. Random House Canada.

Efran, J. S., Lukens, M. D., & Lukens, R. J. (1990). *Language, structure, and change: Frameworks of meaning of psychotherapy*. Norton.

Eisenberg, D. M., Davis, R. B., Ettner, S. L., Appel, S., Wilkey, S., Van Rompay, M., & Kessler, R. C. (1998). Trends in alternative medicine use in the United States, 1990–1997. Results of a follow-up national survey. *JAMA*, *280*(18), 1569–1575. https://doi.org/10.1001/jama.280.18.1569

Eisler, R. T. (1987). *The chalice and the blade: Our history, our future*. Harper & Row.

Ekman, P., Friesen, W. V., & Ellsworth, P. (1982). What are the similarities and differences in facial behavior across cultures? In P. Ekman (Ed.), *Emotion in the human face* (2nd ed., pp. 128–143). Cambridge University Press.

Elkins, D. N. (2009). *Humanistic psychology: A clinical manifesto: A critique of clinical psychology and the need for progressive alternatives*. University of the Rockies Press.

Embleton Tudor, L. (2022). Breath and the dynamics of connection and disconnection: A neuro-scientifically informed perspective. *Person-Centered & Experiential Psychotherapies*, *21*(2), 112–128. https://doi.org/10080/14779757.2022.2067780
Epstein, M. (1993). Awakening with Prozac: Pharmaceuticals and practice. *Tricycle: The Buddhist Review*, *3*(1), 30–34. https://tricycle.org/magazine/awakening-prozac/
Eysenck, H. J. (1952). The effects of psychotherapy: An evaluation. *Journal of Consulting Psychology*, *16*(5), 319–324. https://doi.org/10.1037/h0063633
Eysenck, H. J. (1983). The effectiveness of psychotherapy: The specter at the feast. *Behavioral and Brain Sciences*, *6*(2), 290.
Farber, B. A., Brink, D. C., & Raskin, P. M. (Eds.) (1996). *The psychotherapy of Carl Rogers: Cases and commentary*. Guilford Press.
Farson, R. (1975). Carl Rogers: Quiet revolutionary. In R. I. Evans (Ed.), *Carl Rogers: The man and his ideas* (pp. xxviii–xliii). Dutton.
Farson, R. (1978). The technology of humanism. *Journal of Humanistic Psychology*, *18*(2), 5–35. https://doi.org/10.1177/002216787801800202
Feigl, H. (1959). Philosophical embarrassments of psychology. *American Psychologist*, *14*(3), 115–128. https://doi.org/10.1037/h0047912
Ferguson, M. (1986, August 18). [Keynote speech]. Conference of the Association for Humanistic Psychology, San Diego, USA.
Fiedler, F. E. (1950). A comparison of the therapeutic relationship in psychoanalytic, nondirective and Adlerian therapy. *Journal of Consulting Psychology*, *14*(6), 436–445. https://doi.org/10.1037/h0054624
Fitzgerald, F. S. (2017). The crack-up. *Esquire*. https://www.esquire.com/lifestyle/a4310/the-crack-up/ (Original work published in 1936)
Flasher, B. (1983, November). A monkey speaks out. *Association for Humanistic Psychology Newsletter*, p. 19.
FMS Foundation. (1993). Scientific issues. *FMS Foundation Newsletter*, *2*(7), 1–15. http://www.fmsfonline.org/newsletters/fmsf_1993_july_v2_n7.pdf
Fonseca, A. H. L. (1983, October). Psicologia humanista e pedagogia do oprimido: Um dialogo possivel? [Humanistic psychology and pedagogy of the oppressed: A possible dialogue] [Conference presentation]. First Latin American Meeting on the Person-Centered Approach, Petropolis, RJ, Brazil.
Foucault, M. (1965). *Madness and civilization: A history of insanity in the age of reason*. Random House.
Freire, P. (1970). *Pedagogy of the oppressed*. Seabury Press.
Freire, P. (1979). *Conscientização* [Critical consciousness]. Cortez & Moraes.
Freire, P. (1980). *Education for critical consciousness*. Continuum.
Freire, P. (1981). Unpublished transcript of a talk given in Itaquaquecetuba, São Paulo, Brazil.
Freire, P. (1982). *A importância do ato de ler* [The importance of the act of reading]. Cortez & Moraes.
Freud, S. (1955). Group psychology and the analysis of the ego. In J. Strachey (Ed. & Trans.). *The standard edition of the complete psychological works of Sigmund Freud* (Vol. *18*, p. 110). Hogarth. (Original work published in 1920)
Friedan, B. (1963). *The feminine mystique*. W.W. Norton.
Friedman, M. S. (1985). *The healing dialogue in psychotherapy*. Jason Aronson.
Funtowicz, S. O., & Ravetz, J. (1990). *Uncertainty and quality in science for policy*. Kluwer.
Gadamer, H.-G. (1975). *Truth and method*. Crossroad.
Ganoe, H. W., & Kirwan, J. (1984). Magicians, scientists, and physics: The foot is quicker than the mouth. *The Skeptical Inquirer*, *8*(2), 133–137.
Gazzaniga, M. S. (1992). *Nature's mind: The biological roots of thinking, emotions, sexuality, language, and intelligence*. Basic Books.

Geertz, C. (1979). From the native's point of view: On the nature of anthropological understanding. In P. Rabinow & W. M. Sullivan (Eds.), *Interpretive social psychology* (pp. 225–241). University of California Press.
Gergen, K. J. (1991). *The saturated self: Dilemmas of identity in contemporary life*. Basic Books.
Gergen, K. J. (1994). Exploring the postmodern: Perils or potentials? *American Psychologist*, *49*(5), 412–414. https://doi.org/10.1037/0003-066X.49.5.412
Giddens, A. (1991). *Modernity and identity: Self and society in the late modern age*. Stanford University Press.
Gilligan, C. (1982). *In a different voice: Psychological theory and women's development*. Harvard University Press.
Gilligan, S. (1997). *The courage to love: Principals and practices of self-relations psychotherapy*. W. W. Norton.
Goble, F. G. (1970). *The third force: The psychology of Abraham Maslow*. Pocket.
Gone, J. P. (2022). Four principles for cultivating alternative cultural paradigms in psychology: Summary reflections on innovative contributions. *Journal of Humanistic Psychology*, *62*(4), 614–623. https://doi.org/10.1177/00221678211050725
Gordon, T., Grumman, D. L., Rogers, C. R., & Seeman, J. (1954). Developing a program of research in psychotherapy. In C. R. Rogers & R. F. Dymond (Eds.), *Psychotherapy and personality change* (pp. 12–34). University of Chicago Press.
Gore, A. (2009). *Our choice: A plan to stop the climate crisis*. Bloomsbury.
Gould, S. J. (1980). Sociobiology and the theory of natural selection. In G. W. Barlow & J. Silverberg (Eds.), *Sociobiology: Beyond nature/nurture? Reports, definitions and debate, AAAS selected symposium* (pp. 257–269). Westview Press.
Grawe, K., Donati, R., & Bernauer, F. (1997). *Psychotherapie im Wandel: Von der Konfession zur Profession* [Psychotherapy in transition: From speculation to science]. Hogrefe & Huber.
Greenson, R. R. (1960). Empathy and its vicissitudes. *International Journal of Psychoanalysis*, *41*, 418–583.
Greenspan, M. (1983). *A new approach to women and therapy: How psychotherapy fails women and what they can do about it*. McGraw Hill.
Grennell-Hawke, N., Tahu, N., Mutunga, N., & Tudor, K. (2018). Being Māori and Pākehā: Methodology and method in exploring cultural hybridity. *The Qualitative Report*, *23*(7), 1530–1546. https://doi.org/10.46743/2160-3715/2018.2934
Gribben, J., & Gribben, M. (2009). *James Lovelock: In search of Gaia*. Princeton University Press.
Guggenheim, D. (Director). (2006). *An inconvenient truth: A global warning*. Paramount.
Guisinger, S., & Blatt, J. S. (1994). Individuality and relatedness. *American Psychologist*, *49*(2), 104–111. https://doi.org/10.1037/0003-066X.49.2.104
Haldane, J. B. S. (1954). The origins of life. *New Biology*, *16*, 12–26.
Hanna, M. (2008). *An introduction to Kitbag: Building psychological capacity in powerful times*. https://www.internationalfuturesforum.com/reports/iff_kitbag_brochure.pdf
Hare-Mustin, R. T., & Marecek, J. (Eds.) (1990). *Making a difference: Psychology and the construction of gender*. Yale University Press.
Harman, J. I. (1990). Unconditional confidence as a facilitative pre-condition. In G. Leitaer, J. Rombauts, & R. Van Balen (Eds.), *Client-centered and experiential psychotherapy in the nineties* (pp. 251–268). University of Leuven Press.
Held, B. S. (1995). The real meaning of constructivism. *Journal of Constructivist Psychology*, *8*(4), 305–315. https://doi.org/10.1080/10720539508405911
Held, B. S. (1998). The many truths of postmodernist discourse. *Journal of Theoretical and Philosophical Psychology*, *18*(2), 193–217. https://doi.org/10.1037/h0091185

Hill, J. P. M. (2022). *Te whakatere i ngā awa e rua (Navigating the two rivers): A heuristic investigation of Māori identity as a student psychotherapist* [Master's dissertation, Auckland University of Technology]. Tuwhera Open Access Theses & Dissertations. https://hdl.handle.net/10292/15268

Hockney, D. (1988). *David Hockney: A retrospective*. Los Angeles County Museum of Art.

Hoffman, E. (Ed.) (1996). *Future visions: The unpublished papers of Abraham Maslow*. Sage.

Hoffman, L. (1988). A constructivist position for family therapy. *Irish Journal of Psychology, 9*(1), 110–129. https://doi.org/10.1080/03033910.1988.10557709

Horney, K. (1926). The flight from womanhood: The masculinity-complex in women, as viewed by men and by women. *The International Journal of Psychoanalysis, 7*, 324–339.

Hoshmand, L. T., & Martin, J. (Eds.) (1995). *Research as praxis: Lessons from programmatic research in therapeutic psychology*. Teachers College Press.

House, R., Kalisch, D., & Maidman, J. (Eds.) (2018). *Humanistic psychology: Current trends and future prospects*. Routledge.

Hughes, J. (2005, November 14–17). *Changing our minds: Electronic and chemical modification of cognition and emotion* [Conference presentation]. General Assembly of the World Academy of Arts and Sciences, Zagreb, Croatia.

Jacob, F. (1982). *The possible and the actual*. Pantheon.

Jacobson, N. (1995). The overselling of therapy. *Family Therapy Networker, 19*(2), 40–46.

James, W. (1896). *The will to believe: And other essays in popular philosophy*. Longmans, Green, and Co.

Jones, E. (1974). Social class and psychotherapy: A critical review of research. *Psychiatry: Journal for the Study of Interpersonal Processes, 37*(4), 307–320.

Jones, R. L. (1991). *Black psychology* (3rd ed.). Cobb & Henry.

Jordan, J. V., Kaplan, A. G., Miller, J. B., Stiver, I. P., & Surrey, J. L. (1991). *Women's growth in connection: Writings from the Stone Center*. The Guilford Press.

Kanter, R. M. (1975). Women and the structure of organizations: Explorations in theory and behavior. In M. Millman & R. M. Kanter (Eds.), *Another voice: Feminist perspectives on social life and social science* (pp. 34–74). Anchor/Doubleday.

Kaplan, R. D. (1996). *The ends of the earth: A journey to the frontiers of anarchy*. Vintage.

Kearney, A. (1996). *Counselling, class and politics: Undeclared influences in therapy*. PCCS Books.

Kegan, R. (1994). *In over our heads: The mental demands of modern life*. Harvard University Press.

Keller, E. F. (1985). *Reflections on gender and science*. Yale University Press.

Kelley, E. (2005). *Powerful times: Rising to the challenge of our uncertain world*. Wharton School Publishing.

Kelly, G. A. (1969). *Clinical psychology and personality: The selected papers of George Kelly*. Wiley.

Keyes, K. Jr. (1982). *The hundredth monkey*. Vision Books.

King, A., & Schneider, B. (1991). *The first global revolution: A report by The Council of the Club of Rome*. Pantheon Books.

Kintisch, E. (2009, March 14). *DARPA to explore geoengineering*. Science Insider. https://www.science.org/content/article/darpa-explore-geoengineering

Kirschenbaum, H. (1979). *On becoming Carl Rogers*. Dell.

Kirschenbaum, H., & Henderson, V. L. (Eds.) (1989). *Carl Rogers: Dialogues*. Houghton Mifflin.

Koestler, A. (1987). *Janus: A summing up*. Random House.

Kohut, H. (1959). Introspection, empathy, and psychoanalysis: An examination of the relationship between mode of observation and theory. In P. H. Ornstein (Ed.), *The search for self* (pp. 205–232). International Universities Press.

Kohut, H. (1984). *How does analysis cure?* University of Chicago Press.

Kramer, R. (1995). Carl Rogers meets Otto Rank—and beyond. *Journal of Humanistic Psychology*, *35*(4), 54–110. https://doi.org/10.1177/00221678950354005
Kristeva, J. (1980). *Desire in language*. Columbia University Press.
Kuhl, V. (1994). The managed care revolution: Implications for humanistic psychotherapy. *Journal of Humanistic Psychology*, *34*(2), 62–81. https://doi.org/10.1177/0022167894034 2005
Kuhn, T. S. (1970). *The structure of scientific revolutions* (2nd ed.). University of Chicago Press.
Laing, R. D. (1967). *The politics of experience*. Ballantine Books.
Lakoff, G. (1987). *Women, fire and dangerous things: What categories reveal about the mind*. University of Chicago Press.
Lambert, M. J. (1992). Implications of outcome research for psychotherapy integration. In J. C. Norcross & M. R. Goldfried (Eds.), *Handbook of psychotherapy integration* (pp. 94–129). Basic Books.
Laqueur, T. (1990). *Making sex: Body and gender from the Greeks to Freud*. Harvard University Press.
Lasch, C. (1979). *The culture of narcissism: American life in an age of diminishing expectations*. Norton.
Leicester, G., & O'Hara, M. (2009). *10 things to do in a conceptual emergency*. Triarchy Press.
Leicester, G., & O'Hara, M. (2022). *Spaces for growth*. Triarchy Press.
Leonardi, J. (2006). Self-giving and self-actualizing: Christianity and the person-centred approach. In J. Moore & C. Purton (Eds.), *Spirituality and counselling: Experiential and theoretical perspectives* (pp. 204–217). PCCS Books.
Levin, D. M. (1987a). *Pathologies of the modern self: Postmodern studies on narcissism, schizophrenia, and depression*. New York University Press.
Levin, D. M. (1987b). Psychopathology in the epoch of nihilism. In *Pathologies of the modern self: Postmodern studies on narcissism, schizophrenia, and depression* (pp. 21–83). New York University Press.
Levy, S. T. (1985). Empathy and psychoanalytic technique. *Journal of the American Psychoanalytic Association*, *33*(2), 352–378. https://doi.org/10.1177/000306518503300204
Loftus, E. F. (1979). *Eyewitness testimony*. Harvard University Press.
Luborsky, L. (1989). Who is helped by psychotherapy? *Harvard Mental Health Letter*, *7*(2), 4.
Luborsky, L., Singer, B., & Luborsky, L. (1975). Comparative studies of psychotherapies: Is it true that 'everyone has won, and all must have prizes'? *Archives of General Psychiatry*, *32*(8), 995–1008. https://doi.org/10.1001/archpsyc.1975.01760260059004
Lucretius. (1951). *On the nature of things* (R. E. Latham, Trans. & Ed.). Penguin.
Maccoby, E. E., & Jacklin, C. N. (1975). *The psychology of sex differences*. Stanford University Press.
MacIntyre, A. (1981). *After virtue: A study in moral theory*. Notre Dame Press.
Manicas, P. T., & Secord, P. F. (1983). Implications for psychology of the new philosophy of science. *American Psychologist*, *38*(4), 399–413. https://doi.org/10.1037/0003-066X.38.4.399
Mannheim, K. (1997). *Ideology and utopia: Collected works of Karl Manheim. Volume I*. Routledge. (Original work published in 1936)
Marien, M. (1983). The transformation as sandbox syndrome. *Journal of Humanistic Psychology*, *23*(1), 7–15. https://doi.org/10.1177/0022167883231002
Maslow, A. H. (1962). *Toward a psychology of being*. D. Van Nostrand Co.
Maslow, A. (1966). *The psychology of science: A reconnaissance*. Harper & Row.
May, R. (1969). *Love and will*. Delta.
May, R. (1982). The problem of evil: An open letter to Carl Rogers. *Journal of Humanistic Psychology*, *22*(3), 10–21.

McCann, M., & Tudor, K. (2022). Unintentional racial microaggressions and the social unconscious. *International Journal of Applied Psychoanalytic Studies*, *19*(2), 202–216. https://doi.org/10.1002/aps.1753
Meadows, D. (2005). Dancing with systems. In M. K. Stone & Z. Barlow (Eds.), *Ecological literacy: Educating our children for a sustainable world* (pp. 193–205). Sierra Club Books.
Meadows, D. H., Meadows, D. L., Randers, J., & Behrens, I. I. I. (1974). *The limits to growth: A report for the club of Rome's project on the predicament of mankind*. Potomac Associates.
Mearns, D. (1994). *Developing person-centred counseling*. SAGE.
Mearns, D. J., & McLead, J. (1984). A person-centered approach to research. In R. F. Levant & J. Shlien (Eds.), *Client-centered therapy and the person-centered approach: New directions in theory, research and practice* (pp. 370–389). Praeger.
Melzack, R. (1990). Phantom limbs. *Scientific American*, *266*, 120–126. https://www.scientificamerican.com/article/phantom-limbs-2006-09/
Michael, D. N. (2000). Some observations with regard to a missing elephant. *Journal of Humanistic Psychology*, *40*(1), 8–16. https://doi.org/10.1177/0022167800401002
Miller, R. B. (1992). Introduction: Philosophical problems of psychology. In R. B. Miller (Ed.), *The restoration of dialogue: Readings in the philosophy of clinical psychology* (pp. 31–33). American Psychological Association.
Miller, S., Hubble, M., & Duncan, B. (1995). No more bells and whistles. *Family Therapy Networker*, *19*(2), 52–58.
Ministry of Education, Singapore. (2021). *Our mission and vision*. https://www.moe.gov.sg/about-us/our-mission-and-vision
Moustakas, C. E. (1990). *Heuristic research: Design, methodology, and applications*. Sage.
Narváez, D. (2014). *Neurobiology and the development of human morality: Evolution, culture, and wisdom*. W. W. Norton & Company.
Narváez, D., & Bradshaw, G. A. (2023). *The evolved nest: Nature's way of raising children and creating connected communities*. North Atlantic Books.
Nathan, O., & Norden, H. (Eds.) (1960). *Einstein on peace*. Schocken Books.
National Commission on Terrorist Attacks Against the United States. (2004). *The 9/11 Commission report: Final report of the National Commission on Terrorist Attacks Upon the United States (9/11 Report)*. GovInfo. https://www.govinfo.gov/app/details/GPO-911REPORT
Neimeyer, G. J. (1996). Changes in attitudes, not in the platitudes. *Contemporary Psychology*, *41*(7), 697–698.
Neimeyer, R. A., & Stewart, A. E. (2000). Constructivist and narrative psychotherapies. In C. R. Snyder & R. E. Ingram (Eds.), *Handbook of psychotherapy* (pp. 337–357). Wiley.
Neville, B., & Tudor, K. (2024). *Eco-centred therapy: Revisioning person-centred psychology for a living world*. Routledge.
Newman, F. L., & Tejada, M. J. (1996). The need for research that is designed to support decisions in the delivery of mental health services. *American Psychologist*, *51*(10), 1040–1049. https://doi.org/10.1037/0003-066X.51.10.1040
Newsline. (1996). *APA Monitor*, *27*(9), 10.
Nicolescu, B. (2002). *Manifesto of transdisciplinarity*. State University of New York Press.
Nisbett, R. E. (2003). *The geography of thought*. Free Press.
Nowotny, H. (2003). *The potential of transdisciplinarity*. Interdisciplines. www.interdisciplines.org
NPR News Hour. (2010, October 7). *Flooding, Taliban create uphill battle to educate Pakistani girls*. https://www.pbs.org/newshour/show/flooding-taliban-create-uphill-battle-to-educate-pakistani-girls
Nuffield Trust. (1999). *Policy futures for UK health: Pathfinder*. https://www.nuffieldtrust.org.uk/sites/default/files/2017-01/policy-futures-consultation-web-final.pdf

Obama, B. (2006). *Audacity of hope*. Random House.
Obeyesekere, G. (1985). Depression, Buddhism, and the work of culture in Sri Lanka. In A. Kleinman & B. Good (Eds.), *Culture and depression* (pp. 134–152). University of California Press.
O'Hanlon, W. H. (1993). Possibility therapy: From iatrogenic injury to iatrogenic healing. In S. Gilligan & R. H. Prices (Eds.), *Therapeutic conversations* (pp. 3–17). W.W. Norton.
O'Hara, M. (1973, February 2). The right to abortion. A personal, moral decision. *The Oberlin Review*, *101*(27), 3.
O'Hara, M. (1976). *Different paths: Journeys of sexual self-discovery* [Unpublished doctoral dissertation]. Union Graduate School.
O'Hara, M. M. (1982). Person-centered approach as conscientização. *Journey*, *2*(2).
O'Hara, M. M. (1983a). A hundredth monkey myth. *Association for Humanistic Psychology Newsletter*, November, 20–21.
O'Hara, M. (1983b). Patterns of awareness: Consciousness and the group mind. *The Gestalt Journal*, *6*(2), 103–116.
O'Hara, M. M. (1984a). Person-centered Gestalt: Towards a holistic synthesis. In R. F. Levant & J. M. Shlien (Eds.), *Client-centered therapy and the person-centered approach: New directions in theory, research and practice* (pp. 203–221). Praeger.
O'Hara, M. M. (1984b). Reflections on Sheldrake, Wilber, and 'new science'. *Journal of Humanistic Psychology*, *24*(2), 116–120. https://doi.org/10.1177/0022167884242007
O'Hara, M. (1985a). Comment on Carl Rogers's 'Toward a more human science of the person'. *Journal of Humanistic Psychology*, *25*(4), 25–30. https://doi.org/10.1177/0022167885254003
O'Hara, M. (1985b). Of myths and monkeys: A critical look at a theory of critical mass. *Journal of Humanistic Psychology*, *25*(1), 61–78. https://doi.org/10.1177/0022167885251004
O'Hara, M. (1986). Heuristic inquiry as psychotherapy: The client-centered approach. *Person-Centered Review*, *1*(2), 172–184.
O'Hara, M. M. (1987, November). *Carl Rogers: Scientist and mystic* [Paper presentation]. Symposium honouring Carl Rogers, University of California Extension, Los Angeles.
O'Hara, M. (1988). Science, pseudoscience and mythmongering. In R. Basil (Ed.), *Not necessarily the new age* (pp. 145–164). Prometheus.
O'Hara, M. (1989a). A new age reflection in the magic mirror of science. *Skeptical Inquirer*, *13*(4), 368–374.
O'Hara, M. (1989b). Constructing emancipatory realities: Towards a feminist voice in humanistic psychology. *AHP Perspective*, August/September.
O'Hara, M. (1989c). Person-centered approach as conscientização: The works of Carl Rogers and Paulo Freire. *Journal of Humanistic Psychology*, *29*(1), 11–36. https://doi.org/10.1177/0022167889291002
O'Hara, M. (1989d). When I use the term humanistic psychology…. *Journal of Humanistic Psychology*, *29*(2), 263–273. https://doi.org/10.1177/0022167889292009
O'Hara, M. (1992a). If not now, when? Values for a pluralistic world. *Vital Speeches of the Day*, 59(2), 41–45.
O'Hara, M. (1992b). Relational humanism: A psychology for a pluralistic world. *The Humanistic Psychologist*, *20*(2–3), 439–446. https://doi.org/10.1080/08873267.1992.9986808
O'Hara, M. (1995a). Carl Rogers: Scientist or mystic? *Journal of Humanistic Psychology*, *35*(4), 40–53.
O'Hara, M. (1995b). Constructing emancipatory realities: Towards a feministic voice in humanistic psychology. In W. T. Anderson (Ed.), *The truth about truth: De-constructing and reconstructing the postmodern world* (pp. 151–155). Jeremy Tarcher.
O'Hara, M. (1995c). Is it time for clinical psychology to deconstruct constructivism? *Journal of Constructivist Psychology*, *8*(4), 293–303. https://doi.org/10.1080/10720539508405910

O'Hara, M. (1995d). Streams: On becoming a postmodern person. In M. Suhd (Ed.), *Positive regard: Carl Rogers and other notables he influenced* (pp. 105–155). Science and Behavior Books.
O'Hara, M. (1996a). Divided we stand. *Family Therapy Networker, 20*(5), 46–53.
O'Hara, M. (1996b). Rogers and Sylvia: A feminist analysis. In B. A. Farber, D. C. Brink, & P. M. Raskin (Eds.), *The psychotherapy of Carl Rogers: Cases and commentary* (pp. 284–300). Guilford Press.
O'Hara, M. (1997a). Emancipatory therapeutic practice in a turbulent transmodern era: A work of retrieval. *Journal of Humanistic Psychology, 37*(3), 7–33. https://doi.org/10.1177/00221678970373002
O'Hara, M. (1997b). Relational empathy: From egocentric modernism to socio-centric postmodernism. In A. C. Bohart & L. S. Greenberg (Eds.), *Empathy reconsidered: New directions in psychotherapy* (pp. 295–320). American Psychological Association.
O'Hara, M. (1998). Gestalt therapy as an emancipatory psychology for a transmodern world. *Gestalt Review, 2*(2), 154–168. https://doi.org/10.2307/44390671
O'Hara, M. (1999). Moments of eternity: Carl Rogers and the contemporary demand for brief therapy. In I. Fairhurst (Ed.), *Women writing in the person-centred approach* (pp. 63–77). PCCS Books.
O'Hara, M. (2002). Moments of eternity: What Carl Rogers has to offer brief therapists. In J. K. Zeig (Ed.), *Brief therapy: Lasting impressions* (pp. 337–366). The Milton H. Erickson Foundation Press.
O'Hara, M. (2008). Endorsement. In K. Tudor (Ed.), *Brief person-centred therapies*. Sage.
O'Hara, M. (2010). Another inconvenient truth and the developmental role for psychology in a threatened world. *The Humanistic Psychologist, 38*(2), 101–119. https://doi.org/10.1080/08873267.2010.485915
O'Hara, M. (2018, July 10). *Carpe diem: A transformative turn for person-centered practice?* [Keynote presentation]. 13th World Conference for Person-Centered & Experiential Psychotherapy & Counseling, Vienna.
O'Hara, M. (2024). Social change and cultural transformation. In G. Di Malta, M. Cooper, M. O'Hara, Y. Gololob, & S. Stevens (Eds.), *The handbook of person-centred psychotherapy and counselling* (3rd ed.). Bloomsbury.
O'Hara, M., & Anderson, W. T., (1996, September/October). Divided we stand. *Family Therapy Networker.*
O'Hara, M., & Leicester, G. (2012). *Dancing at the edge: Competence, culture and organization for the 21st century*. Triarchy Press.
O'Hara, M., & Leicester, G. (2019). *Dancing at the edge: Competence, culture and organization for the 21st century* (2nd ed.). Triarchy Press.
O'Hara, M. M., & Wood, J. K. (1983). Consciousness and the group mind. *The Gestalt Journal, 6*(2), 103–116.
Osava, M. (1998, January). *In Brazil, overcrowding, poverty lead to a wave of suicides*. The Black World Today.
Pascual-Leone, J. (1989). Reflections on life-span intelligence, consciousness, and ego-development. In C. N. Alexander & E. J. Langer (Eds.), *Higher stages of human development* (pp. 258–286). Oxford University Press.
Peat, F. D. (2002). *From certainty to uncertainty: The story of science and ideas in the twentieth century*. Joseph Henry Press.
Peat, F. D. (2007). From certainty to uncertainty: Thought, theory and action in a postmodern world. *Futures, 39*(8), 920–929. https://doi.org/10.1016/j.futures.2007.03.007
Pérez Foster, R., Moskowitz, M., & Javier, R. A. (Eds.) (1996). *Reaching across boundaries of culture and class: Widening the scope of psychotherapy*. Jason Aronson.
Plum, A. (1981). Communication as skill: A critique and alternative proposal. *Journal of Humanistic Psychology, 21*(4), 3–19. https://doi.org/10.1177/002216788102100402

Polanyi, M. (1958). *Personal knowledge: Towards a post-critical philosophy*. University of Chicago Press.
Polanyi, M. (1969). *Knowing and being*. University of Chicago Press.
Polkinghorne, D. (1983). *Methodology for human sciences: Systems of inquiry*. State University of New York Press.
Popper, K. (1972). *Objective knowledge: An evolutionary approach*. (Original work published in 1967)
Potterfield, T. A. (1999). *The business of employee empowerment: Democracy and ideology in the workplace*. Quorum.
Rabasca, L. (1999). I'm okay and you're okay, but not sure about Y2K. *APA Monitor*, *31*(1), 1.
Raskin, P. M. (1996). Introductory comments. In B. A. Farber, D. C. Brink, & P. M. Raskin (Eds.), *The psychotherapy of Carl Rogers: Cases and commentary* (pp. 133–141). Guilford Press.
Raskin, J. D., & Leitner, L. M. (2010, August 12–15). Bad-mouthing talk therapy for fun and profit. In B. D. Robbins (Chair), *Science and politics of the APS accreditation initiative—a cross-divisional response* [Symposium]. American Psychological Association 118th Annual Convention, San Diego, CA, United States.
Raskin, N. J., & Rogers, C. R. (1989). Person-centered therapy. In R. J. Corsini & D. Wedding (Eds.), *Current psychotherapies* (pp. 155–194). F. E. Peacock Publishers.
Ray, P. H. (1996). The rise of integral culture. *Noetic Sciences Review*, *37*, 3–13.
Ray, P. H., & Anderson, S. R. (2001). *The cultural creatives: How 50 million people are changing the world*. Crown Publishing.
Rieff, P. (1966). *The triumph of the therapeutic: Uses of faith after Freud*. Harper & Row.
Rogers, C. R. (1939). *The clinical treatment of the problem child*. Houghton Mifflin.
Rogers, C. R. (1942). *Counseling and psychotherapy: Newer concepts in practice*. Houghton Mifflin.
Rogers, C. R. (1951). *Client-centered therapy*. Houghton Mifflin.
Rogers, C. R. (1954). *Psychotherapy and personality change*. University of Chicago Press.
Rogers, C. R. (1957). The necessary and sufficient conditions for therapeutic personality change. *Journal of Consulting Psychology*, *21*(2), 95–103. https://doi.org/10.1037/h0045357
Rogers, C. R. (1959). A theory of therapy, personality, and interpersonal relationships, as developed in the client-centered framework. In S. Koch (Ed.), *Psychology: A study of a science* (pp. 184–256). McGraw Hill.
Rogers, C. R. (1961). *On becoming a person*. Houghton Mifflin.
Rogers, C. R. (1965). Psychology and teacher training. In D. B. Gowan & C. Richardson (Eds.), *Five fields and teacher education*. Project One Publications, Cornell University.
Rogers, C. R. (1967a). Dealing with breakdowns in communication—Interpersonal and intergroup. In *On becoming a person: A therapist's view of psychotherapy* (pp. 329–337). Constable. (Original work published in 1952)
Rogers, C. R. (1967b). *On becoming a person: A therapist's view of psychotherapy*. Constable. (Original work published in 1961)
Rogers, C. R. (1969). *Freedom to learn*. Charles E. Merrill.
Rogers, C. R. (1970). *Carl Rogers on encounter groups*. Harper & Row.
Rogers, C. R. (1972). *Becoming partners*. Dell.
Rogers, C. R. (1977). *Carl Rogers on personal power*. Delacorte.
Rogers, C. R. (1978). The formative tendency. *Journal of Humanistic Psychology*, *18*(1), 23–26. https://doi.org/10.1177/002216787801800103
Rogers, C. R. (1983). *Freedom to learn for the 80s*. Charles E. Merrill.
Rogers, C. R. (1985). Towards a more human science of the person. *Journal of Humanistic Psychology*, *25*(4), 7–24. https://doi.org/10.1177/0022167885254002

Rogers, C. R. (1986a). Rogers, Kohut, and Erickson: A personal perspective on some similarities and differences. *Person-Centered Review, 1*(2), 125–140.

Rogers, C. R. (1986b). The Rust workshop: A personal overview. *Journal of Humanistic Psychology, 26*(3), 23–45. https://doi.org/10.1177/0022167886263003

Rogers, C. R. (1995a). In retrospect: Forty-six years. In *A way of being* (pp. 46–69). Houghton Mifflin. (Original work published in 1974)

Rogers, C. R. (1995b). *A way of being*. Houghton Mifflin. (Original work published in 1980)

Rogers, C. R., & Dymond, R. F. (Eds.) (1954). *Psychotherapy and personality change: Coordinated research studies in the client-centered approach*. The University of Chicago Press.

Rogers, C. R., & Roethlisberger, F. J. (1952). Barriers and gateways to communication. *Harvard Business Review, 30*(4), 28–34.

Rogers, C. R., & Russell, D. E. (2002). *Carl Rogers, the quiet revolutionary: An oral history*. Penmarin Books.

Rogers, C. R., & Sanford, R. C. (1989). Client-centered psychotherapy. In H. I. Kaplan & B. J. Sadock (Eds.), *Comprehensive textbook of psychiatry* (pp. 1482–1501). Williams & Wilkins.

Rogers, N. (2000). *The creative connection: Expressive arts as healing*. PCCS Books. (Original work published in 1993)

Rogers, N. (2011). *The creative connection for groups: Person-centered expressive arts for healing and social change*. Science and Behavior Books.

Rogers, N., Tudor, K., Embleton Tudor, L., & Keemar, K. (2012). Person-centred expressive arts therapy: A theoretical encounter. *Person-Centered & Experiential Psychotherapies, 11*(1), 31–47. https://doi.org.10.1080/14779757.2012.656407

Roland, A. (1988). *In search of self in India and Japan: Towards a cross-cultural psychology*. Princeton University Press.

Rollins, H. E. (Ed.) (1958). *Keats J.: The letters of John Keats. Vol. 1*. Harvard University Press.

Romanyshyn, R. D. (1982). *Psychological life: From science to metaphor*. University of Texas Press.

Rosenau, J. N. (1990). *Turbulence in world politics: A theory of change and continuity*. Princeton University Press.

Roszak, T. (1981). In search of the miraculous: Science joins the occult. *Harper's, 262*, 54–62.

Rowe, E. C., & MacIsaacs, D. S. (1991). *Empathic attunement*. Jason Aronson Inc.

Ruddick, S. (1980). Maternal thinking. *Feminist Studies, 6*(2), 342–367. https://doi.org/10.2307/3177749

Salovey, P. (2005, August 27). Beyond caricature [speech]. *Yale Bulletin & Calendar, 34*(2). http://archives.news.yale.edu/v34.n2/story3.html

Sarason, S. B. (1981). An asocial psychology and a misdirected clinical psychology. *American Psychologist, 36*(8), 827–836. https://doi.org/10.1037/0003-066X.36.8.827

Schein, E. H. (1985). *Organizational culture and leadership*. Jossey-Bass.

Schmid, P. F. (1997). Prospects on further developments in the person-centered approach. In N. Andrade (Ed.), *IV international conference on client-centered therapy and experiential psychotherapy* (p. 30). University Católica Portuguesa.

Schmid, P. (1998). On becoming a person-centred approach: A person-centred understanding of the person. In B. Thorne & E. Lambers (Eds.), *Person-centred therapy: A European perspective* (pp. 38–52). Sage.

Schmid, P. F., & O'Hara, M. (2013). Working with groups. In M. Cooper, M. O'Hara, P. F. Schmid, & A. Bohart (Eds.), *The handbook of person-centred psychotherapy and counselling* (2nd ed., pp. 223–236). Palgrave Macmillan.

Schofer, E., & Meyer, J. W. (2005). The worldwide expansion of higher education. *American Sociological Review, 70*(6), 898–920.

Seeman, J. (1954). Counselor judgements of therapeutic progress and outcome. In C. R. Rogers & R. F. Dymond (Eds.), *Psychotherapy and personality change* (pp. 196–166). University of Chicago Press.

Segrera, A. S. (Ed.) (1984). *Proceedings of the first international forum on the person-centered approach*. Universidad Iberamericana.

Seligman, M. E. P. (1995). The effectiveness of psychotherapy: The consumer reports study. *American Psychologist*, *50*(12), 965–974. https://doi.org/10.1037/0003-066X.50.12.965

Senge, P. M. (1990). *The fifth discipline: The art and practice of the learning organization*. Currency Doubleday.

Sève, L. (1978). *Man in Marxist theory and the psychology of personality* (J. McGreal, Trans.). The Harvester Press. (Original work published in 1974)

Shakespeare, W. (2021). *As you like it* (M. Hattaway, Ed., 3rd ed.). Cambridge University Press. (Original work published in 1599)

Shepherd, J. (2009). *Geoengineering the climate: Science, governance and uncertainty*. https://royalsociety.org/topics-policy/publications/2009/geoengineering-climate/

Shlien, J. M. (1957). *An experimental investigation of time-limited, brief, client-centered therapy* [Unpublished doctoral dissertation]. University of Chicago.

Shlien, J. (1997). Empathy in psychotherapy: A vital mechanism? Yes. Therapist's conceit? All too often. By itself enough? No. In A. Bohart & L. S. Greenberg (Eds.), *Empathy reconsidered: New directions in psychotherapy* (pp. 63–80). American Psychological Association.

Showalter, E. (1985). *The female malady: Women, madness, and English culture, 1830–1980*. Viking Penguin.

Shweder, R. A. (1991). *Thinking through cultures: Expeditions in cultural psychology*. Harvard University Press.

Shweder, R. A., & Bourne, E. (1982). Does the concept of the person vary cross-culturally? In A. J. Marsella & G. White (Eds.), *Cultural conceptions of mental health and therapy* (pp. 97–137). Reidel.

Singer, B. F., & Benassi, V. A. (1980–1981). Fooling some of the people all of the time. *The Skeptical Inquirer*, *5*(2), 17–24. https://skepticalinquirer.org/1981/01/fooling-some-of-the-people-all-of-the-time/

Smason, I. (1996). Letter to the editor. *APA Monitor*, *27*(8), 4.

Smith, B. M. (1994). Selfhood at risk: Postmodern perils and the perils of postmodernism. *American Psychologist*, *49*(5), 404–411. https://doi.org/10.1037/0003-066X.49.5.405

Smith, D. E. (1991). *The conceptual practices of power: A feminist sociology of knowledge*. Northeastern University Press.

Smith, P. (2004). *The quiet crisis: How higher education is failing America*. Anker Publishing.

Speierer, G.-W. (1990). Toward a specific illness concept of client-centered therapy. In G. Lietaer, J. Rombauts, & R. Van Balen (Eds.), *Client-centered and experiential psychotherapy in the nineties* (pp. 337–359). Leuven University Press.

Standal, S. W., & van der Veen, F. (1957). Length of therapy in relation to counselor estimates of personal integration and other case variables. *Journal of Consulting Psychology*, *21*(1), 1–9. https://doi.org/10.1037/h0043038

Stark, M. (1999). *Modes of therapeutic action: Enhancement of knowledge, provision of experience, and engagement in relationship*. Jason Aronson.

Stavrianos, L. (1976). *The promise of the coming dark age*. W. H. Freeman.

Steele, K. E. (2014). *Sacred space: Embracing the spiritual in person-centred therapy*. CreateSpace Independent Publishing Platform.

Steiner, C. M. (1974). *Scripts people live: Transactional analysis of life scripts*. Grove Press.

Steiner, C. M. (1975a). Power: Part I. *Issues in Radical Therapy*, *3*(3), 7–12.

Steiner, C. M. (1975b). Power: Part II. *Issues in Radical Therapy*, *4*(1), 20–22.

Steiner, C. M. (1981). *The other side of power.* Grove Press.

Stricker, G. (1996). How many psychotherapies? *Contemporary Psychology, 41*(7), 656–657.

Suhd, M. M.(Ed.). (1995). *Positive regard: Carl Rogers and other notables he influenced.* Science & Behavior Books.

Surrey, J. L. (1991). The self-in-relation: A theory of women's development. In J. V. Jordan, A. G. Kaplan, J. B. Miller, I. P. Stiver, & J. L. Surrey (Eds.), *Women's growth in connection: Writings from the Stone Center* (pp. 51–66). The Guilford Press.

Szaz, T. (1970). *The manufacture of madness.* Harper & Row.

Taft, J. (1973). *Dynamics of therapy in a controlled relationship.* Peter Smith. (Original work published in 1933)

Taylor, C. (1989). *Sources of the self: The making of the modern identity.* Harvard University Press.

Taylor, C. (1990). *The ethics of authenticity.* Harvard University Press.

Thompson, D. (1917). *On growth and form.* Cambridge University Press.

Thompson, J. W. (1920). The aftermath of the Black Death and the aftermath of the Great War. *American Journal of Sociology, 26,* 565–570.

Thorne, B. (1991). *Person-centred counselling: Therapeutic and spiritual dimensions.* Whurr.

Thorne, B. (1997, July 7). *Congruence: The cost of transparency* [Conference presentation]. IV International Conference on Client-Centered and Experiential Psychotherapy, Lisbon, Portugal.

Thorne, B. (1998). *Person-centred counselling and Christian spirituality: The secular and the holy.* Whurr.

Thorne, B. (2002). *The mystical power of person-centred therapy: Hope beyond despair.* Whurr.

Toril, M. (Ed.) (1987). *French feminist thought: A reader.* Blackwell.

Totton, N. (1999). The baby and the bathwater: 'Professionalisation' in psychotherapy and counselling. *British Journal of Guidance and Counselling, 27*(3), 313–324.

Toulmin, S. (1990). *Cosmopolis: The hidden agenda of modernity.* Free Press.

Toulmin, S., & Leary, D. (1994). The cult of empiricism in psychology and beyond. In S. Koch & D. Leary (Eds.), *A century of psychology as a science* (pp. 594–617). American Psychological Association.

Toynbee, A. (1972). *A study of history* (abridged ed.). Oxford University Press.

Truax, C. (1961). A scale for the measurement of accurate empathy. *Psychiatric Institute Bulletin, 1*(12), 10.

Truax, C. B., & Carkhuff, R. R. (1967). *Toward effective counseling and psychotherapy: Training and practice.* Aldine Publishing Co.

Tuchman, B. W. (1978). *A distant mirror: The calamitous 14th century.* Ballantine.

Tudor, K. (1997). Being at dis-ease with ourselves: Alienation and psychotherapy. *Changes, 15*(2), 143–150.

Tudor, K. (2000). The case of the lost conditions. *Counselling, 11*(1), 33–37.

Tudor, K. (Ed.) (2008). *Brief person-centred therapies.* Sage.

Tudor, K. (2010a). Building bridges across troubled waters: Regarding humanistic and psychodynamic psychotherapies. *Forum* [The Journal of the New Zealand Association of Psychotherapists], *15,* 8–25.

Tudor, K. (2010b). Person-centred relational therapy: An organismic perspective. *Person-Centered & Experiential Psychotherapies, 9*(1), 52–68. https://doi.org/10.1080/14779757.2010.9688504

Tudor, K. (2011). Rogers' therapeutic conditions: A relational conceptualization. *Person-Centered & Experiential Psychotherapies, 10*(3), 165–180. https://doi.org/10.1080/14779757.2011.599513

Tudor, K. (2015). Humanistic psychology: A critical counterculture. In I. Parker (Ed.), *Handbook of critical psychology* (pp. 127–136). Routledge.
Tudor, K. (2017). Alienation and psychotherapy. In K. Tudor (Ed.), *Conscience and critic: The selected works of Keith Tudor* (pp. 58–70). Routledge.
Tudor, K. (2018a). Aliens, alienists—And alienation: A critical and cross-cultural perspective on psychopathology. *The Journal of Critical Psychology, Counselling and Psychotherapy, 18*(4), 228–246.
Tudor, K. (2018b). From humanism to humanistic psychology and back again. In R. House, D. Kalisch, & J. Maidman (Eds.), *Humanistic psychology: Current trends and future prospects* (pp. 222–236). Routledge.
Tudor, K. (2018c). *Psychotherapy: A critical examination*. PCCS Books.
Tudor, K. (Ed.) (2020a). *Claude Steiner, emotional activist: The life and work of Claude Michel Steiner*. Routledge.
Tudor, K. (2020b). *The book of Evan: The work and life of Evan McAra Sherrard* (E-book edition; K. Tudor, Ed.). Tuwhera Open Access Books. https://ojs.aut.ac.nz/tuwhera-open-monographs/catalog/book/2 (Original work published in 2017)
Tudor, K. (2021). He tangata, he tangata, he tangata: A humanistic relational approach to a people-centred and experiential therapy in and of Aotearoa New Zealand. In *20/20 vision, 2020* (pp. 139–152). Tuwhera Open Access Books. https://ojs.aut.ac.nz/tuwhera-open-monographs/catalog/book/6
Tudor, K. (2022a). Person-centred psychotherapy. *Ata: Journal of Psychotherapy Aotearoa New Zealand, 26*(1), 11–37. https://doi.org/10.9791/ajpanz.2022.02
Tudor, K. (2022b). There and back again: Re-envisioning 'relationship therapy' as the center of a contemporary, cultural, and contextual person-centred therapy. *Person-Centered & Experiential Psychotherapies, 21*(2), 188–206. https://doi.org/10.1080/14779757.2022.2066562
Tudor, K. (2025). *Transactional analysis proper—And improper: Selected and new papers*. Routledge.
Tudor, K., & Cornelius-White, J. (Eds.). (2025). Bernie Neville: Contributions and legacy [Special issue] *Person-Centered & Experiential Psychotherapies*.
Tudor, K., & Rodgers, B. (2023). Can we be of help? Cultural considerations regarding personal growth, relationships, therapy, and life. *Person-Centered & Experiential Psychotherapies*. https://doi.org/10.1080/14779757.2023.2166576
Tudor, K., & Worrall, M. (2006). *Person-centred therapy: A clinical philosophy*. Routledge.
United Nations. (1948). *Universal Declaration of Human Rights*. https://www.un.org/en/about-us/universal-declaration-of-human-rights
Van Belle, H. A. (1980). *Basic intent and therapeutic approach of Carl R. Rogers: A study of his view of man in relation to his view of therapy, personality and interpersonal relations*. Wedge Publishing Foundation.
Van Belle, H. A. (1990). Rogers' later move towards mysticism: Implications for client-centered therapy. In G. Lietare, J. Rombauts, & R. Van Balen (Eds.), *Client-centered and experiential psychotherapy in the nineties* (pp. 47–58). Leuven University Press.
van der Ploeg, J. D. (1993). Potatoes and knowledge. In M. Hobart (Ed.), *An anthropological critique of development: The growth of ignorance* (pp. 209–227). Routledge.
Van Kalmthout, M. (1995). The religious dimensions of Rogers' work. *Journal of Humanistic Psychology, 35*(4), 23–39. https://doi.org/10.1177/00221678950354003
Vanaerschot, G. (1990). The process of empathy: Holding and letting go. In G. Lietauer, J. Rombauts, & R. Van Balen (Eds.), *Client and experiential psychotherapy in the nineties* (pp. 267–293). Leuven University Press.
VandenBos, G. R. (Ed.) (1996). Outcome assessment of psychotherapy [special issue]. *American Psychologist, 51*(10). https://doi.org/10.1037/0003-066X.51.10.1005

Vista Hill. (1995). *All staff.* [Unpublished memorandum].

Wakefield, J. C. (1996). DSM-IV: Are we making diagnostic progress? *Contemporary Psychology, 41*(7), 646–652. https://doi.org/10.1037/004602

Wallerstein, R. S. (1989). The psychotherapy research project of the Menninger Foundation: An overview. *Journal of Consulting & Clinical Psychology, 57*(2), 195–205. https://doi.org/10.1037/0022-006X.57.2.195

Watson, L. (1979). *Lifetide.* Hodder & Stoughton.

Weedon, C. (1987). *Feminist practice and poststructuralist theory.* Basil Blackwell.

Weisstein, N. (1971). Psychology constructs the female. In V. Gornick & K. B. Moran (Eds.), *Women in sexist society* (pp. 133–146). Basic Books.

Whyte, W. H. (1952). Groupthink. *Fortune Magazine, 45*, 114–117, 142, 146. http://fortune.com/2012/07/22/groupthink-fortune-1952/

Wigley, T. M. I. (2006). A combined mitigation/geoengineering approach to climate stabilization. *Science Express, 314*(5798), 452–454. https://www.science.org/doi/10.1126/science.1131728

Wiley, M. S. (1992). Toeing the bottom line. *Family Therapy Networker, 16*(2), 30–72.

Wolfe, T. (1976, August 23). The 'me' decade. The new alchemical dream is: changing one's personality—remaking, remodeling, elevating, and polishing one's very self. *New York.* https://nymag.com/article/tom-wolfe-me-decade-third-great-awakening.html

Wood, J. K. (1980). *Shadows of surrender: Trends in consciousness in person-centered approaches* [Unpublished lecture transcript]. Sao Paulo, Brazil, March 1977.

Wood, J. K. (1984). Communities for learning: A person-centered approach. In J. M. Shlien & R. F. Levant (Eds.), *Client-centered therapy and the person-centered approach: New directions in theory and practice* (pp. 297–316). Praeger.

Wood, J. K. (1996). The person-centered approach: Towards an understanding of its implications. In R. Hutterer, G. Pawlowsky, P. F. Schmid, & R. Stipsits (Eds.), *Client-centered and experiential psychotherapy: A paradigm in motion* (pp. 163–181). Peter Lang.

Wood, J. K. (1997). *Carl Rogers and transpersonal psychology* [Keynote presentation]. The VI International Holistic and Transpersonal Congress, Aquas de Lindoia, Brazil.

Wooten, L. M. (1981). Albert Speer: How to manage an atrocity. *Journal of Humanistic Psychology, 21*(4), 21–38. https://doi.org/10.1177/002216788102100403

World Economic Forum. (2001). *Missed opportunity.* https://widgets.weforum.org/history/2001.html

World Health Organization. (2001). *The World Health Report 2001: Mental health: New understanding, new hope.* https://iris.who.int/handle/10665/42390

World Health Organization. (2002). *The World Health Report 2002: Reducing risks, promoting healthy life.* https://iris.who.int/handle/10665/67454

Yankelovich, D. (1978, May). Attitudes at work. *Psychology Today, 11*(12).

Yankelovich, D. (1981). *New rules: Searching for fulfillment in a world turned upside down.* Random House.

Index

Note: Page numbers in *italics* refer to figures and in **bold** refer to table. Page numbers followed by n refer to notes.

Kolibri 360 GmbH
Ferdinand-Jühlke-Straße 7
99095 Erfurt, Deutschland
produktsicherheit@kolibri360.de